STRONG & FREE

BIGHORN

STRONG & FREE

My Journey in Alberta Politics

TED MORTON

Bighorn Books
An imprint of University of Calgary Press
2500 University Drive NW
Calgary, Alberta
Canada T2N 1N4
press.ucalgary.ca

LIBRARY AND ARCHIVES CANADA CATALOGUING IN PUBLICATION

Title: Strong & free : my journey in Alberta politics / Ted Morton.
Other titles: Strong and free
Names: Morton, F. L. (Frederick Lee), 1949- author.
Description: Includes bibliographical references and index.
Identifiers: Canadiana (print) 20240414373 | Canadiana (ebook) 20240414438 | ISBN
    9781773855974 (softcover) | ISBN 9781773855967 (hardcover) | ISBN 9781773855981
    (PDF) | ISBN 9781773855998 (EPUB)
Subjects: LCSH: Morton, F. L. (Frederick Lee), 1949- | LCSH: Progressive Conservative
    Association of Alberta. | LCSH: Politicians—Alberta—Biography. | LCSH: Legislators—
    Alberta—Biography. | LCSH: Alberta—Politics and government—1971- | LCSH:
    Alberta—Biography. | CSH: Alberta—Politics and government—1971-2015. | LCGFT:
    Autobiographies.
Classification: LCC FC3675.1.M67 A3 2024 | DDC 971.23/04092—dc23

The University of Calgary Press acknowledges the support of the Government of Alberta through the Alberta Media Fund for our publications. We acknowledge the financial support of the Government of Canada. We acknowledge the financial support of the Canada Council for the Arts for our publishing program.

Alberta Government   Canada   Canada Council for the Arts   Conseil des Arts du Canada

Printed and bound in Canada by Imprimerie Gauvin
✪ This book is printed on Enviro paper

Copyediting by Peter Enman
Cover art Colourbox #54633804 and 24776686
Cover design, page design, and typesetting by Melina Cusano

This book is dedicated to Preston Manning, founder and first leader of the Reform Party of Canada. Preston's vision and leadership inspired me and thousands of other Western Canadians to work for new policies and constitutional reforms that would resolve our deeper structural vulnerability to predatory federal policies. Without a Preston Manning, there would have been no Stephen Harper; no Jason Kenney or Danielle Smith; no Pierre Poilievre— a past prime minister of Canada; a past premier of Alberta; the current premier of Alberta; and the current Leader of His Majesty's Loyal Opposition (and hopefully soon, the next prime minister of Canada). Alberta wants in, not out. But we want a new deal, a fair deal, from the rest of Canada. A strong and prosperous Alberta makes for a strong and prosperous Canada. We want both.

TABLE OF CONTENTS

Preface

This book is an autobiography of my three decades in Alberta politics. The chapters are organized chronologically, from 1981 to 2023. Readers may want to go directly to chapters that address their particular interests. Some chapters may be too detailed or too technical for a general interest reader. The primary audiences are Albertans who were active in federal and provincial conservative politics during this period; and political scientists interested in policy development, cabinet/caucus politics, and leadership selection. I also hope that this book will help current and future MLAs and cabinet ministers avoid the mistakes of the Stelmach, Redford, and Prentice governments. For future historians, it also provides a record of thirty years of Alberta politics as seen from the inside by someone who aspired to reach the top and almost did.

My dual perspective—as both a player and an academic (political scientist)—is somewhat unique and hopefully provides some original insights. It might also serve as a cautionary tale for future academics considering jumping into the political ring. As a reporter once observed, I was the intellectual godfather of the political party that ended my career. Quite an achievement! Or, as a friend remarked at my retirement party, by the time I exited, I had managed to alienate most of the members of all four major political parties in Alberta. Politics is a tricky business!

My original title for this book was "The Decline and Fall of the Alberta PC Empire." This remains the principal theme. But as I was completing the manuscript, recent events gave me a more positive perspective on what had occurred on my watch. These included the election of Jason Kenney as the new leader of the PC Party in 2017; his successful merger of the PCs and Wildrose parties in 2018; the election of a Kenney-UCP majority government in 2019; and Danielle Smith's takeover of the UCP leadership in 2022 and her majority government in 2023.

Suddenly, many of the "Alberta Agenda"—a.k.a. "Firewall"—policies and ideas I had championed unsuccessfully had now been supported by two successive conservative majority governments. As I told my supporters in 2006, we may have lost the leadership campaign, but we did not lose the battle for new ideas. The same reforms that were on the periphery of Alberta provincial politics twenty years ago are now front and centre. How these issues will play out remains to be seen, but they are not going away anytime soon.

In the last two provincial elections (2019 and 2023), Albertans have elected majority governments that understand Alberta's structural vulnerability to predatory federal policies and are no longer willing to accept it. There is a fundamental misalignment between Canada's nineteenth-century constitution and our twenty-first-century economy. Canada has changed but our constitution has not. This constitutional disconnect invites federal political parties to win national elections with policies that transfer wealth from energy-rich, voter-poor Alberta to the energy-poor but voter-rich central provinces of Quebec and Ontario. The Liberals' election strategy—"Screw the West. We'll take the rest!"—has worked for the past fifty years. In politics, the beneficiaries of the status quo never willingly give up their advantages. Alberta has never received anything from Ottawa without fighting for it. Change requires push. Albertans have now elected two consecutive governments that are pushing back.

I am often asked if I regretted my decision to leave my academic university life and plunge into the shadowy cave of partisan party politics. The answer is: decidedly not. I have had a lifelong interest in understanding politics, but I knew almost nothing about actually governing—being in government and making the decisions that shape public policy. My work as the minister of Sustainable Resource Development, then Finance and finally Energy gave me experiences and knowledge that I otherwise would never have had. To cut to the chase, this book would not exist if I hadn't taken the opportunity—and its attendant risks—that I had in 2004.

My eight years in government also deepened my knowledge of and affection for Alberta. Alberta is large and unique—so large that most Albertans know only the small corners that we each live in. As an MLA, I met and worked with the communities and families in Foothills-Rocky View that I represented for eight years. As a leadership candidate and minister, I travelled the entire province multiple times. The more I saw, the more Albertans I met, the more I cared about Alberta's future. For the past several generations,

Alberta has been one of the best places in Canada—in the world—to live, to work and to raise a family. I want to keep it that way for future generations—which is another reason I wrote this book.

In 2004 I left federal Conservative Party / Reform Party politics and returned to the Alberta arena with the goal of making the Alberta government more self-reliant, more able and willing to fight unfair federal policies. This didn't happen on my watch, but with the subsequent merger of the PCs and Wildrose parties and the majority UCP (United Conservative Party) governments elected in 2019 and 2023, it has.

I'd like to believe I contributed to this—both while in government and after my exit in 2012. No longer being in government gave me back a freedom of speech I had missed for the prior eight years. I've always subscribed to the theory that in politics, "the pen is mightier than the sword." After eight years of wielding the sword, I have enjoyed picking up the pen again.

Acknowledgements

I would like to acknowledge Dave Snow's invaluable assistance in the formatting of the files that make up this book and Peter Enman's excellent copy-editing of my final manuscript. I would also like to thank the University of Calgary School of Public Policy for managing my trust account and financially supporting the publication of this book. Finally, I want to thank the staff at the University of Calgary Press, especially Press Director Brian Scrivener, for their support and encouragement. For any errors of omission or commission, I take full responsibility.

Select parts of this book draw from previously published material. The discussion of the 2011 PC leadership race draws extensively from my 2013 article "Leadership Selection in Alberta, 1992–2011: A Personal Perspective," *Canadian Parliamentary Review* 36, no. 2 (2013), pp. 31–38, http://revparl. ca/36/2/36n2_13e_Morton.pdf.

The discussion of the North West Upgrader in chapter 7 is an edited and updated version of the study I published in 2015, "The North West Sturgeon Upgrader: Good Money after Bad?" *School of Public Policy Research Papers* 7, no. 3 (April 2015), https://www.policyschool.ca/wp-content/uploads/2016/03/ north-west-sturgeon-upgrader-morton.pdf.

The discussion of the risks of earlier attempts at economic diversification by governments of Alberta in chapter 7 draws from the study I co-authored with Meredith McDonald in 2015, "The Siren Song of Diversification: Alberta's Legacy of Loss, 1973–1993," *School of Public Policy Research Papers* 8, no. 15 (March 2015), https://www.policyschool.ca/wp-content/uploads/2016/03/ siren-song-economic-diversification-morton-mcdonald.pdf.

Illustrations

"Alberta Milch Cow, 1915." Arch Dale, "The Milch Cow," *The Grain Growers Guide*, December 15, 1915. Glenbow Library and Archives NA-3055-24.

TED AND BAMBI
MORTON

YOU ARE INVITED TO A

No More
"Sober Second Thought"
STAMPEDE PARTY

Western Dinner and Patio Two-Step Dancing

Date:	Friday, July 10th	R.S.V.P:	
Time:	Cocktails at 6:00 p.m.	Phone	284-3779
Location:	3319 Upton Place N.W.	Fax	282-4773

"No More 'Sober Second Thought" Stampede party. July 10, 1998.

Dear Fellow Reformers,

As your Senatorial candidate, I would bring to the Party 25 years of study and striving to influence the political process through my writings about Canadian politics. Like you, the more I see, the more upset I become over the steady decline in democracy and accountability in Ottawa. The three worst offenders are the Senate, the Supreme Court, and the so-called "national unity" issue. And like you, I've had enough of unelected senators who do too little and unelected judges who do too much. I've had enough of the national unity "problem" being blamed on those who believe in Canada rather than those who want to destroy it.

The Senate

The Senate is a national embarrassment that must be reformed or abolished. For Western Canadians, reform is the only option. Every federal state worthy of the name has an upper house that represents regions. If we'd had a Triple E Senate in 1980, Trudeau could not have rammed through the Liberals' National Energy Policy (NEP). I am committed to achieving some form of Triple E Senate reform.

The Supreme Court

The Supreme Court of Canada has become the single most serious threat to provincial rights and regional democracy. Simply put, unelected, unaccountable judges are making social and economic policy contrary to the intended meaning of the Charter of Rights. This must be stopped. As your Senator, I will continue to advocate term limits, parliamentary hearings for judicial nominees, and use of the legislative notwithstanding power. We must return the Court to its proper role of interpreting laws rather than making laws.

Ted & Bambi Morton

"Dear Fellow Reformers." Morton Campaign Brochure for 1998 Alberta Senate election.

MARK STEYN: WHAT'S SO FUNNY ABOUT CANADIAN EMBASSIES?

INDEPENDENT VOICE OF THE NEW WEST

WESTERN
STANDARD

www.westernstandard.ca

WHO'S HELPING
THE CRTC CENSOR
CHOI-FM?

HOW ANIMAL
ACTIVISTS GOT TO
THE GOVERNMENT

IS ALBERTA
FINALLY READY TO
SEPARATE?

Ted Morton, academic,
architect of the Alberta
firewall and Senator-elect,
wants to add provincial
politics to his resumé.
Why does that have some
Conservatives feeling nervous?

PREMIER
-IN-WAITING?

August 30, 2004 $4.95

"Premier in Waiting." Cover of *Western Standard*, August 30. 2004. Material republished with the express permission of Western Standard New Media Corp.

"Our Future, Our Choices, Our Premier." Morton Campaign Brochure for 2006 PC Leadership election.

EDMONTON JOURNAL
On Sunday

www.edmontonjournal.com　　　　EDMONTON'S NEWSPAPER SINCE 1903　　　　SUNDAY, NOVEMBER 26, 2006"

MORTON MAKES IT A CONTEST

DINNING FACES SURPRISINGLY TIGHT RACE FOR TORY CROWN, WITH STELMACH 3RD / A3

30.2% JIM DINNING

66 In seven days our party and our province have a choice to make. A choice between tackling tomorrow's challenges, or fighting yesterday's battles. 99

26.2% TED MORTON

66 That message is bold and clear and it's a message I like. Change is on the way. 99

15.3% ED STELMACH

66 When you get to the Olympics, you don't get there and then quit. 99

"Morton makes it a contest." *Edmonton Journal*, November 26, 2006. Material republished with the express permission of: *Edmonton Journal/Calgary Herald*, a division of Postmedia Network Inc.

●CALGARY HERALD   Sunday, November 26, 2006   A5

*pc*Alberta **RACE TO BE** LEADER

Who will be premier?

One of these men is the next Tory leader

Herald Archive, Canadian Press

Calgary Herald Archive

Calgary Herald Archive

| **JIM DINNING** | **TED MORTON** | **ED STELMACH** |
| Front-runner takes aim early at rival Ted Morton | Most conservative contender held firmly to his agenda | Rural-backed candidate quietly reaches runoff |

"Who will be premier?" *Calgary Herald*, November 26, 2006. Material republished with the express permission of: *Edmonton Journal/Calgary Herald*, a division of Postmedia Network Inc.

"Yep Ya Got Me." *Calgary Sun*, January 9, 2010. "Premier Stelmach appoints Ted Morton as the new Alberta Finance Minister." Material republished with the express permission of the artist, Tim Rotheisler.

"Harper Milking the Alberta Cow." *Calgary Sun*, January 17, 2010. "Prime Minister Harper coming to Milk Alberta's New Finance Minister Ted Morton." Material republished with the express permission of the artist, Tim Rotheisler.

Morton quits cabinet for bid to lead Tories

Surprise exit of finance minister starts leadership race

JASON FEKETE
CALGARY HERALD

Stuart Gradon, Calgary Herald
Ted Morton, left, announces he is resigning as Alberta finance minister to seek the Tory leadership after meeting with Premier Ed Stelmach in Calgary on Thursday. Stelmach announced Tuesday he will step down as premier by the fall.

Ted Morton resigned Thursday as Alberta finance minister but will remain in caucus, a move that unofficially fires the starter pistol on the Tory leadership race and has Conservative MLAs conflicted over when Premier Ed Stelmach should exit.

Morton announced his surprise departure — and plans to run for the Conservative party crown — at a hastily called news conference with Stelmach at McDougall Centre in Calgary, following a one-hour meeting between the premier and former finance minister.

The resignation came less than 24 hours after Morton said he had no plans to quit and the same week Stelmach announced he will resign as premier in the coming months.

The two Tory heavyweights said the decision is based entirely on Morton's interest in the party reins, and the need to resign his portfolio to avoid any perceptions he's using his office to advance his leadership aspirations.

"I believe it would be difficult, if not impossible, for me to continue to discharge my duties as minister with the required perception of impartiality," Morton told reporters.

"The media coverage and speculation around the impending leadership contest would be a serious distraction from the process of governing, particularly the passage of the budget."

SEE TORIES, PAGE A5

calgaryherald.com

Visit us online to see video of Morton's announcement

Rural Conservative support wavers

JAMIE KOMARNICKI
CALGARY HERALD
SUNDRE

In Alberta's Tory heartland, retired rancher Archie Stockburger has always enjoyed his coffee black and his politics conservative blue.

Most mornings, the Sundre resident heads to a coffee shop on Main Avenue for his caffeine fix with friends.

Like many longtime Progressive Conservatives in

> (The Tories) squandered an awful pile of money for an awful lot of years
>
> LONGTIME TORY SUPPORTER ARCHIE STOCKBURGER OF SUNDRE

this foothills community of 2,500 — which has elected a Tory since the dynasty began in 1971 — it's the politics he's questioning these days.

A growing provincial debt load, mismanaged resources and an ineffective leader, he says, make him skeptical of the ruling Tories and — for

the first time — eye rival upstart, Wildrose Alliance.

Premier Ed Stelmach's abrupt announcement this week he's stepping down, though, has changed everything for Stockburger.

"It's a coin toss. Depends what the Tories do," the 72-year-old retiree says

between sips of coffee.

"They squandered an awful pile of money for an awful lot of years," Stockburger says, adding: "It's Conservative here, and you can't change it."

Across Alberta, residents have been voicing unease with the ruling Tories.

Recent polls peg the PCs in a dead heat with the Wildrose, setting up a ferocious battle for the right-wing vote.

SEE RURAL, PAGE A4

UNITY MASKS TORY DIVISION
Morton's exit launches most bizarre leadership race in Tory history.
Don Braid, Page A4

POLITICS
WHO IS THE REAL TED MORTON?
Divisive ideologue or unifying force?
Tony Seskus, Page A5

WILDROSE NIGHTMARE
Fiscal hawk Morton presents tough test for Danielle Smith
Editorial, Page A12

"Morton quits cabinet for bid to lead Tories." *Calgary Herald*, January 28, 2011. Material republished with the express permission of: *Edmonton Journal/Calgary Herald*, a division of Postmedia Network Inc.

MUCH OF THE INFAMOUS FIREWALL LETTER HAS TURNED INTO UCP GOVERNMENT POLICY

DON BRAID

The Alberta Firewall Letter, once a joke, has become entrenched reality.

Nearly every demand in the once-infamous letter is now top of the UCP government's agenda.

Nobody is happier than Ted Morton, one of the seven who signed it in 2001, along with Stephen Harper before he became Conservative leader and prime minister.

"It feels good," Morton, retired U of C professor and former PC cabinet minister, said in an interview.

"The Alberta agenda ideas are now pretty deeply embedded in provincial politics, and they're not going to go away.

"How they're going to work out, I don't know. But these ideas have gone from fringe to mainstream."

The letter called for creating an Alberta Pension and withdrawing from the CPP; replacing the RCMP with a provincial police force; collecting personal income tax through a provincial agency; pressing for Senate reform; and assuming provincial control of health care, thus forsaking federal money.

The key points are all UCP aspirations or even encoded in law (the new Police Act.)

The call for withdrawing from the Canada Health Act has no traction today, but don't count it out for tomorrow.

The advocates are persistent and effective as they nudge these plans toward the mainstream.

They include Premier Danielle Smith and her key adviser Rob Anderson. They devised the "sovereignty" pitch — the Firewall agenda under a new name.

Albertans are aware of all this by now. And yet, Smith and the UCP appear to have retained the voter support that won them the election last May.

Morton has a book coming

out in September called Strong and Free; My Journey in Alberta Politics.

It was a bruising trip, especially after he joined the Progressive Conservatives as an MLA and minister.

Premier Ralph Klein's crew — and later Ed Stelmach's — didn't like his vision. "They were very resistant to me and to the ideas I was pushing," he says.

Worse, some of Morton's firewall allies were upset that he joined the PCs.

But he stuck with the governing party, twice running unsuccessfully for the leadership.

"Internal party fights are more bitter than cross-party fights," Morton says, "and politics is hard on friendships.

"I had a couple of friendships destroyed. I watched a couple other people lose friendships over this."

Through it all, Morton never wavered in the beliefs expressed in the Firewall letter.

It caused — appropriately — a political firestorm when the signatories sent it to Klein, who

basically ignored it.

The letter was widely derided as extremist, separatist, divisive and dangerous.

Some people feel that the urgency will go out of this drive if the Trudeau Liberals lose the 2025 election and Conservative Leader Pierre Poilievre becomes prime minister.

Morton doesn't believe that for

a minute. In fact, he thinks Poilievre will be a willing partner in most of Smith's plans.

"The RCMP is already talking about walking away from provincial policing. I think Poilievre would, if not facilitate it, at least certainly not block it.

"On the (federal) gun registry, on the electricity regulations, he's already said he's against most of that.

"The touchy one is the Alberta pension plan ... it has major fiscal implications for the CPP. So, I think he'll be much more careful about that.

"But on most of those other issues, I don't think there's much electoral risk to Poilievre in co-operating with Danielle Smith."

Behind all this is the core belief that the problems are structural and can't be solved until Alberta assumes more power.

A hostile government like the Liberals might inflame the tensions to help win support elsewhere.

A friendlier federal government could give the impression that the system is working.

But eventually, the issues will erupt again because of the political and structural inequities.

That's what Ted Morton and his firewall successors ardently believe. And now, many more Albertans seem to believe it too.
Don Braid's column appears regularly in the Herald.

Ted Morton was one of the seven who signed the Alberta Firewall Letter in 2001, along with Stephen Harper before he became the Conservative leader and, subsequently, prime minister. *DARREN MAKOWICHUK FILES*

From Professor to Politician (1981-1997)

*If liberty means anything at all, it means the right to tell people
things they don't want to hear.*

—The George Orwell Foundation[1]

INTRODUCTION

How does a professor become a politician? I suppose there are as many ways
as there are examples. Some of my friends joke that I was like the anthropol-
ogist who went into the jungle to study the natives, but then stayed too long
and "went native." Some of my critics would say that I was always that way.
There may be some truth in both.

My involvement in Alberta politics was incremental. As I explain in this
chapter, initially it was an extension of what I was teaching in the classroom.
And I was self-consciously cautious about going into the political waters too
fast, too deep. Some of the best advice I was ever given came from one of my
undergraduate professors at Colorado College, Dr. Fred Sondermann: "Don't
get involved in elected politics until you are financially secure. You don't ever
want to be in a position where you have to choose between what you know is
right and what you need financially." I never was.

As for going native, it's true that I've always been interested in and attracted to politics. It may be genetic. My grandfather on my mother's side was
a "New Deal" Democrat in the US Congress from 1937 to 1940. My father
was elected as a Republican to the Wyoming House of Representatives from
1966 to 1980; served as speaker of the house in his last term; and then ran unsuccessfully for governor in 1982. My first-year bio at Colorado College states

that I was "interested in politics, creative writing, skiing, golf and becoming a college professor." That was when I was eighteen, so I've been conflicted from the start.

In this chapter I describe my journey from prof to pol, starting with how I became a conservative; my graduate studies at the University of Toronto in the 1970s; and my early involvement with Preston Manning and the Reform Party in the 1980s and 1990s. In chapter 2, I explain my decision to be a Reform Party candidate in Alberta's 1998 Senate election; my involvement with the Alberta Agenda, aka "Firewall Letter," in 2001; and finally, my decision to seek election as the new MLA for Foothills-Rocky View as the candidate of the provincial Progressive Conservative Party in 2004.

HOW I BECAME A CONSERVATIVE (1967-1980)

The inherent vice of capitalism is the unequal sharing of blessings; the inherent virtue of socialism is the equal sharing of miseries.

—Winston Churchill

Sometime during the 1990s, my mother remarked to me (in a disapproving tone) that I had gone from being a left-winger to a right-winger without ever passing through the middle. As usual, she was pretty accurate in her assessment.

It might surprise many of my friends and former supporters in Alberta that my initial involvement in politics was all on the Left. As a senior in high school in the winter of 1967, I read Arthur M. Schlesinger's then recently published book *Bitter Heritage: Vietnam and American Democracy, 1941–1966*.[2] This inspired me to organize the first (and maybe the last) Vietnam War "teach-in" in Casper, Wyoming. My political engagement continued when I went off to college that fall. I participated in anti-war marches outside of Fort Carson, home base of the US Army's Fifth Infantry Division, a major staging area for soldiers going to Vietnam. In February 1968, after a good friend from high school, Vernon Nix, was killed only twelve days after he arrived in Vietnam, I went to work for anti-war candidate Eugene McCarthy's presidential campaign. (Note: Before his political career McCarthy was an economics professor.)

In the fall of 1968, I was a co-founder of Colorado College's first student chapter of the NAACP (the National Association for the Advancement of Colored People, a civil rights organization). I helped to organize voter registration in minority neighbourhoods leading up to the November federal elections. Later that year I was an organizer and speaker at a "free speech" rally defending the onstage nudity of actors in a recent campus theatre performance, which had ignited a firestorm of protest in the local Colorado Springs media. In the Colorado College 1968 yearbook, there is even a picture of me protesting in support of Cesar Chavez and the United Farm Workers, holding a sign, "NO MORE SOUR GRAPES." The occasion was a speaking event for the then anti-union California governor Ronald Reagan. Yes, the same Ronald Reagan whom a decade later I supported for president of the United States! (As did Eugene McCarthy!) And it should come as no surprise during this time that I tried—and liked—smoking marijuana. Soon after, I also experimented with both mescaline and LSD. In short, I was a stereotypical Sixties campus "hippie radical."

This began to change in 1969 when I went off to Aix-en-Provence, France, for my third year of university. Simply being outside of North America for eleven months gave me a new and different perspective. Like so many young people then (and now), I believed that somehow my generation was "better" than previous generations; that our demands for "Peace Now" and racial and sexual equality represented "progress" and would somehow change the world for the better. My eleven months in Europe began to change this. Walking through the streets of medieval towns like Aix and Avignon made history come to life; made me think about how previous empires had come and gone. I began to understand that we are just a very recent part of a much older and richer human tapestry.

I was particularly influenced by my art teacher, Billy Weyman, a young expatriate American who had moved to the south of France to pursue a career as an artist in the tradition of Paul Cézanne and Leo Marchutz. In addition to introducing me to the joys of drinking French cognac, Billy was the first teacher to make me question whether the subjectivity and moral relativism of twentieth-century art and culture represented progress over the past. Maybe the two were related?

In March, a two-week trip through Morocco also impressed on me for the first time how different—and how much better—life was in Western Europe and North America. It began to dawn on me—what today I now know to be true—that so much of what we take for granted is not found in most of the rest of the world. By this I don't just mean our material comforts, but the institutions that make this possible. Democracy, responsible government, the rule of law, property rights, free and fair elections—all are in short supply or even non-existent in most of the rest of the world. That was in 1970. And it's still just as true today.

Being in Europe that spring also meant that I was out of the US in May 1970, when Ohio National Guard soldiers shot and killed four students during an anti-war protest at Kent State University. This tragedy sparked the largest student protests and campus unrest in American history. Had I been in the US, I would have been in the middle of it. But I was not. And so, when I came back from my year in Europe, I had moved in a more reflective, academic direction, while campus politics had become more radical. During my fourth and final year of university, I was not involved in any public protests or political organizations.

What I did do was to immerse myself in philosophy courses with Dr. J. Glenn Gray and political theory courses with Dr. Tim Fuller. Full-semester courses on Plato and Aristotle; Augustine and Aquinas; Hobbes and Locke; Hegel and Marx. I loved it. And as a result, I did surprisingly well, compared to the lacklustre grades of my first two years. So well in fact that by spring graduation, I was nominated and inducted into Phi Beta Kappa, the oldest academic honour society in the United States.

The Phi Beta Kappa award cemented my decision to go to graduate school to pursue my goal of becoming a university professor. But in conversations with professors Gray and Fuller I decided that I would first do a "wanderjahr"—to return to Europe to explore and to better understand the roots of Western civilization. Upon graduation my student deferment expired, but I had drawn a high number—223—in the US military draft that year. So off I went, with Bambi Lathrop, my then girlfriend and now wife of fifty years. We explored Roman and Greek ruins in Spain, France, Switzerland, Italy, Greece, Turkey, and Israel. To pay for these travels, I worked in restaurants in Spain and France; as a chauffeur/handyman for a wealthy Italian family in Switzerland; picked grapes and peaches in France; and then spent seven months in the winter of 1971–72 working on Kibbutz Yifat in Israel.

I had chosen the kibbutz because I had been attracted by the agrarian utopianism in the writings of Leo Tolstoy. I was also attracted by the "back to the land" movement that was part of the Sixties hippie culture. The kibbutz cured me of both. I was in the "ulpan" program—which meant half-time work, and the other half learning Hebrew. This allowed me to get to know some of the Israeli kibbutzniks my age. The more I learned, the more disenchanted I became. Most were planning to leave the kibbutz, and I soon understood why. About 20 percent of the kibbutzniks were doing 80 percent of the work. That cured me of socialism. And my romantic dream of doing honest labour by day and then reading Tolstoy and Plato by night soon evaporated. After eight hours of picking grapefruit or cleaning chicken coops, all I wanted to do was to eat dinner and go to sleep.

Israel also cured me of the pacifism I had embraced during my involvement in the anti–Vietnam war movement. The more I travelled around Israel, the more I realized how perilous Israel's existence was. My time there was after the Six-Day War of 1967 but just before the disastrous Yom Kippur War of 1973. The entire country was an armed camp—soldiers with automatic weapons on every street corner. It had to be. Israel was (and still is) surrounded on all sides by hostile Arab nations and the displaced Palestinians on the West Bank and Gaza. The only reason Israel had survived was because of its superior air force and the US Sixth Fleet cruising off its coast in the Mediterranean Sea. I came to realize the truth of what Professor Sondermann had taught me in his international relations course: Every country is occupied by an army. The question is: Is it yours or someone else's? Irving Kristol once described a conservative as "a liberal who has been mugged by reality." I went to Israel and got mugged.

This was my frame of mind when I arrived in Toronto in September 1973 to begin my graduate studies. I had chosen the University of Toronto because I wanted to study with Emil Fackenheim in the Department of Philosophy. I had already decided I wanted to do my doctoral dissertation on the German philosopher Hegel, and Fackenheim was the most accomplished Hegel scholar in North America. He was also a Jewish refugee who had fled Hitler's Nazi Germany in 1938; had lost his brother in the Holocaust; and had become a Zionist supporter of Israel. He too had been "mugged by reality" to a degree that I could only imagine. I had read his books before I arrived and thoroughly enjoyed the courses I took with him that first year. Unfortunately, this did not last. After being warned that there were virtually no job prospects for new PhDs in philosophy, I chose to transfer to the Department of Political Science, where I thought I could still do my dissertation on Hegel but with better employment prospects after I finished.

It was there that I first met Walter Berns, and then Allan Bloom. Both had done their PhDs with Leo Strauss at the University of Chicago in the 1950s. Both had been tenured full professors at Cornell University. Both had resigned in protest after the Cornell administration refused to sanction the armed Black students who took control of the Cornell campus during student protests in the spring of 1969. Shortly afterward, both were offered and accepted tenured, full-professor positions at the University of Toronto.

I was unaware of any of this history when I first took courses with them. Berns co-taught a course on comparative Canada-US constitutional law with Professor Peter Russell. I liked the course and both professors. I ended up writing my PhD dissertation on the constitutional law of sexual equality, with both as supervisors. With Bloom, I first audited his undergraduate course on Plato's *Republic* and then was a student in his graduate course on Rousseau's *Emile*.

In retrospect, my continuing evolution to the conservative side of the political spectrum was not that surprising. Leo Strauss was one of the most influential American political theorists of the twentieth century. Also a Jewish refugee from Nazi Germany, Strauss had distinguished himself first as a scholar of ancient and medieval philosophy and then as a skeptic of the widely held belief in progress and the view that twentieth-century liberal democracy is "the end of history."[3] In two decades of teaching at the University of Chicago, Strauss attracted dozens of students who went on to their own academic careers. Loosely described as "Straussians," many of these professors influenced the development of the "neo-conservative" movement in American politics. Berns and Bloom were among these.[4]

With Berns and Russell I came to understand the genius of British, American, and Canadian constitutionalism—democracy, responsible government, checks and balances, separation of powers, federalism, the rule of law, and property rights. I learned that constitutional supremacy does not mean judicial supremacy, and that judges—even Supreme Court judges—are not infallible. The US Supreme Court had once ruled that Negro slaves were not humans but just "property."[5] Several decades later, the same court held that the segregation laws of southern states did not violate the rights of now free Black Americans to the equal protection of the laws as long as the separate facilities were "equal."[6] The Supreme Court of Canada had once declared that as far as the *British North America Act* was concerned, women were not "persons" and so could not be appointed to the Senate.[7] Studying cases like these taught me early on that final courts of appeal tend to reflect the same values and prejudices as the political parties that appoint them.

My studies with Bloom deepened my skepticism of the moral relativism and utopian egalitarianism that was (and still is) fuelling modern progressive thought and politics. Indeed, what we now know as "identity politics" and "critical race theory" was unpacked and dissected by Bloom thirty years earlier in his bestselling book *The Closing of the American Mind*.[8]

More broadly, my years in Toronto cured me of the liberal understanding of Western history as inevitable progress—that as each new generation corrects the faults and prejudices of those who came before, our societies become more just, more democratic, better places to live. Yes, this understanding of history may have been persuasive one hundred years ago. The twentieth century was supposed to be the culmination of the Enlightenment and the democratic revolutions of the nineteenth century. But it did not work out that way. Instead, it became the century of the Nazi Holocaust in Germany and the Communist genocides in Russia, China, and Cambodia. In 1900, Germany was arguably more advanced than any other European nation. But by mid-century, Germany had methodically exterminated six million Jews and started a world war that killed over fifteen million soldiers and twice as many civilians.[9]

The Communist genocides were even worse. The Nazi Holocaust was an industrialized version of old-fashioned ethnic and racial prejudice—a source of conflict on all continents since recorded history began. What Stalin, Mao, and Pol Pot did was new. They executed millions of their own countrymen—over sixty million[10]—because of their politics; because they were "enemies of the people." These new totalitarian regimes persecuted and killed people not for what they did but for what they believed. In this sense, it was a throwback to the religious wars of the fifteenth and sixteenth centuries. But now heresy was defined not as belonging to the wrong religion but as not belonging to the correct political party. So much for the "inevitable" progress of democracy and human rights in the twentieth century. And the outlook for the twenty-first century does not look much better. Freedom House, which has monitored the progress/decline of democracy globally for the past fifty years, reported that as of 2023, support for political rights and civil liberties has declined for the past seventeen consecutive years.[11]

Suffice it to say that by the time that I left University of Toronto, I too was a neo-conservative. I subscribed to both *Commentary* and *Public Policy* and read almost everything Irving Kristol and Norman Podhoretz wrote. I now enthusiastically supported as US president the same Ronald Reagan I had protested against when he was governor of California only a decade earlier. I had become an ardent admirer of Winston Churchill, and of his latter-day successor, Margaret Thatcher. My evolution from the left-wing, counterculture politics of the 1960s to the neo-conservative movement of the 1980s was not unique. It turned out to be a path well travelled.[12]

Nor is this ideological evolution surprising. As Churchill is said to have observed, "Show me a young Conservative and I'll show you someone with no heart. Show me an old Liberal and I'll show you someone with no brains." The quote may be apocryphal, but it conveys that liberalism is romantic and aspirational: our society is broken, and we are going to fix it. As Michael Novak observed, "Socialism is the residue of Judeo-Christian faith, without religion. It is a belief in community, the goodness of the human race and paradise on earth."[13] Who can be against that? The problem, Novak, continues, is that "the saintliness of socialism will not feed the poor."

Conservatism is anti-utopian and practical: Do not let the perfect be the enemy of the good. Since Conservatism is not aspirational, it does not appeal to young people. But as Kristol observed, getting "mugged by reality" leads many of us back to a more conservative perspective.

A sense of history also helps. Liberals tend to take the achievements of today's liberal democracies for granted and are preoccupied with what's wrong with Canada and other Western democracies. Conservatives recognize that the political freedom and economic prosperity enjoyed by Canada and the other Western democracies are a unique historical achievement. We must attend to their preservation—the principles, traditions, and institutions that have sustained our collective well-being. It remains a simple historical fact: Today in Canada, we enjoy more freedom; more security; more prosperity; more toleration and diversity; and more opportunities for women than 99 percent of the humans who have come before us.

ALBERTA: THE EARLY YEARS (1981-1997)

We moved to Calgary in August 1981 when I accepted an assistant professor position in the political science department at the University of Calgary. We moved ourselves and all our belongings in a large U-Haul van. We had three children under the age of seven, a large dog, and soon an even larger mortgage with an 18 percent interest rate. We knew only two people in Calgary—Rainer and Robin Knopff, friends from graduate school at the University of Toronto. Neither Bambi nor I had even been to Alberta until I had flown out in March for an interview. In other words, we were much like the tens of thousands of other Canadians and non-Canadians who had flocked to the booming city in the preceding decades for opportunity and jobs.

In my first decade in Alberta, I had no intention of joining a political party or running for public office. How could I? I wasn't even a Canadian citizen. Plus, I was much too busy with teaching, writing, and publishing; working to achieve tenure at the University of Calgary; raising three kids; junior hockey; and coaching Little League baseball.

My initial teaching assignments included teaching the department's course in American Politics. To better engage my students, I regularly drew comparisons with parallel Canadian issues and events. I emphasized the role that the US Senate plays in protecting the interests of the smaller Western states, many of which are oil producers. Alberta was (and is) in a similar situation—small/poor in population relative to Central Canada but rich in oil and gas. Having grown up in Casper, Wyoming—which at that time described itself as the "Energy Capital of the Rockies"—I appreciated how the US Senate balanced the interest of the less-populated states (two senators for each state) with the practice of "rep by pop" in the House of Representatives.

In 1981, Liberal Prime Minister Pierre Trudeau had implemented a "National Energy Program" (NEP) that kept domestic oil and gas prices well below the higher global price. This policy was popular with consumers/voters in Ontario and Quebec (who together constituted a majority of seats in the House of Commons) but had a strong negative effect on the energy sector in Alberta. Many oil and gas companies closed or sold their operations in Alberta. Jobs were lost and unemployment soared. My lectures used a comparative case study that explained how in the US, representatives from the energy-poor but voter-rich East Coast states had tried to enact similar legislation but were blocked by the Senators from the oil-producing Western states.[14]

Shortly thereafter, a new national political party—the Reform Party—was being formed by Preston Manning and Western Canadians. Their mantra was "THE WEST WANTS IN." And it caught on. Many Westerners were angry about the NEP and its negative impact on their communities. One of Reform's principal policy planks was a demand for "Triple E Senate Reform"—elected, equal, and effective—basically the American model. As I was already lecturing on this issue, I began writing some op-eds for the local newspapers in Calgary that explained how the US Senate had allowed less-populated, oil-producing Western states to avoid an American version of an NEP.

The "northern peso" experience was another one of the factors that led to my early involvement with the new Reform Party. By the time I decided to enter provincial politics, fiscal responsibility was not just an abstract concept. It had become personal. Over the preceding decade, I had lived through two successive government debt crises—one provincial, one federal.

In the 1990s at the federal level, there was a reckoning with bondholders for the runaway spending and deficits of both the Trudeau and Mulroney federal governments. The Government of Canada's accumulated net debt had exploded from $300 billion in 1970 to $1 trillion by the time Liberal Leader Jean Chrétien became prime minister in 1993.[15] These numbers had consequences. The value of the Canadian dollar had plummeted to 63 cents US. In 1995, the *Wall Street Journal* referred to the Canadian dollar as the "northern peso" and described Canada as "an honorary member of the third world."[16]

Again, this had a personal connection for me. When I arrived in Canada in 1973 as a graduate student at the University of Toronto, I had to pay US$1.05 to purchase a Canadian dollar. I was impressed. Having travelled and worked in Europe the preceding two years, I equated a strong national currency with a strong, well-governed country. Canada clearly qualified!

Twenty years later, it was the opposite. In 1993, the year the Canadian dollar bottomed out at 63 cents US, we had just sent our two older children off to universities in the US. Notwithstanding the substantial scholarships they both received, there was still travel and room and board, and this had to be paid in US dollars, which now cost us $1.40 Canadian. We calculated that in that decade (1993–2002), helping to pay the education costs for our three children in US dollars swallowed two-thirds of my wife's after-tax income.

At the provincial level, there was a similar reckoning with Alberta's spiralling debt. In 1993, when Ralph Klein took over the leadership of the PC Party, he inherited a structural deficit of almost $3 billion per year and a net debt of over $22 billion. Interest on the debt was consuming *24* cents of every tax dollar collected in Alberta. The ensuing "Klein Revolution" saw drastic cuts in government spending and services, starting with a 5 percent across-the-board reduction in all public sector salaries. I supported the Klein cuts as the "tough medicine" needed to get Alberta back on track fiscally even though they hit us directly. Both my wife and I were subject to the public sector salary cuts (me at University of Calgary; her as a teacher in the Calgary public system). The "northern peso" experience was one of the factors that led to my early involvement with the new Reform Party.

I also began writing op-eds on the new political role of the Supreme Court of Canada. In 1982, Canada adopted a constitutionally entrenched Charter of Rights and Freedoms. The new Charter applied to both federal and provincial governments, and it explicitly gave the courts the power to enforce it. In the Charter's first decade, the Supreme Court actively exercised this new power to strike down numerous federal and provincial laws—almost all resulting in more liberal policy changes. By 1992, I had published two books on this topic: *Morgentaler v. Borowski: Abortion, the Charter and the Courts* and *Charter Politics* (co-authored with Rainer Knopff).[17] The former won the Alberta Writers' Guild award for Best Non-Fiction Book of the year. Both books explained and critiqued the court's new judicial activism and attracted considerable attention within the academy. I think it was in recognition of this work that in 1995 I was awarded the Bora Laskin National Fellowship in Human Rights.[18]

I was also an outspoken critic[19] of both the 1987 Meech Lake Accord and its successor, the 1992 Charlottetown Accord.[20] Both had strong support among political, economic, and media elites across Canada, but both would have had negative policy consequences for Alberta and Western Canada. Specifically, they would have made reform of the Senate either impossible (Meech) or meaningless (Charlottetown). The then-nascent Reform Party ended up opposing both as well. In the end, both were defeated in part because of strong opposition from Western Canada.

By the mid-Nineties, I was writing op-eds on Senate reform and the courts for both the *Calgary Herald* and the *Calgary Sun*. These caught the attention of Ted Byfield—a staunch Western conservative, a strong supporter of the Reform Party, and publisher of the weekly magazine *Alberta Report*. Soon I was being frequently interviewed and quoted. Byfield loved the Reform Party, and the Reformers all loved and read *Alberta Report*. So it was not surprising that I was soon introduced to the founder and first leader of the Reform Party, Preston Manning.

The introduction was made by Stephen Harper—then just a graduate student in our Economics Department, but already working with Manning.

Harper began to bring Manning to campus to meet with a few professors and graduate students who were interested in the Reform Party's policies. These monthly meetings usually included me and also Tom Flanagan, Barry Cooper, and Rainer Knopff from the political science department, plus some economists such as Robert Mansell. My contributions to these meetings were focused on Senate reform, federalism, and court decisions involving the Charter of Rights.

Manning and his mission impressed me. So having now acquired my Canadian citizenship (1991) and my promotion to full professor (1993), I joined the Reform Party. I began to attend Reform Party events and got to know some of their Alberta candidates. In the 1993 federal election, my wife and I held a "meet and greet" coffee for Stephen Harper, who was now the Reform candidate in Calgary West, our federal riding. Harper easily won, and for the next four years, I routinely had dinner with Stephen whenever I came to Ottawa.

The connections between my writing and the growing strength of the Reform Party did not go unnoticed. In 1992, Jeffrey Simpson, the *Globe and Mail*'s national political columnist, coined the phrase "the Calgary mafia" to describe a group of conservative professors at the University of Calgary. These included Tom Flanagan, Barry Cooper, Rainer Knopff, and myself, all in the political science department; David Bercuson, a historian; and Robert Mansell, an economist. Simpson described us as "controversial, outspoken and conservative," and asserted that we were now "public figures ... [whose] work has influenced those who are active in the Reform Party."[21] A few years later we were described more politely as "the Calgary School" by an American political scientist who wrote, "The works of these scholars are being read across Canada (even in translation in Quebec), and are playing a defining role in the Canadian political debate of the mid-1990s."[22]

Notwithstanding any of these developments, I was still a full-time prof at the university. But while I had never consciously aspired to it, I guess I had become what is now called a "public intellectual," which is a form of political leadership.[23] When I spoke in public, I spoke as an engaged academic, not as an elected politician. This all changed in 1998.

2

From Waiting to Running (1998-2004)

ALBERTA SENATOR-IN-WAITING (1998)

In 1998, the Alberta government decided to hold Senate elections. This was not the first time Alberta had elected senators. In 1989, the PC Government of Premier Don Getty held a Senate election. It was won by Reform Party candidate Stan Waters. The next year Waters was appointed to the Senate by Prime Minister Brian Mulroney in exchange for Alberta's support for the pending Charlottetown Accord. But Mulroney had made it clear that this was a "one-and-done" deal. The Canada West Foundation—led by Peter McCormick and David Elton—had continued to advocate for Senate reform,[1] as of course did the Reform Party.

Senate reform was not a priority for newly elected Conservative Premier Ralph Klein. He was preoccupied with cutting Alberta's deficits and debt. But federal Reform Party members had helped him win the 1992 PC leadership race against the favoured, more liberal candidate, Nancy MacBeth. The PC leadership vote came only five weeks after the referendum on the Charlottetown Accord. Reform was the only national party to oppose the accord, and Albertans had voted 60 percent NO. Macbeth had publicly endorsed the accord, while Klein had not. So when MacBeth and Klein were in a virtual tie after the first round of voting, thousands of Reformers bought memberships to block the "Red Tory" from winning. Klein then coasted to an easy victory with over 60 percent of the votes on the second ballot.[2]

The following year Manning and the Reform Party swept twenty-two of Alberta's twenty-six ridings in the federal election and began to pressure the Alberta government to hold a second Senate election. The politically astute Klein agreed to this request, but on the condition that his party would not field any candidates. This eliminated the risk of any direct electoral competition with Reform. In Alberta's first and only other Senate election in 1989, the provincial PCs did field a candidate—Bert Brown—and he was soundly defeated by the Reform Party candidate, Stan Waters.

As I had been writing and speaking about Senate reform for the past decade, it was not too surprising that some of my new friends in the Reform Party—Monte Solberg and Jason Kenney in particular— approached me to become a candidate. Mel Smith, the former deputy minister of constitutional affairs of British Columbia and a strong advocate for Senate reform, also encouraged me.

Initially I was skeptical, so I consulted several friends. Ralph Hedlin encouraged me. Stephen Harper, who had now left the Reform Party because of differences with Manning, recommended against it. Rainer Knopff and Tom Flanagan said, "Why not?" Alberta (like the other three Western provinces) is entitled to six Senate seats. At that time, all were filled, and there were no prospective retirements (mandatory at age seventy-five) for another three years. So even if I were to win, there would be no immediate change in my life. I would become a "senator-in-waiting"—what a comical term. I would stay in Calgary and continue to teach at the university. Because of this, my wife also agreed.

We launched my campaign on May 27 at the old Highlander Hotel on 16th Avenue, NW.[3] I was given a rousing introduction by fellow Reformer and Calgary lawyer Gerry Chipeur. For the first but not the last time, we used our friends in the media to draw attention to the launch. Peter Menzies had a big piece in that morning's *Calgary Herald* with the headline: "Morton looking to run for senator-in-waiting."[4] And it worked. Both print and television media showed up, and we got lots of coverage. It must have been a slow news day. We didn't see any media again until the end of August!

The next day, I woke up at 4 a.m., got dressed and drove 200 kilometres by myself to Brooks to speak at a 7 a.m. breakfast that Monte Solberg had organized for me. After that, it was on to Medicine Hat for a lunch meeting, also organized by Monte. But after countless cups of coffee, I first had to go to the washroom. When I approached the urinal, I realized that at 4 a.m. I had put my underwear on backwards. So I began to take my jeans off to fix the problem. Monte walked in and said, "What the hell are you doing?!" I explained. He barked: "Forget it. If we get caught in here with your pants down, neither of us will ever get elected to anything again!"

That was pretty much how I spent the next four months, but with my underwear now on properly. We criss-crossed all of Alberta—over 10,000 kilometres in my now not-so-new Ford Explorer—attending dozens of Reform Party summer barbeques and many private receptions organized by supporters. It was retail politics at its best. We had an all-female staff— Janelle Holden, Kim Groenendyk, and Jane Arness—that ran the campaign out of my "campaign office" (i.e., our basement). My travel team consisted of Bambi and an ad hoc collection of young Reformers, mostly undergraduate students at U of C. The average age of our travel team was under twenty-five, which made it fun. One of the most engaging was a young man named Pierre Poilievre, who, twenty-four years later, became the leader of the Conservative Party of Canada. We had a budget of $36,000 raised by my friend and finance chairman Greg Fletcher. This paid (poorly!) for our office staff, some campaign brochures, bumper stickers, and our travel. We practised what we preached—fiscal discipline.

My campaign brochures and speeches were an abbreviated version of what I had been writing about for the previous decade: balanced budgets and debt reduction; curbing judicial activism; pro-family public policies; gun laws that target criminals, not law-abiding citizens; effective law enforcement; conservation of natural resources and wildlife; and improved protection of property rights.

These policies were probably more or less accepted by the other six candidates. What distinguished me from them were my messages on "national unity" and the Supreme Court.

With respect to the former, my brochures declared:

> Canada cannot afford another generation of the "neverendum" on Quebec and national unity. Three decades have proven that payoffs and appeasement just make the problem worse. As your Senator, I would fight attempts to put Quebec first and the West second.

With respect to the courts, my message was simple and blunt: "I've had enough of unelected senators who do too little and unelected judges who do too much."

> The Supreme Court of Canada has become the single most serious threat to provincial rights and regional democracy.

Unelected, unaccountable judges are making social and economic policy contrary to the intended meaning of the Charter of Rights. This must be stopped. As your senator, I will continue to advocate for the use of the notwithstanding power. We must return the Court to its proper role of interpreting laws rather than making laws. [See Appendix 3.]

I also had endorsements and organizational connections that the other candidates did not. Publicly, I was endorsed by sitting Reform MPs Jason Kenney and Monte Solberg, and also by Stockwell Day, then Alberta treasurer. I had media endorsements by columnists Lorne Gunter in the *Edmonton Journal* and Peter Menzies in the *Calgary Herald*. And of course, Ted Byfield and *Alberta Report*. Less publicly visible but important to my eventual success were Dale Blue, president of the Responsible Firearm Owners of Alberta (RFOA); and Brian Rushfeldt, executive director of the Canadian Family Action Coalition (CFAC). Both RFOA and CFAC had membership lists that they mobilized on my behalf.

I also got an unexpected boost at the end of August, when the Supreme Court released its ruling the *Quebec Secession Reference*.[5] The primary issue was whether a unilateral declaration of independence (UDI) by Quebec—i.e., secession—would be legal. The obvious answer was NO. But always wary of offending Quebec, the court hedged its answer with the concession that under international law, success would confer its own legitimacy. The court also added a completely made-up new rule that if the separatists were to win a referendum by a "clear majority on a clear question," then the rest of Canada has a "constitutional duty to negotiate." There is nothing anywhere in Canada's constitution that even remotely supports this. It was judge-made law, pure and simple.

I immediately wrote a column for the *Calgary Sun* criticizing the court's ruling as "useless at best and dangerous at worst." It basically sent the message to the separatists: "UDI is illegal, unless you can get away with it." I concluded with a quotation from a prominent Quebec MP in the Liberal Caucus that the Chrétien government would now "put itself at the service of the Quebec Liberals as they prepare for a provincial election." As for the rest of Canada, I warned, "we can sit back and prepare for another round of French kissing. The Neverendum marches on."[6]

The large headline above my column—MORE FRENCH KISSING—was widely circulated in the media and energized my supporters. It also cost me my weekly column with the *Calgary Sun*. The following week Licia Corbella, then the editor of the *Sun*, took me out to lunch, and apologetically informed me that the order had come down from the Quebecor head office in Montreal to terminate my contact. Given the timing, it was a good trade-off for me.

By Labour Day, we had out-travelled, out-organized, and out-worked the other six candidates. In addition to dozens of functions in Calgary, we were in Edmonton twice, Red Deer twice, Medicine Hat twice, and Lethbridge twice, as well as Onaway, Lloydminster, Ponoka, Wetaskiwin, Camrose, Castor, Hanna, Brooks, High River, Grand Prairie, and Peace River. These smaller and more rural communities were Reform Party strongholds, and I had the tacit or explicit support of the local MPs in almost every one.

In the end there were seven candidates competing for the two Reform Party nominations. Bert Brown was the best known—famous for plowing into his wheat field the message "TRIPLE E OR ELSE"—which was easily viewed by airplanes landing at the Calgary airport. I did not have much name recognition outside of Reform Party circles, and the other five had even less. The summer campaign for the Reform Party nominations had virtually no media coverage and was invisible to the larger public.

This all changed on August 28. A sitting Alberta Senator, Jean Forest, unexpectedly resigned her seat. She also declared that she hoped that the winner of Alberta's October Senate election would be appointed to replace her.[7] The now open Senate seat gave "a new sense of urgency and legitimacy" to the vote that was previously lacking. It was now "the real thing."[8] Over the next two weeks, the Senate election received more media coverage than it had in the previous four months. As one commentator observed, "This development is akin to divine intervention for the Reform Party."[9]

Alberta Premier Ralph Klein immediately declared that the prime minister must honour the Senate election and that any "snap appointment" would be a "provocation" against Alberta.[10] In Ottawa, the Reform Party immediately went to the Federal Court to request an injunction to prevent the Liberal government from appointing any new Alberta senator until after the October 19 election. This was front page news not just in Alberta papers but in the *Globe and Mail*.[11] Predictably, Alberta newspapers piled on with story after story demanding that the prime minister wait to appoint an elected senator from Alberta.[12] Just as predictably, the *Globe* immediately published an unsigned editorial denouncing the application for an injunction as an unconstitutional "pressure tactic." There are "no short cuts to new Senate," the *Globe* sternly warned.[13]

This unexpected burst of media attention provided a new relevance and profile for the Reform Party's Senate convention vote held only two weeks later in Red Deer on September 12. Both local and national media were there to cover it. Over 3,000 votes were cast at polling stations around Alberta, and 700 Reformers came to Red Deer that Saturday evening. When the results were announced, I was the clear winner with 36 percent of the votes. Bert Brown was a solid second with 24 percent, and all the others at or below 10 percent.[14]

For the first time in my life, I had to face the cameras and the bright lights not as a professor but as a politician. But I didn't pull my punches. I promised that if I became a Senator, I would still speak the "plain, unvarnished truths" about Quebec separatism, gun laws, activist judges, prisoner voting, and the anti-family agenda of the gay rights movement.

My most memorable quote of the night was about Quebec and the "national unity" issue. I said that Canada's $600 billion of debt was a result of a succession of Quebec-based prime ministers—Trudeau, Mulroney, and now Chrétien—buying votes in their home province with borrowed money. "It is simply unacceptable," I told the crowded hall, "to have one group of Quebeckers negotiating with another group of Quebeckers about the future of our country. This has to end. My message will be simple: 'No more French kissing!'" Later that night Jason Kenney told me that he had been in the upper-level media gallery when I said this, and the CBC reporters next to him nearly fell out of their chairs.

The next day the results were front page news in both the *Calgary Herald*[15] and the *Edmonton Journal*.[16] It was an exciting night for both me and my team. We had worked hard—very hard—all summer, so now we could celebrate. And we did!

We had hardly recovered from our weekend in Red Deer before another political bombshell exploded. On Wednesday, the prime minister publicly called the upcoming Alberta Senate elections "a joke."[17] The next day, he announced the appointment of Doug Roche to fill Alberta's vacant Senate seat. Rather than dampening interest in the still-pending October Senate election, it sparked a political firestorm.

Premier Klein publicly called it "a slap in the face" to all Albertans.[18] And that was just the start. "We are all mocked," declared the *Calgary Herald*.[19] The *Calgary Sun* headlined the "SLAP IN THE FACE" message, adding that, "In one swift stroke, Prime Minister Chrétien has again revealed the depths of his disdain for the ideas, contributions and aspirations of Albertans."[20] And it got nastier. According to the *Calgary Sun*, "when it comes to Ottawa, there are lies, damned lies, and then there are promises from Jean Chrétien."[21] The Calgary and Edmonton *Suns* launched a "Protest Coupon" campaign. Subscribers could sign it and send it in. For the next two weeks, Dave Rutherford, the conservative talk-jock on QR77 radio, had a field day with this issue. He even agreed to deliver the "Protest Coupons" to Ottawa in person on the day of the vote.

That day was October 19, the same day as Alberta's regularly scheduled municipal elections. The actual voting day was anticlimactic. And much less fun than Red Deer a month earlier. It was clear that Bert and I would win. Alberta's other political parties boycotted the Senate vote. The only two other candidates were "Independents" Vance Gough and Guy Desrosiers, whom Bert and I had already beaten in the Reform's nomination vote. Still, 891,583 votes were cast. Bert finished first with 332,766. I was second with 274,126, while Gough and Desrosiers each received about 140,000.

The *Calgary Herald* did a poll following the election. They reported that 77 percent wanted the winners appointed; and 72 percent agreed that electing two senators was the best way to tell Ottawa that Albertans want Senate reform. On the other hand, 60 percent also said it was a "waste of time" because Prime Minister Chrétien would not appoint the winners.[22] And of course, he did not! Predictably the Senate reform issue soon disappeared in both the Alberta and national media. But this did not mean the election was a waste of time. It influenced future political developments in at least four ways.

First, it strengthened the Reform Party both internally and externally. At the micro-level, adding the Senate election to the non-stop summer barbeque tour created energy and enthusiasm for party activists. At the macro-level, it raised public awareness of the regional unfairness issue.

Second, this experience influenced my decision to run for MLA five years later, and eventually for premier. I had enjoyed the summer barbeque circuit, and for me September 12 was a very memorable day. This positive first experience contributed to my decision to plunge into the political deep end.

Third, it deepened my involvement in partisan politics. As one of Alberta's two senators-elect, I was now invited to all major (and minor!) Reform Party events, including caucus meetings in Ottawa. And as Reform transitioned to the United Alternative and then the Canadian Alliance Party, I spent nine months in Ottawa in 2001 as the party's director of research and policy.

Last but not least, meeting and speaking with hundreds of Reform activists that summer created a strong volunteer and donor base for my 2006 leadership bid. I would never have received the memberships and votes that we received in 2006—over 36,000—without this motivated network.

Did being elected a "senator-in-waiting" change my life? Certainly not much. In the years immediately following the Senate election, I continued to teach, research, and write full time at the University of Calgary. In 2000, my book *The Charter Revolution and the Court Party* (co-authored with Rainer Knopff) won a $10,000 Donner Foundation prize for best book in Canadian public policy. That same week, the *National Post* ran a lengthy article on the Calgary School with the byline "The Bad Boys of Canadian Academia Earn Some Respect."[23] I published a third edition of my widely adopted textbook, *Law, Politics, and the Judicial Process in Canada.*[24] In November 1999, I was invited to speak at the World Congress of Families II conference in Geneva, Switzerland. My topic: "The Family as the Moral Foundation of Freedom: The Forgotten Dimension of Liberalism." (See Appendix 2.) In 2004, I spoke on "Provincial Constitutions in Canada" at a conference at the Rockefeller Center in Bellagio, Italy.[25] In 2001, *Maclean's* recognized me as one of the twenty most popular professors at the University of Calgary.

I spoke at several conferences in Ontario organized by opponents of the Liberals' then-pending same-sex marriage legislation and contributed a chapter to a book about "the dangers in Canada's new social experiment."[26] I gave the Fifth Annual "Mel Smith Memorial Lecture" at Trinity Western University in Langley, British Columbia.[27] In 2002, I spent six months in Australia with visiting fellowships at the University of Melbourne and then the Australian National University in Canberra. At the former, I co-authored a paper with Dr. Brian Galligan (a colleague from my graduate school days in Toronto), comparing the role of courts and legislatures in rights protection in Canada, Australia, and the United States.[28] At the latter I was asked to speak by the Australian Senate on the Senate reform efforts in Canada. My message: "Senate Envy: Why Western Canada Wants What Australia Has."[29] Bottom line: While my byline now often included "Alberta Senator-in-Waiting," I was still working full time as a university professor. But the distinction between "public intellectual" and a politician was becoming blurred.[30]

CANADIAN ALLIANCE LEADERSHIP (2000)

An important exception to this was in 2001. In 2000, when the Reform Party transitioned to the Canadian Alliance Party, there had to be a leadership election for the new party. Understandably, Preston Manning, who was the architect of the transition, ran for leader. But he was challenged by Stockwell Day, the then treasurer (finance minister) of Alberta. I thought that to succeed, the new party needed a new leader. Manning had heroically pioneered Reform from one MP in 1987 to official opposition for the past decade. But in the process, he had made a lot of enemies on the Progressive Conservative side. If we were ever to form a majority government in Ottawa, I knew we would need to win over the PCs. I had also worked with Day on the Klein government's response to the Supreme Court's decision in the Delwin Vriend case[31] and the federal Liberals' pending same-sex marriage legislation. After much deliberation, I chose to support Day and served as the principal organizer responsible for membership sales in southern Alberta.

The leadership campaign itself was short and polite—virtually no personal attacks. But when the votes were counted on July 8, to my surprise and almost everyone else's, Day won. He was younger and more charismatic than Preston, and others must have made the same new party–new leader calculation that I had. But Day had a problem. The new party's caucus were almost all Reform MPs. Most had remained loyal to Manning and did not even know Day. Day had never set foot in the House of Commons, and now he was the leader of the official opposition.

Sensing weakness, the Liberals called a snap election that fall. It worked. With the right-of-centre vote still divided between the Alliance and PC parties, Jean Chrétien won his third consecutive majority Liberal government. While the Alliance increased its seat total from fifty-eight to sixty-six, it was less than expected. Some members blamed this on Day's performance as leader.

During this election at a campaign fundraiser in Calgary for Day, I made a classic rookie mistake. Campaigning in Eastern Canada and trying to be humorous, Jean Chrétien had suggested several times that Day and the Alliance were somehow "different" or "aliens." After conferring with virtually no one, I decided it would be fun and funny to come to the event dressed in a full Darth Vader outfit. This seemed like a good idea until I arrived at the hotel. Two double martinis at the bar on the ground floor quickly restored my confidence. So I got on the escalator up to the event. As soon as I got off, I was immediately apprehended by two RCMP security officers travelling with the Day campaign. It turned out that they were under orders to immediately arrest and escort out of the building anyone showing up at with a mask or face covering. Fortunately for me, Patty Boessert, the event organizer, saw what was happening, explained to the RCMP who I was, and rescued me. I then entered the ballroom, mask removed, to my assigned table. Waiting at the table were Ron and Judy Quigley, large donors to the Day campaign. A horde of media cameras quickly descended on our table. So much for a positive first impression! (As it turned out, the Quigleys thought the whole thing was funny. Five years later, in the 2006 PC leadership contest, they gave us the entire fourth floor of their Gunnar Office Furnishings office building in Calgary for our campaign offices.)

The architect of Day's leadership campaign, and now his principal advisor, was none other than Jason Kenney. As caucus unhappiness grew, the two of them came to me and asked if I would help. I agreed, and I spoke with some of the dissident MPs. In February I visited Manning in his Calgary office. I told him about the problem in caucus, and that much of it came from former Reform MPs who still had a strong sense of loyalty to Manning. My request—which I thought was quite modest—was that Manning make a public statement supporting Day and encouraging the dissidents to do the same. To my complete surprise, he flatly refused. Day, Manning told me, "simply doesn't understand." I walked out of his office in shock.

It did not end there. Several months later, eleven MPs left the Canadian Alliance to sit as Independents. Some returned in the fall, but seven, led by Chuck Strahl and Deb Gray, created a new parliamentary grouping, the

Democratic Representative Caucus (DRC), and formed a coalition with Joe Clark's PCs.

As the caucus situation deteriorated, Kenney and Day now asked if I would come to Ottawa to help the new party. It was an intriguing offer, and, perhaps irrationally, I accepted. So from May to December of 2001, I worked in Ottawa as the party's director of policy and research. This worked well during the summer, but not once my courses started in September. I taught my classes on Mondays and Fridays; flew to Ottawa Monday night; worked Tuesday, Wednesday, Thursday in Ottawa; and returned to Calgary on Thursday nights to teach my Friday classes. As much as I enjoyed and benefited from this experience, it was clearly unsustainable. At the end of December, exhausted, I resigned. In January, I left for Australia on a pre-arranged six-month sabbatical.

By the time I returned in June, Day had agreed to a second leadership race to re-establish his authority as the party leader. It didn't work. With Manning now gone, Stephen Harper decided he wanted to return to the new party. He resigned as leader of the National Citizens Coalition, entered the race to challenge Day, and won.[32] This was awkward for me. Harper and I had become friends during his days as the Reform MP for Calgary West. I had also been working closely with him on the Firewall Letter (see below). But I was equally good friends with Day and Jason Kenney, who had been the de facto director of both of Day's leadership campaigns. As one of Alberta's senators-in-waiting, I was still being invited to Canadian Alliance caucus meetings, where there were still a lot of raw nerves and personal animosities left from eighteen months of party infighting.

For me, there were several takeaways from all this. It was my first (but not my last!) experience that in politics, in-house fights are more personal—therefore more bitter—than disputes with other parties. It also contributed to my decision the following year to jump into provincial politics. With Harper now running the show in Ottawa, I thought it made sense for me to go provincial. Premier Klein was expected to retire in the next few years, and his PC Caucus was clearly not aligned with the more conservative and anti-Ottawa principles and policies that I shared with the growing number of Reform-Alliance supporters in Alberta.

Last but not least, I was quite bitter toward the DRC MPs for taking down Day before he, in my opinion, had been given a fair chance to prove (or not) his leadership abilities. I made a promise to myself that going forward I would never put personal disappointment ahead of maintaining caucus unity. In theory, I still think this is a good principle. But in retrospect it may have hurt me politically a few years later, when I stuck with Premier Ed Stelmach and the PC caucus for as long as I did (see chapter 9).

FIREWALL LETTER (2001)

> *Definition: "A firewall is a part of a computer system or network that is designed to block unauthorized access while permitting outward communication."*

With respect to my evolution from "prof to pol," 2001 stands out for a second reason. In January, I was one of the co-authors of the "Alberta Agenda" letter to Premier Ralph Klein. Obscure at the time it was published, this political manifesto turned out have a direct impact not just on my life but the next two decades of conservative politics in Alberta.

Advancing the Alberta Agenda was my reason for running for MLA for the Alberta PCs in 2004. My 2006 PC leadership campaign was based almost entirely on the Firewall. After my defeat, the Wildrose Party picked it up and used it to win official opposition status in the 2012 provincial election. In 2019, it became government policy under the newly elected United Conservative Party government of Jason Kenney[33] and his "fair deal" policy initiatives.[34] Kenney's successor, Premier Danielle Smith, then went one step further by campaigning for and then enacting the *Alberta Sovereignty Act* (2023).[35] In short, the same Firewall reforms that were on the fringe of Alberta provincial politics twenty years ago are now front and centre (see chapter 12 for a more detailed discussion).

The "Alberta Agenda" was a public letter sent to Premier Ralph Klein in January 2001 urging him to take specific reforms to increase Alberta's political autonomy and self-governance. The reforms were intended to insulate and protect Alberta from harmful federal interference—thus its better-known title, the "Firewall Letter."[36]

There were five specific recommendations in the Alberta Agenda:[37]

1. Withdraw from the Canada Pension Plan to create an Alberta Pension Plan offering the same benefits at lower cost while giving

Alberta control over the investment fund. Pensions are a provincial responsibility under section 94A of the Constitution Act, 1867; and the legislation setting up the Canada Pension Plan permits a province to run its own plan, as Quebec has done from the beginning. If Quebec can do it, why not Alberta?

2. Collect our own revenue from personal income tax, as we already do for corporate income tax. Any incremental cost of collecting our own personal income tax would be far outweighed by the policy flexibility that Alberta would gain, as Quebec's experience has shown.

3. Start preparing now to let the contract with the RCMP run out in 2012 and create an Alberta Provincial Police Force. Alberta is a major province. Like the other major provinces of Ontario and Quebec, we should have our own provincial police force.

4. Resume provincial responsibility for health care policy. Albertans deserve better than the long waiting periods and technological backwardness that are rapidly coming to characterize Canadian medicine. Alberta should also argue that each province should raise its own revenue for health care—i.e., replace the Canada Health and Social Transfer cash with tax points as Quebec has argued for many years. Poorer provinces would continue to rely on Equalization to ensure they have adequate revenues.

5. Use section 88 of the Supreme Court's decision in the Quebec Secession Reference to force Senate reform back onto the national agenda. Our reading of that decision is that the federal government and other provinces must seriously consider a proposal for constitutional reform endorsed by "a clear majority on a clear question" in a provincial referendum.

In one sense, these reforms were quite modest. As noted, most were already being done by Quebec, Ontario, or both. So no big deal, right? Wrong! The very fact that Quebec was the model for these proposed reforms immediately raised the spectre of a hidden agenda—Alberta separatism. While this was clearly not our intention at that time, it alarmed critics. There has always been a small but marginal separatist element on the fringes of Alberta politics. But it was largely rural and associated with leaders no one had ever heard of. The Firewall Letter was different. This was the first time in Alberta's history that reforms of this nature had been publicly endorsed by recognizable public figures.

The signatories included, first and foremost, Stephen Harper, then president of the National Citizens Coalition, but until recently Reform MP and one of Preston Manning's most influential advisors. Also signing were Andy Crooks, a Calgary lawyer and president of the Canadian Taxpayers Federation; Ken Boessenkool, former policy advisor to Stockwell Day; and then three members of the Calgary School—Tom Flanagan, Rainer Knopff, and myself.[38]

The immediate catalyst for the Firewall Letter was the just-completed 2000 Federal election, during which Prime Minister Chrétien had singled out Alberta for particularly harsh criticism, especially on health care reforms. His continued refusal to appoint Alberta's elected senators was another irritant. Chrétien had also signed the Kyoto Accord in 1995 without any consultation with Alberta or Saskatchewan. There were fears even then that this could be the precursor of a second National Energy Program—fears that have turned out to be justified. There was also growing frustration with failure of the "unite the Right" efforts. The continued vote splitting between Reform (then Alliance) and the PCs had just given Chrétien and the Liberals a third consecutive majority government.

The letter was Harper's idea. He'd had a falling-out with Preston Manning and had chosen not to run for re-election as a Reform MP in 1997. According to Tom Flanagan, the letter was part of Harper's "long-term strategy ... to force the federal government back into a more narrowly circumscribed sphere of constitutional jurisdiction."[39] It might have been. But I thought it was also setting the stage for Stephen to take a run at the premier's office in Alberta when Klein chose to step aside, which was then being publicly discussed. I had come to know Stephen fairly well over the previous decade, and I did not think he was finished with electoral politics. I turned out to be right, but in the end, he went federal rather than provincial.

By the time I returned from Australia in June 2002, Stephen had defeated Stockwell Day in the leadership contest for the Canadian Alliance Party. This was good for Stephen and good for the Alliance. But now he (and Flanagan, as his policy advisor) was off to Ottawa and the federal political arena. This left the Alberta Agenda without any public advocate in Alberta.

Enter Pat Beauchamp and Alberta Residents League (ARL). Notwithstanding its innocuous sounding name, the ARL played a crucial role in promoting the Alberta Agenda across the province over the next four years.

I had nothing do to with the creation of the ARL. But in the fall of 2002, I was asked by the late Stan Grad to come to a meeting with Beauchamp. I had met Stan through our mutual involvement in the Reform Party during the 1990s, and he had contributed financially to my 1998 Senate campaign. It turned out that Stan—and his network of affluent friends—very much liked the Alberta Agenda and were financially supporting the ARL. The ARL grew quickly. Soon it had a board of directors,[40] a province-wide advisory committee,[41] and a website. At its peak, the ARL had 2,000 dues-paying members. Beauchamp was a great organizer, but not an effective public speaker. Stan thought I could and should fill that role. And in the end, I did.

In March 2003, the ARL launched its campaign with a town hall meeting in Drayton Valley. Ninety people showed up to hear Link Byfield and myself explain and advocate for the Firewall reforms.[42] By year end, the ARL had held ten such meetings across Alberta. These were well advertised and well attended—an average crowd of over 150 persons. I was usually the featured speaker. These town halls received good local media, and the ARL started getting positive coverage in the Edmonton and Calgary papers from conservative columnists like Neil Waugh, Licia Corbella, Danielle Smith, Link and Ted Byfield, and Barry Cooper. It was at the Drayton Valley meeting that Chris Matthews, a recent graduate of the political science MA program at the U of C, came up with the slogan—MORE ALBERTA, LESS OTTAWA. These four words so succinctly captured our message that we adopted it immediately. By the end of 2004, there were a dozen large billboards across the province projecting this message to everyone who drove by.

The success of the ARL can be measured by the Klein government's response. Initially, Klein all but dismissed it. In February 2001, Klein conceded that while Alberta had been mistreated by Ottawa, he rejected the "sense of defeatism that underlies the notion of building a firewall around this province." "Retreating behind our provincial boundaries is not," he wrote, "a response that would be supported by the vast majority of Albertans."[43]

Fast forward to November 2003. After eleven months of ARL town halls, the Conservatives were beginning to feel some heat on these issues. The PCs' annual general meeting in November 2003 featured a panel on "Strengthening Alberta's Place in Confederation." In his keynote address, Premier Klein criticized the "arrogance of Ottawa Liberals," and "cited a litany of longstanding concerns, including the monopoly of the Canadian Wheat Board, the gun registry, the Kyoto Accord, and senate reform."[44] He then announced the formation of an MLA committee that would hold forums across the province to listen to Albertans on this issue.

Media commentary quickly linked the creation of the committee to the ARL town halls. According to one commentator, the premier admitted that "the Alberta Agenda had captured the imagination of a sizeable chunk of those within his party, as well as many within the broader public." And, the writer continued, "Ralph rarely misreads the mood of his party or his province."[45] According to another, "It's strategically important for the Tories to lead the discussion of firewall issues …. By talking about it themselves, they prevent an Alberta right-wing party from taking over the issue."[46] In the first three months of 2004, the MLA committee held twelve public forums. I appeared before the committee at its final meeting in Calgary. I recommended adoption of the Firewall reforms: "What would be irresponsible about urging the government of Alberta to fully exercise the constitutional powers it already has?"[47]

In the end, the committee's report rejected the reforms proposed in the Alberta Agenda, declaring that it would be more productive "to build bridges rather than firewalls." This response was disappointing but predictable. The committee's public hearings were more an exercise in public relations than a true consultation. Nonetheless, the committee gave new attention and energy to the "more Alberta, less Ottawa" message.

In addition to the ARL, I had also formed my own small advocacy organization, the Alberta Civil Society Association (ACSA). I used the ACSA to support my criticisms of a series of Supreme Court decisions based on the Charter of Rights dealing with issues like prisoner voting, sexual orientation, and same-sex marriage. I criticized these decisions in part because there was no explicit language in the Charter to support them. Indeed, there was clear evidence that the framers of the Charter intentionally chose to exclude these issues. But I also criticized them for weakening, both symbolically and in practice, institutions like family, community, and citizenship that nurture the altruistic and law-abiding citizenry that sustain liberal democracies. The ACSA's most visible impact was a colourful bumper sticker whose message was self-explanatory.

```
┌─────────────────────────────────────────────────────┐
│                          NO Wheat Board               │
│   DEFEND THE WEST        NO Gun Registry              │
│                          NO Kyoto                     │
└─────────────────────────────────────────────────────┘
```

We sold over 18,000 of these, and they were a common sight on the backs of cars and trucks all over Alberta for several years.

In addition to speaking at ARL town halls, I became involved with several grassroots protests on issues of importance to Alberta Reformers. In October 2002, I joined Premier Ralph Klein and several Alliance MPs in Lethbridge to speak at a rally to support the thirteen Alberta farmers who were being arrested for exporting their own grain without the prior approval of the Canadian Wheat Board.[48] Farmers in Ontario and Quebec were free to sell their own wheat however they chose. But farmers from Manitoba, Saskatchewan, and Alberta were required by federal law to sell all their wheat through the Wheat Board. At the time of their arrest, Western farmers could sell their durum wheat south of the border for C$8.50 a bushel, but only C$3.50 if they sold to the board. Surrounded by the farmers and their families, I spoke to about 500 persons who attended the rally in Lethbridge. Behind us was a huge banner declaring: "WELCOME TO CANADA: THE ONLY COUNTRY IN THE FREE WORLD THAT JAILS ITS FARMERS FOR SELLING THEIR OWN WHEAT."[49] And go to jail they did.

I also became involved in the opposition to the Liberals new firearms registry, Bill C-68. Enacted in 1995, Bill C-68 required all gun owners to apply for and maintain a federal licence and also to register with the federal government all hunting rifles and shotguns. These "long guns" are used only for hunting and target practice. They play virtually no role in the criminal use of guns or gun deaths. But C-68 would make duck and deer hunters like myself and tens of thousands of other law-abiding Canadians potential criminals if we did not register our guns. I registered mine—all seven of them—but then joined the grassroots movement calling for the repeal of C-68.

The new federal gun registry provoked a strong negative reaction from gun owners across Canada. In Alberta, the Klein government responded by using its reference power to challenge the constitutional validity of C-68. Alberta argued that this kind of legislation falls within the provinces' jurisdiction over "property and civil rights," not under Ottawa's authority for criminal law. Criminal law addresses actions that harm others, Alberta argued. Simple ownership harms no one and should not be deemed criminal. Alberta's challenge was joined by several other provincial governments and ended up before the Supreme Court.

I had written several op-eds criticizing C-68 on both legal and policy grounds. This led to my meeting the late Dale Blue, the founder and executive director of the Responsible Firearm Owners of Alberta (RFOA). Working with Dale and RFOA, we raised sufficient funds to intervene in the constitutional challenge to C-68 before the Supreme Court. We hired Dallas Miller, a lawyer from Medicine Hat and fellow Reform Party activist, to represent us, and all three of us went to Ottawa for the oral arguments in February 2000.

In June, the court handed down a decision upholding C-68 as a valid exercise of the federal government's section 91 criminal law jurisdiction.[50] We were disappointed but not surprised. Several feminist organizations had intervened to support C-68. We knew that the court—then and now—almost never says "NO" to feminist intervenors.[51] I responded with yet another op-ed: "Gun control legal battle lost, but the war is far from over."[52]

In 2002, I wrote a lengthy (39-page) report on how Bill C-68 could be challenged for violating numerous sections of the Canadian Charter of Rights. This work was funded by the RFOA and its sister organizations in British Columbia and Saskatchewan. I first publicly presented this work at an event organized by the Recreational Firearms Community of Saskatchewan in Saskatoon in October 2002. (After which they arranged for a most successful duck and goose shoot on shores of Lake Lenore!)

Several months later, on a cold and snowy January 1, 2003, I spoke in Edmonton at a rally to support Oscar Lacombe and his refusal to register his hunting rifles.[53] Oscar Lacombe was a 74-year-old Métis veteran of the Korean War and former sergeant-at-arms in the Alberta Legislative Assembly. Working with the RFOA, Oscar had announced that he was not going to register his long guns. As had been advertised, on January 1, Oscar carried his .22 calibre rifle—unloaded, bolt-removed, and sealed in plastic—to the steps of the Legislative Assembly—where he had worked for over a decade—and declared to a cheering crowd: "I won't register this gun, and I won't hide. I will not submit to this unjust and dangerous law. ... Free I was born, and even if you put me in jail, free I will remain."[54] But he was still arrested as soon as he finished.[55] Several years later, the Stephen Harper Conservative government (2006–2015) abolished both the long gun registry and the Wheat Board.

But this was too late to help Oscar Lacombe and the thirteen Alberta farmers who went to jail for their non-violent civil disobedience to protest unjust and ineffective federal laws.

None of these "extra-curricular" political engagements by themselves — the Firewall letter, the six months in Ottawa, the Alberta Residents League, the Wheat Board, or long-gun rallies—led me to take the last step: to seek an elected political office as the candidate of a political party. But their cumulative effect did. With Harper now gone to Ottawa; with Jean Chrétien and the Liberals having won their third consecutive majority government; and with neither Klein nor anyone in his cabinet showing much interest in the Alberta Agenda reforms, I decided that Alberta needed new leadership and that I was the person to provide it.

Several friends and supporters had already encouraged me to seek a Canadian Alliance nomination and go to Ottawa to join Harper. But my six months there as director of research had left me with a sour taste for Ottawa. Like all national governments today, the permanent government—the bureaucracy that administers the modern welfare state—is just as powerful as the elected governments that come and go. In Ottawa, the bilingualism requirement for civil servants means that over half of our federal bureaucracy is French—much higher in the senior positions—with little to no personal experience or attachment to Western Canada. Bilingualism is less about language and more like an ideology that prioritizes national unity, and national unity is understood as keeping Quebeckers happy.[56] During my time in Ottawa, I soon learned that—even in the Canadian Alliance caucus—the first question asked about any new policy or press release was: How will this play in Quebec? For me, that was the problem, not the solution. Besides, Harper did not need (and probably did not want) my help. Alberta did.

So on February 1, 2003, I organized a meeting in Red Deer with people with whom I had worked since the 1998 Senate election. Officially, the invitation was for a meeting on how to advance the reforms proposed in the Alberta Agenda. I invited twenty-four individuals. Several were personal friends and fundraisers. The rest represented a variety of small-c conservative groups I had supported or helped in recent years. In the end eighteen attended, mostly from central and southern Alberta.[57] The groups included Farmers for Justice, Canada Family Action Coalition, Responsible Firearm Owners of Alberta, Alberta Federation of Women United for Families, Alberta Residents League, and Alberta Property Rights Initiative.

The agenda consisted of a variety of strategies on how best to influence public opinion to support the reforms recommended by the Alberta Agenda, plus the more recent issues of the Wheat Board, Kyoto, and the gun registry. Beauchamp said the ARL would continue with its town halls. Byfield and *Alberta Report* magazine were planning a major conference, Western Assembly II. Andy Crooks reported that the Fraser Institute was undertaking a new "Alberta Agenda" research project to flesh out some of the proposed reforms. There was a proposal to form a new, separatist party, but there was much more interest in how to influence the Klein Tories, including nominating new candidates. It was in this context that I announced that I had decided to run for the leadership of the provincial PC party when Klein retired. I explained why and asked for their support. None were too surprised, and all were supportive. I drove back to Calgary that afternoon with a sense of optimism about the journey I was about to begin.

This ended abruptly as I watched the evening news. Earlier that day, NASA's Space Shuttle *Columbia* had disintegrated as it re-entered Earth's atmosphere, killing all seven crew members. In Alberta, seven students from the Strathcona-Tweedsmuir School on a cross-country skiing trip had been buried and killed by an avalanche just west of Rogers Pass. Was all this tragic news a foreboding omen for my new venture?

MLA FOR FOOTHILLS-ROCKY VIEW (2004)

I had asked those who met with me in Red Deer to keep my plans confidential until I publicly announced them. But it did not stay secret for long. In April, Ted Byfield wrote a piece in the *Edmonton Sun*, "Why Ted Morton should become premier."[58] This was a general endorsement and did not mention any specific plans. But by July, the cat was out of the bag when Tom Olsen published a piece in the *Edmonton Journal* with the byline, "Firewall group eyes premier's office."[59] This news would not have been received with any enthusiasm in the Klein cabinet, and it complicated my next move.

My first step was to win a nomination for a Progressive Conservative constituency. The obvious choice was Calgary-Varsity, where we lived. The sitting MLA was Murray Smith, then minister of energy, who was widely expected not to run again in the 2004 provincial elections. This should have been simple. But it was not. It quickly became apparent that Smith was not willing to disclose his plans or co-operate with me. We surmised that this was not by accident; that it reflected advice from Premier Klein, his former chief of staff Rod Love, or both.

Klein's inner circle was not a fan of the Firewall agenda, and they did not want me in the PC caucus. Klein had built a big-tent Conservative party, and they feared I might fracture it—opening up cleavages between the more conservative rural wing and more moderate urban members.[60] Rod Love had additional reasons. It was widely known that Jim Dinning, Klein's former minister of finance, planned to run for leader when Klein chose to step down. Love had already agreed to manage Dinning's campaign. The last thing either man wanted was Ted Morton in the leadership race. Murray Smith obviously shared these views, so the door in Calgary-Varsity was closed tight. But if not there, where?

Fortunately for me, there was another option. Alberta's electoral map had been redrawn based on the most recent ten-year census. The map contained a new riding just West of Calgary: Foothills-Rocky View. It stretched from Crossfield in the north to Turner Valley and Black Diamond in the south. In between, it included the smaller communities of Bragg Creek, Millarville, and Priddis, and the acreage communities of Springbank and Bearspaw. Highway 22, the "Cowboy Trail," ran down the middle.

Foothills-Rocky View was just as beautiful as its name. And the good news did not stop there. All these communities were solid PC supporters provincially and Reform-Alliance supporters federally. The latter opened the door for me, as I had met and worked with many of these conservative activists in Reform Party meetings and campaigns. Both the federal MPs for these areas—Dr. Grant Hill (Macleod) in the south and the late Myron Thompson (Wildrose) in the north—had become friends and now strong supporters.

The bad news was I didn't live there. I would be a "carpet-bagger"—a non-resident coming in from outside the riding. As in most parliamentary systems, this is legal in Canada, but still not popular, especially in rural and small-town Alberta. So that was my dilemma: if I could win the PC nomination, I was all but guaranteed to win in the general election. But winning the PC nomination was far from certain. I needed a local champion—someone lots of people knew and trusted. Enter Harvey Buckley.

How to describe Harvey? Maybe a senior version of John Wayne, except that he was friendly. At six-foot-three, he was tall, lean, and handsome, with a smile that made you smile back. His family had ranched west of Calgary for several generations. Harvey knew almost every rancher in both Foothills and

Rocky View counties. Over the first six months of 2004, he drove me to their front doors and personally introduced me. Harvey had been active in local Reform Party organizing and events, which is how we had first met. He also founded Action for Agriculture, an organization that works to protect native grasslands and minimize the fragmentation of ranch and farm properties surrounding Calgary. Without the hundreds of hours of help and support from Harvey and his wife, Margaret, I doubt that I would have won the PC nomination in Foothills-Rocky View. And I did not win it by much!

There were three other candidates vying for the nomination. Unlike me, none had any public profile outside their own communities. But, also unlike me, they each had a home base in the riding. Tim Anderson was the mayor of Redwood Meadows. Jerry Muelaner was the chair of the Foothills School Division. And Spence Bozak was well known and well liked in the Bragg Creek area. We knew that to win, we would have to outwork and out-organize the other three candidates.

The vote was set for June 18 and 19. The first day of voting was at the Red Deer Lake Community Centre in the south end of the riding; the second at the Cochrane Curling Club in the north. At the end of voting hours in Cochrane, the votes from both polling stations would be counted and the winner announced. The vote was by preferential ballot. Each voter indicated their first and second choice. To win required 50-percent-plus-one of total votes cast. If no candidate achieved that threshold, the candidate with lowest number of votes was dropped and his supporters' second preferences were redistributed to the remaining candidates. We were quite confident of a first ballot win. We had knocked on more doors, sent more letters, and made more GOTV (get out the vote) phone calls than the other three candidates combined. But we were quickly reminded that it ain't over 'til it's over.

As we waited outside the Cochrane Curling Club for the results to be announced, we noticed a small contingent of PC Party operatives in the crowd. These included Thompson Macdonald and Rod Love, Klein's former chief of staff and the unofficial chairman of Jim Dinning's unofficial leadership team. They certainly weren't there to support me, so why were they here? Had the party been helping one of the other candidates? It made us a bit nervous.

Just before 9 p.m., the results were announced. On the first round, I received 309 preferences, well ahead of second-place finisher Tim Anderson at 227—but at 44 percent of the total, still less than the 50-percent-plus-one required to win. We became a bit more nervous. The fourth-place finisher—Muelaner—was dropped, and his supporters' second preferences were counted. This only added 13 votes to my total, but 52 to Anderson's. I was still first but still short of 50 percent-plus-one. Now Anderson was only 43 votes behind me and we were more nervous. So Bozak was dropped, and his supporters' second preferences redistributed. When the count was done— and it was done twice—I had squeaked by with 50.3 percent of the votes: 342 to 338, only four more than Anderson.

We celebrated, but it was more in relief than joy. How had it become so close? Was there an anyone-but-Morton campaign that we were unaware of? That evening, Tim said he accepted the results. He even made the motion to destroy the ballots and make the decision unanimous, which was customary in PC nomination elections. That only lasted forty-eight hours. By Monday, he had changed his mind.[61] He told media that he had reason to believe that persons from outside the riding had participated and that he was going to demand a second election. Constituency President Blair Barkley asked if he had any evidence of this. He said he had none. Barkley communicated to us that he found Anderson's request "highly irregular and serving no constructive purpose." After five days of limbo and media coverage, Anderson suddenly reversed again and declared he accepted the results.[62] We breathed a sigh of relief but became suspicious. Why had he done this? Had he been encouraged to? If so, by whom? And for what reason?

On a lighter note, there was a good story that came out of the June 19 vote count that evening in Cochrane. Part of our group waiting for the results to be announced were Eric and Colleen Lowther. We had become friends in the 1990s when Eric served as the Reform Party MP for Calgary Centre. He and Colleen, along with their two daughters, now lived in Springbank, part of the Foothills-Rocky View riding. They had been active volunteers for my campaign from the start. After the final results were announced, Eric approached me with a big grin. "Ted," he began, "you are going to owe me big time from here on out." He went on to explain that while he and Colleen had voted that morning, their two daughters had been at school. So that afternoon, they then made a second trip out to Cochrane so the two girls could vote. Given my final margin of victory, it was clearly the four Lowther votes that put me over the top. I didn't argue.

I was now the official PC Party candidate. But the anticipated provincial election was at least five months away.[63] It was a forgone conclusion that whoever won the PC nomination for Foothills-Rocky View would be elected. It was a strongly conservative riding. We joked that even my dog Coulee—who often came with me door-knocking—could be elected there. So to say I spent the next five months campaigning would be technically accurate but misleading. It was nothing like the ten hours a day, six days a week campaigning I did leading up to nomination vote. I door-knocked on some Saturdays but not all. I did endless meet-and-greet coffee parties hosted by supporters who invited their neighbours to meet me. When the campaign became official in late October, we opened small campaign offices in Cochrane and Black Diamond; hosted still more meet-and-greet coffee receptions; and participated in two debates with the other three candidates. We ran ads in all the four weekly newspapers. But we did no direct mail or GOTV phone banks. That fall, I taught my normal course schedule at the university, and even went duck hunting a few times with Coulee.

What we did do was to continue to plan for my eventual run to become the leader of the party when Klein decided to step aside. I met with my campaign team on almost a weekly basis. They continued to raise money and build mailing lists. To this end, we organized a major fundraising lunch at the Palliser Hotel in mid-September. Technically it was to raise funds for the constituency association and the upcoming fall election. But candidates for rural ridings outside of Calgary don't hold fundraisers at the Palliser. Everyone knew it was in effect my first public leadership event. Just weeks earlier, the *Western Standard* (the Byfields' successor magazine to *Alberta Report*), published an issue with my picture on the cover with the headline: "PREMIER-IN-WAITING?"[64] Maybe this explains why we were able to sell out the event—over 400 seats at $125 a plate. It also explains the icy reception I got six weeks later at the PC Party's "candidates' school" in Red Deer.

I used my speech at the fundraiser to lay out my vision for the future of Alberta—the "more Alberta, less Ottawa" reforms proposed in the Alberta Agenda. I don't think I even mentioned Foothills-Rocky View. Other than the fact that a smiling Jim Dinning was sitting at a table directly in front of the podium, what I remember most about the event were two funny incidents. The first occurred two days before the luncheon. Our event organizer, Catherine Scheers, insisted that I visit the Palliser to see how she had set up the Palliser's ornate Crystal Ballroom. Because of the rectangular shape of the room, she had to put the screens for my PowerPoint at both ends of the room, rather than behind the podium. I said this was fine and started to leave. Not so fast, she said. As long as we're here, I've arranged for you to taste what we'll be serving for the luncheon. As if I cared! But I demurred and sat down.

The next thing I knew there was a steaming hot roasted chicken in front of me. "Chicken!" I shrieked. "We can't serve chicken! My people eat beef! I'll never get elected to anything if we serve chicken!" Startled, Catherine conferred with the hotel representative and then explained that on such short notice, serving beef would raise the per plate cost by 75 cents. I lost it again. "I don't care if it costs three times that, we have to have beef!" And have beef we did: flank steak, so chewy you could have played hand-ball with it. But nobody (except my wife) cared. And it didn't cost a penny more! Thank you, Palliser!

The second incident was my introduction by Lee Richardson. I did not know Lee well, but he was best friends with my good friend the late Ralph Hedlin. Lee was well connected with many of the big donors to the PC Party, and it was Ralph's advice that it would be good for me politically to be introduced by someone like Lee. Lee was also known for his sense of humour, and he didn't disappoint. He began by reminding the audience of how I had been fighting for a "fair deal" for Alberta over the preceding years: opposing the Meech Lake and the Charlottetown Accords; working for Senate reform and the Alberta Agenda; supporting the farmers who went to jail for their protest against the Wheat Board; standing shoulder-to-shoulder with Oscar Lacombe in his civil disobedience challenging the Liberal gun registry. "As you can see," he concluded, "Ted is very good at getting his friends arrested." The entire room burst into laughter. It was a great icebreaker.

Klein finally dissolved the Legislative Assembly on October 25. This triggered a twenty-eight-day campaign, setting the election date for November 22. The day before the announcement, all PC candidates were summoned to Red Deer for a "candidates' school." The purpose of these "schools" is very simple: To make sure candidates know what the party's official talking points are and not—repeat, NOT—to vary from them anytime over the next four weeks. Here's the script. Read it and stick with it. This is standard fare for all parties in all provinces. The last thing any party wants are rookie candidates freelancing new policy announcements in their local races. I knew this in advance and didn't think I needed to drive to Red Deer to hear it. But of course, I did.

For me, two things made this "candidates' school" memorable. The first was that I almost got killed on the way there. Just east of Bowden, my Ford Explorer hit a patch of ice; did a 360-degree spin; crossed the two southbound lanes; crashed through the guardrail; and plunged nose-first into a water-filled, ice-covered culvert on the other side of Highway 2.[65] An RCMP officer arrived within minutes. Once he ascertained that—somehow—neither I nor Harvey Buckley was injured, he called a tow truck and then told us: When you get to town, buy a lottery ticket, because today is your lucky day. He was right.

But of course, we couldn't go to town and buy a lottery ticket. We had to get to Red Deer, and we did. That too was memorable, but for very different reasons. There were eighty-seven PC candidates there, most with a manager, plus Premier Klein and dozen or so of his campaign team. Of the almost 200 people in the room, I knew fewer than ten. This was a bit uncomfortable. And it didn't get better. Was anyone happy to see me or congratulate me for winning the Foothills-Rocky View nomination? Apparently not. The only party official who greeted me was Peter Elzinga, the president of the Alberta PC Party. The drive home for Harvey and me was pretty quiet. The article in the *Edmonton Journal* two weeks later explained why: "Veteran Tory MLAs are eagerly awaiting Morton's arrival at the legislature after the election, simply so they can cut him down. There haven't been this many knives in a welcoming committee since Julius Caesar dropped by the Senate."[66]

The twenty-eight-day campaign in Foothills-Rocky View was uneventful until the last day. As I was leaving our campaign office in Black Diamond, a television reporter, Darrel Janz from CFCN Calgary, was waiting for me. His first few questions were innocuous enough, but then he hit me with a surprise. "What about the allegations that your nomination election last June was fraudulent, and that even if you win tomorrow, you may not be able to take a seat in the legislature?" I was dumbfounded. My inner voice wanted to say, "What the fuck are you talking about?" But my outer voice prevailed: "That was settled months ago," I calmly replied. "Who told you this?" Janz didn't answer. But he did broadcast the interview on the evening news a few hours later.

This ambush interview was just the beginning of an even more bizarre evening.[67] Just after 7 p.m., I began getting phone calls from members of my campaign team about rogue autodial calls that were repeating the same message to residents in the riding: that there was "a voter fraud investigation targeting PC Candidate Ted Morton's campaign," and that this could disqualify me even if I were to win the election the next day.[68] It turned out that there were approximately 11,000 such autodial calls that evening, all with sophisticated call-blocking that prevented tracing their source.[69] It was a classic eleventh-hour drive-by smear attack.[70]

That was the bad news. The good news was that it had no effect on the outcome of the election. When the ballots were counted the next day, I had carried all fifty-seven polls and won over 60 percent of the votes. I had a total of 6,782 votes, and the next closest candidate, Liberal Herb Coburne, had 1,956.

We filed complaints with both Alberta's chief electoral officer and the Canadian Radio-television and Telecommunications Commission.[71] CRTC rules prohibited autodial calls after 7 p.m. CRTC also requires such messages to identify who the caller is and how to contact them. The Alberta *Election Act* prohibits anyone other than candidates, political parties, and constituency associations from using voters lists. The chief electoral officer asked the RCMP to investigate. The CRTC asked Telus to turn over telephone records for that evening that could show who sent the automated messages.[72] If we could have identified the person or persons who organized the robo-call, we could have also sued them for libel.

In the end, the organizers of the phantom robo-call were never identified, and no one was ever charged. But we were certain that none of the other candidates nor their parties would or could have organized such a sophisticated eleventh-hour robo-call. They had neither the motive—they knew they were going to lose—nor the money to launch such an attack. And for the same reasons, it was not Tim Anderson. He explicitly denied any involvement, and we believed him. This could only have come from someone or some group in the PC Party with access to the voters lists and the money to pay for it. And the motive? Clearly to impugn my integrity and damage my reputation. The leadership race to replace Klein had begun. As Graham Thomson had previously reported, the knives were already out.[73]

At the time, the phantom robo-call incident just made me angry. But in retrospect, it may have been an early symptom of the PC dynasty's decline and fall. The election results clearly showed that Klein and the Tories were losing support on both the Left and the Right. The PCs kept their majority with sixty-two seats, but this was eleven fewer than they'd previously held. Their percentage of the popular vote dropped sharply, from 62 percent to 47 percent. The Liberals won sixteen seats—more than double what they'd held before. Many of these Liberal wins were made possible by growing support for the new, more conservative Alliance Party, which resulted in vote splitting in urban ridings. The Alliance finished second in a number of rural ridings, and elected its first MLA, Paul Hinman. Voter turnout was a historic low—45 percent.[74] Was the Tory "big-tent" party beginning to fragment along old cleavages—Calgary/Edmonton, urban/rural, private sector/public sector—and new cleavages—greater autonomy from Ottawa, social issues like same-sex marriage and climate change?

With the 2004 victory, the PC Party had won ten consecutive elections and governed Alberta uninterrupted for thirty-three years. Alberta had become a one-party province. Outside of a few city-centre ridings, the only path to a seat in the legislature was through the PC Party. Anyone interested in a political career in provincial politics had to don the Tory blue silks. As I was soon to discover, at least a third of the MLAs—maybe half from the Edmonton area—would have joined the Liberals or even NDP in any other province.

This may explain why many of them were not particularly happy to see me come into the PC caucus and may also account for my future lack of success as a cabinet minister in steering the caucus in more conservative policy directions. This in turn led to the rise of the Wildrose Party; still more vote splitting on the Right; and, eleven years later, the end of the PC dynasty. Was this my fault? Or was I just a symptom of a party that was already losing its way? That is the subject of the rest of this book.

3

Life on the Back Bench (2005-2006)

FIRST CAUCUS MEETING

First impressions, as they say, tend to be lasting. This was certainly the case for me when I arrived in Edmonton on December 15 to attend my first caucus meeting following the November 22 election. Two days earlier I had been sworn in as the new MLA for Foothills-Rocky View and the 738th member of the Legislative Assembly of Alberta. Now I was making my first visit to Government House. Constructed in 1912 for the Crown's representative in Alberta, the Lieutenant Governor, it is an imperial, three-storey, sandstone mansion built in the Edwardian Tudor revival style. Perched high on the north bank of the North Saskatchewan River in its own private park, it is an imposing building with an imposing view—literally fit for a King. I was duly humbled to be walking through its ornate front doors to my first caucus meeting. Little did I know what was waiting for me.

The first caucus after the election should have been an occasion for celebration. Ralph Klein had just led the PC Party to its fourth consecutive majority government. But the week before, the Supreme Court had released its decision in the Liberal government's *Same-Sex Marriage Reference*,[1] affirming Parliament's authority and jurisdiction to redefine marriage to include consenting same-sex partners. For Klein and our caucus, this posed a problem.

The Klein government had struggled with the sexual orientation and same-sex marriage issues for over a decade. They had refused requests to add sexual orientation as a prohibited discrimination to the *Alberta Human Rights Act*. Then, in the 1998 *Vriend* case,[2] the Supreme Court ruled that Alberta's decision NOT to include sexual orientation violated the equality rights section of the Charter of Rights. The judges conveniently overlooked the fact that attempts to add sexual orientation to the Charter had been rejected by those who wrote the Charter in 1981–82. But rather than striking down the entire Act as unconstitutional, the judges "read in"—that is, added—sexual orientation to the *Alberta Human Rights Act*. This provoked considerable criticism in Alberta. Klein also voiced his unhappiness with the decision, but he declined calls both from caucus and conservative Albertans (including me) to invoke the section 33 notwithstanding power. Instead, he promised to put "legislative fences" around institutions like marriage[3] and also never bothered to formally amend the *Alberta Human Rights Act* to include sexual orientation.

Two years later, in response to the Supreme Court's ruling in *M. v. H.*,[4] the Klein government enacted Bill 202, the *Marriage Amendment Act*. The Act expanded the common law marriage obligations (or "civil unions") to co-habitating same-sex couples (thus complying with *M. v. H.*), but also amended the provincial *Marriage Act* to apply only to the consenting union of a man and a woman. To prevent any Charter challenges to this defence of traditional marriage, Alberta added the section 33 "notwithstanding clause."

Retroactively, section 33 allows governments to reinstate a law that a court has struck down, when the government thinks the court's ruling is based on a misinterpretation of the Charter or deems the policy consequences of the ruling contrary to the public interest. Prospectively, as in this case, a government can use section 33 to shield new legislation from a future Charter challenge. Just as the Charter creates a judicial check on bad legislation, section 33 places a political check on judicial mistakes. It is a classic—and uniquely Canadian—example of constitutional "checks and balances." In both cases, the immunity from judicial review conferred by invoking the notwithstanding power is valid for only five years. At the end of five years, the government must choose between allowing it to expire or to renewing it for another five-year period.[5] Neither courts nor legislatures have the final word.

Fast-forward to December 2004. This five-year time limit was scheduled to expire in only three months, in March 2005. Klein and his justice minister, Ron Stevens, knew that the media would be waiting for them: What is Alberta going to do now? Will you renew the notwithstanding clause for another five years? Stevens had deflected this question a few days earlier with the comment, "It's now time to meet as a caucus and determine our next course of action."

Caucus opened with a few polite formalities: a congratulations to the premier for leading us to a fourth consecutive majority government; a welcome to all the newly elected MLAs (of which I was one). The agenda then quickly turned to how we might respond to the Supreme Court's ruling. Minister

Stevens began by reading from a policy memo prepared by his justice department lawyers.

I couldn't believe what I was hearing. I knew this file inside out. I had been writing about it for over a decade, and I knew we had more options than what we were being told. I raised my hand to speak and was quickly recognized. I rose, but instead of a restrained, calm deliberative exposition of alternative choices, the first words that came out of my mouth were that the options the minister had given us were "three different ways to surrender." All hell broke loose. Only later did I learn that backbenchers were supposed to be deferential and polite to ministers, and that newbies (like me) were supposed to keep their mouths shut for at least the first few months.

The caucus meeting quickly descended into organized chaos. There were heated comments from all sides. For the first time, I observed a regional pattern that was to repeat itself many times. Most Edmonton-area MLAs cautioned passive acceptance of whatever the federal government chose to do. Most rural MLAs argued for renewing the *Marriage Amendment Act* and its notwithstanding clause. Calgary MLAs were evenly divided. But there was a clear bottom-line majority: that we should do everything we could legally do to defend the traditional definition of marriage.

Caucus ended. Buoyed by these results, I was happily descending the winding staircase until I was suddenly confronted by a media mob waiting for me in the ornate foyer of Government House. They knew what I had said and written on this issue before. Now they pressed me for answers on what I thought the government should do.

With lights flashing and cameras rolling, I tried to repeat what I had said in caucus.

> That these various judicial decisions were wrongly decided; sexual orientation was purposively not included in the list of section 15 grounds of prohibited discrimination.

> That constitutional supremacy does not mean judicial supremacy: judges are not infallible, and that's why we have the section 33 notwithstanding clause.

> That while the definition of marriage clearly falls under federal jurisdiction, the solemnization of marriage just as clearly is a provincial power.

That since the federal government had not yet made a decision, and two out of three Albertans were opposed to redefining marriage to include homosexual couples, the Alberta government was legally and morally justified in re-enacting the Marriage Amendment Act and renewing the notwithstanding clause for another five years.

In retrospect, I can say definitively that this is NOT how a new MLA makes a favourable first impression with the powers that be in cabinet and in the premier's office.

Premier Klein subsequently had to answer the same kinds of questions. To his credit, his answers reflected that he had heard from caucus.

I'm willing to abide by the resolution of our caucus to use all political and legal means available to us to fight this. We'll do everything we can politically. We will use every legal mechanism, absolutely.[6]

When asked if his government would "cave in" if the Liberal government in Ottawa approved same-sex marriage, Klein responded: "What do you mean, cave? You can't cave on this."

This is how my first week in Edmonton began. In many respects, it didn't stop for the next eighteen months. Much of my time up to the 2006 leadership race was consumed by addressing the potential negative consequences of the federal Liberal government's subsequent decision to extend the status of marriage to same-sex couples—specifically, how to protect the freedoms of speech, press, and religion of those who, like me, thought that same-sex marriage was a dangerous new social experiment. Much of my time but not all.

FIRST DAY IN THE LEGISLATURE

After the pre-Christmas caucus meeting, we did not return to Edmonton until March 1, 2005, for the opening of the Legislative Assembly. Like my first caucus meeting, my first day in the assembly also left a lasting impression. The first order of business was the election of a new speaker and new deputy speaker. It was a foregone conclusion that Ken Kowalski would be re-elected speaker of the house. He had served as speaker in the prior two sessions. There being no other nominations, he was acclaimed.

On to the election of a deputy speaker. There were two nominations—Richard Marz, a rural MLA from Olds-Didsbury-Three Hills; and Shiraz Shariff, MLA from Calgary-McCall. Richard had contacted me shortly after the November elections asking for my support. While I hardly knew Richard, I told him I would support him. His district was adjacent to mine, and it included several smaller towns where we knew I had strong supporters for the future leadership election. I hoped that by supporting Richard now, I would be able to get his support later. Shiraz also phoned me, but several weeks later. I explained to him that because I had already pledged my support to Richard, I could not support him, but wished him well.

Onto March 1st and the election. Votes were cast. Votes were counted. And the clerk announced that Richard had won. Shiraz was seated in the row of seats directly below me. I could see the tears begin to roll down his cheek, and then he began to sob. We recessed shortly thereafter, and I approached Shiraz in the government lobby. Putting my arm on his shoulder, I tried to console him, urging him not to take it personally. His response was brief and to the point: "Ted, I spoke to every member of caucus, and you were the only one who told me that he would not support me." Lesson learned, not to be forgotten. For the next eight years, I never took private offers of support from any of my fellow PC MLAs as something I could rely on.

FOOTHILLS-ROCKY VIEW CONSTITUENCY

As a new MLA, I was also busy getting to know the communities I now represented in Foothills-Rocky View. Both the towns and municipal districts were experiencing the same mega-growth as Calgary, and the accompanying problems of housing, traffic, schools, water, and sewer—all of which required assistance, funding, or both from the provincial government. And they all looked to their new MLA to help them get it.

When the legislature was in session, I would be in Edmonton Monday through Thursday; meet with constituents Friday in my new constituency office at the Springbank Airport; and often spent Saturdays visiting constituents to see first-hand what their issues looked like. I was especially busy in the spring of 2005, when flooding on the Elbow, Highwood, and Fish Creek rivers damaged many homes and communities. I was learning first-hand how much more work and time is required of rural MLAs compared to those from the larger cities. I'm not sure how I would have handled all of this without the organizational genius and calm demeanour of my constituency office manager, Margaret Lepp.

DE-KLEIN: OVERSPENDING

When it came to government spending and budgets, I was of two minds. On the one hand, I respected the vision and commitment that had allowed Klein and his ministers to slay Alberta's deficit dragon and then (by 2005) retire the $22 billion of net debt inherited from the preceding PC government of Don Getty. Yes, the return of higher energy revenues helped, but it took some heavy lifting—and very thick political skin—to even be in position to benefit from the energy price rebound of the early 2000s.

On the other hand, I became increasingly concerned about how much we were spending. The more revenue we took in, the more we spent. The senior MLAs and ministers seemed to think that after years of restraint and sacrifice, now they were entitled to spend a little. The problem was, we were spending a lot more than a little.

By 2005 and 2006, the prices of both natural gas and oil were hitting historic highs, and so were the Government of Alberta's non-renewable resource revenues (NRRR). The government's NRRR jumped from the $7 billion/year range to $14.3 billion in 2005 and $12.3 billion in 2006. For Budgets 2005, 2006, and 2007, government spending was increasing faster than Alberta's GDP growth, something that clearly was not sustainable. The Fraser Institute described it as the "Beginning of the end of the Alberta Advantage."[7] Shirley McClellan was treasurer and deputy premier, and she kept warning caucus that we could not continue at his rate. But continue we did.

The most blatant example of our overspending was the famous prosperity bonus cheques announced in September 2005. Rising NRRR pushed our projected budget surplus for 2005–6 from $2.8 billion to $6.8 billion. Premier Klein announced that 20 percent of this increase—$1.4 billion—would be doled out in $400, one-time cheques to each and every Albertan. While these "Ralph Bucks" were popular at the time, in retrospect they were a huge mistake. They were also another symptom of the PC Party's loss of focus and Klein's own shrinking, short-term horizons.

What the public did not know was how this decision was made. Earlier that month we had a caucus retreat at Cold Lake / Bonnyville. At the top of the agenda was what to do with the anticipated budget surplus. At the outset, the premier told us that this was "one of the most important caucus decisions we've ever made." For the rest of the morning, we had a vigorous discussion of our options. First and foremost, and my favourite, was to save it in the Heritage Fund. But there were others: reduction of personal income tax rates; elimination of health care premiums; new infrastructure investment; upgrading Kananaskis and other provincial parks; a "windfall tax rebate" to Albertans. Klein indicated that he liked this last option but did not push it. The scheduled lunch break arrived, and we were told we would finish this discussion when we returned. MLAs quickly were off to the dining area, but I lagged behind as I was still finishing my notes. Then, as I passed through the central foyer on my way to the dining hall, I saw that the premier was holding a press conference. I stopped to listen. I could not believe what I was hearing. With great enthusiasm, Premier Klein was announcing the prosperity bonus cheques! The press releases had already been printed.

When I got to lunch, I told whoever was at the table what I had just heard. There were raised eyebrows and shaking of heads in disbelief. But when the caucus meeting resumed, there was no outcry of protest. I was in disbelief. I didn't say anything then, but later that week I criticized the "Ralph Bucks" plan in an interview with one of my local weekly newspapers. A week later I was summoned to the premier's office, and his chief of staff gave me a stern lecture about "teamwork" and "loyalty." Outwardly, I acquiesced. But my inner voice was saying: The real problem is in this office.

While my concerns about growing dysfunction in the Klein inner circle were justified, from another perspective, this was just an example of what Canadians political scientists were already describing as "policy-making by announcement."[8] It reflects the growing concentration of power in the offices of prime ministers and premiers, both Liberal and Conservative. "The reality of Cabinet government is that the truly crucial decisions are made by a small handful of ministers, advised by an equally small handful of senior public servants."[9] This was my first unpleasant encounter with this reality but not my last.

Other than my public criticism of "Ralph Bucks," I more or less went along with this spending spree. As a new backbench MLA, there was nothing I could do to stop it. Plus, I was trying to make some friends—and future allies—in caucus for the anticipated leadership race that would occur when Klein retired. I enjoyed a few small victories. In the caucus debates over Budget 2006, I teamed up with Minister of Finance Greg Melchin to persuade caucus to lower the corporate tax rate from 11.5 percent to 10 percent in exchange for not opposing the finance minister's proposal to raise the cap on energy revenues that could be diverted to general revenue spending.

In terms of Alberta's larger macro-economic health, our continued overspending was putting us at risk. As long as oil and gas prices kept rising, we could get away with it. But I knew this could not last. It never does. In my subsequent 2006 leadership campaign, I promised to cap the growth of public spending at less than private sector growth and to direct 30 percent of our energy revenues to the Heritage Savings Fund. But I did not win, and that did not happen. Two years later, the inevitable did happen.

The US housing mortgage bubble burst, sending energy prices into the tank. In 2008–9, the Alberta government recorded its first deficit budget since 1994. This was followed by thirteen more deficit budgets, as Alberta went from debt free to $100 billion of debt. This is the subject of chapters 6, 7, and 8.

MAIDEN SPEECH AND THE LEADERSHIP RACE

At the outset of the 2004 election, Klein announced that this would be the last time he would lead the PC Party into an election. But he did not specify whether he would stay for four more years, or only one or two. Whatever Klein might have intended, this ambiguity meant that the "unofficial" leadership race began the day after the votes were counted. Klein's former minister of finance, Jim Dinning, had been organizing support for his leadership bid since at least 2002. Mark Norris, an Edmonton PC MLA, was also raising money and even running newspaper ads. And, as noted earlier, my ambitions were no longer secret after August 2004, when the *Western Standard* published their cover story about me as the "Premier-in-Waiting."

The public visibility of the leadership issue notched up again on March 9, 2005, the day I gave my "maiden speech" in the Legislative Assembly. Every newly elected MLA is offered the opportunity in his or her first term to make such a speech. The newly elected legislature had convened on March 1, and my opportunity came only four days later.

Most maiden speeches are filled with platitudes about the members' appreciation of those who helped them get elected and flowery statements about the towns and communities that they represent. Mine certainly began that way. But I quickly segued into a review of Alberta leaders and premiers who from our very beginning had fought to protect Alberta from predatory and harmful policies of the federal government: Haultain, Brownlee, Aberhart, Manning, Lougheed, and now Klein. My conclusion:

"Our Alberta strong and free did not happen by accident; it happened on purpose. It happened because of the wise and deliberate choices made by the statesmen who have served as premier of this province."

No one in the building could miss the implicit connection between the Alberta Agenda and my praise of these past Alberta premiers. Certainly not the thirty or so guests sitting in the members' gallery. Inviting guests for a member's maiden speech is normal. What was not normal was the reception at the Mayfair Golf and Country Club immediately following. The Mayfair is the oldest and most prestigious club in Edmonton. Our reception there had been arranged by Keith Alexander, a former MLA and one of my earliest and strongest supporters. Prior to delivery, we had also leaked copies of my speech to several Alberta journalists we knew to be sympathetic to my leadership plans. Some even attended the reception.

The speech received favourable coverage across the province. Paul Stanway previewed it before I had even delivered it: "The undeclared race to succeed Ralph Klein is about to get a little more crowded today," he wrote in that morning's *Edmonton Sun*. Morton's message: "Everything we have in Alberta right now, all the prosperity and wealth we enjoy, is the result of some very hard-fought battles." And the reception? "You can consider this his coming out party."[10]

Nigel Hannaford was equally blunt: "Morton sets out his leadership case," read the headline in his column in the *Calgary Herald*. "What Morton did was talk of famous Albertans. The message: These guys had the right idea. If you want more of the same, I'm your guy."[11] This was echoed a week later by *Calgary Sun* columnist Paul Stanway. Morton, he wrote, is "the best intellect in PC caucus … a force for change… [who] leads the fight for democratic renewal."[12]

Less than a month later, Klein removed the ambiguity around when he intended to step aside. In April, at the annual PC Convention, Klein casually announced, "If I'm alive, I'll be around for another three and a half years." We were surprised, but happy. As Ted Byfield correctly pointed out in his weekly *Calgary Sun* column, for Morton to win, he needs time. Klein's announcement was "appalling news for both Dinning and Norris. … That's because the man whom both of them fear could be 10 times more dangerous to them in three years than he is now. That man is Ted Morton." Byfield had read my maiden speech and liked it. This was hardly a surprise. Much of my understanding of

Alberta's history and relationship with Ottawa had been shaped by reading Byfield's *Alberta Report* magazine and his eleven-volume history of Alberta. Morton, he wrote, is "a man with a message and a program for Alberta ... More Alberta, Less Ottawa."[13]

Klein's decision to stay *was* good news for me. But it meant that in addition to my new responsibilities as the MLA for Foothills-Rocky View, I was now going to be campaigning full time for the next year and a half. And so we did.

Under the banner "Friends of Ted Morton," we opened a small campaign headquarters next to the Safeway in Bowness. We quietly raised money. We developed a TedMorton.ca website, with copies of my articles, speeches, and favourable newspaper columns (those referenced above). The same materials were collected in a ten-page brochure under the heading "Our Future. Our Choices." Both had contact information along with requests for donations. And I travelled the province almost non-stop after the spring session of the legislature ended in May 2005.

My travel partner and driver for most of these trips was Gord Elliott, a retired engineer from NOVA Chemicals. Because our budget was tight, we usually shared motel rooms. That's the bad news. The good news is that during the second summer, Gord met Marilyn Brown, also a Morton supporter, whom he ended up marrying. (In fact, theirs was the third marriage that began through first encounters on my various political campaigns!). Several years later, at Gord and Marilyn's wedding, I toasted the two of them, telling Marilyn that up to this point, I had spent more nights with Gord in cheap motels than anyone else, but I was now happy to relinquish that privilege to her. Marilyn's reply was short and to the point: "Ted, they won't be cheap any longer."

BILL 208: PROTECTING FREEDOM OF SPEECH AND RELIGION

I was heavily involved in the same-sex marriage issue during my first two years in Edmonton. As noted above, it started at my first caucus meeting in December 2004. When we returned to Edmonton in March for the opening of the legislature, the same-sex marriage issue was still front and centre. In February, the federal Liberal government had introduced Bill C-38, legislation to redefine marriage to include same-sex couples. At our March 17 caucus meeting, Minister Ron Stevens again presented the justice department's legal advice that re-enacting the *Marriage Amendment Act*—even with a renewal of the notwithstanding clause—could not and would not win if challenged in court. The Supreme Court had stated correctly that the definition of marriage falls under federal jurisdiction. If there were a conflict between the province's definition of marriage and federal definition of marriage, the latter would prevail in a court of law. And the notwithstanding power would be of no use, as it applies only to Charter of Rights issues, not to issues of federal-provincial jurisdiction.

Legally speaking, this was all correct. But my point, which I argued again, was that this was much more than a legal issue. The Supreme Court had ruled that Ottawa could redefine marriage, but not that it was legally compelled to. The court had also confirmed that the "solemnization of marriage"—the issuing of marriage licences—is an exclusive provincial jurisdiction. We could still use the notwithstanding clause to defend the latter, even if Ottawa chose to legislate same-sex marriage. The Liberals had introduced Bill C-38 a month earlier, but it was not yet enacted. Until it was, the centuries-old common law definition of marriage continued to be the law of the land. I argued that this was not only Alberta's opportunity to defend it, but also our duty, as recent polls indicated two-thirds of Albertans still opposed same-sex marriage. There was vigorous argument, pro and con, but again my arguments carried the day in caucus. And as he had before, even the premier grudgingly went along.

My opponents in caucus immediately leaked the outcome of this meeting to the press. And their friends—my critics—in the local media seized upon the story to criticize the premier for lack of political will and to tarnish me and my supporters as religious fundamentalists pursuing a fight the province could not win.

I contacted the *Edmonton Journal* to tell them that their "columnists have done a disservice to your readers through inaccurate and misleading reporting" and requested an opportunity to respond. They printed my response in their April 4 edition. I repeated the arguments that I'd made in caucus, but I specifically challenged their claim that renewing the notwithstanding clause was a "mean, empty gesture." To the contrary, I argued:

> It is a bold, positive affirmation of Canada's federal democracy. The notwithstanding clause exists because of former Alberta

Premier Peter Lougheed. In 1981 Lougheed had the foresight to insist on the notwithstanding clause as a democratic check on potential judicial misinterpretations of the Charter of Rights. It is precisely such judicial misinterpretations of the Charter that have driven the homosexual marriage issue. Sexual orientation, much less a right for homosexuals to marry, cannot be found in the text of the Charter. Both are judge-made law—precisely what the notwithstanding clause protects us against.[14]

After reading this over my morning coffee, I happily went off to our morning caucus meeting, even expecting some high-fives from some of my fellow MLAs. That changed quickly. Caucus began with a clear message that we would not be renewing the notwithstanding clause. This time the message was delivered by Government Services Minister Ty Lund, and it clearly had the backing of the premier. The "don't fight a losing battle" message from ministers like Stevens and Hancock had now carried the day. The return of Rod Love, Klein's chief of staff, who had missed the March caucus meeting, was also a factor. Rod was famous for running a tight ship and was not a fan of bottom-up caucus policy making. And not surprisingly, he was no fan of mine. After caucus, the media were given the same blunt message. "I had to put my foot down today," Klein told reporters. "You cannot incorporate into a law something that is unlawful, something that simply cannot be enforced. … As far as I'm concerned, it's dead."[15] Liberal political columnist Graham Thomson celebrated Klein's reversal as a political loss for me.

> Klein was forced to flip-flop. Consequently, he looked like he was losing control of caucus to the more right-wing elements who were emerging as the voice of Alberta conservatism—MLA Ted Morton inside government and Alberta Alliance MLA Paul Hinman outside. … The tail seemed to be wagging the dog. On Monday, Klein brought the dog to heel. The Morton-led flip-flop has flopped. … If Morton thought he was leading the charge on this issue he'll have to take shorter steps. Klein just cut him off at the knees.[16]

It was true. I'd certainly lost the battle. But not necessarily the war. I knew that a majority of caucus still agreed with me that judicially imposed same-sex marriage was both bad law and bad policy. Was there an alternative path forward that would allow Alberta to comply with the Liberals' Bill C-38 but still protect those of us who disagreed with the new policy it had created?

***

It turned out that there was. The rules of the Alberta Legislative Assembly allow for what are called private member's bills. In parliamentary democracies such as Canada, all bills are normally introduced by government ministers. This is the privilege given to the party that "forms government" with a majority of the members of the legislature. To offset this "monopoly" of the legislative agenda, Alberta allows twenty private member's bills each session for those MLAs who are not in cabinet or who are in opposition parties. Private member's bills also affirm the principle that the function of an elected member of a legislature is to represent constituency interests, not just follow party discipline.

Eric Taylor and David Williams—two young staffers assigned to support backbench MLAs—first brought this option to my attention and then helped me to develop what eventually became Bill 208. First, I had to apply for the private member's bill draw held in July 2005. This is a random draw, so I was lucky to even be drawn. I then had to navigate my proposal through two separate approval streams. One—through Parliamentary Council and the speaker's office—was basically procedural: ensuring that the right forms were completed and filed by the right dates. The second was internal to caucus: Agenda and Priorities Committee in the fall; Standing Policy Committee in fall/winter; Private Members' House Strategy Committee in the winter; and finally, caucus approval. Suffice it to say that if it had been a priority in the premier's office to stop Bill 208, there were numerous opportunities to do so. Tellingly, that never happened.

There had been important political and policy changes since the demise of the *Marriage Amendment Act*. The Liberals had enacted Bill C-38, and same-sex marriage was now the law of the land. The Stephen Harper-led Conservatives had defeated the Liberals in January 2006, but with only enough seats to form a minority government. Harper had decided that any attempt to revise Bill C-38 would only be done by a free vote, which meant that it would fail. This meant that same-sex marriage was now a done deal, and that there was no going back.

But as I had warned a year earlier, achieving same-sex marriage was not the endgame for its proponents. Instead, it became a launching pad for a new round of attacks on those who still disagreed with the new law and were not afraid to say so publicly. In British Columbia a teacher, Dr. Chris Kempling, had been suspended without pay because he publicly disagreed with the Liberal government's same-sex marriage law. Also in British Columbia, the Knights of Columbus had been sued and fined because they refused to rent their hall to a same-sex wedding party. In Ontario a leading gay rights activist had called on the government to cut off funding to the Catholic separate schools and all other private schools that did not include same-sex marriage in their curriculum. Even in Alberta, the respected Bishop Fred Henry of Calgary had been charged not once but twice with so-called hate speech crimes for publicly advocating the defeat of the federal Liberals' same-sex marriage bill.

It was clear that the new "progressive" definition of diversity demanded not silence but public affirmation—government enforced if necessary. The traditional liberal definition of toleration—agreeing to disagree and leaving each other alone—was no longer sufficient. It was these kinds of threats to core liberal democratic freedoms that my private member's bill, Bill 208, was designed to thwart.

❖ ❖ ❖

Bill 208 consisted of a preamble and amendments to three different Alberta statutes: the *Alberta Human Rights Act*, the *Marriage Act*, and the *School Act*. The preamble to Bill 208 affirmed the fundamental rights of freedom of conscience and religion. It declared that these freedoms protect any church official from being forced to perform a same-sex marriage contrary to his or her religious beliefs or conscience. It also declared in straightforward, clear language that "it is not against the public interest to hold and publicly express diverse views on marriage." The wording of this preamble was virtually identical to the preamble of federal Bill C-38.

The first section of Bill 208 amended the *Alberta Human Rights Act*. It stated that no person or organization shall be deprived of any benefit or be subject to any other obligation or sanction under this or any other law of Alberta solely because of their publicly stated views on same-sex marriage, whether they oppose or support same-sex marriage. It protected both sides of this debate. This protection would be added to section 11 of the existing *Alberta Human Rights Act*, which is the section that provides a number of legal defences against complaints of discrimination. In layman's terms this meant, at least in Alberta, that there would be no more hate speech prosecutions like the Bishop Fred Henry case; no Knights of Columbus or Chris Kempling job loss incidents such as had occurred in British Columbia; and no cutting off funding to separate or private schools that exclude same-sex marriage from their curriculum.

The second section of Bill 208 proposed an amendment to Alberta's *Marriage Act*. Again, it had the same intent as the corresponding federal provision in Bill C-38. It protected church officials from being forced to perform same-sex marriage against their religious conscience. It also protected marriage commissioners from losing their jobs for refusing to perform same-sex marriages. The Supreme Court had clearly stated that since solemnization of marriage is an exclusive provincial power, only provinces can protect this right. Bill 208 provided such protection.

The third and final section of Bill 208 proposed an amendment to Alberta's *School Act*. As education is an exclusive provincial jurisdiction, there was no parallel provision in C-38. While the amendments to the *Alberta Human Rights Act* also extended to the *School Act*, for further clarity this amendment ensured that the freedoms of conscience, expression, and religion were explicitly protected in the context of Alberta's public, separate, and private education.

❧ ❧ ❧

On April 6, 2006, I introduced Bill 208, "Protection of Fundamental Freedoms (Marriage) Statutes Amendment Act, 2006." This was exactly one year after my loss in caucus in April 2005. Just a week earlier, Premier Klein had received only 55 percent support at our PC annual general meeting. He subsequently announced that he would step aside after what would now be a fall leadership contest. I had voted for him to stay on. But his announced departure was not bad news for me. As a lame-duck premier, Klein no longer had either the influence or the incentive to dictate the fate of Bill 208. It would not be a repeat of May 2005.

First reading is simply a procedure to introduce a bill, with no debate. The action starts with second reading, which for Bill 208 was—how appropriate—May 1. I began by repeating what I had said three weeks earlier:

> Thank you, Mr. Speaker. I'm honoured to open debate today on Bill 208. ... The most important right in a free society is the right to disagree and criticize govern policy. For this reason it has been protected in every major rights document in Canada's illustrious political lineage: the Magna Carta, the English Bill of Rights, the American Bill of Rights, the preamble to the British North America Act, the Diefenbaker Bill of Rights, and most recently the Canadian Charter of Rights and Freedoms.[17]

I continued:

> Despite this noble pedigree of freedom, this most fundamental right, the right to disagree with and criticize government policy, is under attack across our country. ... These incidents are all clear violations of Canadians' rights of freedom of speech, press, religion, and conscience.
>
> Mr. Speaker, Bill 208 would prevent these types of rights abuses. Bill 208 would ensure that when it comes to public discussion of the same-sex marriage issue, no individual will be punished, no community group will be sued, no school will lose their funding, and no student or teacher will be coerced or punished for publicly disagreeing with same-sex marriage. What Bill 208 does not do is interfere with the legal right of gay people to get married. This is the law of Canada, a federal law, and there is little that this Assembly can do about it.
>
> There is something that we can do about the use or, rather, the abuse of courts and human rights commissions to silence and punish public disagreement with same-sex marriage as a matter of public policy. This is precisely what Bill 208 does. ... In the drafting of Bill 208 I followed as closely as possible the wording of similar rights protection provisions in federal legislation as evidenced by the documents that I tabled earlier this afternoon.

When the Liberal government of the day embarked upon the mission to redefine marriage, they were warned that there was a risk that the new same-sex marriage law could come into conflict with the traditional rights of freedom of speech, religion, and conscience. To remedy this, the Liberals initially sought to add specific protections in their own bill to address this conflict. However, in 2004 the Supreme Court of Canada ruled that protecting these rights against provincial infringement could only be done through provincial legislation. If you imagine the protection of fundamental freedoms in this context as a circle, what the Supreme Court did was draw a line through the middle of the circle and say that half is federal and half is provincial. The feds have filled in their half. Bill 208 would fill in Alberta's half, using the identical wording to the extent possible. Mr. Speaker, Bill 208 merely completes what Parliament wanted to do but was prevented from doing by its jurisdictional limitations. It ensures that extending the rights to one group does not restrict the rights of other groups. ...

Mr. Speaker, good public policy is often a question of striking the right balance between competing claims and interests. Bill 208 strikes such a balance. It would ensure that creating the new right to same-sex marriage does not lead to restrictions on the rights and freedoms of those who disagree with same-sex marriage. ...

Mr. Speaker, if this Assembly fails to enact Bill 208, we will have provided less protection for the fundamental freedoms of Albertans than the Liberal government of Paul Martin provided for the rights of Canadians. Surely Albertans expect and deserve better than this. Accordingly, I would ask all members of this Assembly to support Bill 208.

Thank you, Mr. Speaker.[18]

Debate ensued for the next hour and a half. Five speakers from the Liberal and NDP parties spoke against the bill. Five Conservative members—Tony Abbott, Dave Rodney, Ray Prins, George Groeneveld, Len Mitzel, plus Paul

Hinman, the lone Alberta Alliance MLA—spoke in support of Bill 208. The opponents were clearly willing to accept new restrictions on our fundamental freedoms of speech, association, and religion to promote the progressives' new "social justice" agenda. The supporters were not. Supporters did suggest that Bill 208 might be too broad, and suggested possible amendments that would limit Bill 208 to simply the *Alberta Human Rights Act*, since this would still extend the protection to both the *School* and *Marriage* Acts. In closing I indicated that I was open to accepting such amendments when we next met in Committee of the Whole.

I was pleased with the support Bill 208 was getting both in caucus and now in second reading. But I was concerned that with the PC leadership now scheduled for the fall months, there would be no normal fall session of the legislature, and thus not enough time to get Bill 208 through to third and final reading and a vote.

On May 3, only two days after second reading, I sent a letter to the speaker requesting "early consideration" of Bill 208 in Committee of the Whole, which was scheduled for May 8. The following day this request was discussed in caucus. It carried, but not without vigorous opposition from the usual suspects—including several cabinet ministers. At one point, Premier Klein intervened in favour of my request, and I thought that this helped me win. He normally did not intervene in caucus debates, so afterward I sent him a note thanking him and stating: "I think that Bill 208 as amended establishes the principle that Albertans cannot be punished or harassed."

Later that day I received an envelope from the premier's office. When I opened it, it was my earlier note, with a comment from Ralph scribbled across the top: "I agree. Advise Ted." I smiled. From the start, I knew he agreed with me on the broader policy issues, but that he was reluctant to ignore the legal advice he was getting from Justice. Now that he knew he would be leaving Edmonton before the end of the year, I think he decided to go with his heart rather than his head. Actually, this wasn't the first time. It was part of Ralph's character that had made him such a popular premier.

My request that Bill 208 be given "early consideration" still had to be accepted by the Legislative Assembly. Predictably, both the Liberals and the NDP opposed it. Neither wanted to see Bill 208 come to a vote, because they knew it would pass, even with ten or so PC members voting against it. So when May 8 arrived, they began what in effect became a filibuster to prevent it from ever coming to a vote. Citing precedents from Alberta Hansards, they argued that my request for "early consideration" was inconsistent with past precedents and should be rejected.[19]

The speaker was not persuaded and ruled that it was time to proceed to Committee of the Whole and Bill 208. But before he could even sit down, NDP MLA Ray Martin rose to request an emergency debate on adequate funding for long-term care. An important issue, but hardly an emergency. This chewed up another 20 minutes. This was immediately followed by Liberal MLA Laurie Blakeman, who requested a second emergency debate on health care issues in Fort Chipewyan.[20] These requests were clearly designed to delay, not to enlighten, and the speaker knew it. But under the rules, he was obligated to accept them. Add in other time-consuming motions and speeches, and by the end of the day—at 11:50 pm on a Thursday evening—there was no time left for Bill 208.

❊ ❊ ❊

A week later, the legislature recessed for the summer and did not meet again until August 24 for the shortened fall sitting. The weather had changed but the opposition strategy had not. Monday afternoons are reserved for private member's bills, and Bill 208 was the first in line on Monday, August 28. It is standard practice each day to allow MLAs from all parties to introduce any guests they have in the public galleries. Not by accident, the Liberals and NDP had close to one hundred guests that afternoon, and it took forty-five minutes to introduce them all. Question period followed, and that took another hour and half. Then the filibuster began in earnest: more requests for emergency debates, not one but two: the Liberals on the need for more infrastructure spending; the NDP on funding for more affordable housing.[21]

Even some of Conservative MLAs joined in. Thomas Lukaszuk, one of the most outspoken opponents in our caucus, brought a "point of order" on whether the Liberal MLA from Calgary Varsity was in violation of the assembly's dress code because it "appeared" that he was not wearing a necktie. Debate ensued. We learned later that Dave Hancock, our house leader, had co-operated with the Liberals and NDP in the filibuster strategy. (A decade later NDP Premier Rachel Notley appointed Hancock as a provincial judge in 2017.)

By 4:30, Speaker Kowalski had had enough. He condemned the filibuster but could not stop it.[22] He pointed out that the primary objective of allowing private member's bills was to benefit opposition parties—to give them the opportunity to showcase their policy priorities to the electorate. But now the opposition's filibuster tactic was setting a precedent that could be used to silence them in the future—to everyone's detriment.

> There's no hope in hell this afternoon that any private member's bill is coming up. Right after I call Orders of the Day, we have 16, 17 written questions or motions for returns, and even at five minutes for each one, it'll be after 5:30. I know what has transpired in the last Monday allocated for private members' day. I know what's transpired today. I applaud all the parliamentarians in the room for knowing the rules, applying the rules, and using the rules. …. But just remember what the future will be for private members because I think that the new system now is that no private member's bill will ever be dealt with on any Monday in the future, period, and that to me is unfortunate. I couldn't care less what the subject is. That's totally immaterial to me. It's the principle of what Parliament is.[23]

Bill 208 thus died without ever coming a vote.[24] The Liberal-NDP filibuster had worked. But that was still not the end. By the end of August, the PC leadership campaign was in full swing. Both my supporters and my critics knew that Bill 208 could still influence the outcome of this race—and who would be the next premier of Alberta.

Graham Thomson, a columnist in the *Edmonton Journal*, celebrated the demise of Bill 208, but warned that "Morton may be cheering his bill's demise." The Liberal-NDP filibuster, he feared, might have boosted my leadership bid by giving me "a cloak of martyrdom."[25] Colby Cosh, a conservative columnist, echoed Thomson's alarmist prediction but gave it a positive spin. He described Bill 208 as a "cunning bill" that signalled to Albertans the threat to their freedoms by the "tolerant of everything but intolerance clique." According to Cosh, the Liberal and NDP "panic-mongering and cheesy parliamentary tactics" had "served Morton's interests … by reminding Albertans that progressives and the human rights establishment seem to regard freedom of religion as nothing but a pernicious obstacle."[26] Kelly Cryderman reported a similar view: that I was using Bill 208 as a "wedge issue … a brilliant political strategy sharply distinguishing himself from the other eight candidates in the race to become the next premier."[27] Paul Jackson went one step further, writing in the *Edmonton Sun* that "right now, I'm repeatedly told that Ted Morton has nudged himself into the lead over former provincial treasurer Jim Dinning."[28]

Alarmed by such predictions, Naomi Lakritz wrote a blisteringly negative column warning that "anyone who needs proof that Ted Morton should never become the premier of Alberta should read his Bill 208."[29] This was countered by Paul Stanway in the *Edmonton Sun*, who described the filibuster as "a double blow [to] the rights and freedoms of Albertans." Echoing my warnings, Stanway concluded that "gay activists don't want passive acceptance. They want ... official endorsement—with all the legislative enforcement that implies."[30]

The public debate ignited by Bill 208 did not disappear after Labour Day. The first round of voting was now only three months away. The prospect of my winning the leadership vote and bringing back Bill 208 was a motivating force for some of my strongest supporters but also for many of my strongest opponents. The result was the largest voter turnout ever in a PC leadership race—the subject of the next chapter.

As far as same-sex marriage goes, as I knew even then, it was not the endgame for gay activists and the identity politics / social justice movement partisans. It quickly became a staging area for an even more aggressive campaign not just to "normalize" what became known as "LGBTQ" behaviour and relationships, but to silence and, when necessary, to punish any public disagreement with this "new normal." Sacrificed on this new progressive altar have been the traditional liberal rights of freedom of speech, freedom of religion, the rights of parents, equal protection of the laws, and due process of law. In short, the very freedoms that Bill 208 was intended to protect. For a more detailed account and vindication of Bill 208, see Appendix 1.

4

PC Leadership Campaign: The Accidental Premier (2006)

The true soldier fights not because he hates what is in front of him, but because he loves what is behind him.

—G.K. Chesterton

KLEIN'S LONG GOODBYE

Premier Klein had announced in April 2005 that he intended to remain as premier until the next scheduled election in 2008. Over the next twelve months, this all changed. Under PC Party rules, a leadership review had already been scheduled for March 2006 at the party's AGM. In the past, Klein had easily won these with over 90 percent approval ratings. But this time it was different. There was a growing sense that Klein was staying on simply because he enjoyed being premier. There was no longer a sense of purpose or direction. In the 2004 election, the PCs had lost both seats—eleven—and popular vote, from 62 percent to 47 percent. Party members began to worry that under Klein's "long goodbye," PC losses in the next election could be worse.

In an attempt to quell this unrest, in early March 2006, Klein announced that he would resign at the end of October 2007. It didn't work. A week later, Brooks MLA and cabinet minister Lyle Oberg told his constituency association that he would not tell them to vote for Klein to stay at the upcoming AGM. This leaked to the media, and by week's end, the PC Caucus expelled Oberg from the government. Oberg apologized, but also said it was still time for Klein to leave; that the party could not survive another eighteen months of an unofficial leadership race. The same week, Klein received sharp negative media for losing his temper during question period and throwing a copy of the Liberals' policy book at a young parliamentary page.

I had been careful, both in public and in private, not to say that Klein should leave. I was in no hurry for a leadership race. But most of the other would-be candidates were, especially the Dinning camp. Klein's former chief of staff, Rod Love, was now the de facto director of the Dinning campaign. He knew that more time helped me, and he had huge sway within the PC Party machine. Everyone expected Dinning to win, and when it came to appointments and contracts, they wanted to be on Rod's friends list. Given that public approval of Klein was still above 70 percent in mid-March, it seemed probable that the Dinning machine was encouraging NO votes in the leadership review.

Still, going into the 2006 AGM, no one expected Klein to get any less than 70 percent approval. But when the votes were counted, Klein received only 55 percent. Less than a week later, he announced that he would step aside in the fall.[1] This conveniently allowed him to remain as premier for the already scheduled visit by Queen Elizabeth II in June. It also gave me and my team the green light to move our backroom, low-profile, low-budget leadership campaign into high gear.

MORTON CAMPAIGN TEAM

My informal "advisory committee" now began morphing into a more formal campaign organization. Greg Fletcher remained my primary fundraiser and treasurer. Stan Church, Rick Sears, Andy Crooks, Don Watkins, Keith Alexander, and Robert Anderson continued to fundraise and advise. Actual operations of the campaign were shared between Sam Armstrong and Rod Blair. Gord Elliott had stepped forward to be my driver and travel companion for the "unofficial campaign" during the summer of 2005 and remained a key aide and advisor. Doug Main, a former MLA from Edmonton with a prior career as a television reporter, had stepped forward to assist me, and soon began managing our media and messaging.

We had already opened up a small campaign office in Bowness in the fall of 2005. We had been able to hire and to pay Devin Iversen and Rob Griffith to build our database and run our direct-mail efforts. They had done the same for Harper's successful campaign to win the leadership of the Canadian Alliance Party in 2002. Along with Iversen and Griffith, we picked up Matt

Gelinas, Dustin van Vugt, Hamish Marshall, and Jayce Johnson, all of whom had worked on the Harper leadership campaign.

These younger team members were critical to our success. Unlike myself and my other advisors/fundraisers, they understood how to use direct mail and telephone banks to sell memberships. With them we also acquired old federal Reform/Conservative membership lists, complete with names, addresses, telephone numbers, and emails. These lists allowed my campaign team to orchestrate a sophisticated phone-bank / direct mail / email campaign that was essential to our first ballot success in November.

Our campaign also got a big boost from the generosity of Ron and Judy Quigley, the owners of Gunnar Office Furnishings. The Quigleys gave us the entire top floor of their beautiful new office and showroom building located just off Deerfoot Trail in southeast Calgary. This allowed us to move our campaign office from the tiny, second-floor one-room rental in Bowness to the spacious and luxurious fourth floor. Having seen many campaign offices over the past few decades, I can confidently say that none came close to this. With lots of room, windows, sunshine, and free parking for the dozens of volunteers who ran our phone-bank and direct-mail operations, it made "coming to the office" enjoyable. This was a big factor in our success. During the final weeks of the campaign, our volunteers were working thirty-two phones, nine hours a day, six days a week.[2]

The only downside of our team's transition was the loss of Rod Blair. From the very start of my campaign in 2003, no one had put in more time and effort than Rod. He had been invaluable in helping me win the Foothills-Rocky View PC nomination and organizing my earlier leadership events and media. We had become good friends. But Rod was used to having his way and proved unable or unwilling to work with—and cede some authority to—our expanded campaign team. If we were going to run a successful campaign, Rod had to go. For me, Rod's departure was a sad experience. It was the first time, but not the last, that I learned politics can be hard on friendships.

CANDIDATES

From the outset, Jim Dinning was the overwhelming favourite to become the next PC leader and premier. He had held cabinet positions under both Premiers Klein and Getty. He had the support of the party establishment and thirty-seven caucus members. He had been running an "unofficial" campaign since 2004 and had already raised over $2 million. He'd been dubbed by the media "The Prince" and the "Premier-in-waiting," and his campaign team was confidently predicting a first-round victory. Dinning had one liability. Being the clear front-runner gave the other seven candidates an incentive to focus their criticisms on Dinning. For most of the campaign, the "any-one-but-Dinning" message was present but low key. This all changed after the first round of voting.

By summer, there were seven other leadership candidates, none of whom were given much of a chance of winning. From the Edmonton area there were four, none of whom had much profile or support outside of the capital region.

- Ed Stelmach, MLA, Fort-Saskatchewan-Vegreville; a farmer with no post-secondary education; a likeable but undistinguished cabinet minister under Klein. Stelmach was endorsed by thirteen MLAs, but he was virtually unknown south of Edmonton. In the first round of voting, he finished third with 14 percent of the votes, so went on to the second round.

- Dave Hancock, MLA, Edmonton-Whitemud. Trained and practised as a lawyer prior to politics. Hancock had served in several cabinet posts during the Klein dynasty, including minister of justice / solicitor general, but again had little profile outside of Edmonton. He had no support from other MLAs; finished fifth on the first ballot with only 7 percent of the votes; and subsequently endorsed Stelmach.

- Mark Norris, a businessman and one-term MLA from Edmonton-McClung. He was the only cabinet minister to lose re-election in 2004. Marc was affable but had no support from other MLAs. But he was the only candidate who voiced any support for my version of the Alberta Agenda. He finished sixth with 6.9 percent of the vote in the first round, and then endorsed Stelmach in the second.

- Gary McPherson, Edmonton. Gary was a lifelong paraplegic and inspiring advocate for people with disabilities. But he had no prior electoral politics experience and was never a serious contender.

The large number of candidates from Edmonton virtually guaranteed that because of vote splitting, no one candidate was likely to win. But when Stelmach finished third in the first round of voting, all the Edmonton-area candidates then endorsed him for the second round of voting, contributing to his eventual victory.

A sixth candidate was Lyle Oberg, the MLA from Strathmore-Brooks. A physician by training, Oberg had a decade of cabinet experience in the Klein governments. Oberg was arguably the most articulate and experienced candidate other than Dinning, but with no supporters in the PC caucus. For most of the campaign, Oberg was expected to do well in rural southern Alberta and to finish in the top three. When he finished fourth with only 12 percent of the vote, he threw his support to Stelmach in return for a promised appointment as the next minister of finance.

A seventh candidate was Victor Doerksen, the MLA from Red Deer-South. An accountant and banker prior to politics, Victor was elected four times as MLA from Red Deer-South. The previous term he'd served as Klein's minister of innovation and science. A relatively quiet and soft-spoken man, Doerksen had no MLA endorsements; he finished seventh with less than 1 percent of the votes. He declined to endorse any candidate in the second round.

Last, and in many respects least, was me. I was another one of the long shots. I had only been elected as an MLA two years earlier. I had no PC Party history; no caucus supporters; and no experience as a minister. At the outset, the *Calgary Herald* gave me 500-to-1 odds of winning.[3]

But I had one thing that none of the other seven candidates had: a province-wide, grassroots following among the tens of thousands of Reform Party and now Canadian Alliance Party activists. They knew me for my victory in the 1998 Alberta Senate election; my extensive field work for Stockwell Day in the first (2001) Alliance leadership race; and my close association with Stephen Harper, a co-signatory of the 2001 Firewall Letter and now, as of January 26, the newly elected prime minister of Canada.

I also had friends and supporters from the more recent work I had done on the same-sex marriage and parents' rights issues. This included several evangelical organizations and the extensive Mormon network in southern Alberta. For the same reasons, I also received the endorsement of the Islamic Supreme Council of Canada and its leader, Syed Soharwardy. My public role in supporting gun owners' rights and the thirteen Alberta farmers who went to jail for challenging the Canadian Wheat Board monopoly also created support networks that helped us sell memberships (see chapter 2).

There was plenty of overlap between these broad groups of potential supporters, but this was good for me. Individuals and families that were part of both groups would be even more inclined to purchase PC memberships and to vote for me. Our challenge was how to mobilize these potential supporters into card-carrying PC members. But with our new team, new technology, and extensive collection of old Reform/CA membership lists, we believed we could do it. And almost did.

ISSUES: THE FIREWALL CANDIDATE

In terms of issues, my campaign was already defined by what I had been writing and speaking about for the previous six years. I was, first and foremost, the "Firewall candidate." If elected, I promised that I would act on the reforms called for in the 2001 Alberta Agenda manifesto: a provincial police force; collecting our own income taxes; and withdrawing from the Canada Pension Plan and creating our own Alberta pension plan. These "More Alberta, Less Ottawa" policies were reforms that would strengthen Alberta's policy autonomy vis-à-vis the federal government. When my opponents criticized these as radical and dangerous, I would simply point out that Quebec already did all of these. How radical is that?

I also campaigned on the issues and principles that were embodied in Bill 208. Same-sex marriage was now the law of the land, but that did not mean that the coercive power of the state should be used to silence or punish those who disagreed with it. I believed that freedom of religion and freedom of speech, school choice, and parents' rights are all fundamental to a free and democratic society. If elected, I promised I would protect them.

I was more outspoken on democratic reforms than the other candidates. I advocated for term limits for premiers, a lobbyist registry, citizens' initiatives, and referendums. I also promised greater health care reform—specifically, more publicly funded, privately delivered health care. My message was clear: Equal access to a waiting list is not equal access to health care. Unlike the other candidates, my platform also included several specific environmental commitments: strengthening our Water for Life strategy; protecting the Eastern Slopes; and ending the unrestricted out-of-season hunting and fishing allowed by the recently enacted Métis Harvesting Agreement.

Fiscal issues played an important but not a leading role in my leadership campaign. With Dinning having served as Klein's minister of finance during the budget-cutting years of the 1990s, there was not much strategic advantage for me in the fiscal policy field. My fiscal policy commitments included:

- Not allowing Alberta to fall back into the deficit/debt hole that Ralph Klein had dug us out of.

- Capping the growth of public sector spending at less than annual private sector growth.

- Keeping our combined personal and corporate taxes the lowest in Canada.

- Saving 30 percent of our non-renewable resource revenues in the Heritage Savings Trust Fund, as Peter Lougheed had intended.

- Increasing Alberta's tax credit for charitable donations.

The last two policies were the only ones that set me apart from the other candidates. Increasing the tax credit for charitable donations reflected my belief in the need to support policies that strengthen, not weaken, civil society. Whether it's the arts, the vulnerable, health care, or education, voluntary, private-sector charities and non-profits are always competing with the public sector for service delivery. These non-profits also engage citizens in their communities, thereby strengthening civil society. The stronger the institutions of civil society, the less the need for new government programs and bureaucracies.[4] (See Appendix 2.) The flip side is equally true: the more we cede these responsibilities to the state, the larger it becomes, and the weaker civil society becomes.[5] This connection is well recognized in US scholarship but has generally been ignored in Canada.

Private sector provision of services—both non-profit and for-profit—provide citizens/taxpayers with alternatives, and this competition forces their public counterparts to improve.[6] And they need to improve—not just in Alberta but in all modern welfare states. It is an unpleasant truth that public sector bureaucracies tend to be run more for the benefit of the civil servants than for the citizens they are supposed to be serving. Hospitals are run first and foremost for the benefit of doctors and then nurses. Universities routinely prioritize the interests of professors over the interests of students. The same trend is found in our public schools. This tendency is exacerbated by public sector unions that instinctively lobby (and strike) for reduced hours and higher salaries. They also prioritize protecting their poorest-performing members from being dismissed.

My wife and I knew all this first-hand from our decades of teaching— me at the University of Calgary and my wife in the Calgary public school system. We have friends and neighbours who are doctors and nurses, and they reported the same experiences. And it's not because teachers, nurses, and professors are "bad people," but rather because they are completely normal people: they look after their own interests first. This is the Achilles heel of public monopolies. There is nowhere else for unhappy patients, parents, or students to go. Competition from private sector alternatives provides the antidote and forces greater accountability on publicly funded services like education and health care.[7]

CAMPAIGN AND ENDORSEMENTS

In the fall, the PC Party organized seven leadership debates across the province—Calgary and Edmonton; but also Fort McMurray and Grande Prairie in the north; and Red Deer and then Lethbridge and Medicine Hat in the south. As far as debates go, they were deadly boring—both for the audiences and for the candidates. With eight candidates, each candidate had to be given the opportunity to answer each question—which limited responses to two minutes per candidate. This format guaranteed short, superficial, answers—"talking points," as campaign strategists like to call them. Each candidate was given time for an opening and closing statement, five and three minutes respectively. But by the time you listened to eight of them in a row, you tended to tune out. Especially if you had already heard them five or six times.

The more interesting aspect of these debates was not what was said but who showed up. Every debate created the opportunity for each campaign to demonstrate their level of support and organization in that city or region. A strong turnout of supporters would hopefully generate some positive media and build new momentum. With the exception of the Edmonton debate,[8] it was becoming clear that the Dinning and Morton campaigns were winning on the ground. But there was a clear difference between the two campaigns.

The turnout for Dinning was always clean, crisp, and organized. It would include whatever local MLAs were supporting him, as well as some local dignitaries and high-profile men and women from the business community. His supporters were vocal but polite.

The "I'm supportin' Morton" crowd, many wearing our black-and-white T-shirts, was different. Actually, very different. We were numerous and well organized. But the similarities ended there. Many were not quite as clean cut and well dressed as the Dinningites. We were not impolite, but definitely louder and more enthusiastic.

If the Dinning campaign was a top-down organization filled with people who were content with the status quo, the Morton supporters were the opposite—a bottom-up movement that wanted change. The *Lethbridge Herald* noted that Dinning's events "drew a crowd of who's who made up of civic leaders, former and current politicians and business owners." Morton's event, by contrast, "was a gathering of ma's and pa's, parents with children … the ones who shop at the businesses owned by those who attended Dinning's rally."[9] As another journalist put it: "If Dinning supporters believe in the man, Morton supporters believe in the cause."[10]

This contrast was captured in the final weeks of the campaign by a song we received as an in-kind contribution from Bobbie Norman, a Cochrane songwriter and a Morton supporter. Recorded by one of her friends in Nashville, it caught on quickly: "Ted Morton is The Man."[11]

> Trouble so endless, answers so few/Need a cool-headed man with a steady-hand crew/ Someone who studied life's little plan/Don't look any further, Ted Morton is the Man.
> CHORUS:
> Who do you want? Ted Morton!
> Who do you need? Ted Morton!
> Who do you like? Ted Morton!
> Who's gonna make a stand? Ted Morton is the Man.
> He's gonna care for a future with pride/where the east blowin' wind won't knock us off stride/Protecting us all the best way he can/A vote for tomorrow, Ted Morton is the Man.
> CHORUS
> He's Albertan by choice, now runnin' for premier/He'll guard our future, and all we hold dear. Ted Morton is the man with a plan/Ted Morton is the Man.
> CHORUS

The lyrics were corny, but the tune itself was catchy. You can still find it on YouTube.[12] And soon it was playing loudly at all our events.

While I didn't realize it at the time, we had tapped into Albertans' recently dormant but deeply rooted populist political culture. Alberta's political history is characterized by realigning elections in which feelings of Western alienation fuel a populist surge that destroys the incumbent governing party and replaces it with a party that hardly existed before. The United Farmers of Alberta did it in 1921. Social Credit did it in 1935. More recently at the federal level, in 1993, Preston Manning and his brand-new Reform Party—marching under the banner "The West Wants In!"—swept Alberta. In 1988, Brian Mulroney and the PCs had won twenty-five of Alberta's twenty-six federal seats. In 1993, they did not win a single riding. Reformers won twenty-two.

My candidacy embodied the same phenomenon. I was not a new party, but I represented a clear break with the thirty-five-year PC dynasty. The decade of Reform Party ascendancy federally had created an appetite for change at the provincial level. I became the vehicle for that change.

The summer was spent on an endless road trip covering all of Alberta, not just once but twice. My road team consisted primarily of Bill Bewick and my daughter Cally Morton. I had met Bill and his parents through Reform Party politics during the 1990s. Bill was from Calgary, but he had done his undergraduate studies at the University of Alberta. He then did an MA there with Dr. Leon Craig, and went to do a PhD in political theory at Michigan State with Dr. Arthur Meltzer, another Straussian. Suffice it to say that Bill and I had similar world views. I valued Bill not just for his political advice but also his collection of musical CDs—mostly newer, alternative country and western like Corb Lund—which we enjoyed as we criss-crossed Alberta. He also damn near saved my life in the last week of the campaign when the semi-trailer truck we were passing suddenly moved into our lane and pushed us into the snow-filled median!

Cally had graduated from Queen's University in Kingston, Ontario in 2003, and then gone to Ottawa to work for the newly created Conservative Party of Canada. There she had the good fortune to meet and work for Vida Brodie on the 2004 Harper campaign. Vida assigned her to Harper's advance team. This meant that Cally had more actual front-line campaign experience than either me or Bill and this made her a valued part of our team. Those who know Cally won't be surprised to read that she was not reluctant to give me advice.

While the local weeklies usually covered my visits and meetings, our campaign was invisible in the Calgary and Edmonton media. This changed in mid-September when over 300 supporters turned out for our "official" campaign launch party. As reported in the *Calgary Herald*:

> The room is brimming and buzzing with more than 300 people—an eclectic mix of well-manicured yuppies, serious suits, flannel-clad farmers and teenagers with complicated haircuts. … But when Ted Morton finally takes the stage, the applause isn't polite. It's thunderous.[13]

Suddenly, the big-city media began to pay attention. By mid-November, my nemesis in the *Edmonton Journal*, Graham Thomson, warned his readers that my campaign was showing "surprising strength."[14] But our big media breakthrough came two weeks later, with the front page headline in the *Calgary Herald*, "Dinning, Morton virtually tied in Tory race."[15] The *Herald's* polling of 800 PC members found that Dinning was leading at 21 percent and that I was second at 18 percent. But with a 3 percent margin of error, it was a toss-up. Oberg and Stelmach followed well behind with 11 percent and 10 percent.

These polling numbers sent a clear message. No candidate was going to get the 51 percent to win on the first round. And with the top three going to a second-round runoff, the anyone-but-Dinning scenario was no longer just a theoretical possibility. For the Dinning team, which only six months earlier had been predicting a first-round victory, this poll was alarming. For us, it was another momentum builder.

By the final week before the first round of voting, official endorsements began to be announced. Dinning got almost all of them: the *Calgary Herald*, the *Calgary Sun*,[16] even the *Globe and Mail*.[17] Former PC Premier Peter Lougheed also stepped out of retirement to endorse Dinning.[18] This did not faze us. Everyone knew that Dinning was the establishment candidate. We laughed that in Alberta, being endorsed by the Toronto-based *Globe and Mail* might actually be a negative. We were also encouraged that Premier Klein endorsed no one. This left the door open for someone other than Dinning.

My endorsements were fewer and less high profile. But they were from individuals my populist base listened to: Lorne Gunter in the *Edmonton Journal*;[19] Link Byfield in the Citizens Centre for Freedom and Democracy; Joe Woodard in the *Western Standard*;[20] the Canadian Taxpayers Federation; and Licia Corbella in the *Calgary Sun*.[21]

Corbella's endorsement was especially interesting because she revealed that she had written the *Sun's* unsigned editorial endorsement of Dinning just a few days earlier. But in her own mind, she told her readers, "I'm supportin' Morton," and went on to say, "PC members should jump in bed with Ted." This colourful metaphor did not get her in trouble, but it almost did our campaign. We thought it was so funny that we immediately ordered 500 black-and-white T-shirts emblazoned with "Get in Bed with Ted." When they arrived forty-eight hours later, more sober voices prevailed, and the new T-shirts were quickly consigned to the garbage bin.

We also had to spend some money we didn't have. In Alberta rural weekly newspapers, paid advertising must be bought a week before the paper actually appears. Because the rural vote was so central to our strategy, we had planned to purchase over $30,000 worth of advertising in these weeklies, both the week before round one and the week before round two. This meant that we had to purchase the second week before we even knew the first-round results. What if I didn't even make it to the second round? Plus, we were out of money. Contrary to all my talk about fiscal responsibility, we crossed our fingers and went ahead and bought it all.

FIRST-ROUND RESULTS

November 25 finally arrived. It was bitterly cold—minus 20°C. This made our last minute GOTV even more important, and our phone bank ran full bore right up to the polls closing. We then all filed down to the Roundup Centre at the Stampede Grounds to wait for the results. We easily had several hundred supporters there to cheer on the results. But I was nervous. Two days earlier, my campaign staff had sat me down to tell me that we had sold just over 16,000 memberships. By historical comparisons, this was a lot. But was it enough? They told me they didn't know. So as the results began to trickle in and be posted on board at the front of the room, we held our breath and hoped for the best.

And we got it. By 10 p.m. it was clear. Dinning was nowhere near a first-ballot victory. And I was clearly going to finish second. We started celebrating long before the final numbers confirmed our success. Dinning won with 29,470 votes, but this was only 30 percent of the votes. I trailed closely behind with 25,614, or 26 percent, and Stelmach was a distant third with 14,967, or 15 percent. Under the rules, only the top three finishers moved on to the second round of voting. It was exciting, and we celebrated well into the evening. Which was good. Because the very next day, a whole new election began, and there were only seven days before the second round of voting.

The voter turnout was huge—96,000 voters, almost double the number who voted in the last PC leadership contest held in 1992. The results tracked geography as well as ideology. Dinning won every riding in Calgary except Calgary-Montrose. Edmonton was badly fragmented, with Norris, Hancock, Dinning, and Stelmach each picking up several ridings. Stelmach also won four more rural ridings further east of Edmonton. We swept virtually all of central and southern Alberta. Of the twenty-one rural ridings south and west of Edmonton, I won all but four. I also carried the two urban ridings in both Medicine Hat and Red Deer.[22]

The voting system for the second round was a preferential ballot. Voters are instructed to indicate both a first and a second preference on their ballots. To win, a candidate needs 50 percent-plus-one of first preferences. If no candidate receives that on the first count, then the third place finisher is dropped and his/her voters' second preferences are redistributed to the two remaining candidates—one of whom now has the required majority and wins.

We thought this system would help us. Given Dinning's weak lead in the first round, it was now obvious that he was going to finish well short of the 50 percent-plus-one of first preferences needed to win in round two. The winner was going to be decided by the second preferences of the third place finisher. The "anyone but Dinning" strategy suddenly took on a whole new relevance.

As I was the most obvious beneficiary, I quickly became its most vocal proponent. My message to PC voters was that they should no longer consider Dinning a viable candidate to be the leader of our party: "Conservatives in Alberta had a long hard look at Jim Dinning, and 70 percent of them said no."[23] That left only Ted or Ed. We immediately began to message to our PC voter lists: "Vote Ted and Ed. Or Ed and Ted." We assumed, not unreasonably, that Stelmach was too far behind to catch me in the second round. So long as he didn't, then I would get his supporters' second preferences, which would then push me past Dinning.

Dinning's team had obviously made the same calculation but to the opposite conclusion. Suddenly, there was now a very explicit and loud "anyone-but-Morton" campaign. Dinning was "taking the gloves off," declared the *Calgary Sun*. The very night the first-round results were announced, Dinning declared that Albertans had a choice between a leader "that can bring people together" or a leader "who is determined to fight the battles of the past and build firewalls."[24]

These attacks heated up in the days that followed. Graham Thomson reported that Dinning was "running a campaign of fear."[25] Dinning warned that I was "too extreme"; that a Morton win "would take the progressive out of Progressive Conservative. … Ted Morton's Alberta is not my Alberta."[26] By election day Saturday, Dinning was running full-page ads in both the *Calgary Herald* and *Edmonton Journal* under the headline: "Choose the Alberta <u>You</u> Want," followed by a list of "scary" campaign promises I had made.

Predictably, the worst mudslinging was done by proxies hoping to collect a cabinet appointment if Dinning won. Campaigning with Dinning, Gary Mar predicted that if I became the party's leader, the PCs would lose the next election. He declared that he could not support a Ted Morton government and that he would not run again if I became leader.[27] This message was echoed in liberal media stories such as the Friday headline in the *Globe and Mail*, "Is this man too 'scary' for Alberta?"[28]

Dinning's public messaging was complemented by a quiet outreach to Calgarians who traditionally voted Liberal.[29] The message: If Dinning doesn't win, the next premier of Alberta will be your worst nightmare—a pro-life, anti–gay marriage social conservative named Ted Morton.

The *Calgary Herald* reported that in the Calgary arts community both patrons and staff were being encouraged to purchase PC memberships and vote for Dinning.[30] Not coincidentally, Dinning had quietly promised to double public funding for the arts. This last-minute recruiting of Liberal voters clearly had some effect. "Temporary Tories cast leadership votes to head off Morton," reported the *Edmonton Journal*.[31]

My response to the Dinning campaign's personal attacks was that they were a sign of their desperation and would not work. I drew a parallel to the recent federal election. "It didn't work when Paul Martin tried it on Stephen Harper, and it won't work if Jim Dinning tries it on Ted Morton."[32] I continued to portray Dinning as "Liberal-lite" and way too closely tied to the "Calgary mafia"—a wealthy group of corporate insiders who had financed and advised Ralph Klein. I also pointed out more than once that Dinning had delivered a $50,000 cheque to Paul Martin in the 2004 federal Liberal leadership campaign. And when Anne McLellan, the Liberal MP from Edmonton, endorsed Dinning, I happily assured PC voters that no Liberals were endorsing me.

Stelmach stayed above the fray. He pitched himself as the "unity candidate" and stayed out of the Dinning-Morton dogfight. He had concluded—correctly—that he was potentially its biggest beneficiary. If Stelmach could somehow beat one of us on first preferences, and both our supporters chose him as their second preference, he could sneak up the middle and win. But this was a big if. He had finished far behind both of us in the first round. A quarter of his support came from just two ridings—his own and the one next door. In Calgary, he did not receive more than 93 votes in any riding. How could he possibly catch up?

Well, he started by getting the endorsements of the losing candidates. Hancock and Norris immediately endorsed their fellow Edmontonian, Stelmach. Would their supporters follow their advice? Normally, this is far from certain, especially in one-person, one-vote primaries, as opposed to a leadership convention. But in this case, it was effective. Almost overnight, Ed's third place finish mobilized a new issue, a new message: that it was Edmonton's turn to have a premier.

It was no secret around Edmonton that the Klein inner circle was very Calgary-centric. His chief of staff, Rod Love, and most of his major fundraisers were Calgarians. When the legislature was not in session, Ralph clearly preferred to be in Calgary and work from his southern office at McDougall Centre. It was widely rumoured that he had once remarked, "Edmonton is not the end of the Earth ... but you can see it from there." True or not, it fed a feeling of benign neglect in the north. Now suddenly, with Dinning and Morton pounding each other, Ed Stelmach opened the window for a premier from the north.

Oberg's endorsement was more calculated. Most of his supporters came from the same areas that I'd done well in—communities in rural central and southern Alberta. In the PC Caucus meetings, seating is assigned alphabetically, so I had been sitting next to Oberg for the past two years. We had become friendly. With his decade of experience, he often was able to explain procedural and organizational issues that were new to me. In retrospect, I think his helpful manner was partly motivated by Oberg's belief that when the time came for the leadership, he would finish ahead of me and be able to persuade me to throw my support to him. At the time, that was not an unreasonable assumption. But now the shoe was on the other foot.

I wanted his support. I phoned Oberg Saturday night, and several more times Sunday morning. He never picked up the phone. That evening, he announced that he too would be supporting Stelmach. It later came out that Oberg had offered his support to Stelmach in return for a promise to appoint him as the next minister of finance. Stelmach agreed. But it did not end the way Oberg planned.

> After he won, Stelmach did appoint Oberg as his finance minister. But he also appointed his close friend and supporter Lloyd Snelgrove as President of Treasury Board and transferred most key spending decisions to him. This hollowed out the influence that past finance ministers had enjoyed, leaving Oberg with the title but not the power he had hoped for. Not surprisingly, Oberg resigned his post before the next election and left the party. He apparently had not learned what I learned my first day in the legislature.

On the Monday following the first round, we set out on our last road trip of the campaign. We were optimistic. A number of Alberta MPs from the Harper government had returned to Alberta to help us get out the vote. Jason Kenney, Monte Solberg, Rob Anders, and Stockwell Day all helped out. As the front page of the *Calgary Herald* observed, it was "bordering on a war between federal and provincial Tories."[33] This was okay with us. Canadian Alliance members outnumbered PC members three to one.

I also picked up two last minute endorsements from Tory MLAs: Hung Pham, Calgary-Montrose, and Tony Abbott, Drayton Valley-Calmar.[34] Tony had helped me win this rural northern riding in the first round. Pham told us that he had sold 9,000 memberships to the Vietnamese community in northeast Calgary to support Lyle Oberg in the first round of voting. Now he was ready to support me.

Our spirits were also buoyed by the large number of unsolicited cheques and donations that were being hand delivered to our campaign office on Monday morning. A lot of people who had ignored us for the past twelve months suddenly wanted to be on our "friends list." That was fine with us. We suddenly had more money than we knew what to do with. We easily paid off all the bills for the advertising in the rural weekly newspapers that we'd had to buy before the first round of voting. For the first time in the entire campaign, we actually thought we had a good chance of winning.

This thought actually created a problem. What if I did win? What does a "premier-elect" do in his first days and weeks? Choose a cabinet? I'd never been in a cabinet. Messaging to the press? To party members? To Albertans from their new premier? First impressions are important. This is all part of "the transition"—something we had not given a moment's thought to. To this end, we were able to get Bill Boyd, a Saskatchewan Party MLA, to meet me in Medicine Hat to discuss some of the start-up decisions that a new premier needs to make. Bill was part of Brad Wall's inner circle, and, like Brad, was supportive of the "More Alberta, Less Ottawa" themes of my campaign.

Within a day and a half, we came up with a plan. Sunday afternoon, we would hold a press conference. Messaging to the party: unity—everyone is welcome. Messaging to the province: business as usual. Spring session and budget would commence in February, as scheduled. Also on Sunday, establish liaison with the premier's office: request a meeting with Klein as soon as possible and also a meeting with senior civil servants. By end of day Monday, cobble together a "transition team" of seven current MLAs I thought would be supportive and strengthen the party unity message. This included leadership candidates Stelmach, Hancock, and Norris (sending a message to Edmonton and the north that they would be at the table). Mel Knight and Doug Horner were also on this list—both of whom were also from northern Alberta and had helped me with Bill 208. For this same reason, I wanted Greg Melchin, a Calgary MLA and Klein cabinet minister. I also wanted MLA and Minister of Finance Shirley McLellan for her expertise and influence. This transition team was to be introduced at a press conference in Edmonton on Tuesday. Less urgent but not less important, we began discussing the recruitment of new PC candidates for the next election. These would be individuals who had helped my leadership campaign and supported my Alberta Agenda policies. At the top of my list was Danielle Smith. If only...

Predictably, the last week held some unscripted funny moments. In our visit to Medicine Hat, we were met by Dean Shock and his family. Dean was from the Hat and had played an invaluable role in our Calgary campaign office by providing IT and programming assistance. Now, in front of dozens of flashing cameras, Dean's daughter Danielle approached me and presented me with her new four-month-old Jack Russell terrier. She had named it Tedmorton! Our picture was not only in the *Medicine Hat News*[35] the next day, but also the *Calgary Herald*.[36] What other campaign had a mascot!?

Hung Pham's endorsement also entailed a surprise. In return for his endorsement, Hung wanted my assurance that, as premier, I would support a matching grant for a proposed seniors' retirement home being developed by the Vietnamese community in Edmonton. This led to a marathon end-of-day bargaining session in Edmonton with representatives from the Vietnamese community. During the campaign, I had stated repeatedly that, unlike the other candidates, I would not make spending promises in return for votes. So I was uncomfortable with what Pham was asking me to do. As I dithered, my daughter Cally, who was part of my road team, started kicking me under the table. She shared none of my qualms. She just wanted to seal the deal and get the votes. I finally said yes. Then came the surprise. To celebrate the agreement, we were escorted off to an eleven-course Vietnamese wedding feast. This was not on our agenda. And we didn't get back to Calgary until well after midnight.

This may help to explain why I began to come down with a cold and sinus infection later in the week. I made it through the last debate of the campaign Thursday evening, but then spent Friday just making telephone calls (which I hated) and visiting the volunteers at our phone bank (which I loved). But by Saturday, voting day, I was really sick, with a temperature over 39°C. That afternoon we flew up to Edmonton in a private plane generously provided by my friend Archie Nesbitt. I was such a mess that nobody wanted to sit next to me. My campaign team went immediately to the Alberta Aviation Museum, where the results would be announced that evening.

I went with my family to the Hotel Macdonald, where we had booked a suite of rooms in anticipation of an exciting night. In addition to Bambi and Cally, my son Hutch had now joined us, as had my mother. My brother Allen and his wife, Morgan, had flown in just for the weekend. Bambi, of course, had planned a wonderful dinner in the beautiful Macdonald dining room. I managed to dress, but even after two more Tylenol, I knew I had to save what energy I had left for the rest of the night. So as everyone else enjoyed a wonderful dinner, I remained in my room. Lying on our bed, suit and tie, shoes on, eyes closed, I contemplated what was about to happen.

SECOND-ROUND RESULTS

When we entered the Alberta Aviation Museum just after 8 p.m., our initial reception was very positive. Hundreds of supporters were there to greet us and cheer me on. But before an hour had passed, it became apparent that what we had planned for was not happening. Early returns from the Edmonton area indicated a huge increase in votes for Stelmach. We hoped this was just a regional anomaly. It wasn't.

A wave of new voters—over 44,000—propelled Stelmach from a distant third to a virtual tie with Dinning on first preferences: 51,764 to 51,272. We had increased our vote total by more than 16,000, but with only 41,243, I was eliminated. Per the rules, the second preferences of my supporters were then counted, and 86 percent went to Stelmach, making him the new PC party leader. As we were in Edmonton, there were large numbers of Stelmach supporters at the event, and they were jubilant. As the headlines in the newspapers the next day announced, sometimes nice guys do win.

	First Ballot	Second Ballot	Preferential Ballot
Dinning	29,470	51,272	55,509
Morton	25,614	41,243	—
Stelmach	14,967	51,764	77,577
Others	28,639	—	—
Total	98,690	144,279	133,086

Stelmach's jaw-dropping vote surge was a shock. I was right about Dinning being finished, but completely wrong about Stelmach's ability to catch up with us. It was hard to say who was more surprised by this outcome: Dinning, me, or Ed Stelmach! How did this happen?

On one level, the Stelmach strategy was simply better and more effective. Publicly, Stelmach had avoided the negative rhetoric and personal attacks. Privately, his campaign launched a massive new membership sales initiative, reminding potential supporters that Dinning had been Klein's hatchet man in the painful budget cuts of the 1990s. Stelmach also benefited from the large and connected Ukrainian population in and around Edmonton. This overlapped with a whisper campaign that "It's Edmonton's turn now," which in turn tapped into the anti-Calgary sentiment latent in both Edmonton and rural Alberta. Stelmach also received the support of the three candidates eliminated in the first round. Together, they positioned Stelmach as a moderate, likeable, positive candidate, a better alternative to the two warring "fiscal hawks." This message played well with public sector unions and municipal politicians, both of whom depend on Government of Alberta largesse. For all of this, the Stelmach strategy deserves high marks.

But there were also structural factors in the PC leadership selection process that allowed this to happen. In a three-candidate runoff election with a clear front-runner such as Dinning, the only plausible path to victory for second and third place candidates is to join forces to prevent the front-runner from crossing the 50 percent threshold on first preferences. That's what we did. In a two-candidate run-off election, this incentive would not occur. Given that at the outset of the leadership race Dinning was a heavy favourite to win, this structural factor contributed to his defeat.

A second structural factor was the lack of any cut-off date for purchasing party memberships prior to the voting day. Often described as an "open primary system," this rule opens the door for a candidate to sell large numbers of memberships to people who are not party members, not just on the first ballot but also in the one-week window before the second ballot.

This rule clearly benefited me on the first ballot. I was able to recruit large numbers of former Reform Party and Alliance Party supporters who had never held memberships in the provincial PC Party. Going into the first day of voting, my campaign had identified 16,784 supporters and sold 11,230 memberships. By the end of the day, I had received 25,614 votes—more than double the number of memberships we had sold prior to voting day. In Canadian nomination elections, this kind of "conversion rate" (i.e., ratio of memberships sold to actual votes cast) is unheard of. We attributed this very pleasant surprise to the "moccasin telegraph," the informal but tightly knit network of Alberta Reformers.

In the second round, it was the Stelmach campaign that benefited from the "gate crashers." The number of voters in the second round was 48 percent higher than in the first round. Stelmach more than tripled his first-round votes—from 14,967 to 51,764. Some members of my team still believe that if membership sales had been cut off after the first round of voting, I would have won. Dinning would still have been the vote leader, but well short of 50 percent-plus-one. Stelmach would not have caught up with me, and so many—we'll never know how many—of his voters' second preferences would have gone to me. The "Ted or Ed" or "Ed or Ted" strategy might have worked. But the membership sales were not cut off, and the number of new voters was much larger than the total number of voters for the candidates eliminated in the first round. Where did these new voters come from?

Public sector unions were leery of both Dinning and me. Dinning had been Klein's minister of finance in the mid-1990s when the Tories imposed an across-the-board 5 percent pay reduction to all public sector employees— including teachers and nurses. I had campaigned on the promise of fiscal responsibility and opening up Alberta's health care system to more private delivery and contracting out to non-unionized providers. Not surprisingly, the Alberta Union of Public Employees (AUPE), the Alberta Teachers' Association (ATA), and the United Nurses of Alberta (UNA) did not warm to the idea of two self-proclaimed "fiscal hawks" leading the next government of Alberta. The Stelmach campaign privately exploited this anxiety to sign up thousands of new members— "two-minute Tories"—who tore up their PC membership cards as they exited the polling stations.

Third, the "two-minute Tory" window in the second round had a left-wing bias. In a dominant one-party province like Alberta, the winner of the PC leadership race immediately becomes the new premier of the province. This creates an incentive for traditional Liberal Party supporters to buy a PC membership just to help to elect the "least worst" Conservative candidate. As noted above, the Dinning campaign encouraged this. It helps to explain how Dinning increased his votes from 29,470 in the first round to 51,272 in the second.

But the left-wing bias of the second round is structural as well as circumstantial. The window for selling new memberships is open for only one week. Time is short. This creates an incentive for leadership campaigns to target their recruiting efforts on organized interests that can be quickly mobilized through pre-existing membership lists with telephone numbers, addresses, and emails.

For Stelmach, this meant reaching out to public sector unions to block the Dinning-Morton "threat." Dave Hancock threw his support to Stelmach and used his ATA contacts to sell PC memberships to teachers. Stelmach's other "secret weapon" was the Alberta Association of Municipal Districts and Counties (AAMDC), the trade association for elected officials from rural Alberta. Stelmach had begun his political career at the municipal level. He was the former reeve of Lamont County, and had been active in the AAMDC, as had several of his MLA supporters. Led by Sherwood Park MLA Iris Evans, they mobilized significant support through their extensive networks of rural officeholders and employees, most of whom already knew the likeable Stelmach.

These structural factors clearly contributed to Stelmach's come-from-behind victory. Behind its front page headlines—"STELMACH WIN STUNS TORIES," the *Edmonton Journal* went on to explain that Stelmach had gone "from 'Mr. Nice' to 'Mr. Premier' because of a swell of support in Edmonton and northern Alberta."[37] This was partly true. The 300 percent increase in Stelmach's first preferences—from 14,967 to 51,764—did come mostly from northern Alberta. But this only brought him even with Dinning. It was my supporters' second preferences—86 percent of which went to Stelmach—that made Ed Stelmach Alberta's new premier-elect. In this sense, I had made Ed Stelmach the new premier of Alberta; a thought that haunted me until, four years later, I was the one who deposed him. (See chapter 9.)

ED STELMACH: THE ACCIDENTAL PREMIER

Round one was a referendum on Jim Dinning, and he lost. But round two was a referendum on Ted Morton, and I lost. A quarter-million dollars of negative advertising worked. Just as Dinning had underestimated the support I was to receive from former federal Reform Party members, I had underestimated how many Liberals were willing to become "two-minute Tories" to defeat me. I was clearly perceived as a threat to the political status quo in Alberta, and its beneficiaries mobilized quickly to ensure my defeat.

While we lost the leadership race, we did not lose the battle for new ideas. We proved that campaigns matter. We went from 500-to-1 odds at the beginning to almost winning. Plus, we chose who did win. If membership sales had been cut off after the first round of voting, I might have won. Longer term, my campaign changed the culture and composition of the PC Party. As noted earlier, "Dinning supporters believe in the man, Morton supporters believe in the cause."[38] The man was gone, but the cause was not. And neither were my supporters.

My campaign had brought the values and policies that animated federal Reformers into the provincial PC party. First and foremost, this meant the Alberta Agenda: the demand for a new deal—a fair deal—from Ottawa. If not Senate reform, which looked increasingly unlikely, then the "More Alberta, Less Ottawa" policy initiatives I had campaigned on.

While I didn't recognize this at the time, I benefited from the new federal CPC's de-emphasis of Western issues. Stephen Harper did not seek the leadership of the Canadian Alliance and then the CPC to lead a Western rump protest party. Harper and his team wanted to win a majority government, and this meant a new emphasis on issues that played well in Ontario and Quebec. Many first-wave Reformers who did not like what they saw as the abandonment of Reform's founding principles gravitated to my 2006 leadership campaign and, later, the Wildrose Party.[39]

We also grew and energized the social conservative wing of the party. These new PCers wanted policies that would protect them and their children from the rapidly expanding policy demands flowing from the Supreme Court's same-sex marriage ruling. My supporters were looking for a party that would protect their freedom of speech, freedom of religion, parents' rights, and expanded school choice.

Both the "More Alberta, Less Ottawa" and social conservative issues were especially popular in rural and small-town Alberta. Outside of Calgary, I swept virtually all of central and southern Alberta. This regional concentration of my support was essential to my success in the first round of voting. But when in the second round I did not prevail, it laid the groundwork for the future growth of the Wildrose Party (see chapters 9 and 10.)

Both Dinning and I were defeated by voters who were not normally PC party members. So where did that leave the PC Party? The "two-minute Tories" were clearly not staying. They went home to the Liberal and NDP parties. But what about the 41,000 Reformers who bought memberships to support me?

The risk going forward was whether we could keep these conservatives in the PC Party. Losing Red Tories to the Liberals was not a risk. We saw that in 1993, when Nancy Betkowski, after losing the leadership race to Ralph Klein, crossed the floor and joined the Liberals. This made no difference in the next election. What the PCs could not afford were defections to a new right-of-centre party. Dividing the conservative vote was—and is—a recipe for defeat. In BC, the split between Social Credit and the BC Liberal Party gave the NDP a free pass for the entire decade of the 1990s. Federally, the Reform-PC split gave Jean Chrétien and Liberals three easy victories and eleven years of majority government in Ottawa.

Was premier-elect Ed Stelmach up to this challenge? Publicly, I said he was. I was trying to be a gracious loser. I said that his win "probably made it easier to hold the party together"; that he would be "a very good leader—lots of experience and practical judgement."[40]

Privately I was not so optimistic. I knew then what others said later: that Ed was an "accidental premier"—elected as the default candidate between the two warring wings of the PC Party. In the second round, two-thirds of the voters had cast their first preferences for someone other than Ed. Would he be able to hold together a party that was now so clearly divided? Policy-wise there was nothing novel or inspiring about his campaign. In the public debates, he was awkward and inarticulate. Would Ed Stelmach have what it would take to keep the party together? Only time would tell.

Legislating Conservation: Success and Failure (2007-2009)

> *Conservation means development as much as it does protection.*
> *I recognize the right and duty of this generation to develop and*
> *use the natural resources of our land; but I do not recognize the*
> *right to waste them, or to rob, by wasteful use, the generations*
> *that come after us.*
>
> —U.S. President Theodore Roosevelt (1910)[1]

Following Stelmach's surprise victory in the 2006 PC leadership race, he was sworn in as the thirteenth premier of Alberta. His first task was to assemble a cabinet. Based on my strong showing of support in the leadership race, it was obvious that Stelmach would have to include me in his new cabinet. The question was, which ministry? Many of my key supporters were hoping for Finance, Energy, or Health (the latter based on my campaign promises to bring in more publicly financed but privately delivered health care). When Stelmach named me as the new minister of sustainable resources development (SRD), they were disappointed. I was not.

During the extended 2006 leadership race—and the unofficial campaigning that went on through all of 2005—I had become acutely aware of Albertans' concerns over the helter-skelter pace of development with no apparent plan or guidelines. The pressures of hypergrowth were visible everywhere. Alberta's population had jumped from two million to three million in just twenty-five years and was projected to reach five million by 2026. (Most recently, in 2023, we are the fastest-growing province in Canada with a population of 4.7 million.) More people mean more activities on the land.

The number of cars and trucks on Alberta roads had spiked from 1.6 million to 2.6 million over the same time. Registered all-terrain vehicles (ATVs) had quadrupled—from 17,000 to 82,000.

The surge in population and recreational activities was being driven by economic growth. The price of oil had jumped from $28/barrel in 2000 to $140 in 2008, and natural gas prices spiked from under $3/mcf in 2000 to over $12 in 2008 (both before collapsing by 2009). The number of drilling rigs operating in Alberta reached record highs in 2007—26,000, double the number two decades earlier. Capital investment in oil sands projects reached record levels—$32 billion in 2008, up from $7 billion in 2000. In less than a decade, oil sands production had doubled from 668,000 barrels/day in 2000 to over 1.3 million in 2008.[2] [Note: Over the next fifteen years, by 2023, oil sands production grew to over 3.4 million barrels/day.]

Alberta's growth surge was not confined to the energy sector. The number of cattle in feedlots had jumped from 2.8 million to 6.4 million. The forestry industry was booming, with the amount of lumber growing from 1 billion board-feet to 3.2 billion in two decades. In the 1980s, Alberta produced no oriented-strand board (OSB). By 2007, Alberta was the third largest source of OSB in North America, with over 3 billion square feet produced annually. Forty thousand people were moving to Alberta every year, and new subdivisions on the outskirts of Calgary and Edmonton, Red Deer and Lethbridge, and Grande Prairie and Fort McMurray couldn't be built fast enough to house them. The Boom was booming, and there was no end in sight.

Since arriving in Alberta in 1981, I had spent a lot of time with family and friends in the outdoors—camping, fishing, hunting, skiing, and hiking. For me, the "Alberta Advantage" was not just about annual GDP growth, but also our recreational quality of life supported by Alberta's amazing mountains, foothills, and prairies. During the last years of the Klein government, there were growing demands for a provincial land use plan to protect this part of the Alberta Advantage. I was also educated toward more sustainable land use policies by Harvey Buckley, my campaign manager in Foothills-Rocky View in the 2004 provincial election. Harvey had founded Action for Agriculture, a group that advocated for policies that protected agricultural lands from loss to urban sprawl.[3] Harvey in turn had introduced me to Brad Stelfox, whose ALCES PowerPoint presentations made a graphic case for the need for such policies in southern Alberta.[4]

By the end of the 2006 leadership race, every candidate—including Stelmach and me—had committed to pursuing more sustainable land use policies if elected leader. So I was quite pleased to be named the new SRD minister and that my ministerial "mandate letter" explicitly tasked me with the development of a new land use framework for the province. (Having Fish and Wildlife officers guiding me to some of the best / hardest to access fishing holes in the province turned out to be icing on the cake!)

Over the next three years, framing and implementing a land use policy was my primary ministerial focus—culminating in the *Alberta Land Stewardship Act* (ALSA, 2009) and the first of its seven regional plans—the Lower Athabasca Regional Plan (LARP). In addition to ALSA, I initiated—or tried to initiate—a number of other policy changes involving conservation, stewardship, hunting, and fishing. Some succeeded and some failed. In this chapter, I briefly describe each of these initiatives, and explain their respective success or failure. This format is intended not just to preserve a historical record of what was achieved (or not) during my tenure, but also for the benefit of future Alberta governments and ministers. Those who want to pursue policies that promote stewardship of Alberta's natural capital can hopefully learn from my experiences.

Below is a chronological listing of the ten policy initiatives covered in this chapter.

- OH Ranch Heritage Rangeland Status (2008): Success
- Sunday Hunting and Provincial Hunting Day (2008): Success
- *Hunting, Fishing and Trapping Heritage Act* (Bill 201) (2008): Success
- Land Use Framework (2008) and *Alberta Land Stewardship Act* (Bill 36) (2009): Success
- Alberta Land Trust Grant Program (2009): Success
- Kids Can Catch Trout Pond / Bow Habitat Station (Livingston Fish Hatchery) (2009): Success
- Hunting for Habitat (2010): Failure
- Recreational Access Management Plan (RAMP) (2008): Initial success, but later cancelled
- Upland Birds Alberta (UBA) (2010): Success
- Micrex Mine/Livingstone Range (2010): Success

To explain the relative success or failure of these policy initiatives, I've identified seven factors listed (roughly) in order of their importance.[5] They were not mutually exclusive, but rather interacted to make it more or less difficult to achieve policy innovation in this policy area. For example, a policy initiative that entails new budgetary expenditures is more likely to be scrutinized by the premier's office and other ministers.

- Support/opposition/indifference from the premier's office
- Support/opposition/indifference from other ministers
- Budgetary implications
- Instrument of change (order-in-council, ministerial order, or statute)
- Stakeholder support/opposition
- Partisan political advantage/disadvantage/irrelevance
- Support/resistance/indifference from caucus

Support or opposition from the premier's office was decisive. Opposition meant defeat. Support meant success, while indifference meant it was possible. Stelmach's refusal to take our advice on the Marie Lake horizontal-drilling issue ended the conversation.[6] Conversely, his support for ALSA (delivered in caucus through Deputy Premier Ron Stevens) stifled eleventh-hour opposition from some rural MLAs. Similarly, the premier's support for the OH Ranch Heritage Rangeland decision helped to override opposition from Minister of Energy Mel Knight. Lack of opposition from the premier's office—i.e., indifference—contributed to the success of the policies I initiated unilaterally through ministerial orders (MOs) and orders-in-council (OCs).

Support or opposition from other ministers could be a factor. My failed attempts to cancel the Government of Alberta's (GOA's) biofuel subsidy program was led by ministers who had biofuel projects in their ridings and/or canola farmers who benefited financially from the program. Conversely, I was able to thwart Minister Mel Knight's support for the Micrex mining project in the Livingstone Range by leaking to the media. But ministerial support/opposition may be completely irrelevant if the premier's office wants to go in the opposite direction. Examples include Stelmach's Marie Lake decision (see note 6 in this chapter) or my failed attempts to block or revise the North West Upgrader project (see chapter 7).

Support or opposition from caucus members was mostly irrelevant. Caucus was indifferent to most of these initiatives, which was fine for me. The exception occurred when caucus opposition was allied with opposition from a minister, as in my attempts to cancel biofuel subsidies. In the several instances where some caucus members voiced opposition by themselves—such as the final approval of ALSA—it was quickly suppressed by the premier's office.

Budgetary implications for any new policy initiative are critical, especially in times of fiscal restraint and budget deficits. With the exception of RAMP, none of the policy innovations I advanced entailed new expenditures, which made them easier to get through cabinet and caucus. RAMP was initially approved when we were still running large budget surpluses. By 2010, when we were facing our third consecutive deficit—and I was no longer minister of SRD—RAMP was cancelled. The Land Trust Grant program was self-financing, and I was able to cover the expenses for the Kids Can Catch trout pond with a private sector fundraiser and a matching federal grant.

Instrument of change is also important. Policy change through a ministerial order (MO) is the easiest to achieve. A minister, working with his deputy minister, can unilaterally issue an MO that implements a minor regulatory change under existing legislation. An MO does not require cabinet notification or approval. More significant policy change under an existing statute usually requires an order-in-council (OC). An OC must be approved by cabinet and signed by the Lieutenant Governor. An OC does not have to be introduced or approved in the Legislative Assembly. Whether a regulatory amendment is made by an MO or an OC is determined by the enabling authority in the applicable statute, not the scope of the amendment. Major policy change falling outside existing legislation—or entailing changes to existing legislation—requires the Full Monty: cabinet and caucus approval; introducing a bill in the legislature and passing three votes; and then royal assent and proclamation by the Lieutenant Governor. Each of these stages represents a potential veto-point for opponents of the proposed change. Only the *Alberta Land Stewardship Act* (ALSA) had to run this gauntlet.[7]

Stakeholder support also played a role in achieving (and blocking) policy change in this field. There were components of the Alberta PC electoral coalition that strongly supported these initiatives. These included our blue-collar, hunting and fishing, gun-owning supporters, but also more educated, more affluent, more urban PC supporters. Groups like Nature Conservancy of Canada, Ducks Unlimited, Trout Unlimited, Pheasants Forever, and Delta

Waterfowl were enthusiastic supporters of ALSA, the OH Ranch, the Land Trust Grant program, RAMP, Open Spaces, Upland Birds Alberta (UBA) and the Kids Can Catch trout pond. An important exception was the Alberta Fish & Game Association (AFGA). The AFGA loved my removal of the century-old, blue-law ban on Sunday hunting in central and southern Alberta and my expanded youth hunting opportunities. But they strongly opposed my Hunting for Habitat initiative, which they saw as a threat to Alberta's tradition of "free public hunting." With our polling numbers dropping during 2010, the premier's office requested that we drop Hunting for Habitat.

Environmental groups like Sierra Club and the Alberta Parks and Wilderness Association also supported ALSA and the Land Trust Grant program. However, because their members tended not to be PC supporters, their support did not carry much weight inside caucus and cabinet. It was a very different story with ALSA. After its passage in 2009, there was a serious backlash from rural, ranch-farm interests because of ALSA's perceived threats to property rights. Because these rural voters were an integral part of our electoral coalition, their opposition was taken seriously. Bill 10, enacted in the 2011 legislative session, amended several sections of ALSA to try to address these concerns.

Partisan political advantage or disadvantage played almost no role in any of these policy innovations, with the important exception of ALSA, and subsequently Bill 10. As noted above, there was a strong backlash against ALSA because of its alleged infringements on the property rights of farmers and ranchers. As explained below, the new Wildrose Party was both the cause and the effect of this backlash. Through social media and organized public meetings, the Wildrose Party sparked concerns about property rights and ASLA, and then harnessed the growing opposition to ALSA to recruit new supporters.

In recent years the "environment" understood as climate change policy has become a sharp divider between left- and right-of-centre political parties. However, during my tenure as MLA and then minister (2004–2012), it had not yet reached this point in Alberta politics. In 2007, we did enact Canada's first carbon tax—the Specified Gas Emitters Regulation (SGER)—but this policy change was carried by the energy and environment ministers, with no involvement from SRD or me.

The following table summarizes how these seven factors influenced (or not) the relative success or failure of the ten policy initiatives.

	Premier's Office	Other Ministers	Caucus	Stakeholders	Budget	OC, MO Statute	Partisan Advantage
OH Ranch	+	--	0	+	+	OC	0
Sunday Hunt	0	0	0	+	+	MO	0
Hunting Heritage	+	+	+	+	+	Statute	0
LUF& ALSA	+	+	0	+	+	Statute	0
Land Trust	0	0	0	+	+	OC	0
RAMP	0	0	0	+	--	MO	0
Hunting Habitat	--	--	--	--	0	n/a	--
KidsCanCatch	0	0	0	+	+	n/a	0
UBA	0	0	0	+	+	n/a	0
Micrex	0	--	0	+	+	n/a	0

0 = no influence
+ = support/positive influence
-- = opposition/negative influence

OH RANCH: HERITAGE RANGELAND (2008)

My first significant conservation project was to persuade cabinet that the Crown grazing leases on the historic OH Ranch west of Longview should be given "Heritage Rangeland" status and thereby placed off limits to any future development, including oil and gas drilling.[8] This did not sit well with either energy department officials or their minister, Mel Knight.

As the minister of SRD, I was responsible for the management of all Crown (public) lands, which include grazing leases. Grazing leases are public lands—usually native grasslands—that are leased to cattle ranchers for an annual rental fee. Ownership remains with the Crown/GOA, but the day-to-day use of the leased lands is given to the lessee for grazing cattle, per regulations that are mutually agreed to prior to signing the lease agreement. The Crown/GOA owns all subsurface minerals (i.e., oil and gas) on public lands and can sell access to these minerals to oil and gas exploration companies. The latter, however, have to negotiate with the leaseholder for surface access and compensate the lessee for surface disturbance, loss of use, nuisance, etc. If the leaseholder and the energy company cannot reach a mutually acceptable agreement on compensation, the decision is referred to the Surface Rights

Board, whose decision is binding on both parties. The leaseholder keeps the surface compensation payments.

Five months after becoming SRD minister, I was approached in May 2007 by Jim Smith, who was representing Daryl "Doc" Seaman. Doc was an icon of the Calgary oil patch. Coming off a farm in Rouleau, Saskatchewan, and four years of service as a bomber pilot in the Royal Canadian Air Force during World War II, Doc was a self-made millionaire. He was a key player in bringing the NHL Flames hockey team to Calgary in 1980 (the year before I arrived in Calgary). In 1986, the OH Ranch was about to be sold to the Department of National Defence, which planned to use the ranch for an artillery range. Doc intervened to save the historic ranch, and now, twenty years later and approaching the end of his life, he wanted to protect the natural integrity and beauty of the OH for perpetuity.

> Doc illustrates one of my favourite Alberta jokes: Question: "What do you call a guy from Saskatchewan who moves to Alberta looking for work?" Answer: "Boss!"

Jim explained that Doc had been in discussion with the GOA for several years but had made no headway under the previous minister in the Klein government. I was immediately receptive. I had hunted elk on the OH with my friend Barry Cooper in the 1980s, when it was still owned by the Kingsford family, and I knew what a gem it was. Doc's proposal also fit well with where I was headed with the Land Use Framework, which identified protection and preservation of native fescue grasslands as a high priority. I also knew Doc through politics. He had been an early supporter of the Reform Party and had made a donation to my successful effort to win the Reform Party nomination for Alberta's 1998 Senate elections. He had also written a cheque to my PC leadership bid in 2006.

Doc wanted to do a deal with the GOA. He was willing to place conservation easements on the deeded portions of the ranch (lands that he owned) if the government would designate the grazing lease portions of the ranch as "Heritage Rangeland Status," with the same restrictions on surface access that he would place on the deeded lands. The home ranch west of Longview was roughly equal in deeded (9,500 acres) and leased (7,000 acres) area, but the other properties that were further east were heavily weighted toward grazing leases (22,000 acres to 12,000). Nearly all of the lands comprising the ranch had been evaluated by Environment Canada and had been determined to be eligible under the federal Ecological Gifts Program as ecologically sensitive. There was virtually no cultivation on any of the properties, and all were rich in different varieties of native fescue and wildlife.

Location	Deeded Acres	Leased Acres (White Zone)	Total Acres
Dorothy (15 mi. SE of Drumheller)	2,500	17,500	20,000
Bassano (between Brooks and Bassano on the north side of TransCanada Highway)	9,500	0	9,500
Longview (west of Longview)	9,500	7,000	16,500
Pekisko (south of Longview)	800	3,200	4,000
Totals	22,300	27,700	50,000

The stumbling block was that Doc wanted to place broader restrictions on future oil and gas development than would normally apply. Conservation easements on deeded lands do not preclude surface access for oil and gas development. On grazing leases, designation as "Heritage Rangelands" curtails future issuance of subsurface mineral interests but existing holdings are honoured. Doc wanted new restrictions placed on management of existing holdings and no new oil and gas exploration. This is why he had made no progress with the previous minister. Energy department bureaucrats had gone into "turf protection" mode and said allowing these additional restrictions would set "a dangerous precedent" of sterilizing land for future oil and gas development. The result had been several years of stalemate.

Why did it turn out differently this time? Having a more sympathetic minister at SRD obviously helped. After my initial meeting with Jim Smith, I met with Doc twice at the OH—once to discuss the terms of his proposal, the second time for a guided horseback tour of the ranch, along with Minister of Parks Cindy Ady. I was already on board, and Cindy concurred enthusiastically.

But there was still a problem: Minister of Energy Mel Knight's vocal opposition. This is where support from the premier's office made the crucial difference. Even as early as 2008, Stelmach was aware of his political vulnerability in Calgary and southern Alberta. Doc Seaman was an icon of the Alberta oil and gas industry, a co-owner of the Calgary Flames and a long-time financial supporter of the PC Party. Standing shoulder to shoulder with Doc would help Stelmach in Calgary PC circles, and there was no partisan downside. The project fit nicely with the land use framework initiative that all opposition parties supported at this stage. Another plus was that there were no immediate budget implications. All that was required was cabinet approval of my order-in-council. The stars were all aligned.[9]

On a sunny Saturday afternoon, September 13, 2008, several hundred of Alberta's oilpatch and ranching elites gathered for a barbeque at the OH Ranch to watch Premier Ed Stelmach stand shoulder to shoulder with Doc Seaman and announce his government's support for the new Heritage Rangelands status for the Crown lands on the OH Ranch.[10]

Doc died shortly thereafter, in January 2009, leaving $110 million to the Calgary Foundation. The OH was purchased by another Calgary millionaire philanthropist, Bill Siebens. Siebens then donated the Longview properties to the Calgary Stampede Foundation, a gift valued at $11 million, the largest ever made to the Stampede. Today, the ranch is used to raise stock for the annual Calgary Stampede and for field trips for primary school students in southern Alberta. Doc got what he wanted, and the rest of us are the beneficiaries.

SUNDAY HUNTING AND PROVINCIAL HUNTING DAY (2008)

One of my first priorities as the new SRD minister was to repeal the ban on Sunday hunting. I started hunting in Alberta the year I arrived—1981. And for twenty-five years my hunting friends and I had been frustrated by the fact that we were effectively limited to only one day a week of fall hunting.

Like most Albertans, I worked Monday through Friday. In those early years, we also had three children under the age of ten. Getting away early on Fridays was not easy. Successful hunts depend on prior scouting. Whether it's birds or big game, you need to know ahead of time where they are and when they come. You also need to get landowner permission on privately owned farms and ranches. This takes time, and we did not have much.

Living in Calgary meant that we were usually looking at a two-hour drive to get to wherever we were headed—whether it was Stettler, Oyen, Hanna, Brooks, or Warner. This meant that most of our hunts consisted of getting up at 4 a.m.; driving several hours; finding where the game were; getting permission from the landowner; setting up; hunting all day; and then driving another two hours in the dark to get home. Not exactly a relaxing weekend.

Now I could do something to change all this. And it turned out, this was not too difficult. As I quickly learned, I was only the most recent in a long line of ministers who wanted to open up more Sunday hunting. The ban on Sunday hunting in Alberta dates back to when Alberta became a province in 1905. It was just one example of the "blue laws" that prohibited most commercial and entertainment activities on Sundays. But in recent years, this ban has been steadily rolled back. In 1969, the government opened Sunday hunting in the Green Zone—roughly north of Peace River, Slave Lake, and Athabasca— for big game. The next year the same areas were opened for upland game birds, and in 1987 for waterfowl. Almost all of these lands were Crown forests, which meant that the policy changes did not affect many private landowners or municipalities. The Alberta Fish & Game Association (AFGA) continued to push for more Sunday hunting, and more Wildlife Management Units (WMUs) in northern Alberta were opened in the 1980s. But when I arrived, there was still almost no Sunday hunting allowed from Edmonton south to the Montana border.[11]

In my first month as the new SRD minister, I told my deputy minister that extending Sunday hunting to central and southern Alberta was a priority for me. To his credit, he facilitated the changes. Alberta's hunting rules have the legal status of administrative regulations. This means that they can be changed unilaterally by the minister, via ministerial order, in consultation with the relevant civil servants in the department. These officials consulted with both hunters and landowners. Of course, the AFGA supported the proposed changes, and most landowners did not object. An exception was made for some Crown grazing leases in the southern foothills areas that often still have cattle on them in November. With these exceptions, I signed Ministerial Order 08/08 on May 7, 2008, and in September, Sunday hunting came to central and southern Alberta. For the next few fall hunting seasons, I rarely had to pay for my own beers in small-town bars in southern Alberta.

The *Hunting, Fishing and Trapping Heritage Act* was mostly symbolic. It did not change any existing policies or practices. It simply gave legal recognition and status to the long-standing role of these outdoor activities in Alberta. The AFGA had asked—unsuccessfully—the preceding four SRD ministers for such legislation. When they came to me, of course, I said yes. The legislation was brought forward as a private member's bill, Bill 201 (2008), by Len Mitzel, the MLA for Cypress-Medicine Hat. I knew Len before coming to Edmonton through my hunting and farm friends in southern Alberta, so I was happy for him to carry the bill. It was introduced on May 15, 2008, and received Royal Assent less than a month later—surely some sort of record!

There was no opposition in any of its three readings in the Legislative Assembly. But we did have some fun supporting it. At committee of the whole, I had this to say:[12]

> Now, moving away from liberals and coming closer to home, I want to pick up where I left off last time, with the *Calgary Herald* article of April 19, the going green section and recommendation 4, "Eat local". ... The average meal on a Canadian's plate travels thousands of kilometres to get from wherever it starts to your plate. ... Fruit and vegetables from Mexico and South America, lamb from Australia, wines and fizzy water from France, olives from North Africa, rice from Asia: for each of those items it's burning up thousands of litres of gas and diesel to bring that food to our plates. So heed what the *Calgary Herald* says: eat local.

Then I got personal:

> Compare what the alternative is, particularly what the hunting and fishing heritage act provides opportunity for: a tasty mule deer from Milk River Ridge, a delectable pheasant from Brooks, an elk from Ya Ha Tinda, a tasty roast mallard from Stettler, or perhaps a juicy moose roast from McLennan or the Peace River area. Eat local. Nothing is more local than our local fish and game.

Then I got professorial:

> Dr. Lee Foote, one of the outstanding wildlife biologists at the University of Alberta ... has pointed out the following merits

of wild game and wild fish from Alberta: it's locally produced without artificial insemination; there are no antibiotics, no steroids, no artificial growth hormones; its production required no land clearing, no fencing, no fertilizer or feedlots; the animal was never confined, transported, or kept in crowded conditions; the lean meat, before it goes into the oven, was never wrapped in plastic or Styrofoam packaging, and no nitrates or sulphides were applied to prevent discolouration. Once again, eat local.

And I closed by invoking the Lord's blessing:

[W]hen we have friends over at our house for a wild game dinner, I begin the meal by asking our guests to bow their heads and give thanks for our meal, and I end by saying: let us prey, p-r-e-y.

Four months later, on September 13, I announced Provincial Hunting Day—an annual celebration of Alberta's hunting heritage to be held on the fourth Saturday of September. Its purpose is to promote hunting and public awareness of the important role that hunting and hunters play in wildlife management and conservation. As part of Provincial Hunting Day, I added a new youth hunting opportunity. This policy allows resident Alberta youth, ten to seventeen years of age, who have passed the Alberta Hunter Education Instructors' Association (AHEIA) hunter safety course, and who are accompanied by a licensed adult hunter, to hunt upland birds without a licence. In conjunction with Alberta Hunting Day, the AHEIA now organizes other hunting mentoring opportunities for first-time hunters across the province.

LAND USE FRAMEWORK AND *ALBERTA LAND STEWARDSHIP ACT* (2009)

The *Alberta Land Stewardship Act* (ALSA) was my most important policy initiative at SRD. It may have been the most significant—certainly the longest—piece of legislation enacted during the Stelmach years. There was no trouble getting this on the new government's agenda. The push for greater land use planning predated my appointment; was endorsed in principle by all candidates during the 2006 PC leadership race; and was the number one task in my ministerial mandate letter. Some public consultations had already been held by the previous minister. My challenge was to move it from talk to policy.

I spent my first six months at SRD getting up to speed on what the civil servants had already done; meeting with affected stakeholders—environmental activists; municipal governments; and affected businesses such as oil and gas, ranching and farming, and forestry. There were a lot of moving parts and very different if not conflicting interests. My civil servants had done a good job of identifying the many pieces of this policy puzzle but lacked any overarching narrative to explain why this was needed now or any plan on how to knit it all together. By the summer of 2007, we decided to move forward in two stages. The first would be to articulate the need for and the outlines of a new land use framework for Alberta. The second would be to translate this policy document into actual legislation.

Stage one culminated in my presentation to the annual general meeting of the PC Party in Jasper in November 2008. I had decided that the best way to sell the package to cabinet and caucus was first to sell it to our party's base. Using Brad Stelfox's ALCES slides, we developed an effective PowerPoint presentation that graphically portrayed Alberta's explosive growth over the preceding several decades. Alberta had reached a tipping point, I argued, where sticking with the old way of doing things would no longer yield the results we wanted. This was the paradox, I told party members: if we want to keep what we value in Alberta, we have to change the way we make decisions about land use. This worked. My land use framework session was the most heavily attended event at the AGM and was well received. This was duly noted by the premier's office and paved the way for strong support for the draft legislation that followed.

Six months later I introduced Bill 36, the *Alberta Land Stewardship Act*, for first reading. It was a monster bill—150 pages long, almost two inches thick. It amended twenty-five other existing statutes, and explicitly overrode any contrary provincial statutes. But behind its length and complexity, it has seven basic components.

1. Seven Regional Plans Based on Alberta's Major Watersheds
The Act proposed seven regional plans based on Alberta's major watersheds. In central and southern Alberta, water is our scarcest resource. Eighty percent of our water is in northern Alberta (the Peace and Athabasca watersheds), while 80 percent of our population is concentrated in the narrow, twenty-mile-wide Highway 2 corridor running from Edmonton to the US border. Using watershed boundaries to define our regional plans would facilitate assessing our

land use decisions for their cumulative effects on our major rivers and lakes. It would also facilitate the stewardship of the hundreds of streams and rivers that constitute the Eastern Slopes—the headwaters of the major rivers, the Bow, the North Saskatchewan, the Red Deer, and the Oldman—that support our major cities and our irrigated croplands.

This may seem intuitive, but it was a tough sell to my caucus members, who thought in terms of the legal boundaries of the counties and municipalities they represented. After much discussion, I persuaded the majority of caucus of the wisdom of using watershed boundaries. Going forward, water quantity and quality will be one of Alberta's biggest challenges. Defining the regional plans based on our major watersheds will be an important factor in successfully meeting these challenges. (Note: The recently (2024) announced water-sharing and water-consumption reduction agreements are all within the boundaries of the South Saskatchewan Regional Plan.[13] This illustrates the value of the watershed approach to meeting the challenges of future drought and water shortages in southern Alberta.)

2. Cumulative Effects Management

Rather than the traditional one-off approach to approving a new upgrader, dam, pipeline, or subdivision, the cumulative effects approach mandates that decision makers look at development proposals in conjunction with other future developments and how they will interact over time. In what is also known as the "triple bottom line" approach, regional plans are mandated to structure future development decision making in a way that optimizes economic, social, and environmental effects over time.

We emphasized that the goal of cumulative effects management is not to block growth, but to facilitate "smart growth." That is, by minimizing the environmental footprint of today's development, we can leave more room for future growth. A good example of this is urban planning that encourages greater density and public transit, thereby minimizing the amount of adjacent agricultural land that will be lost. While applying cumulative effects analysis will not be easy or without controversy, I strongly and successfully resisted requests from some stakeholders to adopt a "quadruple" bottom-line model—adding culture or spirituality. I deemed this too ambiguous and therefore unmanageable.

3. Regional Advisory Councils

Each regional plan is to be built based on the recommendations from an advisory council appointed by the SRD minister. These councils consist of twelve to eighteen people, drawn from the communities in the region, and representing key private and public sector stakeholders. These would include representatives from the region's important industries/employers and several mayors, reeves, and municipal councillors. The latter are considered important not just for their input, but also for future compliance. Under ALSA, local authorities continue to make decisions to meet local needs, such as municipal development plans, area structure plans, land use bylaws, subdivisions, and development standards. But these must now be consistent with ALSA's new regional plans. In instances of conflict, regional plans override local decision making. During the consultation stage of the Land Use Framework, loss of local control emerged as a major concern. The inclusion of regional office officeholders on the advisory councils is intended to address this concern.

4. Conservation and Stewardship Policy Tools

ALSA strengthens existing tools and creates new tools for the conservation and enhancement of environmental, natural, scenic, and aesthetic values.[14] It strengthens the administration and enforcement of conservation easements on private lands—restrictions that a landowner voluntarily places on future development and use of his or her property. It expands the purpose of conservation easements to include the future protection of agricultural lands from residential subdivision. A new policy tool—the conservation directive—is created to allow regional plans to impose similar restrictions on the future development of private lands. As these directives are non-voluntary, ALSA creates an explicit right to landowner compensation for any decrease in market value of affected lands—making Alberta the first province in Canada to provide this kind of protection to property rights. ALSA authorizes the use of conservation offsets to limit or mitigate the adverse environmental effects of any new development such as a subdivision. It is now common practice in Alberta for residential developers to work with Ducks Unlimited to offset loss of urban wetlands with new rural wetlands. ALSA also authorizes regional plans (or local authorities) to use transfer of development credits to concentrate rural-residential development in a manner that consumes less agricultural land and shares the monetary benefits equitably among local landowners who choose to participate.

5. Political, Not Judicial Enforcement

ALSA explicitly limits the extent to which anyone other than property owners seeking compensation can use lawsuits and the courts to enforce or block regional plans.[15] The Act explicitly states that "[a] regional plan is an expression of the public policy of the Government and therefore the Lieutenant Governor in Council has exclusive and final jurisdiction over its contents." For further clarity, it states that the Act does not create any legal cause of action or confer jurisdiction on any court to enforce regional plans.[16] The model for this type of "privative clause" is the *Workers' Compensation Act*, which also insulates its administrative policy decisions from judicial review.

One of my priorities for ALSA was to prevent its administration and enforcement from being hijacked by anti-development environmental interest groups. I was familiar with how environmental advocacy groups in both Canada and US routinely use litigation to win judicial orders for policy changes that elected governments do not support. I thought that this was wrong—both in theory and practice—and accordingly sought to structure ALSA so that elected governments in Edmonton, not federally appointed judges, would be the primary policy drivers. This aspect of ALSA was an easy sell to both cabinet and caucus, but it was subsequently seized upon by NDP MLAs as a critical fault in the legislation.

Ironically, less than four years after the adoption of ALSA, Ecojustice successfully sued the federal government under the federal *Species at Risk Act* (SARA) to protect sage grouse habitat in southeastern Alberta. Ottawa was forced to issue an emergency order prohibiting the building of new fences or roads and making excessive noise from sunrise to sunset during the sage grouse mating season.[17] There was no compensation for the adverse economic impacts of these restrictions on some affected property owners. If the same restrictions had been imposed through the South Saskatchewan Regional Plan under ALSA, there would have been compensation.

6. Compensation to Landowners for Regulatory Takings

ALSA's sixth pillar was to create a legal right to government compensation for landowners who suffer an adverse financial impact from new restrictions imposed by a regional plan and/or conservation directive. This type of loss is described as a "regulatory taking," as distinct from the older, more explicit form of taking—expropriation—under the ancient common law doctrine of *eminent domain*. Under eminent domain, a government has the legal right to take property from a private landowner for a public purpose—such as a new dam or highway—but is required to compensate the landowner for such a taking at the fair market value of the affected lands. All Canadian governments—federal and provincial—have conformed to this legal practice since Confederation. A regulatory taking, by contrast, does not affect the legal title or ownership of the land, but reduces its market value by placing new restrictions on how it can be used or developed—or not developed—in the future.

As an active member of the federal Reform Party a decade earlier, I had strongly opposed the Liberals' new *Species at Risk Act* (2003), because it did not include mandatory compensation for regulatory takings. SARA simply stated that the minister responsible "may" provide "fair and reasonable compensation" for any losses suffered.[18] Now tasked with building an analogous regulatory system at the provincial level, I insisted that it include explicit compensation for any regulatory takings imposed by regional plans and/or conservation directives.

ALSA does this in Division 3, sections 35–43, which state that landowners have a legal right to compensation for "decrease in market value" and/or "injurious affection"; a right to be notified in advance; a right to appeal to either the Land Compensation Board or the Court of Queen's Bench (now Court of King's Bench); and a right to a further appeal to the Court of Appeal of Alberta; and the explicit liability of the provincial Crown (Government of Alberta) to pay such compensation. This explicit compensation for regulatory taking was a first in Canada, and a necessity for Alberta, where so many critical habitats and watersheds are on private property. Subsequently, however, a successful political campaign was waged by the Wildrose Party against ALSA precisely on the property rights issue.[19]

7. Ten-Year Sunset Clause

ALSA's seventh and final pillar is a ten-year sunset clause for each regional plan, and a mandatory review for each plan at its five-year mark. This requirement reflected our party's commitment to preventing unnecessary or counterproductive regulations. Legally, the sunset clause means that a regional plan expires after ten years unless it is renewed. Practically, it means that a regional plan must prove itself to be worthwhile or disappear. The five-year review requirement simply operationalizes the principle of constant improvement. It acknowledges that almost all public policies have unintended consequences, and provides a safeguard.

On June 2, only two months after its introduction, Bill 36 passed third reading with unanimous support from both the government side and the official opposition Liberals. How did such a far-reaching piece of legislation move through both caucus and the legislature so quickly? Strong support from the premier's office was the single most important factor. When several rural backbench MLAs raised last-minute objections just prior to third reading, they were quickly quashed. Chairing caucus that day, Deputy Premier Ron Stevens curtly cut off further discussion with the simple comment "The Premier wants this." Also important was that ALSA did not require any major new expenditures, so it was not competing for budget dollars with minsters responsible for health or social services.

I also received strong support from my staff at SRD. My deputy minister and assistant deputy minister, Eric McGhan and Morris Seiferling, both devoted hundreds of hours to help make ALSA a reality. In terms of stakeholder support or opposition, all of the organized interests that supported our party—energy, forestry, ranching, and farming—either supported ALSA or were neutral. Some oil sands interests were nervous about potential loss of access to future leases, but they realized that Alberta and the industry were developing a reputation problem, and both had to do a better job in managing the impacts of oil sands growth.

For the same reasons, ALSA had strong support among the more affluent, more urban PC supporters. Groups like Nature Conservancy of Canada, Ducks Unlimited, Trout Unlimited, Pheasants Forever, and Delta Waterfowl all supported ALSA. The Wildrose Party's campaign against ALSA had not yet been launched. The NDP members—all four of them—voted against it because of its anti–judicial review provisions, but their votes did not reflect any organized opposition. The organized environmental groups in the province—Sierra Club, Alberta Wilderness Association, Pembina Institute—all might have wished it went further, but they all supported it. In short, the stars aligned. It was the right policy at the right time and the right place—something that does not happen often in politics in Alberta or anywhere else.

ALBERTA LAND TRUST GRANT PROGRAM AND THE WALDRON RANCH (2009)

The Alberta Land Trust Grant Program should be one of the more important and enduring policy legacies of my time at SRD.[20] It is also one for which I deserve almost no credit. The concept was brought to me by the civil servants in SRD who spotted a "sell high, buy low" opportunity in the way we manage Crown lands.

Rapid population growth had been driving the expansion of Alberta's cities and towns for several decades. As a consequence, there were numerous parcels of Crown land that were now inside urban municipal boundaries. While their original agricultural value was largely lost, they now had substantial commercial value for urban development. The proposal was to sell these parcels to create a dedicated pool of funds that could then be used to purchase private land in rural settings with high environmental value. It was such an eminently sensible proposal that I immediately accepted it. While there is normally a strong political stigma attached to selling Crown lands to the private sector, I could see that it would not apply in this case. The urban lands we would be selling would have low environmental/recreational value, while the rural lands we would be acquiring would have high environmental/recreation value.

A **conservation easement** is a legally binding voluntary agreement between a landowner and a land trust. The easement is placed on the land title to restrict future surface development such as subdivision, housing, or cultivation. The landowner retains the land title and can continue to use the land for its current uses such as grazing and cultivation.

A **land trust** is a not-for-profit, non-government organization that supports the conservation of biodiversity on private lands.

Following the adoption of ALSA, the *Public Lands Act* was amended in 2010 to create the Alberta Land Stewardship Fund (LSF). The Land Stewardship Fund was to be used to assist land trusts to acquire and manage conservation easements on privately owned land. While the LSF can still be used to purchase environmentally valuable private lands, the new option of conservation easements was a significant improvement, since it is much less expensive to pay for an easement on private land than it is to purchase the same lands. A land trust that applies for a grant from the LSF must provide two-thirds of the final funding for the project. Most of the projects that receive funding from the LSF also qualify for federal tax credits under the federal government's eco-gifts program. This creates additional incentives for Alberta ranchers to participate in the stewardship practices supported by the Land Trust Grant Program.

Under the LSF, the placement of a conservation easement on private property is completely voluntary. It cannot be done without the owner's written consent. While the new restrictions on future development lower the commercial value of the affected property, this loss is offset by the land trust's payment to the owner. Neighbouring landowners are usually supportive, since the new restrictions make the land more affordable to other agricultural users by eliminating demand from residential and recreational real estate buyers.

There is no better example of this than the conservation easement that the Nature Conservancy of Canada (NCC) was able to negotiate with the owners of the Waldron Ranch in 2013. The Waldron is one of the oldest and largest ranches in Alberta, dating back to the 1880s. Located south of Longview along both sides of Highway 22, the Waldron consists of over 30,000 acres of largely undisturbed native fescue grasslands in the Eastern Slopes of the Livingstone Range. It is spectacularly beautiful and rich in wildlife—deer, elk, and moose; grizzly bears, cougars, and wolves; and various species of upland birds. To purchase it would have been prohibitively expensive, as it had a market value estimated at $75 million.

In return for placing a permanent conservation easement on their lands, the NCC compensated the landowners (a co-operative of cattle ranchers) with $37.5 million, $12.25 million of which was a grant from the Land Stewardship Fund. The Calgary Foundation contributed another $1 million and the federal government $4 million. At the time, this was the largest conservation easement in Canadian history, and it will protect the Waldron against any future development, subdivision, cultivation, or drainage of its numerous wetlands. More recently, the GOA partnered with the NCC to support an even larger project, the historic McIntyre Ranch on the Milk River Ridge south of Lethbridge, conserving 54,539 acres.

As of 2023, the LSF has awarded $106 million worth of grants to ten different Alberta land trusts for projects that now conserve more than 250,000 acres of land. These LSF grants have facilitated land trusts in leveraging an additional $315 million for these projects. To purchase these same lands would have cost close to $1 billion. So, for roughly 10 percent of fair market value, the Land Trust Grant Program has protected and preserved some of the most valuable and most beautiful landscapes in Alberta.[21]

It should be noted here that both the Waldron and the McIntyre successes contribute to the goals for conservation on private lands in the South Saskatchewan Regional Plan (SSRP)—the plan that was developed for southern Alberta after the adoption of the Alberta Land Stewardship Act. The conservation outcomes and goals for private land in the SSRP are aligned with the LTGP and LSF. And as illustrated here, in practice, the two policies—ALSA and the LSF—have had positive reciprocal effects on each other.

The government's adoption of the Alberta Land Trust Grant Program is not difficult to explain. It was self-financing, making no new requests on the annual budget. It complemented the new Land Use Framework and ALSA, enhancing conservation and stewardship of native grasslands and watersheds. Accordingly, it did not induce any concerns or opposition from the premier's office or other ministers. For the same reasons, there was no partisan downside, and it was supported by all other conservation groups in the province. And, of course, it had the full support of the assistant deputy minister of public lands and his staff, since it was their idea.

BOW HABITAT STATION AND KIDS CAN CATCH TROUT POND (2009)

A river without anglers is a river without friends.
　　　　—Lee Wulff (1905–1991), Famous American Fly-fisherman

Most new ministers inherit at least one train wreck, and I was no exception. Mine was the Bow Habitat Station, a great idea that had imploded during implementation. The concept was to build an eco-interpretive centre adjacent to the Sam Livingston Fish Hatchery. The hatchery is located in Calgary's Pearce Estate Park, along the banks of the Bow River, just east of downtown Calgary. Pearce Estate is a fourteen-hectare "interpretive wetland" that serves as an outdoor eco-systems classroom for Calgary-area schools. The Sam Livingston Fish Hatchery is one of the largest indoor trout hatcheries in North America. Annually it raises up to three million trout—mainly rainbows and browns—which are then used to stock Alberta's lakes and rivers for public fishing.

The proposed Bow Habitat Station would complement and expand the eco-education functions of both facilities with hands-on exhibits linking activities that promote healthy waters for fish and other water-dependent species. The target audience is grade-school students during the school year and families and tourists in the summer months. I loved the concept. It complemented our land-use framework initiative, especially its link between economic development and water quality and quantity issues in southern Alberta. The problem was that the contractor for the hands-on exhibits component of the interpretive centre had gone bankrupt. This left SRD with an empty shell of a building. What do you do with a half-built project whose budget has already been spent?

In June 2007, after the spring legislative session was over, SRD staff took me to tour the site. In front of the new but empty interpretive centre was a big, empty hole. I asked what it was for. I was told that there were plans to build a huge water feature—a pond with jets shooting streams of water into the air—not unlike what you see on the Strip in Las Vegas.

I had two immediate reactions. First, that this was a really dumb idea and a waste of money. The second, why not build instead a catch-and-release trout pond? What better way to get kids interested in the eco-system science that was (supposed to be) inside the centre? What kid doesn't love the excitement of catching a fighting, flopping trout? (Especially if you just put it back in the water and don't have to kill it or eat it!). I still vividly remember catching my first trout with my grandfather at just such a catch-and-release pond. I was hooked. The pond would serve as a beautiful entry into the interpretive centre. And the hands-on fishing would connect the kids to the ecology. It was a perfect fit, both aesthetically and pedagogically. And with the fish hatchery right there, there would be no shortage of fish for the kids to catch. In sum, I thought, cheap and easy. Right? Wrong.

Okay. Half right: we did have plenty of trout. And the manager of the Livingston Fish Hatchery—Craig Copeland—worked endlessly to help make this idea a reality. But the costs turned out to be substantial. I learned that you do not just build a new big pond in the middle of a city. The entire park was in the Bow's flood plain and there were major City of Calgary infrastructure issues in the area where the pond would go. In the end, the price tag for the pond was estimated at $750,000.

If I had known the final price tag in the beginning, I probably would have given up on the idea. But ignorance is (sometimes) bliss. I naively assumed costs would be in the $100,000 range. Surely we could raise this amount privately. All we needed was to organize a fundraising dinner, similar to the ones I regularly attended put on by the Calgary chapters of Ducks Unlimited, Pheasants Forever, and Trout Unlimited. And so, we began down that path.

All three of these organizations agreed to help. With Don Pike from Trout Unlimited Canada (TUC) taking the lead, each group publicized the fundraiser to their membership and contributed items and trips for the live and silent auctions that would be part of the fundraiser. We formed an executive committee, with myself and Dave Byler, president of TUC, as the co-chairs. More importantly, I was able to persuade former Alberta Premier Ralph Klein to be the honorary chair of the event. (Ralph loved to fish and loved to party, so it didn't take much persuading.) Ralph was wildly popular in corporate Calgary, and having him as team captain made raising money much easier. In addition, we had plenty of volunteers from other supporting organizations, including the Bow Habitat Volunteer Society, the Calgary Fish & Game Association, Alberta Conservation Association, and the Angling Outfitters Association of Alberta.

All this organizing and planning culminated on June 17, 2009, in a wonderful evening and dinner/fundraiser at the Hotel Arts in downtown Calgary. The then–Hotel Arts manager, Fraser Abbott, a former student and still a friend of mine, serenaded us into the banquet room with his bagpipes. Over 350 supporters paid $350 a person to join the event. In addition to the silent and live auctions, enthusiasts could pay a beautiful and bountiful mermaid $20 to cast their lures into the adjacent swimming pool to try to hook a floating gift certificate for various overpriced items of hunting and fishing equipment. (It was tough to get Ralph to leave this one!) When the dust settled and the accounts were done, we had raised a staggering $250,000 for the Kids Can Catch fishing pond.

As great as this was, we still needed several hundred thousand dollars more to get the pond built. It wasn't going to come from general revenues or the SRD budget, as by now—2009—we were deep into deficit territory and headed south. (See chapter 6.) At this point, serendipity intervened. One of my former students, Dustin van Vugt, was now working in Ottawa as chief of staff for Lynne Yelich, then Prime Minister Harper's minister of western economic development. One of my executive assistants in Edmonton, Tom Kmiec, knew Dustin because they had both worked on my 2006 leadership campaign. Together, they came up with the idea of getting a matching federal grant for the fishing pond. The Harper government had brought in a new federal infrastructure / economic stimulus program—the Recreational Infrastructure Canada program (RInC)—to encourage children to be more physically active. There was one catch. The RInC list of eligible facilities included hockey arenas (of course!), swimming pools, gyms, and tennis courts, but not fishing ponds. Our initial application was rejected.

Not easily deterred, Tom and Dustin amended the application to include walking paths with handicap access, and then persuaded someone in the Ottawa bureaucracy that fishing is indeed "an outdoor-based recreational activity." To demonstrate the required "municipal support" for the RInC application, we persuaded Calgary mayor Dave Bronconnier to contribute a $50,000 cheque. To prove "provincial support," I was able to use my influence as minister to help the Bow Habitat Station Volunteer Society (BHSVS) receive a $60,000 grant from the Community Facility Enhancement Program (CFEP). The BHSVS had already solicited a $100,000 contribution from BP Canada Energy, and then chipped in another $11,000 of their own. When the dust settled, a beautiful, big cheque for $243,000 arrived from Ottawa to complete the budget needed to construct the pond.

On Saturday, July 7, 2012, the Kids Can Catch fishing pond opened its doors—and its tackle boxes—to the public. Both it and the Bow Habitat Station have been popular ever since. The Discovery Centre begins taking reservations for school programs in late August, and it is usually fully booked for the entire year by the end of September. The pond site is so pleasant that it is also now being booked for weddings and corporate picnics. The fishing pond is open from May 15 to October 31. You can bring your own gear or rent a pole for $5. They even offer "Learn to Fish Clinics" for families in July and August. In recent summers, the pond has averaged 50,000 fishermen annually.[22] The message on its Facebook page sums up exactly what I'd envisioned at the outset: "Just one visit can get kids hooked for life."

The successful completion of the Bow Habitat Station and the Fishing Pond was the result of several factors. The project was already on SRD's policy agenda when I arrived. It began in a period of budget surpluses and was completed with a combination of private funds and a federal grant.

Having a corporate sponsor—BP Energy—was a big help. No legislation or orders-in-council were required. And it was a motherhood issue—Who could oppose teaching kids to fish? There was no partisan risk.

What began as a policy headache ended up being a positive policy legacy of my tenure at SRD. Trout Unlimited's mantra is: "A river without anglers is a river without friends." The Discovery Centre and Fishing Pond are making a lot of friends for the Bow and for Alberta's other rivers.

HUNTING FOR HABITAT (2008)

> *Conservation will ultimately boil down to rewarding the private landowner who conserves the public interest.*
>
> —Aldo Leopold, pioneer of American conservation policy.[23]

Shortly after becoming Minister of SRD, I initiated a program to design some new policies that would create financial incentives for private landowners to keep critical wildlife habitat rather than convert it to agricultural use.

Cynics will suggest that this initiative was just another example of my personal interest in increasing hunting opportunities in Alberta. And there is some truth in this. But the primary motivation was my growing understanding of how the future ecological integrity of much of Alberta rested in the hands of private landowners—Alberta's ranch and farm families. In the White Area of Alberta (see sidebar), 75 percent of the agricultural lands are privately owned. Given the volatility of beef and grain prices, these operators are always under financial pressure to expand their land base by draining wetlands, cutting down woodlots, or clearing brushy slopes. These are precisely the habitats that sustain most of Alberta's wildlife in southern and central Alberta. There are Albertans like Doc Seaman who have the vision and the wealth to voluntarily preserve these landscapes by placing conservation easements on them. But this kind of altruism is as rare as it is admirable, and provides a weak foundation for the conservation of existing wildlife habitat on private lands.

In 1948, at the outset of Alberta's first (post-Leduc) oil boom, the Ernest Manning government divided Alberta into two different zones for planning purposes.

The **White Area** comprises the settled or populated lands in central and southern Alberta, and a small portion in the Peace River country. The White Area covers 39 percent of the province, and three-quarters (75 percent) is privately owned.

The **Green Area** is the mostly unsettled, unpopulated regions in the north, the mountains, and the foothills. It is almost all publicly owned—i.e., Crown lands. These are managed by the Government of Alberta, except for national parks such as Banff, Jasper, Waterton, and Elk Island.

This dilemma is neither new nor unique to Alberta. It describes what has happened on both sides of the border as European settlers moved west and converted the vast North American prairies to agriculture and livestock. As early as the 1930s, Aldo Leopold, a pioneer of American conservation policy, observed, "Conservation will ultimately boil down to rewarding the private landowner who conserves the public interest."[24] Or, to put it more bluntly, "If it pays, it stays," and its corollary: "If it doesn't, it's gone." This is the challenge facing twenty-first-century Alberta: how best to protect the public resource of wildlife on private lands.

I had been introduced to this line of analysis long before seeking public office by my late friend, mentor, and fellow hunter, Ralph Hedlin. Ralph had a distinguished career as a journalist, businessman, and consultant, but he never forgot his agricultural roots growing up in rural Saskatchewan. Three decades earlier, Ralph had written a study for the Western Stock Growers' Association advocating that provincial governments should compensate responsible ranchers for their stewardship of valuable wildlife habitat—or what, two decades later, we began describing as "environmental goods and services" (EGS).

Prior to my appointment as minister, SRD's public consultation on a new land use policy had already identified conservation and stewardship as a distinct issue. In January 2007, I asked my deputy minister to strike a committee to provide recommendations for new programs that would compensate private landowners for the production of EGS. I requested that two of my colleagues from the University of Calgary, Dr. Rainer Knopff and Dr. Cormack Gates, be appointed to this committee. Knopff is a close personal friend. He and I had been graduate students together at the University of Toronto before coming to Calgary. Both he and Gates shared my interest in hunting and my understanding of the micro-economics of agricultural land use, land fragmentation, and wildlife habitat. The result was the "Open Spaces" initiative and the creation of the Land and Wildlife Stewardship Working Group (LWSWG). In addition to Knopff and Gates, the LWSWG included representatives from eleven different stakeholder organizations.[25] The LWSWG met eight times during 2007 and issued their final report in November.[26] Its recommendations were shaped by two guiding principles:[27]

1. Wildlife is a public trust resource to be managed in the public interest.

2. Landowners should not bear the full cost of production and use of wildlife without compensation.

The first meant that there could be no US-style "private hunting" in Alberta. The second meant that landowners who allow hunting should receive some type of compensation. The challenge was how to square this circle.

Working in parallel with the LWSWG and SRD officials, Knopff and Gates developed—and I accepted—two new programs to operationalize these objectives: Hunting for Habitat (HFH) and the Recreational Access Management Program (RAMP). Both were adaptations of similar programs found in Utah and Montana, respectively. Both provided new access to properties that were previously closed to public hunting, and both provided a new revenue stream for participating landowners. LWSWG's research indicated that these programs were popular with both landowners and hunters.[28]

Under HFH, participating private landowners in Alberta would receive 15 percent of available tags (i.e., hunting licences) for both male and female species in their area. They could then sell these tags privately to the highest bidder to create a new revenue stream for their ranching operation. The remainder of the available tags were to be reserved for public hunters under the existing draw system, with the requirement that participating landowners provide equal access to both private and public licence holders.

Representatives from all the relevant hunting associations in Alberta were on the LWSWG, so it wasn't too surprising that details of both HFH and RAMP began to leak out into the hunting community well in advance of a public release by SRD. The response was very negative. In January 2008, an ad hoc group calling itself Alberta Resident Hunters for Justice took to the internet to denounce HFH, saying it would end Alberta's century-old tradition of "free hunting" by introducing paid access hunting for the rich. The group urged members of the Alberta Fish & Game Association (AFGA) to reject HFH at their upcoming AGM scheduled for February in Edmonton.

Sensing trouble, I sent a public letter to the AFGA defending HFH. I emphasized that the "vast majority of tags [would be going] to public hunters through the normal draw process. ... Public hunters would have guaranteed access to participating ranches—many of which have been posted 'No Hunting, No Trespassing' for decades." It seemed to me, I concluded, that this was "a darn good trade-off for resident hunters." It didn't work. Later that month, the AFGA voted unanimously against the entire Open Spaces program.

Following the AFGA's rejection of Open Spaces, a rancher from south of Pincher Creek, Blaine Marr, penned a powerful letter to the editor to the *Pincher Creek Echo* defending HFH. Blaine is a third-generation rancher, a hunter himself, and a former hunting guide. Blaine's ranch borders the Waterton National Park and is in the centre of one of the most ecologically diverse habitats in Canada. (Full disclosure: I know, as I've shot more than a few elk there over the past thirty years.)

> The pie that makes up wildlife and hunting programs today benefits many people such as outfitters, sporting goods dealers, taxidermists, meat processors, rifle dealers and many more [e.g., motels, hotels, restaurants, and bars]. There is no slice in the pie for the landowner, yet he bears the largest cost and liability involved in hunting. OSA along with RAMP and Hunting for Habitat Pilot Projects, try to make the pie bigger for everyone and create long term goals to ensure wildlife and hunting opportunities remain. If existing and future landowners can see a benefit for sustaining wildlife and providing hunter access, then we all win.[29]

I circulated copies of Blaine's letter to all members of caucus, hoping to revive support for HFH. But it was too late. Our government's popularity was being eroded by oilpatch opposition to Stelmach's "New Royalty Framework." The last thing the premier's office wanted was another policy albatross around the leader's neck. With the provincial election just weeks away, Stelmach declared that his government would "revisit" Open Spaces if elected. On March 3, Stelmach and the PCs won a stunning seventy-two-seat majority. Two weeks later, I was asked to pull HFH.[30]

The AFGA leadership's opposition to HFH was short-sighted and narrow-minded. Their "free hunting" slogan was absurd. Nothing is for free. In this case, all the costs are borne by the landowners: the opportunity costs of preserving bush, woodlots, and wetlands versus adding arable acres / grazing pasture; the very real costs of the time dealing with hunters (both those who ask permission and those who simply trespass); and the costs of rounding up the cows that have wandered off through fences that have been knocked down and gates that have been left open. It is hardly surprising that more and more ranches and farms are refusing to give hunters permission to hunt on their land. The predictable consequence is that the number of hunters in Alberta continues to decline. HFH offered a self-financing way to protect an important public good on private lands in a manner that would actually increase access and opportunities for Alberta hunters.

I was more than angry with the AFGA. So angry that, in 2009, I broke with tradition and refused to either attend or to pay for their annual "Lunch with the Minister" in Edmonton. But my being angry didn't change the outcome. HFH was defeated by the negative reaction of the relevant stakeholders and the proximity of the ensuing controversy to the March 2008 election. If we'd had another six months to do the public consultation that had been planned, I believe we could have carried the day and HFH would be a reality today. But we didn't, and it is not.

RECREATIONAL ACCESS MANAGEMENT PLAN (2009)

The second prong of Open Spaces—the Recreational Access Management Plan—survived this political maelstrom. I went back to the drawing board, engaged in further consultations with the AFGA and other hunting organizations such as Pheasants Forever, and was able to roll out a three-year pilot project starting in the fall of 2009.

The RAMP pilot was modelled after the successful Montana Block Program and was limited to just two Wildlife Management Units—WMU

108, the Milk River Ridge triangle south of Lethbridge to the Montana border, bounded by Milk River on the east and Cardston on the west; and WMU 300, the area south of Pincher Creek along both sides of Highway 22 down to Waterton National Park. Again, full disclosure: I knew both these areas and many of the landowners from years of hunting there. As my wife will attest, on most weekends in September through November for the previous twenty-five years, I (and many friends and family) could be found at the farm of Howard and Franki Kaupp outside of New Dayton chasing partridge in September, pheasants in October, and deer in November.

Landowner participation in RAMP was voluntary. Participants agreed to make all or some of their land available for public access and to develop conservation plans for the designated lands. In return, they would be compensated financially according to a formula that combined quantity and quality—how much land was made available and how valuable it was on an EGS scale. Maximum compensation was capped at $20,000 annually, and costs were estimated at $500,000/year for three years. Significantly, the compensation cheques came directly from the government, not from participating hunters. This funding arrangement was added to avoid a repeat of the public relations "free hunting" fiasco that had taken down HFH. It would turn out to be the undoing of RAMP as well, but in a different way.

RAMP Year One was a rollicking success. And then it was cancelled. Twenty-nine properties were enrolled, comprising 131,062 acres of private land. A new, online RAMP website provided the location of each property accompanied by a map detailing the main access road and sign-in station. A participating hunter was required to stop there, sign in with date, time of day, hunting licence number, home telephone, and truck licence plate number. These aspects of RAMP were especially popular with young and new hunters, who may not know where they can hunt and are often reluctant to knock on a stranger's door to ask permission. By season's end, there were 4,240 user-days and an estimated 1,631 individual hunters and anglers. Follow-up surveys indicated a hunter satisfaction rate of 96 percent.

All participating landowners reported a satisfactory experience with RAMP, and were especially pleased with the improved access control with less disruption (thanks to the sign-in stations) and improved hunter behaviour (the former presumably explaining the latter). Total landowner compensation for Year One was only $90,942.08.[31] Even the local Lethbridge Fish and Game Association, which had led the charge against Open Spaces a year earlier, embraced RAMP. Indeed, after it was cancelled, they continued to work with some of local participating landowners to keep the sign-in stations in operation. As recently as the fall 2023 hunting season, I was still "signing in" at several of the former RAMP properties.

So why was RAMP cancelled after Year One? For the same reason as HFH: funding. But in this case, the lack thereof. Initially, RAMP was a ministerial priority with low costs in an era of budget surpluses. This all changed with the global stock market crash of 2008 and the ensuing collapse of oil and gas prices—and thus GOA royalty revenues. (See my account of Budget 2008–9 in chapter 6.) A contributing factor was my departure from SRD to become the next minister of finance, and my replacement by Mel Knight. Knight was grumpy about being moved to SRD. He saw his cabinet shuffle from energy minister as a demotion (it was), as he was unfairly made the scapegoat for Stelmach's New Royalty Framework. He was also a northerner—from the Grande Prairie region—who had little interest in the micro-economics of land use and wildlife habitat on private property in southern Alberta. This is a non-issue in northern Alberta. With his department's budget under pressure, it was easy for him to cancel the next two years of RAMP. If I had stayed at SRD, I have no doubt that I could have scrounged another few hundred thousand dollars to continue the pilot through Years Two and Three.

In fact, I tried. Breaking a cardinal rule of cabinet government that a minister does not interfere in the business of one of his former departments, I contacted several of my civil servants at SRD to try to save RAMP. When Knight found out about this, he sent me a message that any employee of SRD found to be communicating with me would be fired. So I stopped. The bottom line is that having a supportive minister is again a key factor, especially in times of budget deficits.

UPLAND BIRDS ALBERTA AND PHEASANT RELEASE PROGRAM (2010)

Last and perhaps the least of my conservation initiatives was helping to save Alberta's pheasant release program. Last because most of this happened after I left SRD. And least to those who do not consider this a conservation policy. But to those of us who enjoy pheasant hunting, who have and love bird dogs, and who value Alberta's outdoors hunting culture and history, this is not least!

My tenure as SRD Minister ended in January 2011, when I became minister of finance. But this did not mean an end to my efforts to promote environmental conservation and stewardship. The catalyst for my involvement in rebuilding Alberta's pheasant release program was the late Stan Grad. Stan was a successful Alberta-born entrepreneur, initially in the oil and gas business and then as a breeder of purebred bulls. He was an early supporter of the Reform Party and soon became a strong supporter of Ted Morton. Through Stan, I met his extended network of friends and business contacts, many of whom—with Stan's "encouragement"—contributed financially to my 2006 leadership campaign. As I quickly learned, Stan was also an enthusiastic bird hunter—both upland and waterfowl—as were many of his friends.

While they were disappointed that I didn't win the 2006 PC leadership, they were still pleased to see me become the new minister of SRD, i.e., the minister of hunting. They were supportive of my other conservation and stewardship initiatives described in this chapter, but they recruited me to become involved in one more project that had not been on my agenda: saving Alberta's pheasant release program.

When I arrived at SRD, the government's pheasant release program was on its way out the door—scheduled to be discontinued in 2012. Without the release program, Alberta's 100-year tradition of pheasant hunting would effectively end, and with it, the spinoff economic benefits that hunter tourism brings to many smaller towns in rural Alberta.

Pheasants are not native to Alberta. They were first introduced in 1908, and then flourished for the next eight decades. While Alberta's harsh winters take a heavy toll on pheasants, during these early years there was ample habitat to sustain and grow the pheasant population. Post–World War II, Alberta competed with US states like South Dakota as a pheasant hunting destination for hunters on both sides of the border. Hollywood celebrities such as Bob Hope came to Alberta every year to go pheasant hunting. It is estimated that during the 1950s, as many as 140,000 birds a year were being harvested. This hunter tourism—both resident and non-resident—became an important part of the fall economies in southern Alberta communities like Brooks, Medicine Hat, and Taber.

This all began to change in the 1970s and 1980s. By the 1990s, the number of pheasants harvested by hunters had dropped to 20,000 annually. The explanation was twofold: fewer released birds and loss of habitat.

Large-scale, more intensive farming practices took a heavy toll on pheasant habitat—both the quantity and the quality. The original homestead farms that dotted every quarter-section began to disappear, and with them, the windrows of trees and bushes that homesteaders planted as shelters from the freezing prairie winds—cover that also provided critical winter habitat for pheasants and other upland birds. The average acreage of cultivated farm-lands doubled and doubled again during these decades. Next-generation, more efficient tractors and combines were (and are!) more expensive. To pay for them, a farmer needed an entire section (today, more than this) to cover these capital expenses. Sloughs were drained, abandoned homesteads bull-dozed, fences torn out—all meaning less and less habitat for pheasants and other upland birds.

The second cause was the decline of the GOA's pheasant release program. In 1945, the GOA built a pheasant hatchery in Brooks. The Brooks hatchery provided the birds for the pheasant release program over the next forty-five years. During the 1980s, 120,000 pheasant chicks were produced annually. Between 1976 and 1989, a total of 641,000 adult pheasants were released, an average over the fourteen-year period of 45,786 annually.

In 1990, the hatchery was sold to a private company. The government continued to purchase pheasants for the release program from the new owners, but there was a steady decline in the number of pheasants produced, sold, and released. By the time I arrived at SRD in 2007, the number of roosters ordered and released had dropped to 11,750—a quarter of what it had been when I started hunting in Alberta in the 1980s.

Predictably, as the number of pheasants declined, so did the number of pheasant hunters. During the 1980s, Alberta hunters purchased an average of about 15,000 pheasant licences annually. By 2006, it was less than 6,000. It was a vicious circle: fewer pheasants meant fewer hunters, which in turn meant fewer licences and thus less revenue to pay for next year's birds. The end of the program was fast approaching.

This is why Stan Grad and his friends formed a new group, Upland Birds Alberta (UBA), to rescue the pheasant release program.[32] I was already work-ing with some of the UBA founders on the Recreational Access Management Plan (RAMP) during my first years at SRD. As explained above, RAMP was a three-year pilot project in WMUs 108 and 320 that compensated farmers and ranchers who volunteered to protect specified habitat and allowing public hunter access. In WMU 108—a triangular area south of Lethbridge to the Montana border, with Milk River on the southeast corner and Cardston on the southwest corner—the focus was on pheasant hunting and habitat. Year

One of RAMP was a success—both for hunters and landowners. But then it was cancelled in 2010 because of budget cutbacks after I left SRD for Finance. The RAMP experience—both its success and then cancellation—was a catalyst for the formation of UBA.

In May 2011, I attended a UBA organizational meeting at the Busted Shoulder Ranch just east of High River. This led to a more formal "Stakeholders Meeting" in June at the headquarters of the Alberta Hunter Education and Instructors Association (AHEIA) in Calgary, hosted by Bob Gruszecki, the AHEIA's director. UBA had hired Ken Bailey to prepare a policy briefing binder that laid out the past, present, and now pessimistic future of pheasant hunting in Alberta. In addition to the AHEIA, participants included ten other conservation and hunting NGOs[33] and three government departments—SRD, Agriculture, and Tourism. There was a strong consensus that immediate action needed to be taken to rescue the pheasant release program. Two decisions were made. The first was to hire Ken Bailey to coordinate and manage UBA business going forward. The second was to hire a third-party consultant to assess the economic benefits of pheasant hunting to Alberta's rural communities.

UBA subsequently hired Serecon Consulting out of Edmonton to do this study. Serecon released its study in December 2011.[34] I was able to facilitate some GOA assistance in completing this study. Alberta SRD mailed out survey questionnaires to all hunters who purchased a pheasant hunting licence in 2010. Alberta Finance helped by modelling the economic multiplier effects from the initial expenditure data derived from the hunter survey.

The seventy-page report confirmed that pheasant hunting tourism creates significant economic benefits to both Alberta's private sector—restaurants, bars, motels, guides, sporting goods stores—and to provincial and county governments. Over 1,000 pheasant hunters completed the survey. Over 94 percent replied that they would do more pheasant hunting in the future if the opportunities improved. Sixty-one percent said that they would support an increase in the cost of pheasant licences if the additional revenues were dedicated to increased pheasant release.

In February 2012, UBA submitted a formal proposal to the GOA to increase the pheasant release program. Drawing on data in the Serecon study, UBA's message to the government was clear:

The demise of Alberta's pheasant release program would bring an end to decades of tradition, meaning the elimination of significant economic benefits for the province and many rural communities. Alternatively, retaining the program, and growing it to the levels of the 1980s, would re-establish Alberta as one of the premier pheasant hunting destinations in North America. ... [with] material economic benefits to a wide range of stakeholders.[35]

But change was already afoot. With me no longer at SRD and the GOA now running large deficits, the pheasant release program was on SRD's budget chopping block. UBA strongly protested and volunteered to run the program until a more permanent solution could be developed. SRD agreed, and in 2011, off-loaded the administration of the pheasant release program to UBA along with an annual operating grant. Supplemented by some additional fundraising by UBA, this arrangement continued for the 2012 and 2013 fall hunting seasons. This interim arrangement kept the pheasant release program alive, but it was clearly not sustainable. UBA had neither the desire nor the capacity to permanently run the GOA's pheasant program.

In 2014, UBA recommended to SRD that the pheasant program be transferred to the Alberta Conservation Association (ACA). The ACA is what is known as a delegated administrative organization. Since 1997, the Alberta government has delegated to the ACA certain responsibilities to conserve, protect, and enhance Alberta's fish and wildlife populations and their habitats for Albertans to use and enjoy. The ACA manages its various programs independently of the government, but it must report annually to the minister on its policies and budget. In this case, SRD sought to delegate the administration of the pheasant release program to the ACA.

The new SRD minister, Robin Campbell, accepted the UBA proposal, but the ACA initially declined because SRD did not offer to provide annual grants for pay for the program. Following further negotiation, the ACA agreed to take over the program, but to return the management of the Aerial Ungulate Survey Program to SRD. ACA would then use the funds previously allocated to the ungulate survey to pay for the management of the pheasant release program. This meant that there was there was no net change in SRD's annual funding for ACA. It was complicated but it worked.

Under ACA management, there have been significant improvements in the pheasant release program. The number of pheasants released annually has doubled—from 13,900 in 2011 to an average of over 28,000 during the years 2018–2022. Similarly, the number of pheasant hunters has also doubled, averaging over 10,000 annually over the same time compared to 5,700 in 2012. The ACA has revived the 4H Pheasant Raise and Release Program—recruiting farm and ranch children active in 4H. Most recently, this program is raising and releasing 18,000 hen pheasants annually.

The number of release/hunting sites has also been significantly increased—up to forty-one as of fall 2023. These sites are continually re-evaluated and adjusted. There are now more sites in central and northern Alberta than before. The ACA has also initiated new habitat projects with private landowners and municipalities. The Municipal District of Taber has been especially active in upland habitat restoration projects.

The Taber Pheasant Festival has also experienced a dramatic increase in participants. In 2011, its first year, the festival drew 500 hunters with a release of 3,000 birds.[36] Most recently, there were 700–800 hunters chasing 5,600 pheasants in forty different release sites on land owned by twenty-five different landowners.[37] It is now the largest hunting festival in Canada, lasting an entire week and drawing hundreds of hunters, including many first-time, youth hunters.

In sum, quality pheasant hunting has returned to Alberta. And Stan Grad's UBA initiative was the catalyst. In addition to Stan, Ken Bailey, and UBA, credit for this recovery also goes to Todd Zimmerling and his team at the ACA. Pheasants Forever, Ducks Unlimited, and the AHEIA also played important roles. I was just a middle man in all of this—helping to connect the key players. But I was happy to be a part of this revival of another great Alberta tradition.

MICREX MINE AND THE LIVINGSTONE RANGE (2010)

Most accounts of a minister's career are based on what he or she achieves in terms of new policies. This is understandable and is reflected in the structure of this very chapter. But what the public usually doesn't see—which is often just as important—are the policies or decisions a minister prevents. For me, this was the proposed Micrex Mine—a proposal to build an open-pit magnetite mine on the flanks of the Livingstone Range. The Micrex file came across my desk the first year I was at SRD—2007—and, as it turned out, was the last thing I did going out the door in December 2010.

Magnetite is a heavy magnetic iron ore used for coal upgrading and steel production. It is not in short supply and so is relatively cheap. To be profitable, a magnetite mine needs to be large to benefit from economies of scale. That is what did not make sense about the Micrex proposal. Their original plan called for a mine to cover thirteen square kilometres of public lands in the Livingstone Range. But by the time I became minister, the proposal had been scaled down to just 5.5 hectares—barely larger than a football field. It wasn't too difficult to figure out why. At that reduced size, it did not trigger a legal requirement for an environmental impact statement (EIS) under the *Public Lands Act*. However, Micrex had actually purchased 36 square miles, or 56,909 acres of land. The smaller, revised proposal looked suspiciously like a toe-in-the-door strategy that would lay the foundation for future expansion.

There were good reasons for Micrex to avoid any type of EIS. The Livingstone Range is certainly the steepest and arguably the most dramatic front range in all of Alberta's Eastern Slopes. If you've never experienced it, view the online video provided by the Livingstone Landowners' Group.[38] Or drive down the North Burmis Road, just to the west of Highway 22. Better yet, go for hike there, or take a trail ride with one of the local outfitters.

The proposed mine was in the middle of the designated DU Ranch Heritage Viewscape. It provides home habitat to a prolific mix of bighorn sheep, elk, moose, deer, and the usual mix of predators that feast on them—grizzly bears, black bears, and cougars. The proposed smaller mine site was adjacent to the spring lambing grounds of a resident herd of 200 bighorn sheep. The access roads required by the mine would destroy native grasses and be difficult if not impossible to restore. Storing topsoil on slopes that regularly experience 100-kilometre-an-hour winds would be either impossible or very expensive. The new access roads would also increase hunting pressure on the wildlife mentioned above—especially by Indigenous hunters who are not subject to legal limits or seasons and can hunt year-round. And of course, there are water issues. The Micrex properties cover much of the headwaters of the Connelly Creek watershed, a significant tributary to the Crowsnest River, which flows into the Oldman and then the Bow. Erosion from the mine and the access roads would inevitably degrade water quality.

It quickly became evident that Micrex did not make sense either economically or environmentally. Even at full production, the proposed mine would pay virtually nothing in Crown royalties—several million dollars a year—and create fewer than ten full-time jobs. The bottom line was neatly summarized by a letter to Minister Knight, myself, and other ministers, signed by 125 local residents in the Livingstone Landowners Group:

> There is a proven economy in this area already. … It is based on ranching, home businesses, tourism, hunting, fishing, and equestrian outfitting – all things that would be negatively impacted by a mine, no matter its size.

I agreed! And so it's time again for full disclosure. I know this area and many of its landowners quite well. My colleague and friend, Rainer Knopff, has lived there on and off since 1992. Through Rainer, I met Dan and Puff McKim, who operate the historic DU Ranch, a purebred Hereford bull operation just off North Burmis Road. With Rainer and his sons, I have hunted the Livingstone slopes for elk, moose, deer, and grouse. In the summer, my wife joins us for hikes above the DU ranch and fly-fishing in the Crowsnest River. The McKims are active in the Livingstone Landowners' Group.

In the 2008 Alberta election, many of these same people helped to elect Evan Berger as the new MLA for Livingstone-McLeod. I had met Evan during my 2003 "More Alberta, Less Ottawa" speaking tour, and he had helped in my 2006 leadership bid. Evan, a third generation Alberta rancher, runs a mixed livestock-grain operation west of Claresholm. I immediately appointed Evan as my parliamentary assistant because I knew he could be a constructive bridge to the rural landowners as we implemented the South Saskatchewan Regional Plan, which included all of Livingstone-McLeod. Evan was an effective advocate for his constituents, almost all of whom opposed the mine.

In my mind's eye, when I imagined the Micrex Mine, what I saw was a second industrial scar on Alberta's Eastern Slopes—like the Lafarge limestone quarries and cement plant in Exshaw. The Lafarge plant is located 80 kilometres west of Calgary, at the gateway to Banff, Lake Louise, and the Canadian Rockies, a UNESCO World Heritage Site. It is the largest cement plant in Canada. It's located less than a mile from the Trans-Canada Highway, so you can't miss it as you approach Canmore. And it is just plain ugly and totally out of place—a huge scar on the face of the Rockies, with large stacks belching smoke.

In 1906, when the mine and plant were first opened, it made good sense. Alberta was the poorest of all the Canadian provinces, with a mostly rural population of less than 200,000. And the Lafarge plant has served Alberta well, providing most of the cement that has built the province into the wealthiest province in Canada with a population of 4.8 million. One hundred years later, however, you would never build the same plant at the gateway to a UNESCO World Heritage Site. So I decided that such a thing damn well wasn't going to happen again on my watch.

The question was how. While I could have engaged either or both the energy and environment ministers (as there was overlapping jurisdiction), I decided the path of least resistance was simply to rope-a-dope it to death with one administrative delay after another. Without initial public-lands sign-off from SRD, it couldn't go anywhere. While most of the delays were achieved simply by foot dragging on administrative technicalities, there were two potential deal-stoppers for Micrex. One was the then-pending South Saskatchewan Regional Plan (SSRP), being developed under the newly adopted *Alberta Land Stewardship Act* (ALSA). The SSRP encompasses all the watersheds feeding the Bow, Elbow, Sheep, Highwood, Crowsnest, and Oldman rivers—basically everything south of Calgary and the Trans-Canada Highway. The advisory committee for the SSRP, which I had hand-picked, would never recommend approval of project like Micrex, as it failed both the Act's environmental (water and wildlife) and economic criteria.

The second trump card that I could have played was to refer the entire project for a full cost-benefit analysis by Alberta's Natural Resources Conservation Board (NRCB). The NRCB reviews non-oil and gas natural resource development projects and any other development projects referred to it by cabinet. At a minimum this would have added at least another year to the approval process. It was also highly unlikely that Micrex could ever pass a full NRCB cost/benefit analysis, and the Micrex team knew this. Just the referral would have been enough to kill the project.

While I never played either of these cards in my multiple meetings with the Micrex lobbyist, I made her aware that I considered them as viable options. This worked as long as I was minister, but that came to an end in January 2010, when I was moved to Finance. My replacement at SRD was Mel Knight. Mel was a northerner and had little interest in either ALSA or conservation issues in southern Alberta. In the thinly populated north, when someone wants to invest millions of dollars in a new mine, they are welcomed. The

Micrex promoters were alert to the opportunity presented by a new minister and were quickly in Mel's office lobbying for SRD sign-off.

For the rest of 2010, I was much too busy at Finance to pay any attention to the Micrex file. I spent twelve months trying (unsuccessfully) to build a two-step budget process to get us "back in the black" by Budget 2012—an election year. In addition to four painful weeks lost to shingles in May, I was immersed in budget meetings with my officials and Treasury Board (see chapter 7). But as December approached, I was informed by Evan Berger, now minister of agriculture, that Mel was getting ready to approve the Micrex licence. Mel subsequently confirmed this to me, stating that the government could not and should not stop all development in the province until the land use planning process was completed. I responded that while this was true in the abstract, it was completely unacceptable in the specific context of Micrex. But Mel was not persuaded.

The Federal, Provincial, Territorial (FPT) Finance Ministers' semi-annual meeting was in Kananaskis on December 19–20. So, as I prepared for my second (and presumably last) FPT meeting, I decided to do something I had never done before—leak a self-serving story to the media. There were several cabinet ministers who did this regularly to curry favourable treatment by the legislative reporters. We all knew who they were, and I held them in contempt. However, given that I had already made my decision to resign from cabinet the following month (see chapter 9), I figured I had nothing to lose.

I phoned Kelly Cryderman, then the legislative reporter for the *Calgary Herald*. Kelly is a cousin of Sonia Arrison, whom I knew through her public policy work at the Fraser Institute in Vancouver. I had developed a cordial professional relationship with Kelly, so I was comfortable asking her for a favour: Would she mind asking me a question about how Minister Knight was handling the Micrex file? She responded, correctly, that this had nothing to do with the FPT meeting and would violate the unspoken rule of ministers not publicly commenting on each other's work. I replied simply that I was asking a favour.

The FPT meeting in Kananaskis went according to schedule on December 19–20. As is customary at the end, there was a joint media scrum. Most questions focused on the about-face that federal Minister of Finance Jim Flaherty had done on Canada Pension Plan reforms—now favouring Alberta's position of allowing private sector alternatives rather than increasing CPP premiums (see chapter 7).[39] But, just as the scrum was breaking up, Cryderman asked me about Micrex. She then did me the favour of quoting me verbatim in her subsequent *Calgary Herald* article:

> Morton said, "It would be premature to approve a project like this before the regional plan for the South Saskatchewan region is finalized. ... If you look at the policy document for the land-use framework, it identifies the Eastern Slopes in terms of priority use, as watershed and recreation—not mining." ... Morton suggests the company's application may be subject to review by the province's Natural Resources Conservation Board.[40]

Less than twenty-four hours later I received an angry phone call from Minister Knight. What the hell did I think I was doing? I replied that I was just repeating what I had told him before the Christmas break. He was not impressed. While this tactic unfortunately cost me my friendship with Mel, it did get the policy results I wanted. Cryderman's article triggered a flood of phone calls and emails to both Knight's office and to the premier's office—all opposing the Micrex mine. It took several months to grind through the formal process, but in April, SRD announced cabinet approval of an order-in-council (OC) mandating a full NRCB review of the Micrex proposal. But it never happened. Knowing that it could never pass the NRCB review, Micrex placed the project on hold.

So how was I able to block the Micrex mine? I'd like to say because it was so clearly without merit. But we all know that governments routinely enact poor policy. Just look at the Stelmach government's New Royalty Framework and North West Upgrader (see chapter 7). The primary factors in the Micrex defeat were that it did not have any champions in the cabinet, in the civil service, or in any influential business stakeholder groups. Contributing factors were the lobbying and public relations efforts of local residents—the Livingstone Landowners Group—which were effectively communicated by their MLA, Evan Berger. While these factors probably would not be enough to establish a new program, they were sufficient to allow a motivated minister—me—to block a project that clearly violated our government's stewardship and conservation goals.

After the 2012 election, in which both Evan Berger and I were defeated, Micrex almost succeeded in resurrecting their mining project. They applied for a mining permit on a piece of property adjacent to their earlier proposal.

Since it was a different block of land, the requirement for the NRCB review did not technically apply to it. The Livingstone Landowners Group communicated this to me in November 2012, and I immediately passed on their concerns to Ken Hughes, the new minister of energy in the Redford government. Ken was a long-time friend of mine. He had grown up on a ranch near Longview, where his family had settled in the 1890s. He knew and loved the Foothills. I pointed out that the "new" Micrex proposal was not new at all, but just a clever attempt to bypass the requirement of the NRCB review. All the environmental issues were the same. Once Ken became aware of this, the permit was denied.

POSTSCRIPT

Looking back, I am disappointed that stewardship and conservation have slipped off Alberta conservatives' priority list over the past decade. Disappointed, but not surprised. It's been a tumultuous decade.

There have been four provincial elections, five different premiers, and four leadership races in the PC/UCP parties. There was a decade of recession, during which GOA revenues from oil and gas sharply declined. By 2020, successive PC/NDP/UCP governments had run up $100 billion of new provincial debt. Companies went bankrupt. Jobs and homes were lost. For the first time since the 1980s, more people were leaving Alberta than arriving.[41] Stewardship and conservation concerns became secondary to creating jobs and growth. COVID then trumped all other issues for almost two years. There was a loss of institutional memory in the civil service. Sustainable Resources Development (SRD) was dissolved, and its responsibilities—including the *Alberta Land Stewardship Act*—were transferred to three different ministries—Environment, Agriculture, and Parks. Last but not least was the emergence of global climate change as the most important environmental issue. In both Edmonton and Ottawa, provincial stewardship issues took a back seat to the politics of reducing CO_2 emissions.

Much of this was beyond the control of any Alberta government. Boom and bust are inherent in the energy sector. Today, the price of oil and gas—and thus capital investment in new exploration—is a function of global economics and geopolitics. No one in the world saw COVID coming. The decline and fall of the Alberta PC Party? Well, read the rest of this book! But there are two takeaways that I would leave with the readers.

The first is coming to grips with Alberta's boom and bust economy. We prioritize conservation and stewardship during periods of growth, but then slip into neutral when the next energy bust hits. The Lougheed government implemented important new conservation and environment policies during the growth years of 1970s. But these issues were then mostly ignored during the Getty-Klein years in the 1980s and 1990s. This pattern was repeated during the growth years of the Stelmach government (as recounted in this chapter), but stewardship then slid back into the policy basement after 2013.

Once we recognize this problem, we can do something to correct it. Not completely, of course. Governments rightly prioritize policy areas that directly impact the daily lives of Alberta families: job security, a stable and strong economy, health, education, and community safety. But this does not mean ignoring conservation and stewardship issues. As I stated at the outset of this chapter, the "Alberta Advantage" is not just about annual GDP growth. The quality of life Albertans enjoy also includes the recreational opportunities—hiking and camping; fishing and hunting; skiing and snowmobiling—all made possible by Alberta's amazing mountains, foothills, prairies, rivers, and lakes. There are very few places on the face of the Earth that enjoy what we Albertans too often take for granted. Stewarding them for future generations must never drop off any future government's agenda.

My second takeaway is a more realistic approach to the challenges of climate change. One is not a "climate change denier" to insist that the reduction of CO_2 emissions must be balanced with both affordability and energy security. The price of oil and gas is not just about driving our cars and turning on the lights. It affects the cost of everything we do—the food we eat, the clothes we wear, the homes we live in. The building blocks of all modern economies—cement, steel, plastics, and ammonia (fertilizer)—all require oil and gas.[42] The cost of energy impacts the bottom line of every family's monthly budget and the balance sheets of every Canadian company. Affordability must be part of our climate change calculations.

As for energy security, Russia's invasion of Ukraine in 2022 should have been a wake-up call. Europe's reckless dependency on imports of Russian natural gas was exposed as a dangerous strategic mistake.[43] And Hamas's brutal October 2023 attack on Israel and the ensuing chaos/slaughter in Gaza is a tragic reminder of the West's energy insecurity. Global supply chains only work during times of peace. Almost all of Canada's allies are dangerously dependent for global oil supply on the Arab nations of the Middle East.[44] The emerging China-Russia-Iran triad is threatening the relative peace and prosperity enjoyed by much of the world since the end of the Cold War in 1991. Going too far, too fast on government mandates to reduce oil and gas production will have dangerous consequences on energy security for both Canada and our allies.

Canada's response to climate change must also be tempered by the recognition of the unpleasant fact that what we do makes little difference. Canada emits less than 1.5 percent of global CO_2 emissions. We could shut Canada down and all leave, and it would not make much difference. By contrast, we can control what we do here at home. How well we steward and conserve our forests, foothills and plains, rivers and lakes—and the wildlife they sustain—will make a positive difference in the lives of our children and grandchildren.

6

How I Became Finance Minister (2009)

Indeed, it has been said that democracy is the worst form of government except all those other forms that have been tried.

—Winston Churchill

THE KLEIN LEGACY

From 2007 through 2009, my priorities were to address the challenges and opportunities I now had as the new minister of sustainable resources development—the subject of the previous chapter. For Ed Stelmach, the number one priority was to ensure that he—that we—would win the provincial election scheduled for 2008. At the outset, this appeared quite doable.

Thanks to Ralph Klein, the government Ed Stelmach inherited was not only debt free, but also had a new $2.5 billion "Sustainability Fund" to cover off any short-term deficits in a low revenue year. To ensure that future Alberta governments didn't make the same mistakes as the Getty years, the Klein government also enacted a new balanced budget law that made deficits illegal.

The Klein government also terminated or wound down the dozens of failed "economic diversification" programs inherited from the Lougheed and Getty era.[1] Klein also set in motion reforms that took responsibility for managing the Alberta Heritage Fund away from government ministers and vested it in an independent and professional management team—the Alberta Investment Management Corporation (AIMCo).[2]

The Klein Government commissioned a study on how to get Alberta public finances back on a stable, long-term track. That report, *Moving from Good to Great: Enhancing Alberta's Fiscal Framework*, highlighted the structural risks inherent in how Alberta was spending its oil and gas royalties and associated energy revenues.

> The commission also recognizes the increasingly important need to reduce our province's reliance on non-renewable resource revenues. … A new fiscal framework should provide for a gradual but sustained reduction in our reliance on natural resource revenues and a focused attempt to build financial and other strategic assets to maintain and improve the Alberta Advantage.[3]

In response, the government amended the *Fiscal Responsibility Act* in 2002 to allow only the first $3.5 billion of resource revenues to go into general revenues, and directed the rest, if any, to the new Sustainability Fund (capped at $2.5 billion), which would be available to supplement a shortfall if energy revenues did not reach $3.5 billion in a future year. The primary purpose of these amendments was to reduce GOA reliance on non-renewable energy revenues and to escape the "stop-and-go" capital-spending pattern of recent years.

If Stelmach had followed this new fiscal road map, his premiership would have ended more happily. But in his defence, the failure to do this started even before he became premier.

When I first joined the government in 2005, the prices of both natural gas and oil were hitting historic highs, and so were the GOA's resource revenues. As shown in Table 1, energy revenues jumped from the $7 billion/year range to $14.3 billion in 2005 and $12.3 billion in 2006. For Budgets 2005 and 2006, GOA spending increased an average of 10 percent a year, a rate that clearly was not sustainable. Shirley McClellan was treasurer and deputy premier— and she would keep warning caucus that we could not continue at this rate. But continue we did.

	2002	2003	2004	2005	2006	2007	2008	2009	2010	2011
Resource Revenues (billions)	$7,130	$7,676	$9,774	$14,347	$12,260	$11,024	$11,915	$6,768	$8,428	$11,636
Total Spending (billions)	$20,529	$21,751	$24,153	$26,991	$29,507	$33,588	$36,663	$36,690	$38,444	$39,566
Surplus / (Deficit) (billions)	$2,133	$4,136	$5,175	$8,551	$8,510	$4,581	($852)	($1,032)	($3,410)	($2.3)

As noted above, the government amended the *Fiscal Responsibility Act* to allow only the first $3.5 billion of resource revenues to go into general revenues, and directed the rest, if any, to the new Sustainability Fund. No sooner had we put these new rules in place than we began to break them. Or rather, to change them. In 2004 (before I had even joined caucus), the government legislatively amended the amount of resource revenues that could be directed to general revenues from the original $3.5 billion to $4 billion. Once I joined government, we did this twice more—raising the limit to $4.75 billion in 2005 and to $5.3 billion in 2006. At the same time, the "rules" governing what to do with resource revenues in excess of $2.5 billion mandated for the Sustainability Fund were soft and vague. "Surplus funds" could be directed into additional savings, but they could also be directed into the Capital Account or into "balance sheet improvements," which turned out to mean just more program spending.

In the last Klein budget, 2006, GOA energy revenues were $12.3 billion. $5.3 billion was used for budgeting and $7 billion was transferred to the Sustainability Fund. From the latter, $4.8 billion was transferred to the Capital Account; and $900 million was spent on disasters (drought relief, forest fires, pine beetle) and natural gas rebates. All that was left for savings was $1.2 billion. In short, during its last two years, the Klein government failed to follow the new budgeting and spending rules it had just adopted. Would it be different under Stelmach?

I neither liked nor approved of this overspending. But as a new backbencher, I could do little about it. I was also inclined to cut Klein some slack. His government's sharp budget cuts in the 1990s had subjected him and his cabinet members to strong protests, some that got way too personal. Maybe it was understandable that with the Getty debt now paid off, Klein, ever the populist, wanted to go out as a more popular premier. But after the leadership race—and all the candidates' commitments to fiscal responsibility—I expected the Stelmach government to follow the new rules. This did not happen.

STELMACH: BUYING THE 2008 ELECTION

In 2007 and 2008, resource revenues remained high. As before, spending followed. While officially only $3.5 billion in resource revenues were supposed to be spent annually, the true amount was much higher. In Stelmach's first budget, virtually every resource dollar was spent. The explanation was not hard to find.

Stelmach wasted no time keeping his campaign promises to increase GOA program and capital spending. His first budget—2007—saw a \$4 billion spending increase, and the next—2008, an election year budget—saw another \$3 billion increase. In 2008–9, when energy revenues were \$11.9 billion, over \$10 billion was spent on operating and capital, double the \$5.3 billion "limit."[4] Much of this was driven by generous contract settlements with the public sector unions. Stelmach apparently wanted to pay back the "two-minute Tory" supporters who had helped him win the second round of voting in the 2006 PC leadership race.

Between 2008 and 2012, the average weekly earnings of all Alberta provincial public sector employees—29,387 in number—increased by 17 percent. The sweetest deal was given to the Alberta Teachers' Association (ATA). With the ATA threatening a province-wide teachers' strike to coincide with the 2008 provincial election, Stelmach and Minister of Education Ron Liepert gave the ATA a five-year contract, conveniently taking us beyond not just the 2008 election but also the 2012 election.[5] The contract guaranteed annual salary increases equal to the provincial "weekly wage index," which, once the 2008 recession hit, was substantially more than inflation. On top of that, the GOA assumed the \$2.1 billion unfunded liability in the ATA's pension fund and made a \$1,500 lump-sum payment to each teacher.[6] No wonder so many teachers voted PC in the 2008 election!

I had one positive influence on Budget 2008. I successfully argued for increasing Alberta's tax credit for charitable contributions, a policy plank in my 2006 leadership campaign. We raised the provincial tax credit from 12.75 percent to 21 percent, a 60 percent increase that made Alberta number one in Canada in this respect.[7]

Where was all this money going to come from? Stelmach had an answer: from the oil companies. During the course of the PC leadership contest in 2006, all the candidates agreed that given the surging increases in oil prices, it was time to review the royalty rates for the oil sands operations. A decade earlier, when falling bitumen prices threatened to shut down the oil sands, the government had cut royalty rates to help keep the industry afloat. Now, with prices at record highs, it made sense to revisit this arrangement.

As premier, Stelmach went one big step further. He appointed a five-person committee to review the royalty rates on all oil and gas wells in Alberta, not just the oil sands. There were early concerns that that the committee had an anti-industry bias. It was chaired by Bill Hunter, a former executive in the forestry industry, a sector with a long history of poor relations with the oil and gas sector. There was only one member of the committee with personal experience in Alberta's energy sector. While Minister of Finance Lyle Oberg announced the members of the committee, it was widely known that the five members were hand-picked by the premier's office.[8]

The meaning of all this became clear at the 2007 Calgary Stampede, when a draft of the report was presented to caucus. The leading slide depicted a "Daddy Warbucks" lookalike labelled as "Big Oil" holding the puppet strings to elected politicians. While this type of negative caricature might be standard at a Liberal or NDP caucus meeting, it shocked many of us who saw the energy sector as the key to Alberta's prosperity, and a friend of the PC Party.

Three months later—and just five months before the anticipated spring 2008 election—the Stelmach government released the final version of the New Royalty Framework (NRF).[9] It ignored the oil and gas sector's private communications that they were willing to accept some modest royalty increases. Instead, the NRF sharply increased royalties and projected a resulting increase of $1.4 billion in royalty revenues by 2010, a 20 percent increase over the current year.[10] In retrospect, this turned out to be a huge miscalculation. Plummeting natural gas prices and the post–2008 recession collapse of oil prices led to a massive drop in royalties by 2010—over $2.5 billion less than 2007. But that was not until 2010.

In the run-up to the 2008 spring election, the New Royalty Framework—named and marketed as "Our Fair Share"—was wildly popular. Stelmach embraced a populist marketing campaign to style the NRF as win-win for all Albertans: "I made a commitment and I delivered. The New Royalty Framework gives future generations of Albertans a fair share from the development of their resources."[11] The "fair share" message worked. It tapped into a latent resentment in many Albertans rooted in the belief that they had not benefited from the energy boom of that decade.

The NRF became the hallmark policy of the Stelmach Government but also led to its ultimate demise. It may have won an additional dozen seats in the 2008 election, but it deeply alienated the oil and gas sector—especially the juniors—many of whom subsequently bankrolled the Wildrose Party in the lead-up to the next provincial election in 2012.

The final pre-election goodie was the cancellation of health care premiums that Alberta had levied since 1969: $1,056 a year for families and $528 for singles. Total savings to Albertans, Minister of Finance Iris Evan crowed, would be $1.3 billion, the equivalent of a 12 percent reduction in personal income tax.[12] Premier Stelmach went out of his way to link the cancellation of health insurance premiums to his NRF:

> The time has come for Albertans to enjoy additional direct rewards of our province's prosperity. This government made a commitment to Albertans to eliminate health care premiums within four years. We said we would do it sooner if we could and that is exactly what we're doing.[13]

Buoyed by this kind of pre-writ spending and tax cuts, in the March 2008 election, we crushed the opposition parties, winning seventy-two of the eighty-three seats. Predictably, the Conservative gains came mostly in the greater Edmonton area, where the PCs achieved our best results since 1982. The Liberals were reduced to nine MLAs, the New Democrats to two. The lone Wildrose MLA, Paul Hinman, lost his seat in Cardston. The Stelmach "investments" had paid a handsome political dividend!

Several weeks after the election, there was an insightful *Calgary Herald* column by a then-obscure professor at Mount Royal College, Naheed Nenshi.[14] (For readers not from Alberta, Nenshi went on to become the mayor of Calgary from 2010 to 2021.) The "real losers," according to Nenshi, were not the Liberals, the Wildrose, or the NDP. The "real losers" were Ted Morton and Jim Dinning, both of whom, he alleged, were waiting in the wings for Stelmach to stumble, ready then to take him down and make a second run at the PC leadership. Factually, Nenshi was simply wrong about me. I had no active plan for a coup d'état. But at another level, he was right. Any hopes I might have had for a quick second chance were dashed. Nenshi was also right about something else. The longer I waited for Stelmach to retire, the more difficult it would become for me to ever lead the PC Party.

> The problem here is that the Stelmach government stands for nearly everything Morton does not. There's nothing conservative about these conservatives. They spend more than any other province—in Canadian history. They have no appetite for private competition in health care. They avoid all questions dealing with social values. They have yet to find a problem that can't be fixed by throwing money at it. Not only must this be frustrating for Morton

> personally, the longer it goes on, the harder it will be for him to move the party
> back to a solidly conservative philosophy.
>
> —Naheed Nenshi, *Calgary Herald*, March 13, 2008.

Flush from a stunning electoral victory that few would have predicted a year earlier, the Stelmach Tories delivered on all our pre-election promises in Budget 2008. Spending was increased by 11.6 percent over the prior year to a new Alberta record—$37 billion. But revenues were even higher, with a projected surplus of $1.6 billion.

South of the border, the failure of Bear Stearns, a well-established New York investment bank, was an early warning sign of the impending subprime mortgage and credit collapse. But in Alberta, projections for oil and gas prices were at historic highs—$78/barrel oil and $6.75/GJ gas prices. The actual market price of oil in April was an even-higher $118, and would reach $148 by July, before the meltdown of the investment banking industry in September 2008.

In January 2008, I accompanied Stelmach on a trip to Washington, DC, to address growing environmental opposition to Alberta's oil sands and to TransCanada PipeLines' then-proposed Keystone XL Pipeline.[15] (As minister of SRD, I was invited to address new US restrictions on imports of Canadian softwood lumber. Minister of Agriculture George Groeneveld was also invited to address the negative impacts of proposed "country of origin labelling" on our beef exports to the US.) We were not happy when the Canadian embassy in Washington told us they were unable to schedule an appointment for us with US Vice President Dick Cheney. We doubted that they had tried very hard. So I then went through my own back channels to arrange a meeting. (Cheney was from Casper, Wyoming, my own hometown, and was a family friend.)

When the Canadian embassy discovered we were about to meet with Cheney without them, contrary to the normal protocol, they became upset and started phoning Cheney's office. Cheney's chief of staff phoned me and asked if we were okay with someone from the embassy joining us for the meeting. Not feeling generous toward the embassy, I said that it would be okay but to keep them waiting—not to tell the embassy until the night before.

When we finally arrived in Cheney's office Friday morning, the vice president walked right past the embassy official, came up to me, shook my hand, and said, "How's your mother doing, Ted?" I kept a straight face, but Stelmach, Groeneveld, and Gary Mar (Alberta's representative in Washington) almost burst out laughing. Once we had composed ourselves, we introduced the embassy official and got down to explaining the strategic value of Canadian oil imports to the US economy and national security. Predictably, Cheney was very receptive.[16]

STAMPEDE CAUCUS 2008: SPENDING $4 BILLION THAT WE DID NOT HAVE

Blithely unaware of what was just around the corner, in Alberta the government spending frenzy culminated at the annual July Stampede Caucus—an event where the entire PC Caucus comes to Calgary to serve pancakes to the public in the small park behind McDougall Centre. In those heady days, it was common to mix business with pleasure. After the pancakes were served, an all-day caucus meeting was held at McDougall Centre before most of the caucus headed off to the Stampede grounds for the chuckwagon races and evening show.

Caucus was told that while Budget 2008 had pegged our projected surplus at $1.6 billion, our first-quarter update now projected that this surplus had increased by an eye-popping $8 billion—driven by historically high oil prices and royalties. There was justifiable concern in cabinet that this news would lead to public demands for even further program spending.

These concerns intersected with early efforts to do something about the new reality of global—and especially US—opposition to the continued expansion of the Alberta oil sands. Under Klein, there was little interest in responding to demands for reductions in CO_2 emissions in Alberta. But now the criticisms became too loud to ignore. Concerns about "social licence" and "market access," terms the Klein cabinet would never have heard of much less used, were now on the table.

To address these concerns, the Stelmach government had undertaken some preliminary policy development around carbon capture and storage (CCS). CCS was a new, unproven, and expensive technology that captures the exhaust gases from coal-fired power plants or refineries and then uses cooling and high pressure to separate out the CO_2. The CO_2 can then be re-injected into underground formations. In spring 2008, the emphasis for the GOA was on "preliminary" and "expensive."

Notwithstanding this, prior to Stampede Caucus, Minister of Energy Mel Knight had presented cabinet with a plan to invest \$2 billion in CCS. The pitch was that we could use the now-projected budget surplus to jump-start the CCS project, thereby pre-empting calls to spend it on other programs.

This caught most of cabinet by surprise, and I was quick to voice my opposition. As a climate-change skeptic, I was opposed to spending this kind of money on carbon reduction. As a fiscal hawk, I was opposed to spending "projected budget surpluses"—money we did not yet even have—on any new projects. Vigorous debate ensued. Eventually, as a compromise measure, I proposed that for every dollar we would spend on CCS, we'd spend an equivalent dollar on expanding public transportation. I argued that taking more cars and trucks off Alberta roads, could reduce our CO_2 emissions in a way that actually improves the lives of everyday Albertans, unlike pumping CO_2 into the ground. This compromise garnered a consensus, and we were told it would be added to the CCS initiative.

It was my understanding that this meant that the new "policy package" would split the proposed \$2 billion equally—\$1 billion for CCS and \$1 billion for new public transit. Suffice it to say that I and others were surprised when we were told the next day in caucus that the GOA would be spending a total of \$4 billion on a new carbon reduction strategy—\$2 billion each on CCS and public transit, subsequently christened "GreenTRIP."

This episode captures how easy it was to spend money in the years leading up to the Great Recession, which began in earnest less than two months after this Stampede Caucus. The final irony—or tragedy—in this episode was that by the time GOA books closed on Budget 2008–9, there was no \$8.5 billion surplus but rather a deficit of \$852 million. In less than seventy-two hours in early July, we had committed to spending \$4 billion that we did not yet even have. And, as it turned out, never would have.

DEFICITS AND DEBT: MEMOS TO STELMACH AND SNELGROVE (2008–2009)

In August 2008, I wrote the first of two internal memos to then–President of Treasury Board Lloyd Snelgrove, with copies to Premier Stelmach and

Minister of Finance Iris Evans. While I had no way of knowing it at the time, it was these memos that would later lead to my appointment as the new finance minister in January 2010; my subsequent dispute with Stelmach over the severity of the budget cuts I was proposing for Budget 2011; my decision to resign as finance minister in January 2011; and Ed Stelmach's subsequent resignation as party leader and premier.

It began innocently enough. In the weeks following the 2008 Stampede Caucus, I took some time to read the "Mintz Report"—a recently released report on GOA finances done by a commission chaired by Dr. Jack Mintz, the then-president and CEO of the C.D. Howe Institute in Toronto.[17] I had come to know Jack in 2001, the year I worked as director of policy and research for the (federal) Canadian Alliance Party, and had continued to read his policy opinion pieces in the *National Post*. The message of the sixty-one-page report was succinct and blunt: "The current fiscal policy (including relatively high rates of spending and low rates of taxation) is unsustainable over the longer term." The only solution, the report counselled, was a significant and sustained commitment to saving more of current non-renewable resource revenues, with a target of saving $100 billion in the Heritage Fund by 2030.

I was persuaded by the Mintz analysis, particularly the urgent need to start a new savings process NOW, while oil and gas revenues were high and we were running budget surpluses. However, I knew from being a member of Treasury Board that a new, longer-term fiscal plan was not high on our government agenda, so I wrote the memo with the purpose of putting it on the agenda. I will let the letter speak for itself.

---

10 August, 2008

To: Hon. Lloyd Snelgrove, President of Treasury Board

From: Hon. Ted Morton, Minister of SRD

Re: Responding to the Mintz Report (Report and
         Recommendations of the Alberta Financial Investment
         and Planning Advisory Commission)

Xc.   Premier's Office; Iris Evans, Minister of Finance

I am writing to request that Caucus be given the opportunity to discuss how we as a Government should respond to the recommendations of the Mintz Report. Having now had the time to read and think about the Report, I am persuaded by its arguments that the GOA does face an

---

impending structural fiscal deficit and that the best way to avert this is by creating and prioritizing a rigorous annual savings program.

I would note that similar analyses and recommendations for increased GOA savings have been delivered by the Canada West Foundation ("Alberta's Piggy Bank: Investing Natural Resource Wealth," 2005); the Alberta Chamber of Resources ("Vision 20/20," 2006); and the C.D. Howe Institute ("Greater Savings Required: How Alberta Can Achieve Fiscal Sustainability from its Resource Revenues," 2008).

I realize that not everyone in Caucus may hold this opinion, but given that the principle of fiscal responsibility is at the core of what it means to be a Progressive Conservative in Alberta, I think this issue deserves a full airing in Caucus. I would ask that you work with the Premier's office to get it on the Caucus's Fall agenda prior to the sitting of the Legislature on October 14.

I realize that given the political pressures for current spending, adopting the kind of savings policy recommended by the Mintz Report carries some short-term political risks to our Government. However, I think these are manageable, given that the Liberal Party of Alberta has consistently supported increased GOA savings.

I think that we could further mitigate potential political risk by taking this issue to the voters of Alberta in a referendum at the next (2010) Alberta municipal election day. We could use the next two, lead-up years to develop a public dialogue on the savings issue, and then give Albertans the choice between three savings options (high, low and midrange). Use of preferential balloting would in effect construct a consensus choice (whichever option gains an absolute majority of first and second preferences). Implementing the results of the Referendum is relatively risk-free, since we would only be doing "what Albertans told us they want."

I would note that the process could be relatively non-partisan, especially if we gave our own MLAs a free-vote on the issue, and then asked them to consult extensively with their constituents on which of the three savings plans they favoured. I would guess that this process would be quite popular with Albertans, and set us up well the next provincial election in 2011 or 2012. Presumably the results would also be praised by all the policy think-tanks listed above that have criticized us for not saving enough. A GOA Heritage Savings Fund with this kind of public endorsement would also be less vulnerable to attacks from the Federal Government, since such attacks would be construed as an assault on the people of Alberta, not just the Government of the day.

I offer these additional thoughts just for your consideration and an indication of what I would probably advocate if we have this discussion in Caucus. My immediate request is simply that we have such a Caucus discussion. Perhaps it could be a part of the Caucus Retreat planned for September?

Thanks for taking the time to considering my request. I would, of course, be happy to discuss this further with you, should you like.

Hope you are enjoying some down-time time here in August. I have.

Cheers,

Ted

The Mintz Report was never brought to either cabinet or caucus for discussion. By the time anyone got around to reading my August 10 memo, the subprime debt, asset-backed securities meltdown was in full collapse, and so were the GOA revenues. As noted above, the Q1 projection of an $8.5 billion surplus for Budget 2008 ended up as an $852 million deficit.

And Budget 2009 looked even bleaker. As introduced in March 2009, it projected revenues to decline by 11 percent, led by resource revenues, which were projected to be $6.4 billion LESS than just the year before. While increases in spending were kept to 3.2 percent, this still translated into a projected deficit of $4.7 billion. After having publicly boasted for years, "Balanced budgets: That's the rule in Alberta," we quietly amended the *Fiscal Responsibility Act* to allow a deficit. Tellingly, two of the big drivers for increased expenditures were higher salaries for teachers (the result of the 2008 pre-election contract) and the $4 billion commitment for CCS and GreenTRIP (made at the 2008 Stampede Caucus)

A small victory for me was that I was finally able to persuade caucus to eliminate the home heating gas rebates that Klein had brought in to help ensure a win in the 2001 provincial election. As a biweekly columnist in the *Calgary Herald*, I had strongly criticized these rebates when they were first adopted.[18] In 2006, when they were up for renewal, I unsuccessfully argued against them in caucus. The largest beneficiaries were wealthier families who owned larger homes and those who kept their thermostats cranked up too high. I knew, because I represented many of these people who lived in their "McMansions" in my Springbank and Bearspaw constituencies. But by 2009, it was only a token victory. The GOA had already doled out over $2 billion in rebates, and by 2009, with the price of natural gas plummeting, no one qualified for rebates anyhow.

The only bright spot in Budget 2009 was that we could point to the $17 billion we had saved in the Sustainability Fund, and tell Albertans that this "rainy day account" could tide us over for two more years of deficits without falling back into debt. We also promised we would be "back in the black" by 2012, in time for the next election.

By the end of first quarter, the numbers were even worse. Revenues were down another $2.1 billion, thanks to the continuing collapse of natural gas prices. This meant that our projected deficit for the year was now a staggering $6.9 billion. It was against this depressing backdrop that I wrote my second memo to the president of Treasury Board, with copies to the premier and the minister of finance. Again, I will let the letter speak for itself. The tone of this letter was much less polite than the first.

---

5 September, 2009

To: Hon. Lloyd Snelgrove, President of Treasury Board

From: Hon. Ted Morton, Minister of SRD

Re: Request for Caucus Discussion of Legislated Spending Cap and Restrictions and mandated Savings

Xc.   Premier's Office; Iris Evans, Minister of Finance

Lloyd, attached is copy of a memo that I sent a year ago, requesting the opportunity for a Caucus discussion of the Mintz Report's recommendations re GOA spending and savings, and its prediction of a pending structural deficit.

Well, we never had this discussion and now we have not a pending deficit, but actual deficits—two and counting. Accordingly, I would like to repeat my request for a Caucus discussion of these issues, per my 2008 memo.

Rather than focus on a savings strategy (Mintz Report), I recommend that we focus on legislated limits on spending. These are two sides of the same policy coin, i.e. the more we save, the less we spend, and vice-versa. But given the current state of our finances, savings is not a short-term option.

More specifically, I would request that we discuss limiting annual spending increases to the combined population growth and inflation rates for the preceding year, as recommended by the Canadian

---

Taxpayers Federation (among others). This is a relatively easy initiative since this is what we did in Budget 09-10. The challenge/opportunity is not just to have this rule as a one-off, but to entrench it into our budget process. My reasons for us to lead a public debate followed by a referendum in the 2010 civic election apply equally to this initiative. (See last year's memo.)

Had we adopted this approach in Budget 2005-06 forward (the year after we paid off Alberta's debt and the first year I was an MLA), we would still be running a SURPLUS not a deficit today. Under this spending cap, we could have averaged c. 6% annual spending increases over the past five budgets, rather than the 11.5% we actually spent.

Please note, this is not intended to "blame" you or the Premier. The problem goes back to the last Klein years, and I too have been at the table for the last five budgets. We are all to blame. Maybe we thought it worked for Ralph so it would work for us. Well, it hasn't and it won't, and it's time we as a Caucus and Government have a frank discussion about how we are going to dig ourselves out of the deficit ditch we've dug for ourselves. It's not good enough to talk about more "belt tightening," cross our fingers and hope for higher gas revenues. The latter aren't coming any time soon. (See copy of my memo to Premier's Office re replacing gas with bitumen.)

I know you have a lot on your plate right now, but I believe it would be a big mistake for us to focus solely on our short-term budget plans for 2010–11 without also making plans for a medium-term road to fiscal recovery. Indeed, today's budget crisis should make it easier for us to agree upon—and Albertans to accept—a much more disciplined spending/savings regime for the coming decades. (i.e. the Obama line: a crisis this big is too good to waste!)

I will miss Cabinet on Wednesday, but am available in Edmonton next Monday, Sept. 14. If you want to talk this week, I would also be pleased to discuss any of this over the phone. (Eric has my contact info.)

Thank you for taking the time to consider my concerns.

Cheers,

Ted

BUDGET 2010 AND THE WILDROSE CHALLENGE

The following four months were eventful, both inside and outside of caucus. Our massive 2008 electoral coalition was rapidly disintegrating. Unhappiness with the New Royalty Framework had spread beyond the Calgary towers and into the fields and small energy-dependent communities, where thousands of workers were now being laid off. Job losses were compounded by the effects of the global economic recession, which by now had driven the WTI price of oil from $148/barrel down to $75. Rightly or wrongly, Ed Stelmach and the NRF were being blamed for all of this. Suddenly, the Wildrose Party was polling higher than the other opposition parties. On September 14, Wildrose Party leader Paul Hinman won the by-election in Calgary Glenmore, previously a safe PC seat. The PC candidate finished a distant third, even behind the Liberals.

Inside caucus, there was growing unhappiness with our ballooning deficit and the perceived insularity of the Stelmach inner circle. The PC Party's AGM was scheduled for November 7 in Red Deer, and as required by the party's constitution, there would be a mandatory leadership review vote. Fanned by media speculation, there were rumours of a caucus revolt, and the prospect that, as with Ralph Klein just three years earlier, the PCs would use the leadership review to dump an increasingly unpopular leader.

The premier's office clearly sensed these risks. Led by Ron Glen, Stelmach's chief of staff, they had organized our fall calendar accordingly. A two-day caucus retreat was planned for mid-September, followed by a two-day cabinet retreat the following week. These were intended to allow us to develop some consensus on how best to proceed, and to be able to present a united front when the fall session of the Alberta legislature opened on October 26, and, perhaps more importantly, at the AGM on November 7.

Ron Glen opened the caucus retreat with an overview of the political landscape. Reflecting on our humiliating third place finish in the Calgary-Glenmore by-election a week earlier, Glen told us what we all already knew: that our principal opponent was no longer the Liberal Party but the Wildrose. To thwart this growing threat on our right flank, he continued, we had to deal with two key issues: the budget deficit and health care delivery. What followed was a two-hour open-ended discussion—really a giant venting session—during which almost every member of caucus gave their two cents' worth of advice.

The gist of the conversation was whether to "stay the course" or change. Policy-wise, these options roughly translated into continue spending or cut spending. By my count, the speakers fell roughly into four equal groups. Led by Ron Liepert's warning "not to overreact" to our by-election loss, about a quarter urged continued spending on education, health care, seniors, and "the vulnerable." As Liepert put it, the PCs are a "centre party [and we should not become] a right-of-centre party."

Another quarter—which included me—stressed the need for serious cuts to program spending to staunch our ballooning deficits and to win back "fiscal conservatives." Our losses were not just "a perception," but a reality. Drilling rigs and investment capital were leaving our province, and disillusioned conservatives were leaving our party. The rest of the speakers were equally divided between those who just said they were going to be defeated in the next election unless we did something different and those who were all over the map without any coherent or decipherable message. (As was often the case, this last group included Raj Sherman and Iris Evans.)

The retreat ended with a strong plea by Ken Kowalski that MLAs should try to ensure "loyalty to the leader" at the upcoming AGM. What did this mean in practice? Luke Ouellette, another Stelmach loyalist, made it clear: each MLA must ensure that the delegates from their constituency association supported the premier. There was no follow-up discussion of this plea (or order?), perhaps because the Kowalski-Ouellette message appeared to be orchestrated from the premier's office. But at the next break, it was discussed in the halls and there was pushback from some MLAs. I certainly didn't agree. Rather than trying to win back disillusioned PC supporters with policy changes—like more fiscal restraint—we would in effect be kicking them out of the party. I remarked to one group of MLAs that if I told my Foothills-Rocky View board that we had to pre-screen delegates to the AGM, they would all resign.

A week later, at the cabinet retreat, the divisions that were latent in the caucus retreat now became more explicit and more personal. I continued to push for a new spending limitations rule as part of our next budget. "Where are we most vulnerable?" I asked rhetorically. On the Right. We need to focus on reducing spending and the deficit. If that requires breaking the 2007 contract with the ATA (teachers' union), then do it. The marginal voters we need to win back care more about our budget problems than about making teachers happy.

A fellow minister quickly challenged me. "Teachers supported us last time. We have to keep our word." My response: "Of course the teachers voted for us in 2008. We gave them $2 billion for their unfunded pension liability and a five-year contract." This was too much for a second minister: "Ted," he growled, "I'm going to take you on." He re-asserted that not only do the teachers support us [the PC Party] but so too do many civil servants. "We can ignore the old Social Credit/Reform Party rump," he told cabinet. "They are not a threat." My response was true but not very statesmanlike: If we were to follow this advice, I told cabinet, we would be the first small-c conservative party in Canada—probably in the world—to base their electoral coalition on public sector unions.

The cabinet retreat ended the same as the caucus retreat the week before, with no resolution of these competing perspectives. As was his way, Stelmach used his closing remarks to try to minimize these conflicts by embracing both sides. Going forward, he told us, we would focus on seven priorities. One was to ensure a balanced budget within three years (by 2012). But others included "protecting the most vulnerable" and not reducing our capital/infrastructure budget.[19] And so we staggered on.

LEADERSHIP REVIEW

On October 21, I received a personal phone call from Chief of Staff Ron Glen. He requested that I phone Don Braid and Rick Bell, the political columnists at the *Calgary Herald* and *Calgary Sun* respectively, and "set the record straight": that I supported the premier and that media reports that I was organizing for a leadership contest were false. I told him that I would be happy to do the latter, since I wasn't organizing anything. But, I added, I did not have much interest in publicly defending policies that I didn't support.

I pointed out that I had intentionally avoided media interviews over the preceding weeks, and that the one time I was cornered by a reporter, at the PC Party's Leader's Dinner in Red Deer, I had publicly defended the premier on CBC Radio. I told Glen that that he was overreacting. Stelmach was not going to lose the leadership vote, because most of the hardcore anti-Stelmach types had already left the party and would not even be at the AGM. I intended to be an observer not a player, and to let the leadership review take its course. This did not sit well with Glen. Nor, in fact, did it play out that way.

Over the weekend, I weighed my options. I could offer to trade my public support for Stelmach in return for the premier agreeing to drop two policy initiatives that I opposed—Bill 50, the controversial and expensive new North-South electricity transmission lines; and "hunt-farms," allowing ranchers who raised domestic elk to sell "hunts" to shoot their large bull elk. Or I could bargain for a future cabinet post—Finance or Energy. But such "trades" had a timing problem: my endorsement had to come first. Once Stelmach survived the leadership review vote, there would be no penalty for not delivering his side of the deal. This could be solved if I demanded the cabinet appointment before the AGM, but this would cost either Mel Knight or Iris Evans their cabinet posts, something I doubted Stelmach would do to such loyal supporters.

The other option was simply to remain silent. But this had its own risks. If Stelmach were to survive the leadership review—as I thought he would—there could be retribution. I had a number of policy initiatives underway that I cared about—the Land Use Framework, the Recreational Access Management Program (RAMP), working with Upland Birds Alberta (UBA) to re-establish Alberta's pheasant habitat and hunting; the trout pond at the Bow Habitat Station—all of which could be sidelined by the premier's office. Or he could simply fire me altogether. In my mind, there was no clear path forward. This all changed quickly the next week.

Don Braid wrote another column reporting that former leadership rival Jim Dinning had publicly endorsed Stelmach, but then noted the "conspicuous silence" of Ted Morton. The following week, on the opening day of the fall session of the legislature, the media scrum was waiting for me, and they wanted an answer. Remaining silent was no longer an option. Speaking carefully, I said that it would be a mistake for the party to ignore our loss in the Calgary-Glenmore by-election (won by the Wildrose Party), but that it would be a bigger mistake to plunge the party into a leadership contest at this time. I declared that I would be voting against a leadership review at the AGM. And, for the record, I did.

BECOMING FINANCE MINISTER

While Stelmach survived the leadership review vote, his fortunes—and thus the party's—continued to sink. A *Calgary Herald* poll published December 11 showed Wildrose leading the PCs 39 percent to 25 percent. In rural Alberta—our traditional stronghold—we were even further behind—44 percent to 25 percent. These numbers fuelled media speculation that a cabinet shuffle was imminent and that some PC MLAs were considering crossing the floor to join Wildrose. In less than a month, both these predictions would come true.

It was in this context that in mid-December I received a message from the premier's office asking me to come down to his third-floor office before I departed for the Christmas–New Year's break. As I had so few private meetings with Stelmach, I knew something was afoot. In a friendly but serious tone, he proceeded to tell me what we all knew: that Mel Knight had become a lightning rod for oilpatch unhappiness with the New Royalty Framework and had to be replaced. A cabinet shuffle was imminent. Would I be willing to serve as his new minister of energy?

My response was simple and direct. Of course, I would love to be the Alberta minister of energy. Who wouldn't? Even under the current conditions. But, I continued, there were two or three others who could competently do that job, and what we desperately needed was a new minister of finance. For this position, I said, there were only two options: Doug Horner or myself. Both Stelmach and the party needed political love in Calgary, and in Calgary, no one even knew who Doug Horner was. So realistically, I was his only choice.

Stelmach was characteristically noncommittal. He thanked me for my frankness and my support and said he would be back in touch after the break. The next day we left for Ventura, California, where we had rented a house to spend the holidays with our three children, all of whom were then working in Los Angeles.

Three weeks later, my cellphone rang. It was Ed Stelmach. A new cabinet would be announced within forty-eight hours. Would I be willing to be his new minister of finance? Yes, I replied immediately, but on one condition: Would my mandate be to ensure that we had Alberta's budget "back in the black" by 2012, in time for our next election? Yes, Stelmach replied, that's why I'm giving you this job. That was good enough for me, and so the deal was done.

The new cabinet was announced on January 12. In addition to me going to Finance, Mel Knight was moved out of Energy and into SRD—my previous portfolio. Liepert—a Calgary MLA—replaced Knight at Energy. Iris Evans, a Stelmach loyalist, was given a soft landing at International and Intergovernmental Relations, with little work and lots of travel. Two other Stelmach loyalists kept their cabinet posts: Doug Horner, Advanced Education; and President of Treasury Board Lloyd Snelgrove,. Horner was also promoted to deputy premier. However, two other Stelmach loyalists, George Groeneveld and Fred Horne, were unceremoniously dropped. A year later, both were early members of the dump-Stelmach faction.

The media's reaction to the cabinet shuffle was consistent and predictable: a premier with sinking support in the polls and in his party tries to reverse the trend. As for my appointment, commentators uniformly described it as an attempt to fend off the Wildrose challenge on our right flank. One, however, gave it a different twist—one that turned out to be prescient:

> Premier Ed Stelmach made a daring move last week in an effort to shore up sagging support for his government. He appointed his most dogmatic cabinet minister, Ted Morton, to the finance portfolio and then told him to take on Ottawa because Albertans are tired of having so much of their tax money funneled into equalization payments for other provinces.

> As the recession took hold and Stelmach's government became more and more unpopular, it was widely rumoured that Morton would defect to the upstart Wildrose Alliance, which was surging in the polls ... . But Morton played his cards cleverly and managed to become such a powerful player that Stelmach could ill afford to ignore him. Now he is in a position to eclipse Stelmach if he so chooses, and stunt the growth of the Wildrose Alliance. ... Morton once said that he is "every liberal's worst nightmare—a right-winger with a PhD." But his star is rising so quickly he could soon become Stelmach's worst nightmare.[20]

I was pleased with my new post. Politically, I knew I was taking a risk. Not only was I tying myself more closely to the Stelmach record, but in less than a month I would have to deliver Budget 2010. That budget was already at the printers and contained the largest projected annual deficit—$4.7 billion—in Alberta's history.[21] So much for my reputation for fiscal responsibility! Still, I thought the challenge that lay ahead was also an opportunity—not just for me but for Albertans. And I was encouraged by the premier's words announcing the new cabinet:

> I have promised Albertans that we will be back in the black in three years, and I have not wavered from that commitment. My new team will tackle Alberta's fiscal challenges with determination.[22]

If only it had turned out that way!

7

Finance Minister (2010)

BUDGET 2010

Stelmach's new cabinet—with me as minister of finance and enterprise—was announced on January 12, 2010. As mentioned, the 2010 budget had already been sent to the printers, so I knew that I would soon be introducing the largest projected deficit—$4.7 billion—in Alberta's history.[1] What a legacy! On February 10, I did just that.[2] Publicly, I tried to make the best of what I privately thought was a bad deal.

My budget speech—"Striking the Right Balance"—employed all the usual clichés that politicians use to deliver the message of short-term pain for long-term gain. Running a deficit in the middle of the worst global recession since the late 1980s did not make us any different than any other province or the federal government. What did make us different, I emphasized, was that our new debt was paying for long-term capital infrastructure, not day-to-day operations. And I repeated the premier's promise that we would be back to a balanced budget by 2012.

Politically, the budget is a big event in Alberta, and quite a few of my friends came to Edmonton see me deliver the annual budget speech. There was a public reception following my speech. We then held a private party afterward, at which Sam and Kristine Armstrong presented me with a four-foot-long authentic samurai sword. The unspoken message was clear: It was time to start cutting spending.

I spent the next eleven months trying to do just that, with the samurai sword on my desk. My goal was to develop a budget for 2011 that would serve as a stepping stone to a balanced budget in 2012—just in time for the next scheduled election. This was a very public commitment Stelmach had made, and one I was determined to deliver. Unfortunately, it did not turn out that way. The how and why of this is recounted in the next chapter, "How I Unbecame Finance Minister."

In this chapter, I recount the other major issues that occupied my year as finance minister: successfully blocking the federal government's attempts to replace the Alberta Securities Regulator and to expand the Canada Pension Plan, but failing to stop the most expensive fiscal mistake in Alberta history—the North West Upgrader. Looking back, it is ironic that I achieved more policy success outside of the PC cabinet than inside.

THE MINISTER'S CAVE

One of the surprising consequences of becoming a minister of the Crown is that you suddenly spend very little time with your fellow MLAs, and much more time with your senior civil servants and the stakeholders whose interests are directly affected by your new ministry. The only MLAs you regularly interact with are the other ministers. And if you're the finance minister, this means them asking you for budget increases for their departments and you telling them, "No way."

The explanation for a new minister's schedule is simple. The first several months are spent getting up to speed on all the policy files and priority issues that he or she is now responsible for. As minister, you are now the boss. But typically, you know very little about your new business. This irony is compounded by the fact that your instructor in this process is your deputy minister. In theory, of course, he works for you. But in practice, knowledge is power. (There is an inside joke amongst senior bureaucrats: that the ministers they work for are just "renters," i.e. , they come and they go.) This means countless hours in briefing meetings with your new deputy minister and his senior executives. In my first two months at Finance, 80 percent of my time was spent with my new administrative team. It also gave me a new appreciation for accountants!

As for the stakeholders, they all want face time with the new minister as soon as possible. They have been working with and sharing what they consider to be important policy information with the relevant civil servants in your department for years. Now they want to tell it to you face to face. And you had better give them some time. If they become unhappy with you, they are quick to go either to the premier's office or to the media to tell them what a poor job you are doing.

One of these meetings I initiated myself. I requested a meeting with Jim Dinning. As Ralph Klein's new finance minister in 1993, Dinning had been given a similar assignment—to slay the GOA's deficit and debt dragon. I thought that I could learn from Dinning's experience. But I was not sure if he would agree to meet with me, as our relationship had become quite adversarial by the end of the 2006 PC leadership race. To Jim's credit, he did meet with me, and his advice was helpful: When asking ministers to cut their budgets, don't accept NO for an answer. I left our breakfast meeting with a new appreciation for Jim Dinning.

Seventeen years later in 2023, Jim accepted Premier Danielle Smith's request to lead her newly created Alberta Pension Engagement Panel.[3] The creation of a separate Alberta Pension Plan had been a centrepiece of my Alberta Agenda, a.k.a. Firewall, that Dinning had so strongly criticized in 2006. When asked about this, Dinning replied with a smile: It shows that I'm smart enough to change my mind. So now I respect Jim Dinning even more!

Some of the stakeholders I met with that year were members of an informal advisory committee that had been assembled by Jack Mintz. In 2008, Jack had left the C.D. Howe Institute in Toronto and had moved to Alberta to form the new School of Public Policy at the University of Calgary. With Jack now in Alberta and me as the new Alberta finance minister, our communications became frequent.

This advisory committee included some of the most influential business leaders in Alberta.[4] Some I knew already through PC Party politics and my own 2006 leadership fundraising efforts. It would be difficult to create a list of more successful Alberta CEOs. Its composition was heavily weighted toward Calgary and the oil and gas sector. But that was fine with me. That's what had powered Alberta's post-Leduc economic boom for the past five decades. Without oil and gas, "Cowgary" would still have looked like a poorer version of Regina.

I met individually with most of these individuals over the course of 2010. Unfortunately, the first time we assembled as group—December 7, for a dinner in Calgary—was also the last. (To understand why, you will have to read the next chapter.)

FIGHTING THE FEDS I: SECURITIES REGULATOR

One of the first files my new deputy minister, Tim Wiles, put on my desk dealt with the federal government's recently announced plan to create a new national securities regulator. Historically, securities regulation has always been deemed to fall under provincial jurisdiction. Each province has had its own securities regulator. Over time, the provinces have worked together to create a "Passport System" that harmonizes rules and standards and provides for "mutual recognition" of each other's decisions. The plan being proposed by Ottawa would replace all of these provincial regulators with a single, new national securities regulator located where else but in Toronto. The rationale for this change was that the Passport System was an inefficient and outdated "patchwork" of ten different systems and that to stay competitive, Canada needed a single national regulator, like the Securities and Exchange Commission (SEC) in the US.

Predictably, Quebec immediately opposed this transfer of power to Ottawa, and had already announced that it would challenge its constitutional validity in court. A month before my appointment, my predecessor at Finance, Iris Evans, had announced that Alberta also opposed the plan and would intervene to support Quebec's legal challenge. Now the file was mine to manage.

The issue was a perfect fit for me. I had been writing and campaigning against federal overreach for years. In addition, just a few years earlier, I had published a study on how both levels of government use strategic litigation to protect or expand their existing policy jurisdictions. My lead example was how former Alberta Premier Peter Lougheed had used Alberta's reference power to successfully challenge a new federal tax on exported natural gas, one component of Pierre Trudeau's hated Nation Energy Program (NEP).[5] Here was my opportunity to do the same.

In February, I announced that the Alberta government would use our reference power to challenge the constitutional legality of the federal plan.[6] I contacted Quebec Minister of Finance and Revenue Raymond Bachand and asked him to intervene to support our challenge. Not only did he agree, but we soon worked out plans for him to visit Alberta and for me to go to Quebec. We believed these visits would generate public awareness that we were working together to protect our respective provinces. I subsequently hosted Bachand at lunchtime Chamber of Commerce meetings in Calgary and Edmonton on September 13 and 14.

We then sent a co-signed letter to other provincial finance ministers urging them not to feel compelled to sign on by September 30, as requested by federal Minister of Finance Jim Flaherty. We pointed out that that no courts had yet even heard evidence as to the constitutionality of the federal proposal. In a joint press release, we declared:

> The deadline imposed by Ottawa is completely arbitrary and is just an attempt to put pressure on provinces and push its agenda forward in the face of mounting opposition. ... There are other provinces, besides Alberta and Quebec, that do not support the federal proposal and others that have not taken a position, and I would urge these provinces not to feel pressured into signing something that will be taken by Ottawa as a sign of support.[7]

To the best of my knowledge, this was the first and last time that a minister in the Alberta government issued a press release whose header included the official symbols of both the Alberta and Quebec governments. As I explain below, I hope it will not be the last.

I also worked closely with Bill Rice, at that time the president and CEO of the Alberta Securities Commission. Bill and his board strongly opposed the federal initiative, as did almost all of the junior oil and gas companies in Western Canada. Our argument was simple: "What works on Bay Street doesn't work in Montreal, and doesn't work out in Vancouver or Calgary. ... Our success has been in raising capital to reflect regional needs and regional economies."[8]

Canada's Passport System was already recognized as among the best in the world. The OECD and the World Bank Group had rated it ahead of both the United States and the United Kingdom—both of whom have a single, national regulator. And for two years in a row, the Milken Institute had ranked Canada first in terms of having the "best access to capital."[9] Our message was simple: If it ain't broke, don't fix it.

For Alberta, the Passport System also contributed to economic diversification. Since the 1960s, Calgary has become the financial services hub for Canada's energy sector. The job-multiplying effect of having a province-based securities commission was well documented in both Alberta and Quebec. As

I wrote in the *Calgary Herald*, "If we let the Alberta Securities Commission get scooped up and transferred to Toronto we can also say goodbye to thousands of spinoff jobs in investment, banking, law, accounting and financial analysts."[10]

We had reliable evidence that the Passport System already accomplished everything that the proposed single national regulator claimed it would, plus additional advantages for each province. Our arguments were supported by Jeffrey MacIntosh, the Toronto Stock Exchange Chair in Capital Markets at the Faculty of Law, University of Toronto;[11] and also by Thomas Courchene, one of Canada's best-known economists, who has held senior public policy positions at both Queen's University and the Institute for Research on Public Policy in Montreal.[12]

Legally, we had a century of constitutional precedent on our side. Securities regulation had always been deemed to fall under the provinces' section 92(13) jurisdiction over "property and civil rights." Allowing the proposed new federal plan to proceed would also set a dangerous new precedent with repercussions far beyond the regulation of securities. Neither Alberta nor Quebec was going to let this happen without a battle.

The good news: We won. Both the Alberta[13] and Quebec[14] courts of appeal ruled that the proposed new federal regulator was an unconstitutional invasion of provincial jurisdiction. Ottawa, of course, appealed its losses. But the Supreme Court of Canada affirmed the lower courts' rulings.[15] In a unanimous decision, the Supreme Court stated:[16]

> It is a fundamental principle of federalism that both federal and provincial powers must be respected, and one power may not be used in a manner that effectively eviscerates another. ... Accepting Canada's interpretation of the general trade and commerce power would disrupt rather than maintain that balance. Parliament cannot regulate the whole of the securities system simply because aspects of it have a national dimension.

So if all three courts found that the federal plan was clearly unconstitutional, why did Ottawa even proceed with this initiative? The answer, of course, is politics. The federal minister of finance was the late Jim Flaherty. Flaherty was from Toronto, and a Bay Street veteran. Home of the Toronto Stock Exchange (TSX), Bay Street had always wanted a single national regulator, but only if it were located in Toronto. Indeed, the Ontario finance minister at the time, Dwight Duncan, had said more than once that if the head office were not in Toronto, then Ontario was not interested. So all the other policy arguments notwithstanding, what Flaherty was doing was bringing home the bacon to his constituents.

This points to the key takeaway from this episode. It is another example of Alberta's vulnerability to the political calculus that shapes decision making in Ottawa. Remember who the prime minister was during this entire affair: Stephen Harper. That this could happen in a Stephen Harper Conservative majority government shows that when push comes to shove in Ottawa—when money and votes are on the table—Alberta gets marginalized. And it doesn't much matter which political party is in power federally. It's the electoral math. Since 1968, the Liberals have never needed any of Alberta's thirty-four seats to form majority governments. The two Conservative governments—Mulroney (1984–1993) and Harper (2006–2015)—simply took Western seats for granted. No party takes Ontario and its 121 seats for granted.

A second important takeaway is the value and importance of having Quebec as an ally when Alberta goes to the Supreme Court. I doubt that Alberta would have prevailed in this case without Quebec's support as an intervenor. The Supreme Court explains its decisions in terms of legal arguments. But judges' choices of which legal arguments to use are shaped by the broader political context and considerations.

When it comes to decisions involving the federal division of powers—as it did in this case—Supreme Court judges are careful not to make rulings that could ignite separatist sentiment in Quebec. Prior to the court's ruling, an op-ed in the *Globe and Mail* warned that if the Supreme Court were to support the federal government's new plan, "the storm that is already brewing in Quebec could turn into a Category 5 hurricane."[17]

While Alberta and Quebec are on the opposite sides of the arguments about equalization and fiscal transfers, Quebec has been a reliable ally of Alberta in federalism disputes with Ottawa. In the 1980s, Alberta Premier Peter Lougheed worked closely with Quebec Premier René Lévesque—the leader of the Quebec separatist party—to protect provincial autonomy from the centralizing thrust of Pierre Trudeau's *Constitution Act, 1982*. Together, Lougheed and Lévesque successfully demanded the addition of section 92A to Canada's constitution—affirming "exclusive" provincial jurisdiction over the exploration, development, conservation, and management of natural resources and hydroelectricity.

More recently, Quebec intervened to support Alberta's constitutional challenges to the Liberals' new carbon tax[18] (2021) and Bill C-69—the *Impact Assessment Act* (2023), or as its critics call it, the "no more pipelines ever" act.[19] Quebec Premier François Legault has stated that "it should be up to the provinces to decide" how to manage their carbon emissions. "We have often seen the federal government step on the jurisdictions of the provinces. We must be prudent in health, in education ... we must jealously guard the powers of the provinces."[20]

This attitude makes Quebec a reliable ally for Alberta in the politics of Canadian federalism. Governments often use the reference power to go to the courts to protect or to expand their jurisdiction. The constitution does not speak for itself. In the end, it means what the judges say it means. So governments can and do attempt to amend constitutional rules through litigation and judicial interpretation rather than through the formal amending process. In political science, this is called "strategic litigation." Lougheed used it successfully to challenge Ottawa's natural gas export tax in the 1980s. And we used it successfully to block Ottawa's attempt to impose a new national securities regulator in 2010–11. Going forward, Alberta governments should remember that their chance of success in such cases is enhanced if they have Quebec as an ally.

FIGHTING THE FEDS II: PENSION REFORM

By January 28, I had been moved into my new, much larger office on the third floor of the Alberta Legislature Building, and was meeting with my new deputy minister, Tim Wiles, and his executive team. The stack of policy briefing papers they left on my desk was more than a foot high. But the file that immediately caught my attention was the federal government's new initiative to address perceived shortcomings in Canadians' savings for retirement.

One of the options being floated was to expand the Canada Pension Plan. A central plank of my 2006 leadership campaign was for Alberta to withdraw from the CPP and to create our own Alberta Pension Plan (APP), like Quebec. The reasoning was simple. As a consequence of Albertans' younger average ages and higher rates of workforce participation, we pay into CPP much more than we receive back. A recent study found that between 2009 and 2018, the net annual difference was $2.941 billion each year.[21] That's right: $2.9 billion each year. A 2023 study commissioned by the UCP governments of Kenney and Smith found that Albertans' total net contributions to the CPP account for $334 billion, or 53 percent of all CPP assets.[22]

With an APP, this money would stay in Alberta, and could be used to reduce premium payments for both employers and employees; increase retirement benefits; or some combination of both. The last thing that I wanted to do as Alberta's new finance minister was increase the net fiscal drain to Ottawa.

The federal initiative was driven by a new concern over the adequacy of Canadians' savings for retirement. Canada compared well with the US and European democracies when it came to income security in retirement. But the 2008–9 stock market crash had erased a lot of savings, both in pensions and private savings such as RRSPs. Ottawa had struck a task force to study this issue and to report back to all federal and provincial finance ministers at their semi-annual meetings. In 2010, the first of these was scheduled for PEI in June and the second in Kananaskis, Alberta, in December. Fortunately for me—and for Albertans—the federal task force was chaired by Dr. Jack Mintz.

Mintz's studies found that when it came to savings for retirement, the most vulnerable were Canadians who worked in the private sector, especially those in smaller companies; and the self-employed. Nearly three-quarters of private sector workers had no employer pension plans. The least at risk were government employees, who enjoyed secure pension plans, plus their RRSPS and other savings. Also at risk were younger workers—those in their twenties and thirties—who were not saving as much as they needed for retirement.

More specifically, those most at risk were those earning between $40,000 to $100,00 annually. Those earning over $100,000 did not need any help. Those earning less than $40,000 were helped by top-up programs like Old Age Security (OAS) and the Guaranteed Income Supplement (GIS). This suggested that an efficient response would be to target this middle-income group and leave the others alone.

What were the possible solutions? The simplest was just to expand the scope of the CPP. It covers everyone who works and is mandatory. It would require higher premiums for employers and employees, and/or raising the ceiling of annual income that is subject to mandatory CPP contributions. This option was supported by the Canadian Labour Congress, the Canadian Association of Retired Persons, and the Federal Superannuates National Association.

The CPP option was opposed by several other stakeholder groups for a variety of reasons. The Canadian Federation of Independent Businesses (CFIB) argued that given the fragility of Canada's economic recovery from the 2008-9 recession, now was not the time to impose what would in effect be a mandatory payroll tax on all businesses.[23] The CPP option would mean higher costs for employers, which would deter new investment and consequently slow Canada's economic recovery. The CFIB recommended policy changes that would incentivize increased private savings outside the CPP. The C.D. Howe Institute opposed the CCP option for the same reasons. It recommended changing the RRSP rules to bring them up to levels already enjoyed by civil servants and politicians. This could be done by increasing the contribution limits from 18 percent to 34 percent of earned income and increasing the maximum annual contribution from $22,000 to $34,000.

Privately, Mintz had told me that the real battle was between pension funds and insurance companies. The former don't have to pay either GST or income taxes, while the latter do. Expanding the CPP would see the private sector taxables further squeezed by the mostly public sector non-taxables— thereby increasing the latter's influence over private sector corporate decision making.

Last but not least, Alberta's senior Finance officials had been working with their counterparts in BC and Saskatchewan on an alternative plan: a joint, voluntary, private sector defined-contribution plan—one that would supplement the CPP, not replace it. It would not be mandatory and there would be no government liabilities.

As I tried to absorb all of this, I was leaning toward a private sector, voluntary solution—one that was more targeted to help those most at risk. The CPP option seemed like another example of federal overreach. But I was looking forward to a vigorous discussion of all options with my federal and provincial counterparts.

This all came to a crashing end two days before I was scheduled to depart for PEI. With no notice to the rest of us, federal Minister of Finance Jim Flaherty and Ontario Minister of Finance Dwight Duncan released public letters endorsing the CPP option. This caught me totally by surprise. In my January briefings, I'd been told that neither Ottawa nor Ontario was interested in the CPP option. I was also angry. The whole purpose of going to Charlottetown was to discuss the pros and cons of each option, not to rubber stamp something that Ottawa and Toronto had already decided.

I called a press conference and declared that Alberta would oppose any moves to increase the scope and size of the CPP.[24] I also noted that "it would have been much more helpful to receive [the public letters] several weeks ago rather than 48 hours before we begin to discuss these options." And just to make my unhappiness clear, I noted that I did not think it was a coincidence that both letters came out at the same time.[25]

So off I went to PEI, hoping for the best but fearing the worst. In the end, it was neither. No final decisions were made. We were hopelessly divided. I made it clear that while Alberta supported reforms to increase retirement savings, we would not support the CPP option. I repeated the arguments that a more targeted response was needed. My only firm allies were Saskatchewan and Quebec. But there was not much enthusiasm for the new Ottawa-Ontario proposal, and no consensus on what a better alternative might be.

To my surprise, Flaherty seemed open to alternatives. At one point, he actually said that he was "open to deferring the CPP option to two or three years down the road." I began to wonder if he had been so busy with other responsibilities that the entire federal proposal had been written by his bureaucrats with little to no input from him. Maybe he could be persuaded to change his mind? I decided that over the next six months, before we would meet again in Kananaskis, I would try to do just that.

Unfortunately, I found that I could not give the retirement income issue the time it deserved. It was now being crowded out of my agenda by other, more pressing business. The budget process for 2011 began in earnest after July, and as recounted in the next chapter, for me it was all consuming. I was also trying to stop Stelmach from signing off on the North West Upgrader project, and to stop Mel Knight from approving the Micrex mine project in the Crowsnest Pass area (see chapter 5). I failed in the former but succeeded in the latter. All of this left little time to rally support for an alternative to the CPP enhancement option.

However, thanks to my deputy minister and his staff, we did maintain communications with both Ottawa and our provincial allies—Saskatchewan and Quebec. We basically fleshed out the arguments we had made at the meeting in PEI:

- Canada's retirement income system is not broken.
- The majority of Canadians are well served by the policy status quo.
- There are definable demographics who need help.

- The scope of the solution must be tailored to match the scope of the problem.
- Expanding CPP would be overkill.
- A CPP increase would increase business costs, deter new investments, and slow Canada's economic recovery.
- In the current economy, job creation is more important than retirement income.
- It's not just a demographics issue but also an issue of intergenerational fairness.
- The CPP is unfair to younger Canadian workers, whose premiums are now being used to pay for their parents' generation's retirement.
- Younger Canadian workers should be given the freedom and responsibility for how best to plan their savings strategies.
- Many if not most would prefer home ownership to the CPP.
- There are several voluntary, private sector savings options that could meet this need.

Would this be enough to persuade Minister Flaherty to abandon the CPP option? On my drive out to Kananaskis, I had my fingers crossed.

The FPT finance ministers meeting was held as scheduled in Kananaskis on December 19–20. But that was the only "normal" thing about this meeting. Flaherty reversed course and announced that he now favoured Alberta's position of allowing private sector alternatives rather than increasing CPP premiums. Canada's economic recovery was still too weak, he explained, to force employers and employees to make higher CPP payments. Instead, Flaherty announced a framework for new "Pooled Registered Pension Plans" (PRPPs).[26]

The proposed PRPPs, Flaherty explained, would "make well-regulated, low-cost, private-sector pension plans accessible to millions of Canadians who have up to now not had access to such plans."[27] It would be voluntary for both employers and employees, and it would benefit those whom the current system underserved—small businesses, their employees, and the self-employed. This narrower focus was especially beneficial for Alberta's economy, given our disproportionately high number of smaller, private companies.

In addition to its policy merits, Flaherty explained that his decision to go forward with the PRPPs was because "not all provinces were on board" for CPP increases. This was a bit ironic, since the finance ministers from at least six provinces—BC, Nova Scotia, PEI, New Brunswick, and Ontario—preferred the CPP option. They later issued a joint statement asking Flaherty to still consider adopting the CPP expansion later as the economy improved.[28] Initially, Alberta and Saskatchewan had been the only provinces to oppose the expanded CPP option, but Quebec had joined us shortly after the June meeting in PEI.

Why did Flaherty change his mind? Was it the result of our six months of low-key, back-channel lobbying? Had one of my friends in Harper's PMO intervened on behalf of Alberta? Or did we win because now Quebec was asking for the same thing? Or both? I don't know the answer. But I do know that having Quebec on board helped; and it demonstrates again how strategically valuable it is for Alberta to have Quebec as an ally when we are challenging federal policies that have an adverse impact on Albertans.

The decision to go with the PRPPs and not an increase in the CPP was praised by the Canadian Taxpayers Federation (CTF) and the Canadian Federation of Independent Businesses (CFIB) but criticized by organized labour. "My big fear is that reform delayed may become reform denied," said Gil McGowan, president of the Alberta Federation of Labour.[29] If the CTF and CFIB liked it and Gil McGowan didn't, then I knew we'd made the right decision.

But the victory was bittersweet. By December 18, I had already made the decision to resign as finance minister the following month. What would happen after that was anyone's guess—and the subject of the next chapter.

FIGHTING THE PREMIER'S OFFICE: NORTH WEST UPGRADER

The third and in many ways most consequential policy issue I dealt with in 2010 was the proposed North West Upgrader.[30] In government policy, as in life, the path to hell is often paved with good intentions. And so it was with Alberta's bitumen-royalty-in-kind (BRIK) program. What had started off as a low-cost, low-risk initiative to incentivize more upgrading of bitumen in Alberta had evolved into a multi-billion dollar plan to construct a new upgrader outside of Edmonton, with the Government of Alberta—and by extension, Alberta taxpayers—holding the bag if it failed.

It began innocently enough in the first year of the Stelmach government. Oil prices were soaring to unimagined highs, and billions of dollars were going into new oil sands production. Most of these investments were to build new in situ steam-assisted gravity drainage (SAGD) operations that could access oil sands that are too deep to surface mine. Unlike in the original mining operations, the new, smaller, less capital-intensive SAGD producers were not building their own upgraders.[31] But unless new upgraders were built, the growing volumes of bitumen production would all be shipped to the US to be refined, with Alberta losing all the value-added benefits.

When Ed Stelmach became premier in 2006, almost 70 percent of the bitumen mined in Alberta was upgraded in Alberta. It was projected that this figure would drop to less than 50 percent by 2017.[32] But no one was going to invest billions of dollars in a stand-alone "merchant" upgrader in Alberta unless they had an ironclad guarantee of at least a thirty-year supply of bitumen—the estimated time required to pay off construction expenses and make a profit. Enter BRIK. Its proponents even had a catchy marketing slogan: "Refine it where you mine it!"

As first proposed under the 2007 New Royalty Framework, BRIK would require bitumen producers to give the Alberta government a portion of their actual bitumen production in lieu of paying the required royalties. Armed with its own stream of bitumen production, the GOA could in turn sign contracts with prospective merchant upgraders to guarantee them the long-term supply needed to attract investors. While integrated producers—those who had already built their own upgraders—didn't like this policy, it was popular with smaller, newer in situ companies. While novel, BRIK was not unprecedented. Earlier Alberta governments had done something similar with conventional oil and gas.

Under this original scenario, the risks to the GOA would be minimal, since it was merely acting as a middleman—collecting bitumen from existing producers and selling it for the same market price to new upgraders. All the risks of building, operating, and then selling the upgraded bitumen would be with the upgraders. The benefits of a more integrated value-added chain within Alberta would include the jobs created during the construction phase and new corporate tax revenues. As public policy, it was low risk, low cost, almost elegant. Build it—or in this case, supply it—and they will come.

At the outset, BRIK appeared poised to achieve all these objectives. Prior to the 2008 recession, five upgraders were being built or expanded and another six were being planned.[33] In all, the projects represented over $100 billion in capital investment and would have added three million barrels a day (mbd) of upgrading capacity—more than tripling the current capacity. The area east of Edmonton began to be called "Upgrader Alley" in anticipation of a Houston-like "Refinery Row."

Edmonton's euphoria was short-lived. When the 2008 financial collapse hit, oil prices plunged from $140 in July to $40 by Christmas. Investment collapsed. Only three of the five upgraders under construction in 2008 were completed, and five others were either cancelled or postponed. It became apparent that BRIK by itself was not going to build any new upgraders.

From 2007 to 2009, as minister of sustainable resources development, I had been a supporter of the early version of the BRIK program. But I was not directly involved and was only vaguely aware of the post-2008 changes. This changed when I was moved to minister of finance—and was tasked with reining in our ballooning deficits. Now I was very much involved. And the more I learned about the new deal, the more I opposed it.

Eager to keep one of the premier's signature commitments, the Stelmach government proceeded to sweeten the deal to keep the one remaining project afloat—the North West Upgrader (NWU) in Sturgeon County.[34] Under the original scenario, the government would simply ensure ongoing bitumen supply, and leave it to North West to take their upgraded products to market at whatever prices they could get minus whatever costs they incurred to build and operate.

Under Stelmach's new deal, the GOA committed to retain ownership of the bitumen up to the point of sale of the upgraded products; pay North West a processing fee or "toll" for upgrading it; and then sell the upgraded products into the market. By now—2010—construction costs were estimated to be $5.7 billion (up from an earlier estimate of $4 billion). Eighty percent of the capital costs would be borrowed, with payment on these bonds effectively guaranteed by the GOA's thirty-year "take or pay" tolling contract. This new arrangement effectively transferred the risk of upgrading to the government—a liability estimated to cost $19 billion in tolls over the thirty-year contract.

This is the deal that I inherited when I became finance minister. I was immediately assigned to the cabinet NWU "working group."[35] During my January policy briefings, my deputy minister flagged the NWU file as a priority. It soon became clear that Energy officials were much more enthusiastic about this project than Finance. My officials' concerns were that for the GOA, the risks far outweighed the rewards. The more I learned, the more I agreed.

My concerns were amplified by correspondence I had not previously seen, but that was now privy to me as the minister of finance. One industry player had written a letter indicating that while his company was interested in participating in the "new" BRIK, their own forecasts for bitumen upgrading in Alberta indicated poor returns and financial risks that were greater than the potential benefits. The only reason they were prepared to proceed, he emphasized, was that the new request for proposals shifted all those risks to the GOA.

Another letter from a leading corporate bond rating agency confirmed that under the "hell-or-high water" monthly tariff arrangement, investors were assured of recovering all costs—both construction and operations—plus a fixed return. All these costs would be included in the "cost of service" tariffs paid by the GOA (75 percent) and energy company CNRL (Canadian Natural Resources Ltd.) (25 percent). Nor would bondholders be exposed to any volume risks. Under the new proposal, the GOA (75 percent) and CNRL (25 percent) had a legal obligation to guarantee the stipulated monthly supply of bitumen to be processed.

This risk shifting was needed in order to achieve a high enough rating on the billions of dollars of bonds that NWU would have to sell to build the upgrader. The higher the bond rating, the lower the interest paid on the bonds, and thus the lower the cost of building the upgrader. Shifting all the risk—and thereby reducing the costs of borrowing—was only way the NWU could ever be profitable.

I also consulted with former energy and finance minister Greg Melchin. Melchin's advice was blunt: "No amount of government subsidy is going to make an unprofitable business profitable. It is only going to transfer the loss to the taxpayer." He also pointed out that if we did the deal with NWU, it would guarantee that no one else would build a privately financed upgrader in Alberta. The precedent of government subsidy would be set. As a less risky alternative, Melchin suggested a royalty rebate on bitumen upgraded in Alberta, possibly accompanied by a hike in the royalty rate. When I suggested this to the cabinet working group, it was immediately rejected.

The financial risk of upgrading depends on three factors: the capital cost of building the upgrader; the costs of operating it; and the "spread" between the price of bitumen and the price of the refined products. The first two are simple: the more it costs to build an upgrader and the more it costs to operate an upgrader, the higher the processing costs—the "toll"—needed to recover these costs and not lose money.

The spread factor is more complicated. The wider the spread, the greater the opportunity for profit. The narrower the spread, the greater the risk of loss. If the combined costs of the bitumen plus the upgrading "toll" is greater than the going market price of the refined products, then you lose money.

While the spread had varied over past decades, by 2012 recent trends suggested a narrower spread in coming years. The new technologies of directional drilling and multi-stage fracking were dramatically increasing the supply of sweet, light crude in the North American market—keeping its price below the world price. And of course, the upgrader itself contributes to narrowing the spread by increasing the demand for bitumen (making it more expensive) and increasing the supply of refined products (making it less expensive). In short, there's a reason that financial advisors tell their clients to avoid investments that depend on a price spread that moves at both ends.

I was particularly concerned with the "hell-or-high water" conditions around the proposed processing contract. I contended that it was reckless for the government to sign a contract that committed us to pay the monthly tolls even if the upgrader were not operating. To my way of thinking, this amounted to a de facto government guarantee of the debt bonds North West would need to sell to build the upgrader. I argued that this violated Alberta's 1996 *Business Financial Assistance Limitations Statutes Amendment Act*, which prohibits such government guarantees.

Energy officials insisted that the contract was not technically a "loan guarantee," and they were supported by officials brought in from Justice who told the cabinet working group that "section 72 is clear in that it does not prohibit" such contracts. My response was that this interpretation was self-serving, and that it was not the same as saying that the Act "authorizes or permits" such contracts. I lost.

At a subsequent meeting, our discussion went to the issue of making the tolling payments conditional on the upgrader's performance. Present at the meeting was a representative from Moody's, who was there to advise us on finances. He was quick to tell us that to sell the bonds at an interest rate low enough to allow North West to be profitable, there would have to be a "direct, irrevocable and unconditional guarantee of the Crown." This directly contradicted what our own justice department lawyers had told us. I felt vindicated. But I was hopelessly outnumbered, and I lost again.

Not only was the North West Upgrader one of the premier's priorities, but it was also championed by newly appointed Deputy Premier Doug Horner. This was hardly surprising. The proposed upgrader was to be built in Horner's constituency of Sturgeon County. The project was also buoyed by the same pro-Edmonton, anti-Calgary sentiment that had helped Stelmach defeat Jim Dinning and me in the second round of the 2006 PC leadership race and that subsequently led to Stelmach's ill-fated royalty review.

In the end, all the crucial decisions were made by our cabinet working group and the relevant senior bureaucrats, all coordinated through the premier's office. Prior to our final meeting before the plan was to go to cabinet and caucus, I had persuaded two of the ministers to join me and vote against it. The day of the meeting, one did not even show up. When I asked why the next day, the response was blunt: "I can count. The fix was in." When it came time to vote, my one other erstwhile ally voted to support the deal. I didn't bother to ask why.

The North West Upgrader saga clearly affirms what Canadian political scientists have been saying about cabinet government for quite a long time: "The reality of Cabinet government is that the truly crucial decisions are made by a small handful of ministers, advised by an equally small number of senior civil servants."[36] The earlier successes I had enjoyed at SRD in developing new policies were made possible by the indifference of the premier's office.

An interesting sidebar to this in-house decision-making process is that over that summer I was approached in a social setting by a senior executive from NWU who pressed me on my opposition to their project. It is interesting because, of course, these were cabinet deliberations that were supposed to be confidential. Who had he been talking with?

A short but polite conversation ensued. I remarked that no private company would take on this type of risk, so why should the government? My interlocutor acknowledged that over time there would be some good years and some bad years, but only the government has the ability to commit for thirty years. Sensing my lack of enthusiasm, he pointed out that the government's risk is really only an "opportunity cost," since it receives the bitumen in kind (in lieu of actual royalties). This means that there is no public record of profit or loss. I replied that I doubted that energy analysts in Calgary would be fooled by the lack of public records. Even I could figure out the dollar value of the bitumen we would take in-kind, and then compare that to the price we would get later when we sold the upgraded bitumen.

His final foray was that the upgrader would be a hedge against future low prices for bitumen. This continues to be a favourite "fall-back" position for upgrading supporters. I replied that we already would have that hedge even if the amount of bitumen upgraded in Alberta dropped to 50 percent. Besides, 50,000 b/d of upgrading would hardly be much of a hedge, when daily bitumen production in Alberta hits two or three million b/d. Our conversation ended there.

So, in the end, the new NWU arrangement—packaged as "Refine it where you mine it!"—was presented to cabinet and caucus as a done deal that would deliver on the premier's promise to incentivize more upgrading in Alberta. Caucus heard a lot about capturing the "value added," but was told almost nothing about the significant financial risk the GOA was now assuming. I am certain that the majority of caucus did not even understand the changes that had been made to the original deal.

But I did not voice my objections. After six months of losing these arguments with the premier's office, I was not going to take him on in front of the entire caucus. I was still his finance minister, and I was going to need his support for the spending cuts I would be proposing in upcoming Budget 2011. Cheered on by Edmonton-area ministers and MLAs, the package got a free pass in caucus. The one concession my objections had produced was a hard cap on the GOA's liability on construction costs. By 2011, capital costs were estimated at $5.7 billion. The plan approved by caucus included a guarantee that any cost overruns above $6.5 billion could not be added to the GOA's processing toll.

❖ ❖ ❖

Six months after my defeat in the 2012 election, NWU sanctioned phase one of the new upgrader. Over the next decade, all my worst fears about the NWU came true. Despite promises, costs continued to rise. North West's CEO Ian MacGregor acknowledged that cost overruns were a risk but assured an all-party committee of the Alberta legislature:

> We plan to build it for $5.7 billion, and our fee structure runs out at $6.5 billion. I get a lot of questions about: what happens if this costs more than $6.5 billion? My answer is: 'It's not going to. We meant $5.7 billion when we said it, and here's the planning and the amount of work.' We spent $800 million proving that we can do it for that. I mean, those are the things you have to meet.[37]

This cap was confirmed in the Report of the All-Party Legislative Committee in May 2013.[38] Five months later in October, Premier Redford participated in the official ground-breaking ceremony. There were smiles all around.

Two months later, the smiles were gone. In a press release just days before Christmas (when governments hope that no one is paying attention to the news), the GOA quietly announced that cost overruns had driven the total construction costs to $8.5 billion, and the expected completion date was extended twelve months to 2017. In addition, the GOA would now loan NWU $300 million to help with interim financing. The original $6.5 billion cap was nowhere mentioned. By 2020, construction costs had risen to $10 billion, and by 2023, to $11 billion.

In 2013, an independent study done by the respected energy-consulting firm IHS CERA concluded that "the province creates more jobs and benefits by not upgrading bitumen."[39] It cited the additional demand that constructing NWU would put on Alberta's already-constrained labour market. Building the upgrader, it concluded, would result in higher costs for other oil sands projects because of higher labour costs. These higher costs in turn result in decreased royalties and taxes to the GOA.[40]

Higher construction costs mean higher tolls that the GOA was (and is) legally obligated to pay for processing its bitumen. By 2023, the toll had increased from the original figure of $19 billion to $35 billion over the next sixty years. Yes, *sixty* years, to 2083. To accommodate the spiralling costs and tolls, the GOA agreed to extend its commitment from thirty years to sixty. Needless to say, there are multiple risks in this new commitment, not the least of which is whether there will still even be a market for the diesel fuel that NWU produces.

Then do the math. Rather than paying a toll of $39 per barrel, the new toll works out to $73 per barrel. According to the Energy Resources Conservation Board (ERCB), North West Upgrader could still be profitable at this rate, if all its optimistic assumptions prove accurate. But if they don't, the GOA is on the hook for $35 billion in tolls and paying all remaining debt.[41] And as for things not working out, for nine months in 2018–19, the NWU had operational difficulties and could not process any bitumen. But thanks to the "take or pay" provisions I had fought so hard to delete, the GOA was still paying $750,000 a day in tolls, even though no bitumen was being processed.[42]

This was the "bitumen boondoggle" inherited by Rachel Notley and the NDP in 2015; and then Jason Kenney and the UCP in 2019. Kenney's mandate to his new energy minister, Sonya Savage, was to try to stop the financial hemorrhaging. They hoped that the GOA could simply cancel the contract. But of course, they couldn't. So as a least-worst option, Minister Savage engineered a buyout in which the GOA purchased a 50 percent ownership share in NWU. $425 million was paid to North West (Ian McGregor's company) and $400 million to CNRL. As an owner, the GOA is now on both sides of the deal: it is on the receiving side of the tolls that it pays to have its bitumen upgraded. But it also means that the GOA is now fully in the bitumen upgrading business for the next six decades.

The only bright side of this affair is that it could have been twice as bad. During the first six months of 2011—while I was occupied with the leadership race to replace him—Stelmach had been persuaded to approve a second upgrader project in the Edmonton area. It was to be financed the same way as North West—with all the risks on the GOA. As the new energy minister in the Redford government, I vetoed it as soon as I learned about it. (See chapter 10.)

POSTSCRIPT

The BRIK/NWU project spanned five different PC energy ministers[43] (including myself) and four different PC premiers. It took on an inertia of its own, sustained by its bureaucratic supporters in the ERCB, Edmonton-area MLAs, and most of the Edmonton business community. Over these eight years there was a glaring lack of effective government oversight and due diligence. While I did not realize it while I was in government, the NWU is just the most recent installment in a long "legacy of loss" in the GOA's attempts at economic diversification and valued-added initiatives.[44] The twisted tale of how the NWU came to be is wholly consistent with the economic literature on "forced growth."

Forced growth denotes government-led initiatives to use public funds—whether in the form of grants, subsidies, loan-guarantees, tax-breaks, or some combination of all four—to attract private sector companies to develop new companies or other forms of economic activity within their jurisdictions. The forced-growth literature reveals a pattern of economic failures. The factors contributing to this pattern of policy failure include the following:

- Such projects tend to be motivated more by politics than by actual or potential economic viability.

- Typically there is no high-quality, independent, professional assessment of the proposed project's long-term economic viability, which results in an underestimation of the risks.

- Unequal expertise means that governments tend to be out-negotiated by their more experienced private sector counterparts.

- As a result, there is a tendency for governments to take most of the risks, provide most of the capital, and receive little of the profits, when there are any.[45]

Evidence of all of these factors can be found to varying degrees in the eight-year genesis from the original low-cost, low-risk BRIK policy to the high-cost, high-risk North West Upgrader. Future Alberta governments should think long and hard before succumbing to future versions of diversification siren songs like "refine it where you mine it."

8

How I Unbecame Finance Minister (2010)

The opposition occupies the benches in front of you, but the
enemy sits behind you.

—Winston Churchill

The issues recounted in the preceding chapter were all important. They had both short- and long-term consequences for Alberta. But a finance minister's number one priority is the government's annual budget. For me, that meant reining in our ballooning deficits and debt and returning to a balanced budget by 2012.

Accordingly, after delivering the 2010 budget in February (and then sneaking off to British Columbia for three days of backcountry snowcat skiing with my son), I spent the next five months immersed in meetings with my new deputy minister, Tim Wiles, and his executive team.

For those first six months, I felt like a bear that couldn't come out of its den. In addition to all the budget information I had to understand and absorb, there were the policy issues described in the preceding chapter—the Northwest Upgrader plus planning how to stop Ottawa's proposed national securities regulator and expansion of the Canada Pension Plan. Then there was the third session of the 27th Legislature from February through April. This meant preparing for question period four days a week and then the media afterward. The latter, of course, are only interested in reporting bad news. Good news is not news. So don't say anything stupid in question period. Oh yes, I also came down with shingles in May, which kept me in bed for a week and at low energy levels for another month after that. At times I began to ask myself: Why did I ever ask for this job?

Delivering Budget 2010 was unpleasant but easy. It was preparing for Budgets 2011 and 2012 that was hard. And it began the day after my budget speech. We spent the next month working with President of Treasury Board Lloyd Snelgrove reviewing revenue and expenditure projections for the coming years. The scenario was bleak. In March, together we sent a memo to all cabinet ministers and Caucus Policy Committee (CPC) chairs that we were adopting a new policy for dealing with anticipated revenue shortfalls:

> You will now be required to identify options and provide a recommendation on how any new costs will be accommodated within your ministry's existing Budget 2010 spending targets.

Instead of me having to meet one-on-one with twenty different ministers to say "NO" to their requests for increased funding, this was a way of saying "NO" to all of them at once.

RECESSION

It was not until September 20, at our first full caucus meeting following the August break, that I had to start breaking the bad news to caucus. I used a PowerPoint presentation to explain the seriousness of our fiscal situation. Our first quarter update (Q1) showed that declining revenues now put us into a deficit situation for Budget 2012. But that was minor, compared to the longer-term forecasts for both the Sustainability Fund and the Heritage Fund. I reminded everyone that it was the $18 billion surplus in the Sustainability Fund that had allowed us to declare that we had "balanced the budgets" in 2009 and 2010, as we could cover those deficits with a transfer from our "short-term" savings. But what if the Sustainability Fund is drawn down to zero? That was what our projections showed was going to happen by 2014.

This was a difficult message to get across, as our projections also showed us returning to a modest ($600 million) budget surplus by 2013. This apparent contradiction is explained by the fact that our accrual accounting rules for capital construction only allow us to record annual depreciation as an in-year expenditure, but the cost of the new building, road, etc. must be paid in full. That dollar difference is drawn out of the Sustainability Fund. This is something that every first-year accounting student knows—CapEx is greater than Depreciation—but that neither I nor most of caucus had ever been told or understood. This hadn't made much difference for the years we were running multi-billion-dollar surpluses, and most of those surpluses were being deposited in the Sustainability Fund. But given the "new normal," those days were long gone. The bottom line was that just to keep the legally required minimum balance of $3 billion in the Sustainability Fund, we had to achieve budget surpluses of at least $2.5 billion a year—not $600 million—starting in 2013.

The forecasts for the Heritage Fund were equally bleak. In the wake of the Great Recession, the Heritage Fund had lost $2.6 billion in 2008–9—its largest loss ever. In 2009–10, the fund rebounded and earned $2 billion. But because of our long-standing policy of transferring all the Heritage Fund's annual earnings to general revenues, these 2009–10 earnings did not offset the losses of the prior year. Going forward, this meant that during periods of economic growth, the real value of the fund stays the same, but one bad year of losses meant a permanent and non-recoverable drop in the fund's value.

The takeaway for caucus was, in my mind, simple: faced with lower than earlier projected revenues for 2011–13, and the need for larger than projected surplus to keep the Sustainability Fund afloat, we had some serious budget cutting ahead of us. As for the Heritage Fund, in the short term we were too cash-strapped to stop taking out all the annual earnings. But it was imperative we commit to start taking less by mid-decade. As that fall evolved, both of these became principal planks of my proposed "Renewed Fiscal Framework."

THE NEW NORMAL

Two weeks later I was back before caucus as part of a marathon two-day budget session. I basically had two objectives. The first was to rally caucus support for major cuts to ministry budgets by illustrating the financial train wreck that would happen if we didn't. Klein had made across-the-board 5 percent cuts to government expenditures during the 1990s. Why couldn't we do it now?

The second objective was to give the caucus an understanding of the fiscal constraints now facing Alberta—what I dubbed the "New Normal." I hoped that to the extent that caucus would buy into the "New Normal," it would help us to achieve our first objective and could then be used by our MLAs to explain to Albertans the difficult cuts that would appear in Budget 2011.

As part of the annual budget process, Finance sends each ministry a target budget number in August. Each department is asked if they can meet this target, and, if not, what are their "pressures" and "asks"—i.e., "Why not?" and "How much more do they need?" We now had received and aggregated all the departments' responses, and, predictably, the "Pressures/Asks" exceeded the budget targets by huge amounts: $1.4 billion for 2011; $2.2 billion for 2012; and $2.8 billion for 2013. Lesson learned: no civil servants are going to voluntarily cut their own budgets.

We had run these numbers through our budget models, and the results were shocking. Under a budget scenario in which 50 percent of the pressures/asks were met, we would run deficits every year until 2014. If 100 percent of the pressures/asks were met, we would run deficits every year until 2016. Under both scenarios, the Sustainability Fund would be depleted in 2013, and we would need to borrow just to cover operating expenses starting in 2013.

Hoping that caucus was duly alarmed by such numbers, we then spent the better part of two days slogging through the pressures and asks of each ministry. The main culprits were Health and Education, but one by one, every minister had to stand and present. As each MLA had a right to speak his or her mind, it was a chaotic process, lurching from one issue to another, often with little connection. The most charitable thing I could say about the whole process was that it may have served as a sort of "group therapy" for backbenchers, as they had ample opportunity to unburden themselves. This assessment sounds cynical, but its accuracy is borne out by the fact that the premier and Ron Glen, his chief of staff, were absent for most of it. They knew that final budget decisions would be made by a much smaller group, which they would hand-pick.

Wedged into this two-day process was my presentation on the "New Normal"—a short and simple summary of six new economic and political realities that were squeezing—and would continue to squeeze—public finance in Alberta.

THE NEW NORMAL

1. Sharp decline in royalties because of Shale Gas Revolution

In less than four years, the combined effect of directional drilling and multi-stage fracking has almost doubled North American natural gas production and cut its price from over $10/mcf to less than $3. The

---

knock-on effect on GOA revenues has been staggering. As illustrated in the graphic below, the GOA's non-renewable resource revenues (NRRR) dropped from an average of $12 billion/year (2004–2008) to $8 billion/year (2009–11). The collapse of natural gas royalties accounted for almost all of the drop. The $4 billion difference is—not by coincidence—almost exactly the size of the Government's projected deficit for 2010. Nor is this going to change anytime soon. Abundant and therefore cheap natural gas is here to stay for North American consumers. But its impact on GOA revenues is devastating.

Problem II
Energy Revenues – the "New Normal"

- 2004/05 to 2008/09 – averaged $12 billion
- 2009/10 to 2012/13 – forecast to average $8 billion —— $4 billion shortfall
- U.S. has 250 year reserve of Shale Gas

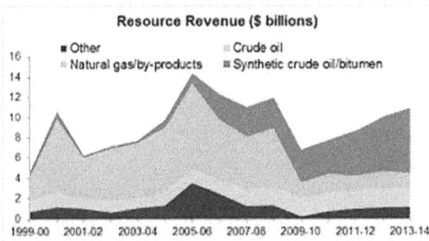

Resource Revenue ($ billions)

■ Other   Crude oil
Natural gas/by-products   ■ Synthetic crude oil/bitumen

Alberta

Government of Alberta

2. "Loonie"/Currency parity with the US dollar

Over the past decade, the exchange rate for the Canadian dollar against the US dollar has risen from less than 70 cents to virtual parity. This has negative consequences for GOA revenues. For every 1 cent increase in the value of the "Loonie," the GOA's NRRR declines by $215 million. This is because all oil and gas exported from Alberta to the US is paid for in US dollars. A weak Loonie means higher revenues for Alberta oil and gas exporters, which means higher royalties for the GAO. A strong Loonie—such as we are currently experiencing—means lower revenues.

3. Canadian Exports to US reduced by recession

The 2008 Recession has damaged the US economy more than Canada's, but this is reducing demand for Canadian exports to the US. Currently the US economy is characterized by high unemployment, high consumer debt, high government debt, and a housing market foreclosure glut. There is no certainty regarding how soon the US economy will recover. Reduced US demand translates into weaker economic growth in Canada and reduced revenues for Canadian governments from both corporate and personal income taxes.

4. Demographic time bomb in Alberta means sharp increases in costs for government-provided health care and senior services

The first wave of Baby Boomers (born in 1945) will turn 65 in 2011. The ranks of Baby Boomers becoming seniors will grow by 2,000 a month for the following decade. Today, there are 400,000 seniors in Alberta. By 2020, there will be 610,000; and by 2030, 800,000—more grandparents than grandchildren.

5. Underfunding of public sector pensions

There is a systematic understatement of the accrued liabilities of public sector pension funds in Canada. Using private sector "fair value" accounting rules, the C.D. Howe Institute reports that that while the "official" liability for Alberta is $49 billion, the "fair value" liability is $61 billion. For the Government of Canada, the official liability is $143 billion, while the "fair value" is $208 billion. This underfunding reflects the changing composition of our workforce. During the 1960s, the ratio of workers to retirees was 7:1. By 2025 it will be 3:1. This underfunding is aggravated by recent stock market losses and historically low interest rates. Governments are liable for covering the shortfalls of public sector pensions.

6. Increased environmental scrutiny—especially on CO_2 emissions

Prior to 2000, Alberta's environmental policies were mostly an inside-Alberta issue. Today, Alberta is the focus of national and international scrutiny because of global warming concerns. Stopping or slowing the growth of oil sands production is the objective of well-financed campaigns by ENGOs such as Greenpeace, Forest Ethics, Sierra Club, Tides USA and Tides Canada. Today and going forward, Alberta's "social license" and "market access" are at risk.

Taken together, these six economic and political realities constituted the "New Normal" for Alberta. They explained in part the budget deficits we were now running. I emphasized that none of these were going to disappear anytime soon, and there was little to nothing we could do about any of them. What we could do—and what we had to do starting in 2011—was to control our spending. The details of how we were going to do that would be the focus of a future presentation—the new "Fiscal Framework."

A NEW FISCAL FRAMEWORK

From the outset, I viewed my challenge at Finance as not just to get us to "Back in Black by 2012," but to put in place a new set of budgeting and accounting rules that would prevent a repeat of what had happened since 2005, which in turn was almost a carbon copy of what had happened in the 1980s under the Getty government. By November, with a great deal of assistance from Deputy Minister Tim Wiles and his staff, I had put together a package of fourteen rules I wanted to see put into legislation as part of Budget 2011. Collectively, we called these "A New Fiscal Framework for Alberta."

The Fiscal Framework would achieve three much-needed reforms to the annual budget process: mandatory minimum contributions to both our short-term and long-term savings accounts, the Sustainability Fund (rules 1 to 4) and the Heritage Fund (rules 5 and 9); new restraints on spending (rules 6, 7, 8, 11, and 13); and a procedural barrier to tax increases (rule 10). It also increased the GOA's annual reporting requirements (rules 12 and 14). The Fiscal Framework did not include the most-needed reform—the mandatory retention of a fixed percentage of NRRR in the Heritage Fund each year, such as the 30 percent rule that Lougheed had originally established in 1976. In the context of the "New Normal" and our desire to balance the budget by 2012, this was deemed too steep, and so was deferred.

A Renewed Fiscal Framework for Alberta

or

Alberta TAXPAYERS' Protection Act

Summary of rules/principles included in Fiscal Framework

1. No deficits allowed unless they can be paid for out of the Sustainability Fund (SF). [current]

---

2. Budget must ensure that there is a minimum balance of $3 billion in the Sustainability Fund for the Budget year. [part current, part new]

3. To replenish SF, GOA's Budget must be "cash balanced" by Budget 2014. [new]

4. Beyond 2014, SF should be rebuilt to a balance equal to 30 percent of operating budget (c. $10 billion). [part current, part new]

5. Heritage Fund growth must be established through mandatory retention of a higher percentage of earned profits. [part current, part new]

6. Spending restraint will be achieved by requiring allocations to savings [SF and HF] first; operating and capital spending can only be made from funds that remain. [part current, part new]

7. Spending restraint will be achieved by limiting in-year spending increases to 1 percent of total annual budget ["total expenditure"] and including capital expenditures (grants and investments) in this 1 percent. [part current, part new]

8. Spending restraint will be achieved by requiring repayment of current debt borrowed for capital purposes as it becomes due, beginning in 2014. [new]

9. Heritage Fund must be protected by requiring any changes to allowable withdrawals or to the retention rates to first be approved by an act of the legislature. [part current, part new]

10. Any increases to personal income tax rates or the adoption of any sort of general sales or consumption tax (e.g., PST) must first be approved by referendum. [part current, part new]

11. Future borrowing for capital must be accompanied by a plan to repay the debt incurred over a specified time frame. [part current, part new]

12. All "off-book" financial obligations of the Government must continue to be reported annually as part of the Government's Consolidated Financial Statement/Annual Report. [current]

13. The Capital Plan must include amounts for deferred maintenance reflecting a percentage of the three-year average value of capital built in the province [part current, part new].

14. Government will report annually on labour settlement provisions including compensation and benefits, including salaries, bonus, pension contributions, and other provisions for which additional costs

are borne by the government (i.e., working conditions, attraction, and retention programs, etc.) [part current, part new]

Note: If a rule is already government policy, it is indicated as "current." If a rule represents a new requirement, it is indicated as "new." If the rule combines existing practice with a new requirement, it is indicated "part current, part new." Of the fourteen proposed rules, only two are "new," two are "current," and ten combine a component of existing policy with a new requirement.

While I had consulted with both Snelgrove (Treasury Board) and the premier's office on the concept of a new Fiscal Framework during the course of the year, to actually turn it into legislation meant running it through the internal policy approval process of the government caucus. This meant taking it to the Agenda and Priorities Committee (A&P) on November 16; Caucus Policy Committee (CPC) on December 6; and to caucus on December 13.

The purpose of the A&P Committee was to provide political advice and guidance to the premier. Its responsibilities included not just vetting proposed new legislation and budget issues, but anything else "politically relevant." Our agenda for November 16 was unusually busy. Since the Legislative Assembly had begun its weekly sittings again on October 25, we—especially the premier—were getting badly beaten up in question period and in the media on health care issues. In November, Edmonton MLA Raj Sherman, an emergency room surgeon, had been suspended from our caucus after making inflammatory accusations about mismanagement in Alberta Health Services (AHS). These were given credibility by the chaos surrounding the firing of AHS CEO Stephen Duckett that same month.

Sorting out these issues took up most of our allotted time. Ominously for me, it was also at this meeting that several other cabinet ministers first began to make the case for new accounting rules for capital expenditures, changes that would allow us to redefine "balanced budget" as "operationally balanced." I made a brief—ten-minute—introduction to the Fiscal Framework. With little discussion, it was approved to go to the next stage—the December 6th CPC meeting—for a more substantive analysis.

Sensing growing headwinds for my budget, I asked for and was given a meeting with the premier and Ron Glen on November 23. I knew that their active support would be critical to success. My message was simple: A budget by itself is not enough. We need a plan—a multi-year strategy—that will guide

Alberta back to balanced budgets and fiscal stability. The Fiscal Framework is such a plan. It would serve as a sword in dealing with ministers' budget requests. It would also provide a shield—"We can't fix it overnight"—against the inevitable Wildrose attack alleging that the budget is "too little, too late." I said, immodestly, that I represented a significant portion of our party—the business/fiscal conservative wing—that we were at risk of losing to Wildrose. They were looking to me to bring in both a balanced budget (in 2012) and a savings strategy. This Fiscal Framework did this. If you abandon me on this, if you cut me loose, you cut them loose too, at real risk to yourself and to our party.

The very next day my sense of foreboding was validated. At our Treasury Board meeting, the new proposed budget numbers were sharply criticized. One minister called it "an accountant's budget, not a political budget." My quick response was that after four consecutive budget deficits, a balanced budget IS political. Sensing that the majority of Treasury Board members were favourable toward my arguments, a second. minister chimed in: "We need a Cabinet meeting to discuss this ... to give Dave and Doug an opportunity to present their case." A third tried to please both sides, reminding us of our repeated "back-in-the-black" promises but then digressing and ending by saying that a "positive trend" was our goal. I was not reassured.

LOSING THE FIGHT

Caucus Policy Committee met as scheduled on Monday, December 6, and the attacks on the Fiscal Framework escalated. Again, Horner led the charge, arguing for his now well-known preference for dividing the budget into operational and capital spending, and borrowing for the latter. He was supported by Thomas Lukaszuk, an Edmonton MLA, who said our *Deficit Reduction Act* was "not worth the paper it is written on." I had some support for the Fiscal Framework—Doug Griffiths, Janice Sarich, Broyce Jacobs—but nowhere near what I wanted or needed. Especially disappointing was President of Treasury Board Lloyd Snelgrove, someone whose support was essential if I were to succeed. Speaking at length, Lloyd barely mentioned the Fiscal Framework, instead musing on what we needed to do when we returned to fiscal surplus, and ended by saying that he "trusted caucus to set priorities." This was hardly reassuring, as Snelgrove had alerted me earlier that he was going to be out of town when caucus was scheduled to meet the following week.

Following CPC, I called an emergency huddle with my two key staffers, Eric Taylor and Tom Kmiec, and we identified three "go forward" options:

- Drop the Fiscal Framework and just concentrate on Budget 2011.
- Take the Fiscal Framework to caucus and fight it out there.
- Take the Fiscal Framework to caucus but downgrade its rules from statutory requirements to "policy guidelines."

This last option was clearly a step-down position, but we mused that if we were to get it adopted by caucus, we could take it to the next PC Party AGM, and try to get it adopted there as statutory or even constitutional rules.

Things went from bad to worse the next day at Treasury Board, where I reported that our fiscal situation had further deteriorated. Our internal third quarter (Q3) update showed that the deficit for Budget 2010 had now ballooned to $5.3 billion (from $4.7 billion); and that our projected deficit for Budget 2011 was now $3 billion, up from the $1.1 billion we had projected.

The following day, Wednesday, I had a private budget meeting with the premier, Ron Glen, and Lloyd Snelgrove. Glen floated the idea of postponing Budget 2011 until March, to allow us to "consult" with Albertans before tabling a budget. At first I liked the idea, as it would give us an opportunity to take the "New Normal" message public. But I became suspicious when I realized that Glen (and probably the premier) saw it as an opportunity to wiggle out of our "back in the black" commitment. And once again, the idea of separating operational spending from capital spending as a way to "balance the budget" was vetted, forcing me to explain that all our prior "back in the black" commitments had assumed existing accounting practices—revenue less total expenses, not just operating expenses. I warned that any deviation from this would mark a departure from twenty years of practice and attract negative attention from economists and the media.

In retrospect, I can see it was not by accident that when I returned home to Calgary that Friday, I composed the first version of my "Waves" document—a list of MLAs who might come with me if I were to resign, leave caucus, and sit as an Independent.

If the week of December 6 was bad, the next week was worse, but by now I was no longer surprised. Monday was the long-awaited showdown over the Fiscal Framework with the entire caucus. My office had provided each member with two documents the preceding week. The first was a six-page document, "A Renewed Fiscal Framework for Alberta," which summarized and then explained each of the fourteen recommended new rules. The second was a ten-page "background" document that explained why we needed to adopt these new rules to cope with the "New Normal," and then laid out the three options we were to vote on: Option 1, status quo; Option 2, adopt Fiscal Framework; or Option 3, adopt Fiscal Framework and include "Emergencies and Disasters" as a $500 million budgeted expense (rather than paying for them after the fact through the Sustainability Fund). We then recommended Option 2 and provided a brief explanation of how it could be implemented.

I had worked out an informal agreement with the Whip and the premier's office that we would discuss each of the fourteen proposed rules one by one; then take a non-binding vote on each; and then conclude with a non-binding vote to include all those rules that had been approved as part of Budget 2011—basically Option 2. That was the theory.

What happened was far different. Led by Ministers Horner and Hancock, there was a sustained attack on the entire document as unnecessary, too restrictive, and politically damaging. Jack Hayden, Iris Evans, Frank Oberle, and Luke Ouellette, all close allies of the premier, joined the choir. Many MLAs spoke in favour—we had lined up a dozen or so supporters beforehand—but fence sitters saw where the premier's team wanted to go, and joined in. In the end, the nays clearly outnumbered the ayes. The president of Treasury Board was, as expected, absent. At the end of almost two hours of heated argument, Robin Campbell, the Whip, who sits next to the premier at caucus meetings, announced that there would be "no vote," as the issue was "too politically sensitive." Instead, he suggested, we could "get it out quietly," whatever that meant.

Interestingly, the caucus debate was as much about the political value of the Fiscal Framework as it was about its actual contents. As before, I stressed that a longer-term fiscal strategy was necessary to win back the fiscal conservative wing of the PC voter coalition that was drifting off to the Wildrose Party. The critics vigorously rejected this and argued that whatever voters we might lose to Wildrose we would pick up from Liberals and NDP supporters. I replied that this was ridiculous. In the rural ridings, there were no Liberal or NDP voters to pick up.

Critics could say that I was subsequently proven wrong by the next provincial election, when Premier Alison Redford's "spend now, pay later" 2012 budget paved the way for the election of another strong PC majority government. But, as I explain in Chapter 9, the 2012 election also gave the then-fledgling Wildrose Party the rural base they needed to take down first Redford and then Jim Prentice and end the PC dynasty in the 2015 election.

If the Fiscal Framework died at Monday's caucus meeting, my version of Budget 2011 died at Wednesday's cabinet meeting. I had been warned by my officials in Finance that opponents of our proposed budget cuts were planning to use this cabinet meeting as a showdown, and they were certainly right.

I presented the budget numbers that would be needed to keep on track for a balanced budget in 2012. As soon as I finished, the attacks began.

"Forget about back in the black," said one minister, "and just say we made a mistake." He was congratulated by a second minister, who added: "The average Albertan doesn't care." A third said it was "time to be bold... to show confidence in the future" (i.e., spend more money that we don't have). A fourth said that the proposed budget for Health would mean cutting seniors' and children's services, which he could not support. A fifth expanded on this: "Mulroney didn't lose because of his deficits. He lost because of new taxes" (i.e., the GST).

I tried to counter. I said all these arguments were the same ones used by the Getty cabinet in the 1980s and look where that got us: $23 billion of real debt. What was being proposed was not "bold and confident" but "naïve and reckless." But I could see now that it was a lost cause. Once again, the ministers leading the attack were almost all close to the premier and Ron Glen and wouldn't be doing what they were doing without at least tacit support, if not outright encouragement.

In closing, I repeated what I had been saying since I became finance minister: that we must earn the next election, not buy it; that our political risk is on our right flank with Wildrose; and that failure to keep our "back in the black" commitment would hurt us in southern Alberta and Calgary. But I was clearly in a minority.

In retrospect, my failure to win over cabinet was in part a political lesson that I had once known but had since forgotten: when it comes to caucus and cabinet decision making, it is as much about relationships as it is about policy. Over the preceding eleven months, I had picked policy fights with almost every other minister: Liepert and Horner over the North West Upgrader; Hancock over the *Education Act*; Knight over the Micrex project and Bill 50; Zwozdesky over cuts to the Health budget. I still think I was on the right side of policy in each of these battles, but when it came to garnering support for my budget, I had few friends.

STAY OR LEAVE?

Returning to Calgary for the weekend, I pondered my options. It was clear that the spending numbers for Budget 2011 were going to be much higher than I wanted, and, more importantly, would make it impossible—barring some sort of miracle—to deliver a balanced budget in 2012. The latter was non-negotiable for me. My principles and my reputation for fiscal responsibility had already taken a huge hit for delivering the record deficit in Budget 2010. Unless a personal plea—or threat—to the premier could change the situation, resignation appeared to be about the only card left on the table.

My choice was made for me on Monday. In an end-of-year interview, the premier told Sun Media that a balanced budget in 2012 was still the "goal," but that if extenuating factors increased, then there might be a delay: "There's a number of issues, obviously some challenges [in meeting the target]," he said. "These are external factors, nothing we can do anything about. We're going to trend toward a balanced [budget]."[1] Trend toward a balanced budget? Now there's a beauty! Others were more blunt: "Dec. 20, 2010: Budget backtrack."[2] I had been given no prior notice of this policy reversal, nor for that matter did Stelmach ever contact me afterward to explain or discuss it. I just learned about it from a phone call from my staff.

Notwithstanding our many differences and disagreements, I had stuck with Stelmach for the past four years. My loyalty up to now was based on my experiences in 2001 when I was working as the director of policy and research for the newly created Canadian Alliance Party. I was upset with the MPs in our caucus who were Manning loyalists and who took down the party's newly elected leader, Stockwell Day, before he had been given a fair chance to prove (or not) his leadership abilities. As noted in chapter 1, I made a promise to myself then that going forward I would never put personal disappointment ahead of maintaining caucus unity. I still think this is an honourable principle. But even good principles can be abandoned when and if circumstances warrant. And Stelmach's public reversal on a balanced budget by 2012—with no advance notice to me—was the final straw. The question was no longer if to resign, but when and how.

A week later, Stelmach told the *Globe and Mail*: "I watch both sides of the political spectrum ... and there's a saying in rural Alberta: It's the quiet dog that will come and bite you, not the barking dog. ... That quiet dog? Generally, the Left. ... Let's not just focus on one political party to the far right and lose the direction that Albertans want us to go in."[3]

Once again, Ed Stelmach was wrong.

9

The Prairie Putsch (2011)

> *When a leader of the Pack has missed his kill, he is called the*
> *'Dead Wolf' as long as he lives, which is not long.*
>
> —Rudyard Kipling, *The Jungle Book*

WHEN TO LEAVE

While Premier Stelmach's December 20 interview was the final straw in my decision to resign as finance minister, I'd been considering that option for some time. And not just because of the deteriorating budget situation. The defection of two backbench Calgary MLAs—Rob Anderson and Heather Forsyth—to the Wildrose in January was the beginning, not the end, of Ed Stelmach's troubles in 2010. The February budget was unpopular on both the Right and the Left, for opposite reasons. The negative impact of Stelmach's New Royalty Framework was causing layoffs in the oil patch. There was growing unhappiness with the perceived negative effect of the *Alberta Land Stewardship Act* on property rights in the farm and ranch communities. The government's plan (Bill 50) to build two new 500 kV DC power lines between Edmonton and Calgary excited NIMBY opposition amongst thousands of affected landowners.

Now led by the younger, media-savvy Danielle Smith, the Wildrose effectively exploited all these issues. This political turmoil ratcheted up a notch in November 2010, when PC MLA Raj Sherman went rogue and began criticizing his own government for emergency room wait times. Sherman was suspended and then booted from the PC caucus, but not before taking down the CEO of Alberta Health Services (AHS), Stephen Duckett, who had become a lightning rod for all the unhappiness with health care delivery in Alberta. Three AHS board members also resigned. To ice the cake, Duckett received one year's salary for severance—$735,000—sending howls of protests from angry bloggers and tweeters. The Alberta media—sensing blood and hungry for political change—had a field day.

As the PCs' fortunes waned over the course of 2010, prospects for leadership change grew. On December 3, an Angus Reid poll reported that Stelmach's approval rating had dropped to only 21 percent.[1] His approval ratings were consistently ten points lower than support for the PC Party, which now led the Wildrose by only six points.[2]

Just days before Christmas, *Calgary Herald* columnist Don Braid provocatively predicted, "Stelmach is almost certain to face a severe challenge to his leadership in the next few months. The talk is everywhere. Many Tories won't wait any longer for the popularity bounce that never comes." Unfortunately, he then fingered me as the most likely challenger.[3]

Encouraged by key advisors and political friends—and my own ambition for a second opportunity to become premier—I began to make contingency plans in case this happened. As early as September, I had asked my two executive assistants, Eric Taylor and Tom Kmiec, to contact Hamish Marshall to reactivate my political website. A month later, we met again to discuss the deteriorating political situation and how I should position myself. Additional plans were made to do a massive Christmas card mailing—over 3,000—to my 2006 supporters list.

Later in October, I was pheasant hunting with the late Stan Grad, a friend and constituent in Foothills-Rocky View. Also hunting with us were several other friends and financial supporters who had been active in both the UBA and Kids Can Catch Trout Pond initiatives. At dinner that evening, I brought up my concerns about Stelmach and my own future. This provoked a torrent of condemnations of Stelmach and encouragement for the resignation option. I countered that there was no telling what would happen if I resigned. It might be the catalyst for other resignations and the beginning of the end for Stelmach. Alternatively, I might just be kicked out of caucus and be left sitting by myself on the other side of the Legislative Assembly as an Independent. In other words, there was a real risk that it would be the beginning of the end of my political career. Stan's retort: "Ted, this is Alberta. Taking risks is what we do."

I took this advice to heart. Two weeks later, on November 4, I met again with Eric and Tom to discuss the logistics of vacating my office. We would need to get out all my records and files before I resigned, but how and when? We couldn't afford to be seen carting dozens of boxes out of my fourth-floor office in the legislature. (We eventually did this late one night in mid-January when the legislature was not sitting, and the rest of my office staff were still out of town on vacations.) We also decided to do a video Christmas greeting rather than send cards, as it would be less expensive, more effective, and could be delivered after the legislature closed for Christmas. I also agreed that Tom could resign his position effective January 7, to take a new job in Calgary where his wife (and former Morton leadership volunteer), Evangeline Winfield, was about to give birth to their second child.

That same week I met with Devin Iversen and Sam Armstrong, my 2006 leadership campaign managers, and close friends and confidants, to discuss the pros and cons of resigning. By early December, we developed the first version of what we came to call the "Waves" document—a list of other MLAs who were unhappy with Stelmach. If I were going to jump ship, it would be best to have some company. And before Christmas, I met with Greg Fletcher, Stan Church, and Rick Sears—all of whom were major fundraisers for me in 2006—to seek their advice. They all supported resigning.

RECRUITING ALLIES

I actually left the province on December 23 for a previously planned family Christmas holiday in California and didn't return home until January 12. But the "when" and the "how" of my resignation strategy were basically worked out via conference calls and emails over this two-week period.

The metaphor we used—and laughed (nervously) about—was me jumping off "the Good Ship PC," and then the ship just sailing on, leaving me behind and alone in the deep "Blue" sea. To avoid that, I needed some others to join a "mutiny." Since we couldn't push the ship/ocean/mutiny metaphor much further (we were, after all, in the middle of the Prairies), we soon began to refer to the project as the "Prairie Putsch"—again with nervous laughter. We all knew what happens to the "traitors" when a putsch fails.

My objective in resigning as minister of finance was to avoid delivering a budget I could no longer support, but without my resignation becoming a one-way ticket to political oblivion. This meant that my resignation had to be not just the end of one story, but the beginning of another; the catalyst for a chain of events that would eventually end—maybe in several weeks, maybe in several months—with Ed Stelmach being forced to resign because he no longer had the support of his caucus.

In an attempt to recruit some allies, we took what was potentially a risky step, but one that turned out to be well worth the risk. On January 14, we met for lunch with Rod Love, Alan Hallman, and Morten Paulsen in the very private Mary Dover Room at the Calgary Ranchmen's Club. This was basically the 2006 Dinning leadership team—the team that would have won if it had not been for us. While I was far from their favourite PC MLA, we suspected—correctly, it turned out—that they were even more unhappy with Premier Stelmach.

As chief of staff in the previous Klein regime, Rod Love had virtually run the government from the premier's office. Since 2006, however, the Stelmach team had basically frozen Love and his associates out of any access to either the premier or other cabinet ministers. And, like more and more PCs around the province, they were dismayed at the prospects of losing the next provincial election.

By the end of the lunch, they were on board for helping us to make my pending resignation the first step in pushing out Stelmach. The bonus was Rod Love's extensive (and to me, surprising) knowledge of British parliamentary precedents of ministers resigning but remaining in caucus. Rod gave us the historical materials to craft the argument that a minister's disagreement with the leader is not automatically deemed disloyalty to the party—a message that became a central theme in our communications strategy.

We assumed, other things being equal, that my resignation would result in my immediate expulsion from the government caucus. To make my exit from caucus the beginning of the end for Stelmach, I would have to take some other MLAs with me. It did not have to be a lot—only a few to start with. But we believed that once the defections started, the numbers would grow.

We had already identified several "true-blue" Morton supporters who would almost certainly have followed me regardless of the chances for success. But as the previous months' caucus deliberations had proven, "true-blue" Tories were in a distinct minority in the PC caucus. To dislodge Stelmach from the premier's office, we would need to tap into the larger number of MLAs who, out of their own keen sense of political self-preservation, were increasingly anxious to dump the floundering Stelmach before the next election.

To do this, we undertook to craft a communications strategy that would make the initial narrative be about the budget and Ted Morton standing up for his principles, and not about Ted Morton's leadership ambitions. Of course, it was both. But to attract broader support from caucus and PC party members, we believed that for the first few rounds of media coverage, we needed to shape a narrative that was high minded and public spirited, not just another seedy round of ambition-driven caucus assassination of faltering leaders.

To this end, we crafted my resignation letter—and my media talking points—around two themes. The first was the budget, Stelmach's reversal, and my standing on principle. But the second was a strong statement that I wanted to remain in the government caucus. We doubted Stelmach would allow this, but it would look better—support our desired narrative—if he kicked me out than if I left on my own volition. The latter scenario would look like the calculated first step in an intentional leadership challenge. In the former, I would just be a victim of the premier's own insecurities.

Resignation Letter

January 25, 2011

Premier Ed Stelmach

Room 307, Legislature Building

Edmonton, AB T5K 2B6

Dear Premier:

A year ago this month, I agreed to become your Minister of Finance with the understanding that you wanted me to help to design a fiscal strategy that would steer our province back to a balanced budget by 2012 and begin to replenish our short-and long-term savings accounts. This understanding was subsequently affirmed in your Mandate Letter to me of February 2, 2010 (copy attached).

Working closely with the President of Treasury Board, I believe that we were making significant progress toward both these goals until late November. At this time, you began to signal that you were willing to push back our "back in the black by 2012" commitment until 2013. It is certainly your prerogative as Premier to change the mission, but it is a mission contrary to the mandate you gave to me as Minister of Finance and one that I cannot in good conscience support.

If there were some way to ensure that this proposed deferral was only for one year and that by 2013 we would be in a position to balance our

---

books, I might have been persuaded to support it. But of course, it is not possible to guarantee what will happen in the future. The same external forces that are undermining our fiscal strength today could very well persist into 2012 or even 2013, at which point the Sustainability Fund will be exhausted and our operating deficits will become real debt. This, in my view, is not a risk that should be taken with the finances of Alberta.

I do not wish our government to repeat the mistakes of the late 1980s and early 1990s, when the Government of the day continued to spend despite falling revenues. They simply crossed their fingers, and hoped that revenues would rebound. Of course they did not, and the result was seven successive deficits and $22 billion dollars of real debt. While former Premier Ralph Klein deserves full credit for digging us out of the deficit/debt ditch, it was a painful experience that Albertans do not want to go through again.

Avoiding accumulated debt is fundamental to sound public finance. Paying interest on debt erodes a government's ability to provide current services and benefits. But it is more. It is also an obligation—a moral obligation—that each current generation owes to the generations that come after us. It is similar to environmental policy: it is wrong—morally wrong—to leave a mess for our children and grandchildren—whether that mess is financial or environmental.

Over 300 years of British parliamentary democracy has established the unwritten but well-understood constitutional convention that a Minister of the Crown who fundamentally disagrees with a major policy decision of the Government should resign. This historic tradition maintains the legitimacy of government, in so far as the members of Cabinet fully support the policies of the government.

As a consequence of your change of direction on our timetable to eliminate deficit spending; and your lack of support for the savings and spending strategies developed in response to your requests in my Mandate Letter, I now find myself in the position of presenting a budget to Treasury Board today and then Caucus tomorrow that I cannot support. In our system of government, I am left with only one option. Accordingly, I tender my resignation to you effective immediately.

In resigning from your Cabinet, I wish to make it clear that I intend to remain in our Party's Caucus. British-Canadian parliamentary tradition makes a clear distinction between resigning a ministry and remaining a member of one's party's parliamentary caucus. I still strongly believe that the Progressive Conservative Party of Alberta represents the best choice to successfully lead our province into the 21st Century. I also owe it to the voters of Foothills-Rocky View who elected me as a candidate for the Progressive Conservative Party of Alberta. I trust that you will respect hundreds of years of British and Canadian parliamentary precedents that allow a resigning Cabinet minister to remain in Caucus.

It has been an honour to serve as the Minister of Finance and Enterprise and, before that, as Minister of Sustainable Resources Development. I thank you for these opportunities, and I look forward to continuing to serve Albertans, my constituents in Foothills-Rocky View, and the Progressive Conservative Association of Alberta.

Sincerely,

Ted Morton, MLA, Foothills-Rocky View

As a complementary recruitment strategy, we continued to build what we called our "Waves" document—a list of MLAs ranked in order from the least loyal / most unhappy with Stelmach to the most loyal / least unhappy. Our hypothesis was that while the political risk for "first movers"—myself and a few close supporters—was high, there would be security in numbers. The more of us that "abandoned ship," the lower the risk for those who followed. The risk threshold would be different for each MLA, depending on their level of unhappiness with Stelmach and their assessment of the negative effect that his continued leadership would have on their 2012 re-election chances.

Initially, I used the Waves List to approach those at the very top of the list (the most unhappy and/or least loyal) to discuss discreetly my dilemma with the budget, and—if they seemed sympathetic—to broach the possibility of my resigning, and then to assess their reaction. Those who indicated enthusiasm for abandoning Stelmach we categorized as "Floor Crossers," and then further subdivided these into First, Second, and Third Waves—reflecting the order in which we predicted they would follow me to sit (temporarily) as Independent MLAs. The rest were categorized, in descending order, as Sympathizers, Fence-Sitters, and No-Nevers.

These conversations were risky for me, because if I went too far down the "putsch path" with the wrong person, it would get back to the premier's office. Which, in the end, it did. The Waves document went through numerous revisions, but here's what the final version looked like the weekend before I resigned.

The "Waves" Document

Floor-Crossers [15]	Sympathizers [14]	Fence-Sitters [26]	No Nevers [11]
First Wave [5]	*Ron Liepert (C)	*Heather Klimchuk (E)	Genia Leskiw (N)
George Groeneveld (S)	*Alison Redford (C)	*Rob Renner (S)	Teresa Woo-Paw (C)
Ken Allred (E)	*Lloyd Snelgrove (N)	Len Mitzel (S)	Pearl Calahasen (N)
Kyle Fawcett (C)	Art Johnson (C)	Greg Weadick (S)	*Gene Zwozdesky (E)
Doug Griffiths (N)	Neil Brown (C)	Cal Dallas (S)	*Iris Evans (E)
Evan Berger (S)	Barry McFarland (S)	Verlyn Olson (N)	*Luke Ouellette (S)
Second Wave [5]	Arno Doerksen (S)	*Cindy Ady (C)	Hector Goudreau (N)
Tony Vandermeer (E)	Ty Lund (S)	Art Johnston (C)	*Doug Horner (N)
Doug Elniski (E)	*Yvonne Fritz (C)	Wayne Cao (C)	*Ray Danyluk (N)
Dave Rodney (C)	Janis Sarich (E)	*Lindsay Blackett (C)	*Jack Hayden (S)
Mo Amery (C)	George VanderBurg (N)	Robin Campbell (N)	*Ed Stelmach (N)
Fred Lindsay (N)	*Mary Anne Jablonski (S)	Jeff Johnson (N)	
Third Wave [5]	Manmeet Bhullar (C)	Diana McQueen (N)	
Ray Prins (S)	*Len Webber (C)	Richard Marz (S)	
Jonathan Denis (C)		Frank Oberle (N)	
*Janis Tarchuk (S)		Wayne Drysdale (N)	
Broyce Jacobs (S)		David Xiao (E)	
Alana DeLong (C)		Naresh Bhardwaj (E)	
		Peter Sandhu (E)	
		*Dave Hancock (E)	
		Fred Horne (E)	
		George Rogers (E)	
		Carl Benito (E)	
		Dave Quest (E)	
		*Thomas Lukaszuk (E)	
		*Mel Knight (N)	

N: North

S: South

C: Calgary

E: Edmonton

*Cabinet Minister

HOW TO LEAVE

In the end, we came up with three options. The first was the "solo" option: for me to resign as finance minister, and also as the Foothills-Rocky View MLA. I would return to my position at the University of Calgary and then wait to see how events unfolded up to and including the 2012 election. If the PCs lost or did poorly—which seemed certain—Stelmach would have to resign, and then I could return to enter the next leadership race, reputation intact. We abandoned this for several reasons. We would have little to no control of how events would unfold. Secondly, I wanted to be able to run in the 2012 election against David Swann while he was still leader of the Liberal Party because he was so beatable. Also—and most ironically in retrospect—we were nervous that Jim Prentice, who had just resigned from the federal Conservative cabinet, would run for the provincial PC leadership if the opportunity arose. For those readers not from Alberta, this is exactly what he did—three years later, when the next PC premier, Alison Redford, was forced to resign.

The second option was to assemble a "Committee of Wise Persons"— other disillusioned MLAs—and go to the premier as a group before the caucus meeting scheduled for Wednesday, January 26, and inform him that if he did not agree to resign, we would all leave the PC caucus and sit as Independents. Under this scenario, I would make an impassioned last-ditch effort at Tuesday's Treasury Board meeting for both my budget and the Fiscal Framework. Assuming this would fail (a safe bet), we would then invite a carefully selected number of pre-screened MLAs (See list of "First and Second Waves") to my house that evening to recruit them into the "Wise Persons" plan.

The appeal of this plan was security in numbers and not leaving Stelmach time to plan a counterattack. The downside was that it would come across in the media as a straight power play by an overly ambitious Ted Morton, and the "standing on principle" narrative would be lost. There was also a real risk that our "Wise Persons" committee might suddenly become very small at the last minute, as erstwhile members lost their courage and bailed out.

The third and final option—and the one I chose—we tagged as the "Raucous Caucus." Under this scenario, I was to meet with the premier before Tuesday's scheduled Treasury Board meeting in Calgary and hand him my letter of resignation. A copy of the letter would simultaneously be leaked to Don Braid, political columnist for the *Calgary Herald*. This would ensure that there would be no turning back. The letter would stress that while I could not deliver the red-ink budget that the premier wanted, I wished to remain in the government caucus. My disagreement was with the budget, not the party.

Next, in Wednesday's caucus meeting, a group of supportive MLAs would use my resignation—and the accompanying media storm—as a reason to raise the leadership issue. If I were still in caucus (post-resignation), I would remain silent. Their argument would be that the political bleeding would only get worse, and that it would be better for the party if the premier were to leave now rather than later. While Stelmach loyalists would aggressively challenge this, we believed there would be other MLAs—such as Liepert and Redford—who would join the "resign now" chorus, not out of any love for me or my budget, but because they feared they would lose their seat in the next election.

If Stelmach were to survive the "Raucous Caucus," the First Wavers would either be kicked out of caucus or leave of their own volition to sit as Independents—thus fulfilling their own prediction that it was too late for Stelmach to stop the political bleeding. They would then be followed by "Second Wavers" a week or two later, further undermining Stelmach's position. Regardless of whether I had been kicked out of caucus or allowed to stay in, I would stay out of this debate, thus separating the leadership issue from the budget issue, the ambition narrative from the "standing on principle" narrative. As noted, this is the option we chose to go with. While it had its risks, we thought that—sooner or later—there would be enough defections to force Stelmach to resign. After all, taking risks is what Albertans do.

JANUARY 25: THE PUTSCH

January 25 finally arrived. Officially, my calendar indicated lunch with the Walton Group at a downtown event featuring the ex-governor of California, Arnold Schwarzenegger; the Treasury Board meeting in the afternoon; and later a dinner with Bill Rice, CEO of the Alberta Stock Exchange. These were left on my calendar to make my day look normal, but we had already arranged phone calls to cancel the first and last.

My wife was still in California, so I woke up, showered, dressed, and had coffee by myself. When I put the envelope with my resignation letter in my jacket pocket, I felt like an assassin holstering a concealed weapon. At 7:45 a.m. sharp, as planned, Eric arrived to pick me up and drive to McDougall Centre. On the ten-minute drive to the underground parking garage at

McDougall, neither of us said a word. There was nothing left to say. Plus, both of us were too nervous to make small talk.

At the garage door, Eric rolled down his window and pressed the speaker box to ask security to let us in. We could see the security cameras activate as we pulled up. When security responded, Eric said in a loud, cheerful voice: "Hi, Eric Taylor here with Minister Morton for our morning meetings." As the door opened, we both involuntarily roared with laughter. We were laughing so hard we were almost crying. But again, neither of us said a word to the other. We were more than a little nervous. We quickly composed ourselves and went upstairs to meet with Tim Wiles, my deputy minister, to prepare for the Treasury Board meeting later that day—a meeting I had no intention of attending.

The premier was supposed to be flying down from Edmonton and was scheduled to arrive at McDougall by 10:00 a.m. I was planning to meet him then to hand him my resignation letter. At 9:30 and again at 10:00, we were told that his plane was delayed because of weather. This was not unusual, and I was not concerned. But then at 10:30, we were told that the premier had scheduled a televised press conference for 11:00. That news sent my blood pressure soaring. A televised press conference? These aren't planned at the last minute. Clearly, we had been intentionally misled by the earlier messages. We realized immediately that someone must have leaked my resignation plans to the premier's office.[4] The only reassuring thing was that everyone else at McDougall seemed equally mystified.

As we crowded into the premier's McDougall office suite—the only room that had a television and was also large enough to handle the dozen or so of us—I was prepared to watch myself be fired on television. Instead, to the shock of everyone in the room, Stelmach announced his intention to resign later in the year. Instead of firing me, he was firing himself. For me, the irony was palpable. Four years earlier, I had effectively made Ed Stelmach premier with my supporters' second preferences. Now, I had deposed him.

A tired-looking Ed Stelmach told Albertans that "after twenty-five years of public service," he and his family had decided that he would not run in the next provincial election, scheduled for 2012. The Progressive Conservatives would have to choose a new leader, and to give the party time, he would retire later this year. He did not give a date. Stelmach said he was tired of "personal attacks," criticized "US-style wedge politics," and warned against the threat of "an extreme-right party." But, he said pointedly, he would remain premier long enough to deliver the next budget, a budget that would allow Alberta to return to a balanced budget in 2013, not 2012.

This was the premier's official version of events. But the media was not buying it. The unofficial version was that his finance minister, Ted Morton, had planned to resign that morning. If Stelmach then kicked him out of caucus, Morton would take at least a dozen PC MLAs with him. This would precipitate a war of attrition within the caucus, a war Stelmach could not win and a war the party could not afford. It was not an accident that the unofficial version bore a strong resemblance to our "Raucous Caucus" plan. Armstrong and Iversen had leaked all of this to *Globe and Mail* reporter Josh Wingrove by mid-morning, and his story was online by mid-afternoon.[5]

This made for a very awkward moment later that afternoon when I made the mistake of leaving McDougall Centre alone and on foot. I was swarmed by a media scrum demanding to know if the "unofficial version" was accurate. Without any aides to fend off the media, I did my best to avoid answering that question, as I sprinted two blocks down Fifth Avenue to the hotel where Iversen and Armstrong were waiting in a fifth-floor suite to figure out our next move.

But what was our next move? In one sense, we had won and won big. Stelmach was leaving, and I hadn't even resigned. But that was the problem. I was still finance minister with a budget I could not support. With a new leadership contest now guaranteed, it was even more imperative that I NOT deliver Budget 2011, as it would destroy whatever base I had left with fiscal conservatives in both the PC and Wildrose parties. To resign on principle now, as originally planned, would simply confirm the "unofficial version" of events, and make me the ambitious political assassin who took down the likeable Ed Stelmach. In a perverse but clever way, Stelmach's surprise resignation had boxed me in. That evening in Calgary, Ron Glen was overheard boasting that this was exactly what he and Stelmach had done. But this lasted less than twelve hours.

That evening we took a break to watch the 10 p.m. local news. Most of it was a rerun of the earlier 6 p.m. news, covering Stelmach's surprise announcement and reactions from other party leaders and talking heads. But our ears perked up when we heard the one piece of new news. In an interview with a local Edmonton radio station, Stelmach had said that any of his current cabinet ministers who planned to run to replace him should resign in order to avoid the perception of any conflict of interest in the exercise of their ministerial powers. Bingo! This was my way out of the "box" predicament, and we immediately set to work drafting a new resignation letter. Stelmach's comment, while no doubt sincere, had to have been completely unscripted, and must have driven his advisors wild. But unscripted comments were Ed's specialty.

Resignation Letter (Take Two)

January 27, 2011

Premier Ed Stelmach

Room 307, Legislature Building

Edmonton, AB T5K 2B6

Dear Premier:

Early in the 2006 leadership race, you were the first Minister to resign from cabinet to avoid the appearance of conflict of interest and to facilitate a smooth transition in the operation of your ministry. At the time, I was one of many Albertans who admired the principled position you took. It was the right thing to do then—and it is the right thing to do today.

It is my intention to seek the leadership of our Party upon your departure. While I have not yet stated this publicly, it is widely perceived to be the case.

Under these circumstances, I believe it would be difficult, if not impossible, for me to continue to discharge my duties as Minister with the required perception of impartiality. The media coverage and speculation around the impending leadership contest would be a serious distraction from the process of governing, particularly the passage of the upcoming budget. The planned Cabinet Tours would compound this problem with the perceived use of government resources by a leadership candidate. Needless to say, the same principle should apply to any other minister planning to seek the leadership of our party.

Accordingly, I tender my resignation to you effective immediately.

In resigning from your Cabinet, I wish to make it clear that I intend to remain in our party's caucus. As you know from your own experience, there are hundreds of years of British and Canadian parliamentary precedents that allow a resigning cabinet minister to remain in caucus. I still strongly believe that the Progressive Conservative Association of Alberta represents the best choice to successfully lead our province

---

into the 21st century. I also owe it to the voters of Foothills-Rocky View who elected me as a candidate for the Progressive Conservative Party of Alberta.

It has been an honour to serve as the Minister of Finance and Enterprise, and before that, as Minister of Sustainable Resources Development. I thank you for these opportunities, and I look forward to continuing to serve Albertans, my constituents in Foothills-Rocky View, and the Progressive Conservative Party of Alberta.

Sincerely,

Ted Morton

MLA, Foothills-Rocky View

RAUCOUS CAUCUS

First thing Wednesday morning, I went to McDougall Centre and met with the premier. I handed him my letter of resignation and explained that, based on his comments the previous night, I felt compelled to resign now, before delivering the budget, because I knew already that I would run for the now open leadership. I was surprised at how friendly and relaxed Stelmach was, and he accepted my resignation amicably. When he called in Ron Glen to inform him of my resignation, I could see that his chief of staff was anything but happy. Glen saw that I had escaped the trap he had laid.

What followed was the most bizarre press conference I have ever been part of. Just before noon, Stelmach, Lloyd Snelgrove, and I met with the media to announce my resignation. Stelmach explained that Snelgrove, who was already president of Treasury Board, would become the new minister of finance and deliver the 2011 budget. We assured them that there was no bad blood between us; that my resignation was just normal protocol for a minister planning to run for leadership; and that it was all business as usual. Of course, none of them believed us.[6]

I also stated that my intent in running for the leadership would be to bring back Wildrose conservatives to the PC Party. I warned of the risks of vote splitting on the Right. Since many of my friends and supporters from the 2006 leadership were now with the Wildrose, I was optimistic that I could succeed in bringing us back together. Danielle Smith, who was present at the press conference, immediately threw cold water on that idea. She dismissed the prospects of a merger as "highly optimistic and also a little patronizing. ... I gather he figures he'll win the leadership and then I'll just roll the party into the PCs. I think that is pretty delusional."[7]

Reflecting back now, I have to wonder what might have happened if Smith had embraced my resignation, worked with me to help win the PC leadership, and then joined a Ted Morton–led PC government. Three years later she did just this—joining the Jim Prentice–led PC government. But by then it was too late to stop the vote splitting on the Right, which led to the demise of the PC dynasty in the 2015 election.

Following the press conference, we proceeded directly to the previously planned 1 p.m. caucus meeting. The premier explained his own decision, and then informed caucus that he had just accepted my resignation. As with the press conference, he assured everyone that this was all business as usual. As with the press conference, no one believed him. He then announced for the first time that his departure date would not be until October 1. This caught almost everyone by surprise, including me, and provoked a new discussion. Could the government—could the party—survive eight months with a lame-duck premier?

Having caused enough trouble for the day, I chose to remain silent. But others voiced legitimate concerns about the public's reaction to an eight-month caretaker government, while now-former cabinet ministers were slugging it out to be the next leader and premier. As was his way, Ron Liepert was the most outspoken, stating that for the good of the party, Stelmach should leave no later than June. Calgary MLA Dave Rodney rose to support Liepert's position but was cut short by the premier. For the first—and last—time in his tenure as premier, Stelmach lost it in front of caucus. He let fly a few F-bombs, at least one of which was about how he was sick and tired of F-ing Calgarians. A stunned caucus went uncharacteristically silent. No one spoke further on the October 1 departure date, and we adjourned shortly thereafter.

Our acquiescence in Stelmach's stubborn and self-indulgent plan to remain in the premier's seat until October 1 was understandable. We all knew Ed Stelmach to be a decent and good man, and he had just been dealt some nasty cards. Some kindness was in order. Understandable, but a huge mistake, not just for the PC party but also for me. By the end of February, my leadership campaign had already raised $100,000, and I was an early favourite to win a short leadership race.

That was certainly my team's plan. But it didn't happen. My electoral base from the 2006 leadership had evaporated. The eight-month campaign created the time needed for long-shot candidate Alison Redford's campaign strategy of buying off public sector unions to win the PC leadership. While Redford's new centre-left strategy helped her to win the 2012 provincial election, it cost her the leadership less than two years later. An eleventh-hour rescue attempt by ex–federal MP Jim Prentice, another Red Tory, failed to stem the tide, and the vote splitting with the Wildrose that I had warned about opened the door for an NDP majority government in 2015. How this unfolded is the subject of the next chapter.

10

Redford and Prentice: The End of the PC Dynasty (2011-2015)

Politics are almost as exciting as war, and quite as dangerous. In war you can only be killed once, but in politics many times.

—Winston Churchill

2011 PC LEADERSHIP: TWO-MINUTE TORIES STRIKE AGAIN

Stelmach announced his intention to resign on January 25. Two weeks later, I was the first to announce that I would be a candidate to replace him. I had high name recognition and was expected to build on my strong showing in the 2006 leadership campaign. I had now served in two senior cabinet positions. Within days I was being labelled as the "front-runner" by media pundits, but with a cautionary title that turned out to be prophetic: "The curse of the Front-runner." The pundit went on to note that "Alberta leadership races have a history of going sideways at the last minute for the person who has the most support, the most money and media attention."[1]

Gary Mar was also an early favourite. During the Klein era, Mar had been an MLA from Calgary and held numerous cabinet positions. During the Stelmach years, he had served as Alberta's trade representative in Washington, DC. Mar was the favourite of the PC establishment, who were no more enthusiastic about me in 2011 than they had been in 2006. Mar enjoyed the endorsement of twenty-seven MLAs. By the end of the leadership campaign, he had out-fundraised the rest of us by a two-to-one margin—raising over

$2 million, mostly from the same people who had bankrolled the Dinning campaign in 2006.

The other four candidates were:

- Doug Horner: another experienced cabinet minister from the Edmonton area and the son of a former PC cabinet minister. Like Stelmach in 2006, Horner was viewed as a regional candidate. Ten of his fourteen MLA supporters were from Edmonton and northern Alberta. Horner clearly had the support of the Stelmach loyalists.

- Alison Redford: a little-known feminist and human-rights lawyer from Calgary. She had worked for former federal PC Prime Minister Joe Clark and had stuck with the PCs during the 1990s civil war with the upstart Reform Party. With a reputation as a Red Tory, Redford tried unsuccessfully to win a nomination to be the federal Conservative Party's candidate in Calgary-West in 2004. She then went provincial, was elected as a Calgary MLA in 2008, and was immediately appointed as minister of justice. Redford had the support of only one MLA and initially was seen as running to position herself for future influence.

- Rick Orman: a former MLA from Calgary (1986–93) who had held three different cabinet positions, including minister of energy. He ran for the leadership of the PC Party in 1992 but finished third and retired from elected politics the following year.

- Doug Griffiths: a thirty-four-year-old MLA for Battle River-Wainwright. When I arrived in the PC caucus in 2004, Doug was the only MLA who had previously been active in the federal Reform Party. He also was an ally in pushing out Stelmach.

In 2006, I had only one MLA endorsement: Tony Abbott. This time I was endorsed by ten sitting MLAs. Five were from Edmonton. David Xiao, Doug Elniski, and Tony Vandermeer had all become disillusioned with Stelmach and supported my effort to force him out. Also from Edmonton were Carl Benito and Peter Sandhu, both of whom were influential leaders in their respective immigrant communities, communities that liked my pro-family policy positions. From Calgary I was supported by Jonathan Denis, who shared my Reform Party roots, and Dave Rodney, who had supported my conservation and stewardship policies. Further south I had the support of

George Groeneveld and Evan Berger. Both represented rural ridings adjacent to mine and were also early Reformers. We had worked together on overlapping constituency issues and had become friends. Both were early supporters of the Prairie Putsch.

My 2011 leadership campaign could not have been more different from my 2006 campaign. In 2006, I was an outsider, trying to break into the party from its conservative wing. To win, I had to attract new members to the PC Party by challenging the status quo. But now I was an insider, a member of the status quo. We assumed that I could keep my 2006 base supporters and finish in the top three in the first round. But to win in the second round, I would have to attract support from more traditional, mainstream PC members. From the start, we prioritized winning the second preferences of those candidates who did not make the cut-off after the first ballot.

My 2011 leadership campaign made little mention of the Alberta Agenda. Why would it? I was now trying to appeal to a new group of PC supporters who never did like the Firewall Letter. The most my brochures said about Ottawa was that I would be "a strong voice at the table in Ottawa." I was at least partly right to de-emphasize the Alberta Agenda. To most Albertans, it no longer made much sense for me to be railing against Ottawa when the prime minister—Stephen Harper—was not only from Alberta but also a personal friend.

This strategy might have worked if I'd still had my former base of supporters from 2006. We simply assumed that I did. If we had done a baseline poll of my former supporters list at the outset—which we were advised to do—we would have seen that I didn't. Not doing this baseline poll turned out to be a fatal mistake. My advice to future leadership candidates: spend this money at the beginning to find out where you have supporters and where you don't.

Shortly after I declared my candidacy for the PC leadership, I was interviewed by *Calgary Herald* columnist Don Braid. Braid wrote that a "kinder, gentler Morton" had moved to the centre to prevent vote splitting on the Right.[2] Being in government, I had told Braid, had been "a moderating experience." As I told another reporter, "In a parliamentary system, governing is a team sport. Puck hogs aren't welcome, so you've got to play as a team and that's how I've played for the last eight years."[3] I concluded, "I'm criticized by some Red Tories as being too conservative and criticized by Wildrose as being too liberal. ... That's not a bad place to be."[4] This assessment turned out to be very wrong. In a general election, vying for the median voters in the middle is usually a good strategy. But in an open primary like the PC leadership election, it is not.

My two primary campaign messages were that as leader I would reunite the Right and bring back the "Alberta Advantage." On the latter, I pledged no more deficit spending; balanced budgets; low personal and corporate income taxes; and restoring investor confidence. I argued that fiscal responsibility was the successful PC brand—built by Lougheed and Klein, but now destroyed by Stelmach. I claimed that I was the candidate with the experience and determination to bring it back. My refusal to bend to Stelmach's spend-now, pay-later policies was the proof. In retrospect, I think this was both accurate and true. But telling families that you are going to tighten up funding for programs they care about is hardly a way to win over voters.

My other primary campaign message was that I was a uniter: the only candidate who could prevent vote splitting with the Wildrose. By the time Stelmach announced his resignation, the Wildrose was polling almost even with the PCs.[5] My message to conservative voters in 2011 was simple and clear: "Remember the lesson of the Federal conservatives: United we stand, divided we fall. The last thing Alberta needs is two conservative parties."[6] While this message clearly did not help my leadership campaign in 2011, four years later it proved prophetic.

I also emphasized the importance of environmental stewardship—especially for water quality and quantity on Alberta's Eastern Slopes. I emphasized the work I had done with the Alberta Land Use Framework and *Alberta Land Stewardship Act* (ALSA). My message: that just as it is morally wrong to leave unpaid bills and debt to our children, it is wrong to leave them with an environmental mess. I also used these issues as a critique of the Wildrose Party. "The single biggest weakness of Wildrose," I told Don Braid, "is that they have no environmental policy. In the 21st century, you'd better have one. You need it to protect Albertans' quality of life, protect our markets, and keep the federal government out of our jurisdiction."[7] Again, this was all true, but its political value in the PC leadership race was marginal. Concerns about ALSA's impact on property rights had alienated many of my former rural supporters.

My campaign brochures also made commitments to:

- Health Care: reducing wait times for elective, non-emergency surgeries by more use of privately delivered but publicly funded surgeries.

- Education: more school choice for parents, and a tuition tax credit program to make post-secondary education more affordable for young Albertans.

- Democratic Reforms: fixed election dates; reducing the size of cabinet from twenty-four to seventeen; holding Senate elections every four years; rolling back Stelmach's pay increase for ministers and MLAs; and strengthening the auditor general's office to police government waste.

- New vanity licence plates with a painting of a Canadian bighorn sheep by my new friend Robert Bateman with the inscription "Alberta Strong and Free."[8]

With the exception of the last (which was my favourite), all of these were mainstream policy initiatives. But the first three did little to distinguish me from the other five candidates. The Bateman vanity licence plates were to cost $60, half of which would go to fund Robert Bateman's "Get to Know" program, which connects children with nature; the other half to an Alberta conservation group of the plateholder's choice. This initiative garnered the endorsements of the Alberta Wilderness Association and Canadian Parks and Wilderness Society. But members of groups like these were not normally PC Party members and were not going to bother to purchase a PC membership to support me.

An early sign of my campaign's weakness was that I never picked up any additional support from PC MLAs. Ten was a lot more than Redford (one), Griffiths (one), or Orman (zero). But it paled in comparison to Mar's twenty-seven MLA endorsements, and even Horner had fourteen.

Another negative indicator was the dramatic reduction in the number of volunteers in our Calgary campaign office. In my 2006 leadership campaign we had over thirty unpaid volunteers working non-stop on our phone banks and direct mail operations. This time we had less than a dozen. All of our phone bank operations were run by paid employees—mostly university students looking for some part-time work. They were there for the pay, not for the candidate.

I was blinded to the implications of these ominous differences by the ease with which we were able to raise money. We raised over $100,000 by the end of February. By the end of the campaign, over $1 million. In 2006, we struggled to meet monthly expenses, and in the last month didn't ... until after the first ballot! In 2011, the more we asked for, the more we got. Another difference was the number and size of donations. In 2006, we had thousands of donations in the $25 to $100 range. In 2011, we had far fewer donors, but many writing big cheques: three for $30,000, the legal maximum; twenty-two for between $15,000 and $30,000; and sixty-nine for over $5,000. In other words, close to 90 percent of our funding came from ninety-four donors. So much for grassroots! But I was not aware of these numbers until well after the campaign was over.

In a similar way, I was misled by the co-operation I received from local PC constituency officers as I campaigned across the province. Wherever we went, PC volunteers were there to greet me and to help organize meet and greets. I interpreted this co-operation as a sign of support. This was naive. Patronage and a friendly ear in the premier's office were the glue that had helped to hold the PC empire together for over four decades. At the end of the day, everyone wants to be on the side of the winner. As I was a high-profile PC cabinet minister and an early favourite to win, it was strategic to help me. I had forgotten what I thought I had learned on my first day in the Alberta legislature. In party politics, people often tell you what they think you want to hear, rather than what they really think.

As the campaign rolled on, I continued to poll well. Mar was usually ahead of me, but not by a significant margin. However, late polling in September predicted Redford as a contender. The two of us actually met privately once in early September to discuss helping one another with second preferences should one of us fail to make the cut-off after the first ballot. Of course, I assumed that would be her, not me.

In July I was endorsed by the *Globe and Mail*.[9] Morton, the *Globe* wrote, "is right wing enough to fend off the Wildrose threat, but moderation is part of his complex character. He would probably govern with considerable fiscal prudence." My campaign interpreted this a sign that we were succeeding in my rebranding as a moderate conservative. I had forgotten that in 2006, I had joked that the *Globe's* endorsement of Jim Dinning was a political kiss of death in Alberta.

My campaign ended on a sour note. Eight days before the first day of voting, the CBC broke what they spun as a "scandal" story that as minister of SRD I had been using two different government emails—the second to avoid FOIP (Freedom of Information) requests for copies of my emails. This information had apparently been leaked by an unhappy bureaucrat in SRD in the hope of damaging my leadership chances.

The first part of the story was absolutely true. I did have two separate emails: Ted.Morton@gov.ab.ca and FLM@gov.ab.ca .The first was my official government email. As it was publicly available from the SRD website, I would often receive hundreds of emails a week from the general public, opining one way or the other on the dozens of issues that were pending decision at SRD. The sheer volume of these emails made it virtually impossible for me to efficiently conduct email correspondence with my office staff and my senior civil servants. So for this purpose, we created the second email for internal communications, and I left it to my office staff to filter and reply to emails from the general public.

As I told the media the day the story broke, "If I was trying to avoid FOIP, I wouldn't have used my real name [i.e., Frederick Lee Morton]."[10] To their credit, when asked, both Premier Stelmach and rival candidate and fellow cabinet member Doug Horner told the media that they too used a secondary email to conduct government business. And I was more than skeptical when both Mar and Redford said that during their time as ministers, they used only their one official government email address. It was simply a matter of the most efficient use of a minister's limited time and had nothing to do with avoiding FOIP requests.

After the initial headlines, the story went nowhere. But playing defence is not the way you want to end the last week of a political campaign. As Calgary columnist Don Braid observed, "For Ted Morton … Thursday was a miserable day in politics, one that could hurt his chances of becoming premier."[11] It certainly didn't help. But neither did it affect the outcome. The die was already cast.

❊ ❊ ❊

None of the six candidates was expected to win the 50 percent-plus-one needed for a first ballot victory, but Mar came close. He took 41 percent and left the rest of us in the dust. His strength was not just wide but deep—winning pluralities in fifty-two of the eighty-three ridings. Redford was a surprise second-place finisher at 19 percent, with strong support in Calgary, while Horner finished third with 14 percent. I finished fourth at only 12 percent, my anticipated support failing to materialize in either my old rural strongholds or in my MLA supporters' ridings in southeast Edmonton and northeast Calgary.

2011 PC Leadership: First Ballot Results*		
Candidate	Votes	Percent
Gary Mar	24,195	41
Alison Redford	11,127	19
Doug Horner	8,635	15
Ted Morton	6,962	12
Rick Orman	6,005	10
Doug Griffiths	2,435	4
Total	59,359	

*Progressive Conservative Association of Alberta, "PC Alberta Leadership 2011," September 22, 2011, archived by the Wayback Machine, https://web.archive.org/web/20110922163053/http://www.albertapc.ab.ca/results.htm.

I was totally unprepared for my poor showing. I had expected to come in second, not far behind Mar, and well positioned to pass him on second preferences. It had never even occurred to me that I would not make the cut-off to the second round. But in retrospect, my demise no longer seems that surprising. My strongest supporters had become disillusioned with the Stelmach government and with me for staying with him as long as I did.

Many of my former ranch and farm supporters were angry with me for the *Alberta Land Stewardship Act* and its alleged infringement on property rights. During 2010 as the minister of finance, I was preoccupied with my new budgetary responsibilities, and had not paid attention to the Wildrose Party's attacks on the property rights issue. I thought then—and still do—that this was a bogus claim. As explained in chapter 4, ALSA made Alberta the first province in Canada to compensate landowners for "regulatory takings"—policies or regulations whose effect is to reduce the market value of the land. But it was too late. As I said later, "The toothpaste was out of the tube, and it's been tough to put it back in."[12] My 2006 supporters had either switched allegiance to the Wildrose Party or simply stayed home. The collapse of my support—from 41,000 votes in 2006 (second ballot) to 7,000 in 2011 (first ballot)—told the story.

The Red Tories that were left had never forgiven me for blocking the "coronation" of the "Prince in Waiting," Jim Dinning. And many of the Edmonton and northern Tories disliked me because I had pulled the plug on Stelmach. Finally, as finance minister, I had annoyed almost every other cabinet minister by rejecting their requests for more funding. From this perspective, it's no wonder I got clobbered.

❋ ❋ ❋

Post–first ballot, I had to make a decision: endorse one of the three candidates advancing to the second round; remain quiet; or leave the party altogether. I met with my advisory group Sunday afternoon—and a very dispirited meeting it was. We discussed each of the three options. Several encouraged me to leave the party to sit as an Independent—or to join the Wildrose. What future was there for Ted Morton in a party that had just chosen the three least conservative candidates to proceed to the second round? If I couldn't live with my conscience in an Ed Stelmach government, what was it going to be like in a Gary Mar or Alison Redford cabinet?

I was not persuaded. I understood the risks associated with starting new parties. I have never regretted my early involvement in and support for Preston Manning and the Reform Party. But I also never had any illusions about what it cost Alberta and conservative voters during the 1990s. Splitting the conservative vote in federal elections had given a free ride to the Liberals for thirteen years. For the past eight months, I had campaigned on the dangers of vote splitting with two right-of-centre parties. At this point, going over to the Wildrose was no longer an option.

Endorsing no one and remaining neutral was the easiest option. But it also seemed like a one-way ticket to the back bench in the next government. If I wanted to stay in the party and have a good chance to remain in cabinet, I had to endorse one of the three. Horner was clearly not going to win. So, would it be Mar or Redford?

It may shock many of my friends and former supporters that on a personal level, I preferred Redford. She was clearly much more liberal than I was. But many of the problems that cabinet deals with are administrative and non-ideological: basically, just trying to make the trains run on time. And when it came to this, Redford had been better prepared, more articulate and demonstrated better practical judgement than most of the Stelmach ministers I'd had to work with. We had maintained a friendly, professional relationship, and this continued throughout the leadership campaign.

I had reservations about Mar. I had not forgotten that he'd served as the Dinning campaign's most vocal mudslinger in the anyone-but-Morton campaign in the final week of the 2006 leadership. He also had a reputation for sleazy backroom deals while serving as a minister in the Klein governments.[13] And I hadn't forgotten how in December 2006, after Stelmach had become premier and did not appoint Mar to a cabinet position, he threw an ugly temper tantrum in the next caucus meeting.

Notwithstanding all this, I chose to support Mar. At 41 percent of first-round support, no one was going to stop him. If the reason I was staying in the PC caucus was to remain a senior cabinet minister, then Mar was the ticket. At a press conference with Orman on Monday morning, we both endorsed Mar. I then left the province for some much-needed rest. I did not return until the second Saturday of voting and so played no role in that segment of the Mar campaign.

Redford's second-ballot strategy was the same as mine had been in 2006. She needed to block the front-runner, Mar, from passing the 50 percent threshold, and then take enough of Horner's second preferences to win. To this end, Redford publicly encouraged her supporters to give their second preferences to Horner. Horner was less direct, but he reciprocated in a widely circulated comment: "When you look at the policies, the platforms, the call for change, where we need to go with this province in the future, I think it's pretty obvious where you would find my second ballot."[14] While these remarks may seem obscure, the message got through to his supporters.
When all three of the eliminated candidates—Orman, and Griffiths, and myself—endorsed Mar, he seemed like a shoo-in to win the second ballot outright on first preferences.[15] But this was not to be.

❊ ❊ ❊

On the second ballot, the number of new voters surged again—this time by 31 percent. Mar's percentage—at 43 percent—hardly budged from the first ballot. By contrast, Redford more than doubled her share of the votes to 37 percent. Horner took only 14 percent, and was thereby eliminated, throwing the outcome to the second preferences of the Horner supporters.

	First Ballot	Second Ballot*	Preferential Ballot**
Mar	24,195	33,233	35,491
Redford	11,129	28,993	37,101
Horner	8,635	15,590	—
Others	15,402	—	—
Total	59,361	77,816	72,592

*Progressive Conservative Association of Alberta, "PC Alberta Leadership 2011," October 4, 2011, archived by the Wayback Machine, https://web.archive.org/web/20111004125849/http://www.albertapc.ab.ca/results2.htm.

**Progressive Conservative Association of Alberta, "PC Alberta Leadership 2011," October 4, 2011, archived by the Wayback Machine, https://web.archive.org/web/20111004153716/http://www.albertapc.ab.ca/results/finaltotal.html.

Then the "curse of the front-runner" struck again. In the second round, 40 percent of Doug Horner's supporters did not even indicate a second preference—suggesting that they did not much care for Mar or Redford. Of those who did, over three-quarters (10,366) gave their second preference to Redford, allowing her to sneak past Mar with 51 percent, and making her the next premier of Alberta. For the third time in a row, an underdog candidate had burst from the pack to take down the party favourite. While these results surprised both participants and observers, the reasons are not hard to discern.

As in 2006, there was a dramatic surge of support from public sector unions, this time for Redford. Early in the campaign, she had publicly broken from the Stelmach government and promised to "restore" $110 million to the education budget. She then promised to help out the underfunded Alberta policemen's pension, which garnered an endorsement from the police association. When front-runner Gary Mar refused to rule out more privately delivered (but publicly funded) health care, Redford denounced him and promised "to keep public health care public." She also promised new "family [health] care clinics" that would accommodate the crowded schedules of working mothers. Redford's policy focus on education and health care sent the message that she might well be the "least-worst choice" for public sector union members who didn't normally vote PC.

What had happened somewhat spontaneously in the 2006 Stelmach campaign became a conscious strategy for Redford in 2011. Her policy promises on health and education issues resonated well with nurses' and teachers' unions. In the last month of the campaign, this "pull" was turned into a "push" by a sophisticated social media campaign that targeted professional working women, a demographic that overlaps strongly with nurses and teachers.[16] In Calgary, the polling stations were filled with "two-minute Tories"—buying their PC memberships on the way in and ripping them up on the way out.

MINISTER OF ENERGY

I left the Edmonton EXPO Centre in shock. Like everyone else, I had never imagined that Redford could catch and pass Mar on the second ballot. The next morning, I packed up our car and headed to Calgary—and, I assumed, soon to the back bench. Any prospect of a cabinet appointment in a Redford government seemed like a complete impossibility. Then, as we passed by the Edmonton airport, my cellphone rang.

On the other end was Ken Hughes, a former Conservative MP from Calgary back in the 1980s. We had met through our mutual friend Barry Cooper and become friends, even after Ken lost his seat in the Reform Party's sweep of Alberta in the 1993 federal election. So why was Ken calling me this morning? He quickly explained that he was in Edmonton helping Redford with her transition planning and that she wanted to speak with me ASAP about a possible cabinet appointment.

I was shocked, but fortunately did not drive off the road. I did, however, do a U-turn, and forty-five minutes later walked through a door at the Chateau Lacombe Hotel. There to greet me were Ken and Robert Hawkes, Redford's ex-husband. They got right to the point: party unity. Redford needed a cabinet that represented all factions of the PC Party. As a Red Tory, she needed a senior Blue Tory in her cabinet. And I was her man. Would I accept an appointment as her minister of energy?

It took me less than a minute to say YES. My year as finance minister had made me acutely aware of how dependent GOA revenues were on a healthy oil and gas sector. In 2011, this meant increased access to global markets and global prices. But the anti-oil sands, anti-pipeline campaign was already underway. The next Alberta minister of energy would be at the centre of this battle. I welcomed the opportunity. As I subsequently joked, being minister of energy in Alberta was like being the minister of wine in France (a job I'd also be willing to accept).

Unfortunately, from the day I became minister of energy, the next provincial election was only five months away. Other than learning my new policy files and meeting with key energy stakeholders, I had little opportunity to do much in terms of new policy. The two exceptions were two new proposed north-south electricity transmission lines and the Teedrum Upgrader.

Earlier, Redford and I had both opposed the new 500 kV transmission project as unnecessary and too expensive. But after reading my minister's briefing notes and meeting with experts, I was persuaded otherwise. Geographically larger, integrated electric systems are less prone to failures and blackouts than smaller, regional systems. An unexpected loss of electricity in one region can be covered by transmission from a different region. With the new steam-assisted gravity drainage systems (SAGD) that were being installed in the oil sands, we had an abundant new source of electricity. But to get it to where it was needed—central and southern Alberta—required new transmission.

No new north-south transmission had been built since the 1980s, during which time Alberta's population had increased by 1.4 million, or 40 percent. Policy-wise, it was time. My explanation: "We're trying to do what's best for the province, not just for the next four years, but the next four decades."[17] But my reversal hurt me politically, as segments of the new lines would be built right through parts of my new riding of Rocky View-Chestermere, and nobody wants sky-high transmission towers in their backyard.[18]

The proposed Teedrum Upgrader came as a complete surprise the day I walked into my new office. I discovered that during the six months of the leadership campaign, Stelmach had been persuaded to sign off on a second upgrader project in the Edmonton area, this one backed by a consortium of Alberta Aboriginal groups led by Enoch Cree First Nation Chief Ron Morin. It had a $6.6 billion price tag and the same bitumen-royalty-in-kind (BRIK) supply and financing arrangements as the now-approved North West Upgrader. As explained in chapter 7, this meant that all the downside risks were on the Government of Alberta. Having just spent most of 2011 trying—unsuccessfully—to block North West, I was damned if I now was going to endorse an identical fiscal calamity. I went immediately to the premier's office and told her I would resign rather than sign off on Teedrum.

To her credit, Redford agreed with me. She had served with me on the ministerial subcommittee that had vetted North West and was well aware of its high financial risk. She arranged for me and Stephen Carter, her then chief of staff, to meet with Teedrum's Aboriginal backers. It was probably the most unpleasant meeting I ever had as a minister. I explained the policy reasons for my refusal to approve the deal. That went nowhere. Its proponents turned to

Carter, looking for a save from the premier's office. To Carter's credit, he said point blank that Premier Redford supported my decision 100 percent. The meeting adjourned less than three minutes later. Unfortunately, Teedrum's Aboriginal backers denounced my decision as "racist."[19] More importantly for Alberta taxpayers, Teedrum never saw the light of day again.

As the April 23 election approached, our caucus became increasingly worried by polls indicating that the Wildrose Party would defeat us. Discussions began about what kinds of voter-friendly new policies we could announce to stem the tide. One suggestion was a price freeze on consumer electricity costs. I'm not sure who came up with this idea, but Ron Liepert, now the new minister of finance, soon became its most vocal supporter. But electricity policy was now in my energy policy portfolio. I spoke strongly against this, declaring that this was something the NDP would do but not Conservatives. Liepert's response was quick and to the point: "We had to out-NDP the NDP." I won the argument that day, but Liepert's exhortation set the tone for the ensuing campaign.

2012 PROVINCIAL ELECTION

The PC campaign for the April election picked up where Liepert had left off (perhaps not too surprising, as Liepert was now Redford's new finance minister). Per her promise during the PC leadership, Redford restored the $107 million for teachers' salaries that Stelmach (and I) had cut in the 2011 Budget. She promised that there would be no cuts to social services (health, education, and other social programs) and full funding for all planned capital projects—new roads, new schools (50!) and new hospitals.[20] In the middle of the campaign, she upped the ante by promising 140 new "family care clinics" with a price tag of $3.4 billion.[21] Just for good measure, she then promised to bring in full-day kindergarten at a cost of another $200 million. All of this, Redford promised, would be done with a balanced budget in the following year, and a $5.1 billion budget surplus by 2015.

This was all wildly unrealistic. The premier knew it. Caucus knew it. And so did the Wildrose. They attacked the PC budget promises as "Alison in Wonderland."[22] And they were right. For the record, the Redford government subsequently ran three consecutive budget deficits totalling $5 billion in new debt. But in the context of a four-week campaign, it was impossible to prove this in any politically meaningful way. These promises clearly helped Redford and the PCs win votes from teachers, nurses, and other public sector workers.

The Wildrose policy book endorsed most of the key reforms recommended in the Firewall Letter. This was not surprising, as much of their policy book had been copied and pasted from my 2006 leadership materials. These reforms included:

- Withdrawing from the CPP and creating an Alberta pension plan
- Not renewing the contract with the RCMP and creating an Alberta police force
- Reducing Equalization and other fiscal transfer programs that were taking $20 billion a year net out of Alberta.

Smith pointed out that we now had a prime minister—Stephen Harper—an Albertan who had helped to write the Firewall Letter, and who would be sympathetic to Albertans' demand for a fair deal. Smith declared that "someone's got to say the system isn't working. Someone's got to tell Quebec and the other provinces they can actually strive for something better."[23] While this no doubt helped the Wildrose recruit my former supporters, it may have hurt them with centrist voters. Redford herself avoided the issue, but her surrogates did not. Stephen Carter, her campaign manager, declared that such policies "would likely wall us off from the rest of the country at a time when we need the rest of the country more than ever."[24]

The PCs also benefited from a series of Wildrose communication blunders in the last weeks of the campaign that raised issues of abortion rights, homophobia, and racism. These remarks were not made by leader Danielle Smith but by several of her candidates. Smith responded by strongly stating that neither she nor her party supported these comments, but the damage was done.[25] The PCs, with the help of the media, capitalized on these blunders and launched a last-minute "campaign of fear": that a Wildrose government would be a dangerous step backward for Alberta.[26]

This media firestorm, plus the complete collapse of support for the Liberal Party, sealed the deal for Redford. In the last week of the campaign, polling showed the Wildrose went from leading the PCs by ten points to trailing by ten points. It's hard to say what was more decisive on election day: Wildrose communication blunders or PC promises. But the results were clear: a decisive victory for Alison Redford and the PCs.

The PCs won sixty-one seats with 44 percent of the vote, a loss of five seats but still a strong majority government. The Wildrose won 34 percent of the vote but only seventeen seats: enough to make them the Official Opposition but a major disappointment given earlier expectations. Bringing up the rear were the Liberals (five seats) and the NDP (four seats), with each party getting less than ten percent of the vote. For the NDP, these results were pretty much par for the course. But for the Liberals, this was a disaster. In the two prior elections (2004 and 2008), the Liberal Party was supported by over a quarter of the voters. Now they were down to only ten percent. This collapse can be at least partially attributed to the incompetence and erratic behaviour of the Liberals' new leader, Raj Sherman.[27]

Subsequent analysis found that many Albertans who normally voted Liberal chose to vote "strategically" and went over to Redford and the PCs to stop the Wildrose.[28] In Edmonton, for example, the PCs won Edmonton-Gold Bar (Liberal since 1982) and Edmonton-Riverview (Liberal since 1997). Both went solidly NDP in 2015. The "campaign of fear" worked. And it helped to replace the thousands of Alberta conservatives who in the past had voted PC, but now, abandoned by Redford, went to the Wildrose. In 2012, this helped Redford win. But it potentially spelled trouble for the future. Historically, the PCs had benefited from vote splitting on the Left—between the Liberals and NDP. But what would happen if there were no longer a viable Liberal Party? We would have to wait until 2015 for the answer to this question.

As for me in Chestermere-Rocky View, I was one of the many PC casualties of the Wildrose sweep of rural southern Alberta. From the start, we knew I was in for a rough ride. Chestermere-Rocky View was new—created by redistricting after the 2008 election. It had the northern half of my old Foothills-Rocky View riding, but then added the Calgary suburb of Chestermere. Chestermere had been part of Rob Anderson's old riding when he was first elected as a PC. Now he was the second most powerful MLA in the Wildrose caucus—Smith's deputy leader—and still had a strong political team in Chestermere.

My opponent, Bruce McAllister, was well known and popular in Chestermere. He was a former television broadcaster. His son was the captain of the local hockey team, and his wife ran the only hair salon in the community. They knew almost everyone. I, of course, was a complete outsider.

To overcome this deficit, we made two strategic decisions before the election even began. One was to mount an intense ground game. By the end of the thirty-day campaign, I had door-knocked almost every Chestermere home twice. We also blanketed Chestermere with direct mail and telephone calls.

Second, my campaign brochures and political advertising in the local weekly newspapers—the *Airdrie Echo* and the *Cochrane Times*—were completely independent of and different from the Redford/PC party media. I tried to run on issues totally different from the PC Party's province-wide campaign. The issues I emphasized fit much better with Wildrose than the Redford PCs. But in the end, it made no difference. I was trounced by the Wildrose Candidate Bruce McAllister by almost a two-to-one margin, 10,168 to 6,156.

I was disappointed but not surprised. Like the rest of us, voters in Chestermere-Rocky View voted party, not person. As one media commentator accurately predicted just days before the election, under the headline "WILDROSE GODFATHER TED MORTON MAY END UP ON LOSING SIDE OF ALBERTA'S CONSERVATIVE CIVIL WAR":

> Ted Morton espouses the right politics, but he sits on the wrong side of history. If the current momentum carries until voting day on Monday, he'll be ousted by a Wildrose Party espousing a political philosophy he helped create.[29]

Wildrose's second-place finish with only seventeen MLAs was a major disappointment to its leaders and organizers. But in a broader context, it was still a significant achievement. For the first time, they were now the Official Opposition—not bad for a political party created only three years earlier.[30] But would the Wildrose have staying power? Was this divide on the Right just a temporary aberration or more permanent?

Evidence suggested that it would be more permanent because it had a regional foundation. The political science is clear that the best way for a new party to establish itself early is by having a strong regional base.[31] The early success of the Manning Reformers came from the concentration of our support in Western Canada.[32] My success in the 2006 PC leadership was based on the regional concentration of my supporters in southern and central Alberta, where Ralph Klein also did well in 1992.[33] On the first ballot, I carried every rural and small-town constituency south of Edmonton except five, and even won two rural ridings north of Edmonton.

In the 2011 leadership contest, this support disappeared. At the time, pundits speculated that this was because my supporters had already gone over to the Wildrose.[34] The subsequent results of the 2012 general election seemed to confirm this.[35] In the April 2012 provincial election, the Wildrose Party won twelve of the twenty-one ridings I had won in the first round of the 2006 leadership vote. Of the seventeen Wildrose MLAs elected, twelve came from ridings I had won in 2006. In some—such as Drumheller-Stettler, Airdrie, and Lac La Biche-St. Paul-Two Hills—the same volunteers who ran my 2006 leadership campaign ran the Wildrose campaigns in 2012.

So if geography matters—and in first-past-the-post electoral systems, it does—then the Wildrose Party was not going to evaporate anytime soon. It now had a beachhead in southern and central Alberta from which to mount future assaults on the Tory dynasty. Add this to the collapse of support for the Liberals and thus the end of vote splitting on the Left, and you might have begun to worry about its implications for Alison Redford and the party she now led.

The forty-year-old Alberta Tory dynasty was founded on a coalition of urban and rural interests, an unlikely marriage between the oil and gas industry and the ranch-farm sector. This unspoken coalition had helped them win twelve consecutive victories. But this coalition was now unravelling. The collapse of my support—from 41,000 votes on the 2006 second ballot to 7,000 in 2011—confirmed that many Blue Tories / federal Conservatives had already left the PC Party for the Wildrose Party.[36]

Would this mean the end of the Tory dynasty? Not necessarily. But it meant that the PCs would have to cobble together a different coalition of interests and groups—a more urban coalition— to continue to win majority governments. One of Redford's campaign ads in the 2012 Alberta general election boasted, "Not Your Father's PC Party." She turned out to be right, but she soon discovered that managing the consequences was not so easy.

THE REDFORD DEBACLE

From the outside, the rise and fall of Alison Redford has been told elsewhere by others.[37] As I was no longer in caucus or cabinet, I have no inside story to tell. The most remarkable aspect was how quickly it happened. Less than two years into her four-year mandate—after two stunning, come-from-behind victories—she was literally chased out of the Alberta Legislative Assembly by her own caucus. It will go down in Canadian history as one of the most humiliating and unpleasant endings for any Canadian first minister. What happened?

Officially, it was a growing list of publicly reported incidents that soured Albertans' view of Redford. These culminated in the disclosure that she had billed the government $45,000 to attend Nelson Mandela's funeral in South Africa, including $10,000 for a private jet to return to Alberta. While none of these incidents by themselves might have been fatal, their cumulative effect was. New polling showed that her approval rating plummeted to only 18 percent—a far cry from the 58 percent she had enjoyed only eighteen months earlier.[38] It created a perception of a premier with a sense of hubris and entitlement.

While the perceived abuse of taxpayer-funded perks helps to explain how Redford lost the support of Albertans, low public opinion ratings halfway through a mandate do not force a premier to resign. With two more years left in her mandate and the support of her caucus, Redford had more than enough time to recover from her poor start.

So why did Alison Redford leave so quickly? It was not just because of the alleged misuse of government aircraft and other perceived abuse of taxpayer-funded perks. Yes, that was the fuse, but it ignited three deeper, more dangerous political landmines.

First, Redford never had the support of the PC party—top, middle, or base. She won the 2011 leadership race not by engaging the PC faithful, but by going around them.[39] She won by promising $500 million of new spending on teachers, nurses, and other public sector workers—people who normally don't vote PC, but who became "two-minute Tories" just by buying memberships on the last day of voting. The night Redford won the leadership, she suddenly found herself in the penthouse of the PC chateau, but the rest of the hotel was empty.

So, job number one was—or should have been—winning over caucus members and the PC rank and file. It never happened. This was landmine number two. Rather than engaging with her new team, she never gave them the time and respect needed to gain their confidence and support. Whether it was cabinet ministers, backbenchers, or party volunteers, they never warmed up to her. It started immediately. While I was still in caucus, she rammed through her "new idea"—never even discussed during the campaign—of lowering the impaired driving limit from .08 to .05, over strenuous caucus opposition. This all but guaranteed the defeat of most rural PC MLAs in the next election. FYI: There are no taxis to take you home in rural Alberta. This lack of communication and consultation with caucus and even ministers continued after I departed.

Next was Budget 2012. Already badly in the red for the fifth year in a row, the province was driven deeper into deficit as Redford added $500 million of new program spending to pay for her leadership campaign promises. Objections were ignored. She made it clear that it was her call, and that she did not appreciate being challenged in caucus. Those who did soon regretted it. This pattern was set early, and on it went.

By summer 2013, disillusioned PC staffers at the legislature were cracking dark jokes about the Stelmach era as "the golden age." There were allegations of bullying and intimidation by the premier's office. In the fall, Redford survived the mandatory leadership review. But her team's aggressive full-court press—and thousands of PC Party dollars used to round up 77 percent of the votes—left a bitter taste for many members.

As the fallout from the $45,000 South Africa trip and other alleged misuses of government aircraft began to swirl around her, Redford retreated into her premier's office, an office now staffed almost entirely with people imported from her old Joe Clark, Red Tory networks in Toronto and Ottawa. Most of them knew little about Alberta or Albertans. Several had hardly been anywhere outside the legislature. The revelation that her chief of staff was living in a $200-a-night room at the Fairmont Hotel Macdonald did not help matters. While the Ontarification of the premier's office was not widely reported, it did not escape the notice of MLAs and PC volunteers, who saw it as yet another sign of her being out of touch.

The third and final strike was the new accounting rules introduced in the 2013 provincial budget. The new three-pronged accounting system—operational spending, capital spending, and savings—just didn't wash. The budget proposed to borrow $4.3 billion to pay to build new schools, hospitals, and roads. According to Doug Horner, her new finance minister, this $4.3 billion expenditure was not counted as part of the deficit since it would create new public assets.

These new accounting rules were missed by most normal Albertans, who are too busy to pay attention to arguments over such technical matters. But it didn't escape the notice of those who follow government finance. As the Canadian Taxpayers Federation commented, the new accounting rules were "an attempt to sow confusion and 'cook the books.'"[40] Or, as the *National Post* reported, "Alberta budget 2013 marked by billions in deficit spending, service cuts."[41] I publicly criticized the new rules the month they were released. Two years later, I joined five other former PC finance ministers in a public letter that challenged all candidates seeking to become the next PC leader to repeal the Redford accounting rules.[42]

The 2013 Redford-Horner budget sent a bitter message to the thousands of PC activists and supporters who remembered the pain and pride of the Klein years—the pain of the spending cuts needed to end the deficits; and pride of balancing the GOA budgets and eventually paying off Alberta's $22 billion debt. For many, myself included, this was one more reason not to come to the rescue of Alison Redford, when or if she ever needed it.

And she needed it soon. By March 2014, Redford's personal approval rating had dropped to 18 percent. Public support for the PC Party was at 19 percent, while the Wildrose was polling at 46 percent. On Thursday, March 13, MLA Len Webber left the PC Caucus to sit as an Independent. On the following Monday, a second MLA, Donna Kennedy-Glans, did the same. A caucus revolt seemed imminent. Redford held an emergency meeting with PC Party executives, but this failed to stem the tide. Ten MLAs publicly announced their intention to meet on March 16 to debate whether to follow Webber and Kennedy-Glans. A group of PC riding association presidents announced that they were meeting later that week to vote on a non-confidence motion in Redford's leadership of the party.

At a hastily called end-of-day news conference on Wednesday, March 19, Redford announced that she would resign as premier on Sunday. She did, but then did not return to the legislature until May 5, creating more controversy, as she was still collecting her MLA salary. This came to an end on August 6, when she resigned as the MLA for Calgary-Elbow and went into political exile, never to be seen again at a PC function.

PRENTICE TO THE RESCUE ... NOT

Redford's sudden departure in March left the PCs leaderless in the middle of the spring session of the legislature. The PC caucus chose Dave Hancock to take the role of interim party leader and premier, but neither he nor the party wanted him to stay for long. He was too closely tied to Redford and way too Red Tory to stem the exodus of PC voters to the Wildrose.

A new leadership election was scheduled for early September, but there were no obvious candidates. The PC coalition was blown apart, and polling now showed them trailing the Wildrose in public support. Who wants to lead a party like this? Nature abhors a vacuum and so do political parties. So several sitting MLAs stepped forward: Thomas Lukaszuk from Edmonton; and Ric McIver and Ken Hughes from Calgary. Hughes was the only one of the three who had any realistic chance of reuniting the party, but he withdrew his name only a month after launching his leadership campaign. Why?

Hughes and Jim Prentice were old friends. Both had worked closely with Joe Clark in the federal PC Party during the Seventies and Eighties. Like Clark, they had refused to join the Reform Party during its ascendancy in the 1990s. Before announcing his leadership candidacy, Hughes had asked Prentice if he intended to run. Prentice prevaricated—not saying that he was running, but never saying that he was not running. When Prentice did jump in, Hughes quickly withdrew—knowing already that neither he nor anyone else was going to defeat Prentice. Only a month after Prentice did win—and despite being promised a cabinet position in the new Prentice government—Hughes resigned from the legislature and the PC Party in September. Politics can be hard on friendships, a lesson that I had also learned.

Into this vacuum swooped Jim Prentice, the former federal MP from Calgary. Prentice had been a Joe Clark Tory dating back into the 1970s. Like Redford, Prentice had refused to join the Reform Party during its ascendency in the 1990s. But after the 2004 merger, Prentice joined Stephen Harper's new Conservative Party of Canada. Prentice held three different cabinet positions in Harper governments, before he retired in 2010 to take a well-paid position as a vice-chairman at CIBC Bank in Calgary.

It was no secret that Prentice had always aspired to political leadership. He had run unsuccessfully in both the 2003 federal PC leadership race and then in 2004 for the leadership of the newly created Conservative Party of Canada. Now, suddenly, a new window opened. Handsome, articulate, and well known to the Calgary business community—with connections in both the Blue and Red wings of the fractured PC party—Prentice appeared as a "dream candidate,"[43] a *deus ex machina* that could rescue the PCs from self-destruction.

The leadership race itself was almost an afterthought. On September 6, Prentice swept to victory with over 76 percent of the votes. McIver and Lukaszuk, never serious contenders, were left far behind.[44] Prentice had won a landslide victory. But there was a problem. Who cared? Only 23,386 Albertans even bothered to vote. Compare this to the vote totals for 2006 (144,279) or even 2012 (72,592). What was left of the once-mighty PC machine?

The challenge facing Prentice was clear. Somehow, he had to win back the thousands of conservatives who had migrated over to the Wildrose. To his credit, he came pretty damn close. Over the next three months, his party won four by-elections, and then achieved something unprecedented in Canadian political history: the leader of the Official Opposition, Danielle Smith, crossed the floor with over half of her caucus to join the government.[45]

Publicly, Prentice and Danielle Smith declared that, policy-wise, they agreed with each other more than they disagreed, and that they wanted to end vote splitting on the Right. Privately, Prentice had cemented the deal with the promise of immediate cabinet positions for both Smith and her deputy leader, Rob Anderson. While this has never been publicly confirmed, the offer to Smith is said to have been appointment as the new finance minister. Together, they now held seventy-two of the eighty-seven seats in the Legislative Assembly. From the outside, it seemed like a brilliant move.

But party politics is played from the inside. And there were some serious miscalculations on both sides of the deal. Smith did not consult party members before agreeing to the deal. This backfired big time. The Wildrose Party had been built from the ground up at the constituency level. Thousands of volunteers had worked their hearts out just two years earlier to defeat the PCs. Nor had they forgotten the PCs' "fear campaign" that stigmatized Wildrose supporters.

Now, with no notice or consultation, they were expected to fold their tents and join the PCs? The situation was further aggravated by the fact that many if not most of its volunteers were ex-Reformers who had not forgotten that Prentice was a Joe Clark loyalist who had never joined the Reform Party wave in the 1990s. Many were furious, and never forgave Smith. For them, the new call to "unite the Right" fell on deaf ears.

On the other side, Prentice ran into an analogous backlash for the same reason: little to no prior consultation with his cabinet or caucus.[46] Given that his preordained mission was to rescue the forty-year-old PC dynasty from losing the election, Prentice naively assumed that his caucus would embrace his new "unite the Right" initiative. He had scheduled only one hour for a meeting with his caucus, and he had already instructed his justice minister, Jonathan Denis, to have the Lieutenant Governor available to officiate the swearing in of new cabinet ministers the next day.

Instead, all hell broke loose. For two years, the PC caucus had sat though question periods watching the Wildrose opposition destroy their leader. Redford's two principal antagonists were Smith and Anderson. They were adept at pushing the QP buttons that would send Premier Redford into (televised) fits of exasperation and anger. The idea that these two might now not only join the PC caucus but immediately assume senior cabinet positions was too much.

Led by Hancock and Horner, Redford's two staunchest defenders, a substantial portion of the caucus let Prentice know that they would not accept this. The planned one-hour caucus meeting stretched on to two and then three hours. While there was no explicit discussion of new cabinet appointments, Prentice got the message. The next day, nine Wildrose MLAs joined the PC caucus, but there were no new cabinet positions for any of them.

This fuelled the anger in the Wildrose base. What policy concessions were Wildrosers receiving in return for Smith's floor crossing? Nothing! In retrospect, Prentice's caving in to the Hancock-Horner protests hurt the PCs in the next election. He could have—and should have—told his caucus critics to shut up or leave. They were the ones responsible for the Redford fiasco. Prentice had come in to rescue the PC Party. He owed them nothing. Had he done this—and given Smith and Anderson important cabinet positions—the subsequent vote splitting with the Wildrose would not have been so devastating. But he didn't, and it was.

Initially, the floor crossing was celebrated as a triumph for Prentice in the run-up to the fast-approaching May election: "Progressive Conservative Premier Jim Prentice crushed Alberta's official opposition and consolidated his hold on power Wednesday," crowed the front page of the *Edmonton Journal*.[47] As mentioned above, Prentice and the PCs now held seventy-two of the eighty-seven seats in the Alberta legislature. The remaining fifteen MLAs were evenly split between three different parties—what was left of the Wildrose, plus five Liberals and five NDP. What could possibly go wrong now? Plenty! Prentice was about to relearn the adage that in politics, a week is a long time.

In less than three months, Jim Prentice's approval ratings went from 60 percent positive to 60 percent negative. His March budget, combined with an early election call, delivered a lethal one-two punch. The pay-more, receive-less budget angered both the Right and the Left. In my opinion, it was the first honest provincial budget presented to Albertans since the 2008 recession. I wrote a column for the *Calgary Herald* that said just this:

> Premier Jim Prentice and Finance Minister Robin Campbell are to be congratulated for Budget 2015. They have told Albertans the truth about our public finance. They have ditched the misleading Alison Redford–Doug Horner accounting rules. They have made it clear that it is time that we live within our means and pay for the services we consume—not leave unpaid bills to our children.[48]

But there is no political reward for telling voters the hard truth about public finances. The PC budget had too many program cuts for liberals; too much spending for the conservatives; and too many tax hikes for everyone except corporations.

Prentice exacerbated the negative reactions to his budget with his offhand comment that if Albertans wanted to understand who was responsible for a decade of government overspending, "we need only look in the mirror." This sparked a viral social media backlash— "Prentice blames Albertans"—that further soured voters' perception of their new premier.[49] His well-publicized purchase of a vintage 1956 Thunderbird convertible for $71,000 during an impromptu vacation stop in Arizona didn't help matters.[50]

Another blow was Prentice's early election call. The next provincial election was not scheduled until April 2016. So, when Prentice announced on April 7, 2015, that he was calling an election in less than a month, he looked cynical and power hungry. Two of the three opposition parties did not even have permanent leaders. It smacked of opportunism and winning cheap. Albertans didn't like it.[51]

Until then, Prentice looked different from the old, take-no-prisoners PC war machine. The "under new management" narrative was working. The early election call killed this. PC MLAs who went door-knocking got an earful.

Prentice no longer looked different. Many Albertans were not willing to tolerate their votes being taken for granted. And that's what the spring 2015 election now looked like. When the dust settled, protest votes, and now a badly divided right-of-centre, resulted in what no one could have imagined a year earlier: a majority NDP government led by Rachel Notley.

2015: THE END OF THE PC DYNASTY

On May 5, the NDP won fifty-four seats and a majority government. The Wildrose, with twenty-one seats, continued as the Official Opposition. The PCs trailed with only nine seats. Shocked and demoralized, Prentice resigned as PC leader and as the MLA for Calgary-Foothills that very night.[52]

The 44-year-old PC dynasty had come to a crashing end. But May 5 did not mean that Alberta had experienced a Jekyll-and-Hyde transformation from right-wing conservatism to the labour-union left. The NDP victory was not so much an "Orange Wave" as the splintering of the right-of-centre vote. Of the fifty-four seats won by the NDP, twenty-one were won with less than 40 percent of the votes. Combined, the PCs and Wildrose won 54 percent of the votes, but only 35 percent of the seats. Contrary to what some have argued, 2015 did not mark the beginning of "the New Alberta"[53]—a fact confirmed by the subsequent election of UCP majority governments in 2019 and 2023.

Yes, Alberta's demographics had changed. Since the Stelmach victory in 2008, Alberta's population had grown by 430,000. There was now a higher percentage of younger Albertans; more with university educations; more urban; and a 50 percent increase in public sector union membership.[54] None of these changes are usually positive for small-c conservative parties.

But by themselves, these changes don't explain the 2015 Alberta election. Alberta's demographics had been changing every decade since 1971. As the late David Taras and others have pointed out, many immigrants choose Alberta precisely because it has had more conservative, business-friendly governments for the past fifty years.[55] This "self-selection" is especially true for the tens of thousands of Canadians who came to Alberta in the 1980s from Saskatchewan and BC in the 1990s—refugees from economies that NDP governments had destroyed. It is hardly surprising that many or most of them chose to elect PC governments in their new home province. In 2015, almost two out of three Albertans still voted against the NDP. Most Albertans were and remain non-ideological. Many who supported NDP candidates were voting *against* Prentice and the PCs, not *for* the NDP.

There was also a deeper flaw in the Prentice team's pre-election strategy. They assumed that the floor-crossing had removed the threat of vote splitting with the Wildrose. Their leader, Danielle Smith, was now in the PC caucus. With both the Liberals and Wildrose parties without leaders, the PCs called an early election, and then focused their campaign on the New Democrats and winning over centre-left voters—the classic "median-voter" strategy. The problem is that this strategy does not work when there is a viable third party on your flank.[56] The PCs assumed there was not, but there was. So, they ended up fighting a war on two fronts—never a good strategy. Like earlier PC leaders, Prentice ignored the cross-cutting issue of Western alienation, which remained a priority for many Wildrose supporters.

After forty-four years of PC rule, a decade of Stelmach-Redford melodramas, and five different PC premiers in less than a decade, many Albertans were simply tired of the PC brand. And there wasn't much left of the brand. As Colby Cosh perceptively observed, "Redford did for the PCs' ethical reputation what Stelmach had done to its managerial bona fides."[57] Albertans were ready for change. And Prentice no longer looked like change. The door was open, and an articulate, intelligent, and affable woman—Rachel Notley—walked through it.

11

The Decline and Fall of the PC Empire: A Post-Morton

In democracies like Canada, all political dynasties have within them the seeds of their own destruction. The demise of the Alberta PC Party in 2015 was not simply the result of Jim Prentice's flawed election strategy,[1] nor the significant shortcomings of his two predecessors, Ed Stelmach and Alison Redford. Yes, each in their own way contributed to the decline and fall of the forty-four-year-old PC empire. But the PC dynasty was much larger than just its leaders. The last three leaders were as much the effect as the cause of the party's demise. There were deeper structural factors that contributed to the party's eventual downfall. What follows is a post-mortem—an autopsy—of five of these larger factors.

FLAWED LEADERSHIP SELECTION PROCESS

Historically, the Alberta PC Party was a unique urban-rural coalition. Its urban wing was grounded in the dynamic, ever-expanding oil and gas sector that has transformed Alberta since 1947. Its rural wing was supported by the prosperous farm and ranch communities that have defined Alberta from its beginnings. For four decades, the Alberta PC Party was the only conservative party in Canada that bridged the urban-rural divide. But as a result of the leadership selection process, this coalition slowly came apart.

The flawed leadership selection process contributed directly to the decline and fall of the PC party dynasty. The party lost control of choosing its own leaders. The "open primary" system, preferential balloting, and lack of any cut-off date for party memberships meant that thousands of Albertans who did not normally vote for the PCs could and did vote in the PC leadership contests. This was aggravated by the one- and two-week windows between leadership votes that allowed strategic "gate-crashers" from the Left to decisively influence the outcome of the last two PC leaderships. For these "two-minute Tories," the "least worst choice" meant the least conservative candidate: Stelmach in 2006 and Redford in 2011.

The "two-minute Tory" liability was magnified by the more liberal leadership candidates' strategy to directly solicit new voters from organized interests whose members could be quickly mobilized. In theory, this bias might be ideologically neutral. It certainly helped me in 2006. But in the context of second-round voting in the 2006 and 2011 leaderships, this meant recruiting primarily teachers, nurses, and members of other public sector unions—all more urban constituencies. The result has been the election of the most "liberal" of the three finalists in each contest. Not surprisingly, a growing number of disillusioned "small-c" conservatives began looking for a new political home and found it in the Wildrose Party. This vote splitting between two conservative parties then opened the door for the NDP victory in 2015.

The 2006 leadership race weakened the PC party by electing a compromise candidate who turned out to be a weak leader. From the outset, Stelmach had low support in Calgary and southern Alberta. On the first ballot, he did not win a single rural constituency in southern or central Alberta. On the second ballot, he received only 14 percent of the votes in Calgary and did not win a single constituency. His subsequent oil and gas royalty policies pushed many Blue Tories and federal Conservatives into the Wildrose Party.[2] If either Dinning or I had won in 2006, it's hard to imagine that either of us would have mishandled the royalty issue as badly as Stelmach. And without the royalty debacle, it's hard to imagine the Wildrose would have garnered the financial support it received in the run-up to the 2012 election.

If the 2006 PC leadership race created the opportunity for the Wildrose, then the 2011 leadership contest sealed the deal. All three finalists were Red Tories (Mar, Redford, Horner). All three eliminated candidates were Blue Tories (Morton, Orman, Griffiths). And the "reddest" of the three Red Tories (Redford) won.[3] These results suggest that the shift had already occurred. In the 2011 PC leadership race, the total number of votes cast in the second round (77,816) was only about half the number cast in 2006 (144,279). As David Stewart and Anthony Sayers discerned: "Almost 60% of the decline in Conservative participation can be associated with the Morton loss of support. If he had simply turned out those who voted for him on the second ballot in 2006, Morton would have led Mar by more than 17,000 votes and the total vote would have exceeded 93,000."[4]

This decline in PC voters was sharpest in southern and central Alberta—where the number of votes cast was only one-third of what it had been in 2006. Almost all the ridings I won in the 2006 PC leadership race were in these two regions. Not surprisingly, so were almost all ridings that the Wildrose won in the 2012 election.[5] The PC establishment had finally gotten rid of me, but a big chunk of their electoral base had also left.

Some commentators predicted that Redford's leadership victory would "renew" the PC party by allowing it to reflect Alberta's changing demographics—younger, more urban, more liberal.[6] This prediction seemed to be confirmed when, nine months later in the 2012 provincial election, Redford led the PCs to a strong majority government. Given these back-to-back successes, Redford has been credited with running sophisticated campaigns.[7]

But this sanguine interpretation of Redford's early successes ignores an important fact. In 2012, the Wildrose established a strategic beachhead by winning nine of the twelve rural seats in southern Alberta and—now with seventeen MLAs—replaced the Liberals as the Official Opposition. This regional concentration gave Wildrose staying power. Over the next two years, the Wildrose effectively destroyed not just the political career of Alison Redford, but the reputation of the PC party itself. By the time Redford's caucus forced her to resign, her approval rating had dropped to 18 percent, and support for the PCs to 19 percent. Support for the Wildrose had risen to 46 percent.[8] A year later, when Jim Prentice's "unite the Right" rescue mission failed, the PCs lost sixty-one of their seventy seats. With only nine MLAs, they did not even achieve the status of Official Opposition. The dynasty was over.

It merits noting here that after the virtual destruction of the PCs in the 2015 Alberta election, the party abandoned the one-member / one-vote leadership selection process and returned to the traditional delegated convention process. They also added a two-week cut-off for membership sales prior to constituency elections to select delegates to the convention. This meant no more "two-minute Tories" crashing the gates on election day to vote for the "least worst" (i.e., the least conservative) candidate.

I would like to think that an article I wrote in 2013 for *Canadian Parliamentary Review* detailing the negative consequences of the open-primary, preferential balloting system contributed to this reform.[9] The irony of this is that I never could have even considered running for the PC leadership in 2006 if it had been a delegated convention. The PC establishment would have controlled the delegate selection process and crowned the "Prince in Waiting," Jim Dinning, as the new leader and premier of Alberta.

VOTE SPLITTING ON THE RIGHT

The 2015 NDP majority government was the result of vote splitting on the Right. In single-member, first-past-the-post electoral systems, winning does not require a majority of votes. To win, a candidate simply needs a plurality, more votes than any of the other candidates. When there are candidates from three or four different political parties, the winner may sometimes have less than 40 percent of the total vote. Of the fifty-four ridings won by NDP candidates in 2015, almost half—twenty-one—were won with less than 40 percent of the vote.

Province-wide, the NDs won 61 percent of the seats with only 41 percent of the votes. This counterintuitive result was made possible by vote splitting on the Right. The PC/Wildrose votes combined equalled 52 percent of the provincial vote, but together, they won only 35 percent of the seats.

In Calgary, the foundation of PC majorities since 1971, the effects of vote splitting on the Right were even more devastating. The NDs won sixteen of the twenty-nine ridings in Calgary and surrounding areas with only one-third of the votes. The PCs and Wildrose combined won 54 percent of the votes, but only eleven seats. If the PC and Wildrose vote totals had been combined, together they would have swept all twenty-nine Calgary ridings and been able to form a majority government.[10]

The NDP majority was augmented by the collapse of support for the Alberta Liberal Party. For decades, the PCs had been the beneficiary of vote splitting on the Left. In the 1997 election, the Liberals (32.8 percent) and the NDP (8.8 percent) combined won 41.6 percent of the popular vote. but only 26 percent of the eighty-three seats (22). More recently, in 2004, the NDP and Liberals combined received 39 percent of the vote, but they won only 24 percent of the eighty-three seats (twenty-two). This ended in 2015. With only 41 percent of the votes, the NDP won 61 percent of the seats (fifty-four). Notley was able to consolidate the left-wing vote. What had been a weak showing for the Liberals in 2012 became a complete collapse of support in 2015: only 4 percent of the vote and one seat. Vote splitting was now a problem for the Right, not the Left in Alberta politics.[11]

DYNASTY SYNDROME: POWER REPLACES PRINCIPLES

The dynasty was over. But it was not simply Jim Prentice's fault. Nor Alison Redford's, nor Ed Stelmach's. In one-party states over time, the dominant party has an incentive to move to the centre. It does this to pre-empt the opportunity for growth of its leading competitor by adopting some of its policies. For the Alberta PCs, this meant moving toward the Liberals and NDP. Policy-wise, this meant appeasing public sector unions' salary and benefits demands in the months leading up to the next provincial election. Both Stelmach (2008) and Redford (2012) did this.

This is how a dominant party tries to ensure that it continues to be win majorities. In political science terminology, this dynamic is known as "convergence," and it reflects each party's attempt to capture the "median voter"—the undecideds or "moderates" in the political middle.[12] It both explains and describes the PC's drift toward the Liberals that began in Klein's last years.

In a one-party state like Alberta, this drift to the centre was strengthened by the fact that the dominant party attracts candidates who simply want to be on the winning side. For them, policies and principles are secondary to winning. In Alberta, from 1971 until 2015, if your goal was to be elected to the legislature—especially if you had any aspirations to ever serve in cabinet—you had to join the dominant party, the PCs. It didn't matter if your values were liberal or conservative, left or right. With the exception of a few central city ridings in Edmonton and Calgary, you had to run as a PC candidate. As Taras notes, it was the only game in town for over four decades.[13]

The result was that the PC party and caucus filled up with people who were not particularly conservative. For them, policy was a way to access power, not vice versa. By the time I arrived in 2004, many of the MLAs were conservatives-of-convenience, people who would have run as Liberals or even NDP in any other province. Or, as it turned out, even in Alberta, if they became unhappy with their prospects in the PC Party. Examples include:

- After losing the 1992 PC leadership race to Ralph Klein, Nancy Betkowski/MacBeth joined the Liberals in 1998, and then became the Liberal leader.

- In 2011, Raj Sherman crossed the floor and joined the Liberals, and soon became the Liberal leader.

- Sandra Jansen crossed the floor and joined the NDP in 2017 after it became clear that Jason Kenney was going to win the PC leadership.

Politely, these types of politicians can be described as pragmatists. Less politely, as opportunists (or worse!). For them, policy is a means to power. You say what you need to say to win the next election. At the other end of the spectrum are what might be called principled politicians. Or, less politely, ideologues. For this type, power is the means to influence policy. The purpose of engaging in politics is to influence public policy. You say or do what you think is "right," even if it costs you votes.[14]

Successful parties require a balance of both types. At different times and in different circumstances, a stronger case can be made for one or the other. But by the time I arrived in 2004, the Alberta PC caucus was top-heavy with "pragmatists." Taras argues that being a "big tent" political party was the PC's deliberate strategic choice and contributed to its success. At best this is only half right. However much this centre-left strategy may have helped earlier PC governments, it contributed directly to the party's demise in 2006–15.[15]

This "big tent" character of the PC Party was more of an effect than a strategy—the effect of the caucus filling up with Red Tories from Edmonton whose prospects for re-election depended on more centrist government policies. This was predictable. Edmonton is a government town and a university town—both communities that are more supportive of left-leaning political parties. To win in "Redmonton," as some of us called it, it helped to be a Red Tory. But the more Redmonton Tories we had in our PC caucus, the further left we drifted. To try to ensure their re-election, in caucus they consistently advocated for more liberal policies. Lukaszuk and Hancock, for example, led the effort to prevent my Bill 208 from coming to a vote in 2006. In the Redford years, Hancock and Horner were her strongest supporters in caucus. My favourite example of this mindset comes not from an Edmonton MLA but from Calgary MLA Ron Liepert's exhortation to the PC caucus that to win the 2012 election, "We have to out-NDP the NDP."

In the post-cutback years—after 2001—this quip captured the mindset of the PC leadership and caucus. It started with Klein after 2000 and accelerated under Stelmach and Redford. Winning the next election became the overriding consideration—policy and principle be damned. This uber-fixation led to the PC party's ultimate demise in 2015. As the PC party abandoned more conservative Conservatives, they abandoned the party. By the time Prentice took the helm, the PC ship was already sinking.

THE RESOURCE CURSE

Ten years from now, twenty years from now, you will see: oil will bring us ruin. ... Oil is the Devil's excrement.[16]

—Juan Pablo Pérez Alfonso (1976), former Venezuelan
minister of energy

The "convergence" theory explains the tendency for successful political parties to drift toward the ideological centre. The competition for the median or undecided voter pulls them there. But for the Alberta PC party, it was exacerbated by the "resource curse"—their overreliance on annual oil and gas revenues to fund annual government services and programs.

To most Albertans, this will sound counterintuitive. Wasn't the political dynasty that Peter Lougheed founded and that then governed Alberta for the next forty-four years built on the ever-expanding oil and gas industry? Yes. Absolutely! But in the end, it also contributed to its demise. How to explain this paradox?

Alberta is a textbook example of what Daniel Yergin describes as the "petro-state"—a nation whose economy becomes overly reliant on oil and gas exports. These exports create significant revenues for the governments, in the form of royalties, taxes, or both. The result, Yergin writes, is, "In a petro-state, the competition for these revenues and the struggle over their distribution becomes the central drama for the nations' economy."[17] This type of politics is described as "rent-seeking." For the petro-state, rent-seeking "means that the most important 'business' in the country (aside from oil-production itself) is focused on getting some of the 'rents' from oil—that is, some share of the government's revenues."[18]

Yergin's leading example of the dysfunctional "rent-seeking" politics of petro-states is Venezuela. But the parallels to Alberta politics are clear. The most obvious example was Ed Stelmach's ill-fated 2007 New Royalty Framework (NRF) and 20 percent increase in oil and gas royalties—projected to increase the government's non-renewable resources revenues by $1.4 billion annually by 2010. It was not by coincidence Stelmach announced his new "Fair Share" policy just prior to the 2008 provincial election. Stelmach publicly linked these new revenues—which in fact never materialized—to payment for his new policy promises: eliminating health care premiums; a five-year contract with the Alberta Teachers' Association (ATA); assuming the ATA's $2 billion unfunded pension liability; and a one-time, $1,500 lump-sum payment to every teacher (see chapter 6).

This new spending did help the PCs win another crushing majority government—seventy-two of eighty-three seats. But it also opened the door for the then-tiny Wildrose Alliance to grow. The negative backlash to the New Royalty Framework in the oil and gas sector pushed many former PC supporters to Wildrose and contributed directly to the party's improved fundraising leading up to the 2012 provincial election.[19]

But Stelmach did not invent the strategy of buying votes with oil and gas revenues. As far back as 1982, Lougheed's home-mortgage interest rebate program—funded by energy revenues that were diverted from the Heritage Savings Fund—helped the PCs win that year's election (see below). Similarly, Klein announced a new program to subsidize the cost of natural gas for home heating just prior to the 2001 election. This strategy went from subtle to obscene in 2005 with Klein's "Prosperity Bonus Cheques." This previously unannounced program doled out $1.4 billion in new energy revenues, with every Alberta resident receiving $400 in what quickly became known as "Ralph Bucks" (see chapter 3).

In 2011, Alison Redford doubled down on this strategy. First, she won the second round of the PC leadership race by recruiting thousands of "two-minute Tories" with her promise to restore the $110 million that had been cut from education in (my) Budget 2010; and to bail out the underfunded Alberta policemen's pension fund. Next, by delivering on these promises in the 2012 general election, Redford won substantial support from the public sector unions (see chapter 10). But like Stelmach's 2008 spending spree, Redford's 2012 budget sent still more disillusioned fiscal conservatives over to the Wildrose Party—contributing to the subsequent vote splitting and the demise of the PC party in the 2015 provincial election.

None of this was lost on Rachel Notley, who in 2015 consolidated the NDP's control of public sector union votes by promising not to cut budgets for health care (nurses); public education (teachers); or government services (government employees).[20] Not by coincidence, Notley's husband sat on the governing board of the NDP and was then a senior communications official for the Canadian Union of Public Employees, a union that had over 12,000 municipal employees and 7,000 K–12 workers in Alberta.[21] Just for good measure, in the newly elected NDP government's first Speech from the Throne, Notley promised a new royalty review to help pay for her spending promises. Just to round out the vicious circle of "rent-seeking" politics, Ed Stelmach then praised her for doing so.[22] In a petro-state like Alberta, no party can afford NOT to be in favour of a "Fair Share" of energy revenues.

A second defining characteristic of the petro-state is what Yergin calls "fiscal rigidity." Global oil and gas prices are inherently volatile. As they rise, government revenues and government spending rise too. "But," Yergin points out, "when world oil prices go down and nations' revenues fall, governments dare not cut back on spending. Budgets have been funded, programs have been launched, contracts have been let, institutions are in place, jobs have been created, people have been hired. Governments are locked into ever-increasing spending. Otherwise, they face political backlash and social explosion."[23] All of the beneficiaries of the status quo—public sector and private sector—fight any government attempts to cut back programs that benefit them.

Yergin wrote this to explain the political instability and economic mismanagement of petro-states like Venezuela. But for anyone who knows Alberta's fiscal odyssey since the 1980s (reread chapters 5 and 7!), this will sound disturbingly familiar. Over the past fifty years, seven consecutive Alberta governments from three political parties have ramped up spending during years of high energy revenues, and then run deficits when oil and gas prices inevitably declined.[24] All of the political incentives are to spend energy revenues, not to save. Spending gives voters more services and benefits without imposing more taxes to pay for them—a politician's dream.

When oil and gas prices tanked in the 1980s, the PC government of Premier Don Getty ran up $23 billion of debt with seven consecutive deficits. PC Premier Ralph Klein then spent the next decade cutting GOA spending by 30 percent to pay off this debt. Klein famously announced during Stampede in July 2004 that Alberta's debt was "PAID IN FULL." "Never again," Klein told the cheering crowd at McDougall Centre, "will this government or the people of this province have to set aside another tax dollar on debt."[25] This lasted less than four years.

Oil prices hit their historical high of $147.27/barrel on July 11, 2008. By Christmas, the price of oil collapsed to $30.28/barrel. Similarly with natural gas: it peaked at $13.06/mcf in July of 2008. A year later it dropped to less than $5/mcf and stayed there—and in some years much lower still—for the next thirteen years. The Stelmach 2008 "Fair Share" budget—whose then record spending ($37 billion) helped the PCs win another majority government in March—had projected a $1.6 billion surplus. By July, spiralling oil and gas prices had pushed the projected surplus up to $8 billion. But by the end of the fiscal year, we were left with a deficit of almost $1 billion.

This set the pattern for the next seven years. By the time the PCs were defeated by the NDP in the 2015 election, Alberta's accumulated debt had reached $11.9 billion.[26] So much for the party of "fiscal responsibility." If it's any consolation, this overspending accelerated during the next four years (2015–2019) of NDP government.[27] When Jason Kenney led his newly created United Conservative Party to a majority government in the 2019 provincial election, he inherited a net debt of $85.9 billion.[28]

But if this addiction to spending is found in all petro-states, then why would we expect Alberta to be any different—regardless of which party formed government? Does the "resource curse" syndrome absolve the Stelmach and Redford PC governments of responsibility for their overspending, deficits, and massive new debt? No, it does not.

As Yergin points out, other petro-states have adopted at least a partial antidote to the resource curse: sovereign wealth funds (SWFs). In boom years, legally required deposits of a specified percentage of energy revenues into a SWF reduces government revenues available for annual budgets, which then curbs overspending. In bust years, the earnings from SWFs can be used to offset declining energy revenues and thus minimize if not eliminate budget deficits. In sum, a properly constructed SWF can act as a stabilizer of volatile oil and gas prices and revenues.

The two most well-known—and successful—SWFs are in Norway and Alaska. In the beginning, Alberta had its own SWF: the Alberta Heritage Savings Trust Fund created by Peter Lougheed in 1976. As originally designed, 30 percent of the province's annual non-renewable resource revenues (NRRR) were legally required to be transferred to the Heritage Fund. In the high-NRRR years of the late 1970s, the Lougheed government complied with these rules, and the Heritage Fund grew rapidly. Between 1976 and 1982, it accumulated assets with a net value of $8.3 billion.[29] Early estimates were that the Heritage Fund could top $50 billion by 2000.

This was short-lived. As the price of oil dropped, NRRR declined. Faced with an election in 1982, the Lougheed government slashed NRRR deposits into the Heritage Fund from 30 percent to 15 percent. The PCs then used the remaining revenues to win the election with a new home-mortgage interest rebate program.[30] Any homeowners (a.k.a. voters) with a mortgage interest rate above 12 percent received government cheques to offset the difference. As I was then an untenured junior assistant professor with an 18 percent mortgage, I remember it well!

Four years later, Lougheed's PC successor, Don Getty, had to deal with another election and even lower oil prices. To help win that election, the Getty government "temporarily" stopped making any deposits in the Heritage Fund. It used all NRRR revenues to help fund the annual budget with no service cuts and no tax increases. This "temporary" policy quickly became permanent. Other than the three one-off deposits in the boom-year budgets of 2005–7, PC governments for the next seventeen years did not deposit a single dollar of NRRR into the Heritage Fund.

The result is that in real dollars, accounting for inflation, the Heritage Fund's current value of $18.6 billion is actually less than it was thirty years ago. Other than the inflation-proofing that began in 2005, under current government policy, virtually all of the fund's realized annual earnings are transferred to general revenues for in-year spending. This means that the fund's value cannot grow as the market goes up. But then when there are down years—such as 2009—investment losses permanently reduce the fund's size. Combine this with the fact that the Alberta government has made only three new deposits in the fund since 1987, and the fund begins to resemble the old Slinky toy—holding steady in good years but dropping down in bad years, slowly but steadily working its way to the bottom.

The Heritage Fund's deteriorating value is even worse when population growth and inflation are taken into account. Prices have increased fourfold since the fund started in 1976. Alberta's population has nearly tripled. In per capita real dollars, the fund's value peaked in 1983 at $12,380 per Albertan. As of 2022, that figure was approximately $4,200.[31]

The sad fact is that of the $263 billion in NRRR that the Alberta government collected between 1977 and 2022, less than 6 percent has been saved.[32] The fund's current value is approximately $18.6 billion. If the $9.7 billion that sat in the Heritage Fund in 1982 had remained untouched (and no further contributions made) and allowed to grow simply at the rate of inflation, the value would have stood at $24.2 billion in 2010.[33] If 30 percent of NRRR had been deposited in the Heritage Fund—per the original design—the fund's value would have been at least $79 billion higher than it is today. Not only were these deposits not made, but most of the fund's annual earnings—over

$39.2 billion since 1976—were transferred from the fund to the province's general revenues to pay for current annual spending.[34]

Oil and gas revenues became the crack cocaine of Alberta politics. The politicians became addicted to spending it. And their "customers"—Alberta voters—became equally addicted to enjoying it; for not having to pay for much of the government services we used. As Ron Kneebone observed, "The taxpayers rewarded them for it."[35] Look what happened to Jim Prentice in 2015 when he made an offhand comment that to understand the past decade of government overspending, "We need only look in the mirror." The next day social media was on fire with the message: "Prentice blames Albertans."[36]

By way of comparison, the Alaska Permanent Fund—created in 1976, the same year as the Heritage Fund—now has a balance of US$79.6 billion. And that's after paying out US$20 billion in dividends to Alaska residents. Norway's NRRR savings fund was started in 1990 and now has a balance of US$1.6 trillion.[37] Even the tiny state of Wyoming—with a population of only 581,000—has its own sovereign wealth fund, created in 1975, with a current value of almost US$10 billion.[38]

How have the Alaska and Norway SWFs succeeded where Alberta has failed? The answer is simple: They were put beyond the reach of the short-term political interests of politicians. The Alaska Fund was created by a constitutional amendment that mandates that 25 percent of annual energy royalties and rents must be deposited in it. To change this would require a constitutional amendment and a referendum. To date, no Alaskan governor has ever proposed this, knowing that it would fail. The Alberta Heritage Fund was created by a statute, which means it can be changed unilaterally by a majority government any time it is politically advantageous.

Norway's fund is not constitutionally entrenched in a legal sense, but it is universally understood to be off limits to the governments of the day. In Canadian terminology, we could say the fund's status as politically untouchable is a constitutional convention—widely recognized and followed. Originally named the Petroleum Fund of Norway, its name was changed in 2006 to the Government Pension Global Fund. While it is clearly not a pension fund in the normal sense (i.e., member-funded), this name change emphasizes that the fund belongs to the people of Norway, not the government of the day. In short, the Alaska and Norway funds were made politician-proof by protecting them from the government of the day's inevitable short-term priority—winning the next election.

The Alaska and Norway funds also differ from Alberta's Heritage Fund in how their principal is managed and invested. They cannot be used for domestic economic development, the kinds of politically useful but economically risky projects that Alberta governments indulged in during the 1980s. In that decade, the Lougheed-Getty governments lost over $2.2 billion using the Heritage Fund to invest in new Alberta start-up companies.[39]

In 1996, the Klein government put an end to using the Heritage Fund for high-risk diversification projects, and instead directed it to be used to maximize long-term returns. The creation of the Alberta Investment Management Corporation (AIMCo) a decade later further insulated the fund from cabinet micromanagement. AIMCo's directive emphasizes that these monies are to be professionally managed for the long-term interests of Albertans, not the short-term interests of the government of the day. Recent developments, however, suggest that the PCs have already forgotten their past mistakes.

Redford's 2014 budget proposed to resurrect the practice of using money in the Heritage Fund for "strategic investments." Bill 1, the misleadingly named *Savings Management Act*, would have diverted $2 billion from the Heritage Fund into a new spending program to "provide government with the financial resources to take advantage of new opportunities, yet to be determined, that may require a large, one-time investment from the province."[40] Such politically driven investments are all but guaranteed to achieve the same dismal results as they did during the 1980s and with the more recent North West Upgrader fiasco (see chapter 7). Following Redford's sudden resignation in March 2014, Bill 1 was never implemented.

Not to be outdone, the NDP's first budget directed AIMCo to invest $540 million from the Heritage Fund into Alberta-based "growth companies" to promote diversification of Alberta's economy. Both of these initiatives are reminders of the Heritage Fund's vulnerability to short-term political objectives.

I have written elsewhere about how a future Alberta government could and should "politician-proof" the Heritage Fund.[41] The rules requiring mandatory annual transfers of NRRR into the Heritage Fund must be entrenched constitutionally, not just statutorily. The models of success—Norway and Alaska—are out there to be adopted by and adapted to Alberta.

To conclude, the "resource curse" may explain why successive PC governments so mismanaged the $263 billion of NRRRs, but it does not excuse it. Since 1986—with the important and praiseworthy exception of Ralph

Klein (1992–2006)—successive PC governments chose to spend Alberta's oil and gas revenues rather than deposit them into the Heritage Fund. This choice is entirely predictable. How many politicians prioritize long-term fiscal responsibility ahead of short-term re-election prospects? Since 2006, the Stelmach, Redford, and then Notley governments chose the latter over the former. And with those choices comes responsibility for the consequences: as of 2022, an accumulated debt of $93.9 billion with annual interest payments of $2.8 billion.[42]

WESTERN ALIENATION

A fifth and final cause of the demise of the PC Party was the refusal of the PC leaders, both elected and unelected, to recognize Alberta's chronic vulnerability to harmful federal Liberal policies, and their consequent failure to embrace reforms that would better protect Albertans' interests. Starting with the 1993 federal election, the Reform Party and its successor parties, the Canadian Alliance (CA-2001) and then Conservative Party of Canada (CPC-2004) dominated Alberta politics federally. Their message to Albertans: That the West wants in! That the constitutional status quo is stacked against Western provinces in favour of Ontario and Quebec—and the Liberal Party governments that these two central Canadian provinces routinely elect.

In the first three decades of the Tory dynasty, Premiers Peter Lougheed and Ralph Klein successfully rode the wave of Western alienation to majority governments—the same wave that Preston Manning rode to take the upstart Reform Party from nothing to the Official Opposition in the 1990s. As Taras observed,

> The Tories' popularity was that they came to be seen as the great protector or Alberta's rights against encroachments by the federal government. ... The best way ... to stand up to Ottawa was to give the Tories a strong majority. Economic interests were therefore merged with identity politics so that, for many, being a strong Albertan also meant being a strong Tory.[43]

Taras's analysis was right as far as it went. But then he ignores the fact that starting with the end of the Klein era, the PCs turned a blind eye to the growing number of Albertans who wanted meaningful reforms to our relationship with Ottawa. Taras correctly notes that "Jim Prentice never played the alienation card."[44] But he ignores the fact that neither did Stelmach or Redford. Taras's account of the "rise and fall" of the PCs does not even mention Preston Manning or the domination of the Reform Party in Alberta's federal elections. Stewart and Sayers make a similar omission. They attribute the success of the PC Party to its rejection of "more right wing candidates" in the 1993, 2006, and 2011 leadership elections.[45] In addition to being wrong about 1993—Klein, the winner over Nancy Betkowski, was clearly the "right-wing candidate"—it was the leaderships of Stelmach, Redford, and Prentice that drove more conservative Albertans out of the PC Party into Wildrose, resulting in the vote splitting that finally destroyed the PCs in 2015. And it has been the election of "more right-wing candidates" as leaders—Kenney in 2019 and Smith in 2023—that has ended vote splitting on the Right and produced two majority UCP governments.

From the mid-1990s on, the PCs not only ignored the Reform Party and its supporters but were actively hostile. Remember the "welcome" I received when I was first elected as the PC MLA for Foothills-Rocky View in 2004. As the *Edmonton Journal* reported, "Veteran Tory MLAs are eagerly awaiting Morton's arrival at the legislature after the election, simply so they can cut him down. There haven't been this many knives in a welcoming committee since Julius Caesar dropped by the Senate."[46] The PC Party's hostility toward me and later the Wildrose Party may be understandable, but it was also a mistake.

This hostility was understandable, because by the time Ralph Klein stepped down as premier, Albertans had enjoyed four decades of growth and prosperity under PC governments and the unique urban-rural coalition that kept re-electing them. Many Albertans, both urban and rural, had done very well, and they were prepared to spend money—lots of money— to protect what was working. The Alberta auditor general's reports document how PC governments have been funded by donations from corporate friends and clients to an extent unprecedented in any other province.[47]

In my early years as an MLA and then minister, I was often surprised that some of the same people I would see at PC party events in the evenings were the people who had come to my office to lobby me in the morning. After a few years, I was no longer surprised. The same people who did business with the Alberta government were well represented at all levels of the PC Party organization.

This is how the PC dynasty sustained itself for forty-four years. The last thing they wanted was a new guy (Ted Morton) from another party (Reform) with a new set of issues (Alberta Agenda) to upset the apple cart. So they strongly supported the PC establishment candidates: Jim Dinning in 2006 and Gary Mar in 2012, both of whom went on to lose. But they lost to candidates—Stelmach and Redford—who continued to ignore the growing support for the Wildrose Party and the threat this posed to the PC's electoral coalition.

In theory, this strategy might have worked. It usually serves the electoral self-interest of a dominant major party like the PCs to suppress new cross-cutting issues, preserve the existing "dimension of conflict in voters' minds, and occupy the position of the median voter."[48] But for the Tories, ignoring Albertans' growing support for change turned out to be a mistake.

Alberta was the birthplace of the Reform Party. Its influential founder, Preston Manning, was the son of popular former Alberta Premier Ernest Manning, who had governed Alberta for twenty-five years (1943–1968). From the Reform Party's beginnings, Alberta has been the financial and intellectual foundation of the Reform/CA/CPC parties. Throughout the 1990s and 2000s, Albertans routinely gave Reform/CA/CPC over 60 percent of our votes and 90 percent of our MPs. Thousands of Albertans of my generation spent decades of "blood, sweat, and tears" to build Reform from an upstart Western fringe party to a national party. Many of our children—including one of mine—went to Ottawa to work with the Reform/CA/CPC parties. And we finally helped to elect Albertan Stephen Harper as the prime minister of Canada from 2006 to 2015.

Yet despite Reform/CA/CPC success in the federal elections, PC leaders never embraced—much less accommodated—either the policies or the people that built the Reform movement in Alberta. The PC Party refused to advance any reforms—such as those proposed in the Harper, Morton et al. "Firewall Letter"—that would address Alberta's constitutional vulnerability to Ottawa and the predatory policies of the federal Liberal Party.

The Liberals' policy attacks on Alberta's energy sector are inevitable. It's how they win elections. As Keith Davey, Pierre Trudeau's campaign manager, summarized their strategy to win the 1980 federal election—the National Energy Program—"Screw the West. We'll take the rest."[49] It worked for the Liberals then and continues to work today.

Predictably, disillusioned Alberta Reformers decided to form their own party—the Wildrose. And once they did, the more the PCs ignored the

Western alienation issue, the more Albertans were attracted to the Wildrose Party. But it was not just the Alberta PCs that contributed to the rise of the Wildrose.

The Wildrose Party also benefited from the federal CPC's evolving de-emphasizing of the Western fairness issue. First Manning, with his United Alternative initiative, and then Harper with the CPC, sought to transform the Reform Party from a Western-based protest party to a competitive national party—a party that had a plausible path to displacing Liberal majority governments in Ottawa. But this meant catering more to voters in Ontario and Quebec. As early as 2005, Faron Ellis predicted that disillusioned Western voters would form a new party.

> Alienated, right-of-centre western voters will again witness a national party they solidly support expend most of its efforts chasing votes in Central Canada. Given the history of western Canadian federal party politics, it also seems likely that as the process plays itself out, at some point in the future, some westerners will again be agitating for a new party to represent their dissenting opinions.[50]

Ellis turned out to be right about a new party, but it turned out to be a new provincial party, not a new federal party. Actually, he was proven right twice. The new Saskatchewan Party and its leaders—Brad Wall and now Scott Moe—also have their origins in the Reform Party movement.

But it was not until 2016, when the PC Party was destroyed by vote splitting with the Wildrose, that Jason Kenney—a first-wave Reformer in the 1990s and never a PC party member—could stride in from Ottawa and take over the party in less than one year.

In a plan that he unveiled only a year earlier, in 2017 Kenney first won the PC leadership contest (March); then the vote to merge PCs and Wildrose (June); and then won the leadership of the new United Conservative Party (October).[51] In the PC leadership contest, he raised over $1.4 million—nine times more than the next highest candidate.

Almost all of Kenney's campaign team consisted of friends and staffers he brought with him from his Reform/CPC years in Ottawa. Other than myself, there were virtually no former PC cabinet ministers or senior PC operatives on the Kenney team in 2016–17. When he later ran to win the leadership of the newly merged UCP, most former PC MLAs and cabinet ministers backed his opponents. Kenney's relationship with the PC caucus was most memorably captured by a leaked email he sent to his fellow Alberta MPs in which he described Thomas Lukaszuk—then Redford's deputy premier—as "a complete and utter asshole."[52]

A less colourful but more reliable indicator of Kenney's complete break with the old PC party is that out of the sixty-three UCP MLAs that were elected with Kenney in 2019, only two—Ric McIver and Mike Ellis—had been in either the Stelmach or Redford governments. Indeed, only eight had ever been in the Legislative Assembly before. When he was sworn in as Alberta's eighteenth premier, Kenney had effectively cleaned house of former PC MLAs.

12

The Alberta Agenda: From Fringe to Mainstream

KENNEY'S HOSTILE TAKEOVER OF THE PC PARTY (2017)

In political science terminology, what Jason Kenney achieved is known as a "hostile takeover": where an existing party is taken over by a new leader—an outsider—with new issues and new supporters. Hostile takeovers become possible when an established party loses control over its candidate nomination process and fundraising for leadership candidates.[1] This concept has been used in US politics to explain how Donald Trump won the Republican Party's nomination for president in 2016. But it accurately captures what happened to the Alberta PC Party in 2017.

The destruction of the PC Party by Wildrose is also consistent with what political science describes as an "invasion from the margin"—where a new party tries to break into a two-party dominant system.[2] To succeed, the new party must successfully promote a new issue that "opens the possibility of breaking up a major party's coalition and winning some of those voters for the minor party."[3]

> The recipe for success is for the new, more extreme party to find a regional base, cut deeply into its nearest rival's traditional base of core voters, and eventually take it over by merger or drive it down to a point where it is no longer relevant or even disappears.[4]

This was written in 2014. The best Canadian example is how the Reform Party first stole the federal PCs' Western voter base in the 1993 and 1997 federal elections, and eventually took it over via Stephen Harper's 2003 merger. But there is a clear parallel with what happened in the 2015 Alberta provincial election, and Jason Kenney's subsequent takeover of the Alberta PC party.

This should sound familiar. It is basically what I tried to do in the 2006 leadership, and why the PC establishment worked so hard to defeat me. In 2017, Kenney succeeded where I had failed. He succeeded in part because he had a well-organized, well-financed campaign. He was also the most effective public speaker Albertans had seen in decades.

But he also succeeded because there was no one left to defend the PC party or its brand. And with the party reduced to nine seats in the legislature and without a leader, there was nothing left to defend. This was the price the PCs paid for ignoring the new issues of Western alienation and the growing number of Albertans who supported the Reform/CA/CPC calls for a new deal—a fair deal—from Ottawa.

EQUALIZATION REFERENDUM AND THE FAIR DEAL REPORT (2019)

In 2019, Kenney led the UCP to a new majority government. With the PCs and Wildrose parties now united—i.e., no more vote splitting—Kenney crushed the NDP, winning sixty-three seats and 55 percent of votes. A central issue in this election was Kenney's commitment to hold a referendum to abolish the federal equalization program. He had initially endorsed the equalization referendum during the 2017 UCP leadership election. But he was a follower on this issue, not a leader.

In March 2017, I had published a column in the *Calgary Herald*[5] (and a more extensive policy paper for the Manning Centre[6]) explaining how the Supreme Court's ruling in the *Quebec Secession Reference*[7] created a constitutional opportunity for Alberta to use a referendum to challenge the equalization program. Several months later, in July, Brian Jean announced his candidacy for the leadership of the newly formed UCP. He promised that, if elected, he would support holding a referendum to abolish equalization.[8]

At the time, Jean, the former leader of the Wildrose Party, was the only candidate who might beat Kenney in the UCP leadership election scheduled for October. Abolishing equalization was popular with Wildrose members, who now would be a key voting bloc in the UCP leadership race. To pre-empt any advantage this might give Jean, Kenney quickly announced that he too would hold an equalization referendum. This certainly helped him win his overwhelming majority—61 percent—of UCP voters in October. But it also meant that the equalization referendum became a key plank of the party he now led.

After he won the 2019 provincial election and became premier, Kenney kept this campaign promise. To minimize costs, the referendum was not held until Alberta's next municipal elections, in October 2020. When the votes were counted, 62 percent supported the proposal to abolish the federal equalization program.[9]

A second catalyst for Kenney's stronger challenges to Ottawa was the Liberals' victory in the October 2019 federal election.[10] Now faced with the gloomy prospects of another four years of Trudeau's anti-oil, anti-Alberta policies, Kenney convened a meeting of several of his key outside advisers—i.e., outside of both his caucus and cabinet. On very short notice, this emergency pow-wow was held in the Jephson dining room at the Ranchmen's Club on October 25. Other than me, the participants were a who's who of Western Canadian conservative leaders: Stephen Harper (former prime minister of Canada); Brad Wall (former premier of Saskatchewan); Scott Moe (current premier of Saskatchewan); and Preston Manning (founder and former leader of the Reform Party of Canada).

Suffice it to say that it was one of the most interesting political meetings that I ever attended. In addition to great food, wine and scotch, there was plenty of advice on how best to counter economically harmful Liberal policies. I found it interesting—but not surprising—that the most animated advice came from Stephen Harper. There was clearly no love lost between Harper and Justin Trudeau!

I was relatively quiet that evening, because I had already given Kenney my advice in a three-page memo. Its core was the four initiatives listed in the Alberta Agenda. I cautioned that there was a risk of going too far, too fast—further alienating Trudeau and jeopardizing Ottawa's support for the completion of the Trans Mountain Pipeline. But I also warned that there was "a risk of not going far enough, quickly enough, and losing support to a new rump Alberta Separatist Party." I specifically referenced a recent op-ed by none other than Danielle Smith—"How Alberta can stop acting like Canada's doormat"[11]—and warned: "We don't want to start dividing conservative voters again."

This advice appears to have caught Kenney's attention. Only two weeks later—on November 9—Kenney announced the creation of the "Fair Deal Panel," chaired by none other than Preston Manning. The panel's mandate was to determine Albertans' support for the reforms proposed in the 2001

Firewall Letter. Seven months later, in May 2020, the Fair Deal Panel released its report.[12] Its recommendations included:

- Cancelling Alberta's contract with the RCMP and creating our own Alberta Police Force, as Ontario and Quebec already have.

- Collecting our own personal income taxes, as Quebec and now Saskatchewan already do.

- Withdrawing from the Canada Pension Plan and creating our own provincial pension plan, something Quebec has already done.

Suddenly, the Alberta Agenda was now the Government of Alberta's agenda. But then COVID-19 hit, and all of this was put on hold. Two years later, in 2022, Kenney was pushed out as PC leader for his handling—or mishandling—of the COVID-19 lockdowns.[13] (For the record, I think that if COVID-19 had not hit when it did, Kenney would have gone on win several more elections. He drew a very bad card, and it was a sad ending to an otherwise outstanding political career.) Ironically, the anti-Kenney revolt was led by many of the same former Reform Party/Wildrose members who had helped him win the UCP leadership in 2019. But then, this is basically what happened to me a decade earlier. It was my former leadership supporters—now Wildrosers—who took me down in 2012.

DANIELLE SMITH AND THE *SOVEREIGNTY ACT*

In a hotly contested election to choose a new leader—there were seven candidates—Danielle Smith came out of political exile to win. A central component of her campaign was her promise to enact an "Alberta Sovereignty Act" to protect Albertans from hostile federal policies. This strategy worked. And the new Smith government's first piece of legislation, Bill 1, was the *Alberta Sovereignty Act*.[14]

While the *Sovereignty Act* helped Smith win the UCP leadership race, it was a potential liability in the upcoming provincial election, already scheduled for May 2023. To moderate voters—including many who had voted for the UCP in 2019—it seemed overly aggressive. Academics warned that Smith's populist approach was "out of step with public opinion" and advised that the "next UCP government would do well to focus less on building Fair Deal firewalls around the province and more on building bridges with the rest of the country."[15] But notwithstanding sharp criticisms from the NDP and much of the media, Smith and the UCP prevailed, winning forty-nine seats, more than enough to form a new majority government.

How this will work out over the next four years remains to be seen. But the Smith majority government clearly marks a turning point in Alberta politics. For the first time, Albertans have a provincial conservative government that explicitly recognizes Alberta's chronic vulnerability to harmful federal Liberal policies, and that embraces reforms that would better protect Albertans' interests. The *Alberta Sovereignty Act* is now law, and it is already being used to challenge the federal government's new clean energy regulations.[16] Recent academic commentary has supported the *Sovereignty Act* and suggests that it may part of a broader "new provincial rights movement."[17] This culminates a thirty-year struggle to persuade Alberta's provincial conservative party to support the reforms that Albertans have been voting for at the federal level.

In her election night victory speech, Smith promised to defend Albertans against harmful federal policies, and explicitly challenged the Trudeau Liberal government to back off on their pending climate change policies—policies that would clearly hurt Alberta's oil, gas, and electricity sectors. The next day in a radio interview Smith was more explicit. Referencing Ottawa's proposed net zero policy for provincial electricity grids and a hard new cap on oil sands emissions, Smith warned: "There's a big fight coming up."[18]

THE NEXT CHAPTER

In one sense, this is history repeating itself. In the 1920s, Premier Brownlee and his UFA government had to fight with Ottawa to gain provincial control of Alberta's natural resources.[19] In the 1980s, Alberta Premier Peter Lougheed went to political war with Ottawa over Pierre Trudeau's National Energy Program and won the addition of section 92A to the constitution—explicitly affirming exclusive provincial jurisdiction over the development of natural resources. Alberta has never won any concessions from Ottawa by asking politely. We have had to fight for them.

But in another sense, Premier Smith and her newly elected UCP majority government are unprecedented. It's been a long march, but there is a historical line—covered with blood, sweat, and tears—from my 2006 leadership campaign to Danielle Smith's 2023 victory. The same reforms that were on the periphery of Alberta provincial politics twenty years ago are now front and centre. And so are some of the key players.

Almost all the people in UCP's 2023 "war room" were involved in my 2006 leadership campaign. Rob Anderson, Danielle Smith's top advisor, was then a law student at the University of Alberta in 2006, and he organized our campus membership sales. (His father, Calgary lawyer Robert Anderson, was on my 2006 fundraising and steering committee.) Another second-generation player was Lauren Armstrong, whose father, Sam Armstrong, was my 2006 campaign director. Lauren is now with Navigator, the influential national consulting company. Rob Griffith, Matt Gelinas, Bill Bewick, and Dustin van Vugt—all key members of my 2006 campaign—were also in the UCP 2023 war room. And of course, their boss, now premier and party leader, Danielle Smith, had been one of the eighteen people at the 2003 meeting in Red Deer where I first announced my intention to run for the PC leadership when Klein resigned.

On a personal level, it has been gratifying to see that many of the reforms that I had written about and campaigned for, but did not achieve, are now being implemented. But it also reflects a qualitative change in Alberta politics: that the Western alienation / Fair Deal movement is here to stay. It now has an intellectual substance and respectability that it lacked before.

In Alberta politics, there have always been angry populist rump parties that could garner ten percent of the votes in provincial elections: the Western Canada Concept Party in 1982; the Alberta Alliance Party in 2004. But both the national and local media could and did dismiss them as single-issue wingnuts that lacked any intellectual substance. With the new United Conservative Party, this is no longer possible.

There are direct links, both in term of policies and personnel, between the UCP and the so-called "Calgary School." (The same is true for the federal Conservative Party of Canada.) Starting in the 1990s, the "Calgary School" has been recognized nationally and even internationally as an important "influencer" in both Alberta and Canadian politics.[20] More recently, our voice has been strengthened by the policy scholarship of Dr. Jack Mintz. Born and raised in Edmonton, Mintz spent most of his career in Ontario, where he taught at both Queen's University and the University of Toronto and was director of the prestigious C.D. Howe Institute in Toronto. But in 2008, he moved to Calgary to found and direct the new School of Public Policy at the University of Calgary.

In 2020, I co-edited a book with Mintz and Tom Flanagan—*Moment of Truth: How to Think About Alberta's Future*[21]—which has become the handbook of the Fair Deal movement. In addition to our own chapters, *Moment of Truth* includes chapters written by recognized, senior scholars and leaders from across Canada. These include one of Canada's former ambassadors to the United States and two members of the Royal Society of Canada, none of them from Alberta.[22] *Moment of Truth* cannot be dismissed as "fringe," and neither can the UCP. Viewed from a different perspective, the Alberta sovereignty movement now has what Quebec has had for the past forty years.[23]

This type of intellectual leadership—while new to Alberta—is an important dimension of politics in all modern democracies. It is what Adam Masters and John Uhr have described as "distributed" political leadership—leadership that includes not just first ministers but also "leading voices in academic research ... politically active people in civil society."[24]

The mainstream media found the Smith-UCP victory alarming. And they should. The Fair Deal movement is here to stay. Smith has not only the solid backing of her caucus, but also support from new allies in the rest of Canada. Saskatchewan Premier Scott Moe is clearly a soulmate. His government has already enacted the *Saskatchewan First Act* and plans to start collecting personal income taxes. Saskatchewan acted before Alberta to protect parents' rights,[25] as has New Brunswick.[26] The Quebec government—always a staunch defender of provincial rights—has recently supported Alberta's constitutional challenges to both Bill C-69 and the federal carbon tax.

And then there is the man who now leads the Conservative Party of Canada and intends to replace Trudeau as Canada's next prime minister—Pierre Poilievre. Poilievre broke with precedent and publicly endorsed Smith and the UCP prior to the May 2023 provincial election. This was not a surprise to many of us. Both Smith and Poilievre began their political careers in the heady Reform Party politics of Alberta during the 1990s. They have both been part of the Long March. They both understand that the West wants in, not out. But they also understand that we want a new deal—a fair deal—from the rest of Canada. The next chapter has begun. And it will be written by the next generation of Alberta leaders.

Power to the Parents: A Vindication of Bill 208

In retrospect, subsequent political developments have vindicated my warnings about the threats to freedom of speech and religion that Bill 208 was designed to mitigate. Same-sex marriage is now a *fait accompli* in most Western democracies. Tellingly, in both Canada and the US, this is the result of decisions by unelected, unaccountable judges.

I still think, as I did twenty years ago, that same-sex marriage is a dangerous social experiment. It ignores the basic biological and psychological differences that define the two sexes. It has never been adopted in any societies in human history prior to the last two decades. It will increase the number of children who grow up without either a mother or a father in their household. As I and others have written (see Appendix 2), this will be to the detriment of both children and society at large. Critics will quickly point out that we will not know whether these risks become realities for several more generations. My response: Yes, but we don't know that they won't become realities, and that is a risk I do not think we should have taken.

What we do know now is that the push for same-sex marriage was not the endgame for gay activists and their woke allies, but a staging area for an even more aggressive campaign not just to "normalize" what quickly became known as "LGBTQ" behaviour and relationships, but to silence and, if necessary, to punish any public disagreement with this "new normal." What now passes for the "progressive" or "woke" agenda of sex and race issues is eroding the traditional rights of freedom of speech and religion; the rights of parents to choose their children's education; equal protection of the laws; and due process of law.

Out of the 193 countries in the world today, only thirty-four countries have legalized same-sex marriage, and virtually none in Eastern Europe, Asia, or Africa—which constitute over 80 percent of the world's population. It is interesting—and a bit frightening—to ask: What are the conditions in Canada and the other Western democracies that gave birth to same-sex marriage and the LGBTQ movement? Are we the pioneers of a brave new world, one that the others will follow into a more egalitarian future? Or are we at the beginning of the decline and fall of the European-Anglo-American empire, a small handful of nations that have been too wealthy, too powerful for too long, and have forgotten the social and political foundations of their success? Have we started down the rabbit hole of George Orwell's *1984* and the "thought police"? I don't know the answer to those questions. But I do know that Canada, unfortunately, is in the vanguard of the woke authoritarian movement. How did we get here so quickly?

UNIVERSITIES

The place to start is with our universities. This is where "identity politics" and the "social justice" agenda originated and has gone the furthest. With the defeat and demise of communism in the 1990s, the academic Left developed a new "narrative" and a new set of categories to retool their critique of Western liberal democracies. In postwar Western democracies, the most dynamic agent of social change has been not Marx's industrial proletariat but an "oppositionist intelligentsia," drawn from and supported by the well-educated, more affluent strata of society.[1]

In post-industrial democracies such as Canada and the US, the "knowledge industry" has become a new source of political power. The socio-economic base of this new knowledge industry consists of "the well-educated and affluent, academics, journalists, professionals and civil servants."[2] But since these groups still constitute a minority of voters, they choose to pursue their policy goals through the courts and human rights bureaucracies rather than through the electoral process.[3]

In the new social justice vocabulary, equity has replaced equality. Justice is no longer equality of opportunity, but equality of result. Justice for whom? The working class? The many poor? Not any longer. Now it is for "historically disadvantaged minorities." Women and "BIPOC"—Black, Indigenous, and people of colour—all of whom are now deemed to have unjustly suffered from sexism and the "white supremacy" that defines Canadian and American "colonialist" societies. Heterosexism—the term invented for prejudice against homosexuals—fits comfortably into the new war against racism and sexism.

It was soon expanded to "transphobia" to include transsexuals and bisexuals—newly defined "gender minorities."

Identity politics is not just wrong as a matter of history. It is also dangerous. It promotes the very differences that modern liberalism made secondary because they have been the source of so much conflict—race, religion, and ethnicity. As Andrew Sullivan—himself an out-of-the-closet gay man—has written, "The goal of our [woke] culture now is not the emancipation of the individual from the group, but the permanent definition of the individual by the group."[4] The belief that adopting these policies will somehow promote greater equality and toleration among groups in the future is delusional.

This is a huge step backward. Legally defining individuals by their religion, race, or ethnicity is what fuelled a century of civil wars between Catholics and Protestants in Europe. More recently, Third-World versions of "identity politics" have fuelled the bloodshed and human tragedies in places like Kosovo, Turkey, Rwanda, Somalia, Iraq, Iran, and now Gaza, Israel, and Sudan.

I saw the identity politics / social justice movement coming back in the 1990s. I described it in my 2000 book, *The Charter Revolution and the Court Party*: how the new progressive left was using litigation and the courts to do an end run around elected "responsible" governments.[5]

By the time I returned to university teaching in 2012, the new woke agenda had gone from a vocal minority of faculty to the dominant institutional culture. In 1995, I was awarded a prestigious national fellowship in "human rights research."[6] In today's new "woke" environment, this could never happen. A snapshot of this new normal is captured by Professor Jordan Peterson's 2022 public letter explaining his early resignation from the University of Toronto (where I did my PhD in the 1970s):

> We are now at the point where race, ethnicity, "gender," or sexual preference is first, accepted as the fundamental characteristic defining each person (just as the radical leftists were hoping) and second, is now treated as the most important qualification for study, research and employment.[7]

What are called the "Diversity, Equity, and Inclusivity" mandates (DEI) now dictate who is hired and promoted. The result, Peterson continues, is that "my qualified and supremely trained heterosexual white male graduate students

... face a negligible chance of being offered university research positions." But it's not just new hires. Existing faculty members—including senior professors with outstanding records of research and teaching—must now "undergo so-called anti-bias training, conducted by supremely unqualified Human Resources personnel, lecturing inanely and blithely and in an accusatory manner about theoretically all-pervasive racist/sexist/heterosexist attitudes." He concludes that this, "combined with the death of objective testing, has compromised the universities so badly that it can hardly be overstated."[8]

Peterson's account of what has happened at Canadian universities mirrors what has happened in American universities. As reported in the *Wall Street Journal*,

> The left has spent decades consolidating power across the institutions of American academic life. The crowning achievement of that effort was the diversity, equity and inclusion bureaucracy—constructed to perpetuate progressive dominance of higher education by keeping conservatives out of the professoriate.[9]

For those in Alberta, the 2012 "cancelling crusade" against my friend and colleague Tom Flanagan—"from respected political scientist to pariah"—was a wake-up call to this new dystopia.[10] The more recent 2022 firing of tenured Professor Frances Widdowson at Mount Royal University is only the most recent example of suppression and punishment of professors who in their teaching and writing do not toe the new line of "political correctness." Widdowson was fired for criticizing the Black Lives Matter movement and for stating that there were educational benefits for Indigenous youth in Canada's residential schools system.[11]

In 2023, the University Calgary announced its new "cluster hiring initiative"—a plan to hire forty-five new professors, all of whom must be members of "equity-deserving groups"—women, Indigenous people, visible minorities, or persons with disabilities.[12]

DEI's consequence for our universities—and by extension, all Albertans—will be negative. More qualified candidates for faculty hiring will be passed over in favour of applicants from "equity-deserving groups." Not only is this unfair discrimination against the more qualified candidates, it will also undermine the competitiveness of our universities—both nationally and internationally.

What happened to hiring based on merit and achievement? Imagine if the players on professional hockey or basketball teams were hired based on DEI rather than skill and merit. Guaranteed last place! For our universities—and our students, who are our future—it will be an academic and economic disaster. I wrote an op-ed for the *Calgary Herald* sharply criticizing the U of C for all of these reasons.[13]

Much to my surprise, the *Herald* did not include my op-ed in their online version, which has a much larger number of subscribers. When I requested that they add it to the online edition, they refused, saying it was a way to "reward" their home-delivery subscribers. I was not persuaded, and so subsequently published an expanded version of the same piece in the *Western Standard*.[14] But I went further, and tried to make my arguments against the U of C's new faculty hiring policy less abstract, more personal, more local:

> The sort of reverse discrimination now being launched by the U of C is not a path that Alberta needs to go down. Over the past six decades, families from all over Canada—and all over the world—have come to Alberta for better opportunities. More importantly, they have stayed. And they stayed because they have prospered. … Alberta has prospered largely because it has been a classic meritocracy. With increasingly rare exceptions, Albertans don't care where you've come from or what colour your skin is. At some point, all our families came from somewhere else. We care if you can do the job and do it well. If you can, you're on our team. This culture has contributed to building the most productive and prosperous province in Canada. … The more diverse we become, the more imperative it is that the government treat everyone equally. It is not only morally right. It works. In Alberta it has worked for the past six decades. And it will keep working if we allow it to.

I ended by endorsing the policy recommendations proposed by the Macdonald-Laurier Institute to bring back freedom of speech and academic integrity to Canadian universities.[15] These include freedom of speech codes for both students and professors; merit-based hiring of new professors; and the prohibition of mandatory DEI declarations as a condition of employment or research funding. And I added one more: "To provide funding for new institutions on university campuses that ensure students have access to the ideas and facts that rebut and disprove the new pseudo-progressive orthodoxies. Fight false speech with true speech. The historical facts are on our side."

The irrationality and harm of this new woke culture is not limited to university campuses. It has spilled over into mainstream media, entertainment, and the corporate world. As Peterson warned, "What happens in the universities eventually colours everything."

HUMAN RIGHTS ACTS

The federal legalization of same-sex marriage in 2005 had immediate consequences for both human rights legislation and for education. It removes the concept of a natural parent from Canadian law; "It disconnects being a parent from its natural basis—the union of a man and a woman, a husband and wife, a father and a mother."[16] As Douglas Farrow notes, "At a stroke, it made parenthood a gift of the state—a legal construct—rather than a natural right."[17] Not only is this dangerous—what the state creates, it can take away—but it has also opened the door to endless new legal definitions of marriage and parenthood with no regard for biological realities. For woke progressives, the very term "biological realities" is itself proof of heterosexism and transphobia.

Feminists and gay rights activists were quick to pressure federal and provincial governments to add not just sexual orientation to their human rights acts but also "gender identity." The general public, of course, had no idea what this meant or what such legal changes would entail, so most governments took the path of least resistance and quietly complied.

Alberta was an exception. The Supreme Court had already ruled in its 1998 *Vriend* decision that not including sexual orientation was a violation of the Charter of Rights, so Alberta had no choice but to add it. But not "gender identity." Now a member of cabinet, I warned caucus that the term "gender identity" was a carefully constructed political and legal time bomb that, if put into legislation, gay rights activists would take to the courts to force precisely the kinds of restrictions on freedom of speech and freedom of religion that Bill 208 had been designed to prevent. Notwithstanding then Minister of Education Dave Hancock's arguments to the contrary, caucus agreed with me. So when the Stelmach government introduced Bill 44 in 2009, we did not include "gender identity."[18] We also went a step further by adding a parental notification requirement if a class were to study "subject matter that deals explicitly with religion, sexuality or sexual orientation," and gave parents the right to exclude their children from such classes.[19]

Other than Alberta, most other provinces went along with the radical new dispensation. At the federal level, to their credit, the Harper Conservatives did not. But in 2016, the newly elected Justin Trudeau Liberals were quick to incorporate such changes into federal law. The Liberals' Bill C-16 added not just "gender identity" but also "gender expression" to the list of prohibited forms of discrimination in the *Canadian Human Rights Act.*

The intentional ambiguity of these terms makes them unintelligible to normal people. But for the woke activists, their meaning is clear. Similar phrasing in the *Ontario Human Rights Act* has already been interpreted to mean that "refusing to refer to a trans-person by their chosen name and a personal pronoun that matches their gender identity" will be deemed illegal.[20]

As Queen's University law professor Bruce Pardy warned in the *National Post*, "Bill C-16 will give transgendered and non-gendered people the ability to dictate other people's speech."

> [F]ailure to use a person's pronoun of choice—'ze,' 'zir,' 'they,' or any one of a multitude of other potential non-words—will land you in hot water with the commission. That, in turn, can lead to orders for correction, apology, Soviet-like 're-education,' fines and, in cases of continued non-compliance, incarceration for contempt of court.[21]

Alberta has not been exempt from controversies over mandatory "re-education." In 2021, the Law Society of Alberta adopted a new rule that required all Alberta lawyers to complete a five-hour online learning module teaching "Indigenous cultural competency," or risk being suspended. A year later, the Law Society suspended thirty Alberta lawyers who failed to complete their "training" in post-modern de-colonization.[22] Critics drafted a petition calling for its repeal. They argued that the Law Society's job is to ensure competency and integrity, not to impose political indoctrination. At their 2023 annual meeting, members of the Law Society defeated a proposal to eliminate the mandatory course.[23]

These types of mandated speech and professional re-education policies are the exact antithesis of one of the oldest and most important human rights—freedom of speech—and more specifically, the right to publicly disagree and criticize government policy. Pardy concludes that "we are in the middle of a culture war, and human rights have become a weapon to normalize social justice values and to delegitimize competing beliefs." In Canadian and American universities, the woke warriors have prevailed. And now they are moving on to primary and secondary schools.

EDUCATION CURRICULUM

In 2021, Ontario escalated the culture war with Bill 67, later re-introduced as Bill 16.[24] Bill 16 seeks to incorporate "social justice theory"—a Canadian variant on its American counterpart, Critical Race Theory (CRT)—for all Ontario K-12 schools and universities.[25] CRT, as Barbara Kay accurately reports, "teaches that we should judge others and ourselves *only* by skin colour, gender identity, DNA (indigenous status), and other group markers." The new goal is not equality of opportunity, but equality of results, now called "equity." Equity is mentioned fifty-four times in Bill 16, but equality not once. This isn't by accident.

> Equity is about finishing lines for groups. If minority groups don't achieve the same outcomes in proportion to their numbers in the population, there can only be one reason: racism or some other form of bigotry exercised by an oppressor group with privilege.[26]

Like its federal counterpart, Bill C-16, Ontario's Bill 16 means that racism need not be overt or intentional. "Those who 'feel' offended decide whether or not an act of racism has been committed. There is no objective threshold, no due process for the alleged perpetrator. If you say you are not a racist, this is deemed proof that you subconsciously are a racist."[27]

❀ ❀ ❀

Alberta has not escaped the campaign to revamp provincial education systems to reflect the new social justice / woke agenda. With my departure in 2012 and the leadership turmoil that ensued (three different premiers in three years), the PC caucus became more susceptible to the lobbying efforts of the

LGBTQ activists and their allies in the province's human rights bureaucracy. Both were still angry about Bill 44's omission of "gender identity" and its requirement for parental notification and the opt-out provision.

In 2014, Conservative MLA Sandra Jansen introduced Bill 10, innocuously titled *An Act to Amend the Alberta Bill of Rights to Protect our Children*. (Two years later Jansen showed her true colours and crossed the floor to join the new NDP government.) Bill 10's benign title hid a cryptic and complex set of amendments to the *Alberta Human Rights Act*. These amendments were crafted to open the door to future, more explicit, and more intrusive policies through bureaucratic regulations, where the media and thus the general public were less likely to notice them.

Bill 10 retained the parental notification / opt-out provisions of Bill 44, but then added a requirement that all Alberta school boards add and support student "diversity" clubs if any student requested one. It contained a parental notification requirement, but only that such a club had been created. Schools were not required to notify parents if their child was participating in such a club. This provided a convenient end run around the parental notification requirement for classroom materials dealing with sexual orientation.

In 2015, the newly elected NDP government was quick to take advantage of Bill 10's bureaucratic back door. In November, Minister of Education David Eggen introduced sweeping new "education guidelines."[28] Ostensibly these "guidelines" were to assist school boards in implementing Bill 10. In reality, they were mandatory, intended to force local school boards to adopt the new "diversity" initiatives. If a school board resisted, unhappy students or parents could appeal to the minister for correction.

The guidelines required all schools—public, separate, Francophone, charter, and private—to adopt the LGBTQ maxim that "self-identification is the sole measure of an individual's sexual orientation, gender identity or gender expression." Following from this alpha principle, all schools were told to revise "policies, regulations and procedures" to ensure they "respected ... sexual orientations, gender identities and gender expressions." Sixteen pages then spelled out in detail what this entails. But the most dramatic change— and the one that sparked the most controversy—was the new requirement that prohibited schools from disclosing to parents any information about their child's sexual orientation or gender identity without first getting that child's permission.[29]

These changes sparked a wave of protests. Bishop Henry, the Catholic Archbishop of Calgary, publicly denounced the guidelines as "the madness of relativism and the forceful imposition of a particular narrow-minded anti-Catholic ideology."[30]

Now back in my university office, I wrote a column for the *Calgary Herald* denouncing it as violating the freedoms of all Canadians, and most specifically parents. The NDP guidelines, I reminded readers, were in clear violation of Article 26 of the United Nations Declaration of Human Rights: "Parents have a prior right to choose the kind of education that should be given to their children."[31] But the most effective and mobilizing resistance came from a new organization—Parents for Choice in Education—and its founder, Donna Trimble.

> Schools are being coerced to isolate parents from their own children, thereby severing the parent-child bond that is essential to the mental health of every child. ... This guideline will only serve to isolate children who are confronting one of the most difficult and confusing moments of their young lives with the cumulative pressure of having to decide when, if ever, to invite their parents into the discussion.[32]

Undeterred—and sensing that they might lose the 2019 election (which they did)—in 2017 the NDP pushed through a second piece of legislation, Bill 24, which further entrenched the LGBTQ agenda in Alberta schools. Bill 24 abandoned the vague and innocuous "diversity" rationale for student clubs and made their purpose explicit: "Gay-Straight Alliance" and "Queer-Straight Alliance." It authorized these clubs to provide sexually explicit materials and prohibited schools from informing parents if their child was participating in one of these clubs.

PARENT POWER: THE DEI BACKLASH

In the United States, these same issues have sparked what is now being called a "culture war." In the 2016 US presidential election, Hillary Clinton's description of Trump supporters as "a basket of deplorables ... racist, sexist, homophobic, xenophobic, Islamaphobic" elicited laughter and applause from her Upper East Side New York City audience. But it also contributed to her defeat, as millions of traditional working-class Democrats felt her contempt and voted for Donald Trump.

More recently, legislators in at least six states have passed laws that restrict teaching about sexual orientation and gender identity in public schools. Their supporters argue that these are decisions should be made by parents.[33] National columnist Peggy Noonan has described these developments as a "parents' rebellion." Noting political victories by anti-woke candidates in the recent Virginia governor's race and a school board recall election in San Francisco, Noonan concludes, "There is a real parents movement going on, and it is going to make a difference in our politics."[34] Noonan's prediction has proven to be accurate. Initially these protests were ad hoc and local. But in 2021, a new national organization, Moms for Liberty, was formed to coordinate and advance the protection of parents' rights in all fifty states.[35]

The backlash against DEI has also grown at the university level. In 2023, Florida enacted a law that prohibits its public universities and colleges from spending public funds on DEI initiatives. A year later, the University of Florida abolished all positions related to DEI—including thirteen full-time administrative positions in addition to appointments for fifteen faculty members.[36] Similar anti-DEI policies have been introduced in thirty other state legislatures, seven of which have now been enacted.[37]

In the United States, growing political polarization over issues like these has been described by Michael Lind as the "revolution from above." Drawn from the more educated, more affluent, more urban classes of society, the new "progressives"—the "managerial elites," as Lind describes them—have three central policy objectives: reducing CO_2 emissions to fight climate change; supporting affirmative action / reverse discrimination policies to promote the equality of results for disadvantaged minorities; and the gay marriage, LGBTQ, gender identity project. Lind neatly summarizes these as the Green Project, the Quota Project, and the Androgyny Project.[38] This "revolution from above," writes Lind, is being implemented primarily by and through the following agencies:

- State bureaucracies—especially the human rights commissions and public schools / teachers' unions

- The courts—especially final national appellate courts

- Universities and colleges—especially law schools

- Public school systems, run and staffed by graduates of universities and colleges
- United Nations and other supranational organizations

The common denominator of these institutions is that they are all unaccountable to voters and to the elected/accountable branches of government. They are aided and abetted by the national media and corporate America—which are also run and staffed by graduates of universities and colleges. Lind describes this as "the new class war," and is blunt about the challenge it poses: "saving democracy from the managerial elite."[39]

The recent forced resignation of the president of Harvard University suggests that the political backlash to identity politics and DEI is gaining strength. On October 7, 2023, Hamas slaughtered 1,200 Israeli civilians, the most Jews killed in a single day since the Nazi Holocaust of the 1940s. Claudine Gay, Harvard's black female president, refused to discipline Harvard students who publicly supported Hamas and its call for the genocide of Jews. In subsequent public testimony, Gay refused to agree that calling for the genocide of Jews is a forbidden form of hate speech at Harvard.

This triggered a public backlash and new scrutiny of Gay, her career, and her academic background. Subsequent research revealed that in some of her earlier academic publications, Gay had plagiarized work from other scholars without footnotes or attribution of her sources. When her plagiarism became public knowledge, she was forced to resign. As Christopher Rufo reported, "The truth finally broke through: Ms. Gay was a scholar of not much distinction who climbed the ladder of diversity politics, built a DEI empire as a Harvard dean, and catered to the worst instincts of left-wing ideologues on campus. The nation's leading university had subordinated *veritas* to politics, compromising its mission. The only choice was to force Ms. Gay to step down."[40]

CULTURE WAR COMES TO CANADA

While what Lind and Rufo are describing has transpired south of the border, the parallels to Canada are clear. In the 2002 federal election, well before Hillary Clinton's "basket of deplorables" remark, Liberal cabinet minister Elinor Caplan described Canadian Alliance supporters as "Holocaust deniers, prominent bigots and racists."[41] (No wonder the Liberals win no seats in Alberta!)

In 2018, *Globe and Mail* columnist Jeffrey Simpson described the surprise election victory of Doug Ford's Conservatives in the Ontario election as a "populist … reaction—or a revolt—against 'identity politics' … for whom the elites' messages of 'inclusiveness' seems to include everybody but them."[42] And now the Ford Conservatives have been elected a second time, again with strong support from the suburbs, smaller towns, and trade-union families.

A recent study by Dave Snow found that while Canada's media coverage of the Harvard University incident followed mainstream US media's favourable portrayal of President Claudine Gay and DEI policies, Canadian editorial opinion did not. Of the fifteen opinion columns that addressed DEI or "woke" policies, fourteen were critical of their influence on universities.[43] Canadian public opinion may also be moving against DEI policies at publicly funded universities and colleges. Survey research by political scientist Eric Kaufmann found that "Canadians largely reject the woke ideology" promoted by so many university and government elites, which presents "a glaring opportunity for conservatives and a glaring risk for progressives."[44]

As well it should. When Jordan Peterson first blew the whistle on the harm that DEI was doing to the University of Toronto, he was a voice in the wilderness. Today, that voice has become a choir. An entirely new think tank has been formed—the Aristotle Foundation for Public Policy—to challenge DEI and identity politics—in the universities, in the media, and in our schools[45] Their first book, *The 1867 Project: Why Canada Should be Cherished—Not Cancelled*, has been on the Amazon bestseller list since it was released in July 2023.[46]

A recent survey of professors at Canadian universities found that many professors now self-censor, not only in what they say but what they teach. Their results supported the claim that "there is a serious crisis in higher education in this country":

> Canadian universities are political monoliths whose lack of viewpoint diversity contributes to serious problems on campus including a weakening of support for academic freedom, a hostile climate for those who disagree with left-leaning values, and significant levels of self-censorship.[47]

These findings were confirmed by a recent article published by *The Hub*, a new and rapidly growing digital news and commentary media outlet. The article is by a senior administrator at a Canadian university. The author reports that "ideology trumps academic integrity" in what has created a "progressive race to the bottom" on campus: "Conformity and accessibility, rather than debate and excellence, define today's university." Tellingly, the author published this anonymously for fear of retribution (i.e., losing one's job). The author ends with the hope that "as the public becomes more aware of what is happening in these elite institutions, there may be some incentive to change."[48]

The Hub has also published another article decrying "the growing disconnect between the ideas and languages of universities and the rest of society," and the resulting tension this is creating: "University administrators and faculty members want it both ways—they want taxpayer funding but they don't want taxpayers to have a say about what happens on campus. ... One cannot help but think that this is no longer a sustainable arrangement. ... Something will likely need to give."[49]

As in the US, backlash against DEI policies is also growing at the primary and secondary school level. In 2023, Scott Moe, the conservative premier of Saskatchewan, introduced Bill 137, *Parents' Bill of Rights*, which requires schools to receive parental permission if a student under sixteen wants to change their chosen name or pronoun.[50] Predictably, this was immediately challenged in court by a "2SLGBTQIA+"[51] advocacy group as a violation of the Charter of Rights. When a judge issued an injunction against the implementation of Bill 137, Moe invoked the section 33 notwithstanding clause to protect the new parental rights policy from any future judicial veto. For this, of course, he has been widely and loudly denounced by mainstream media[52] and academics.[53]

In Alberta, there is also growing support for policies and parties supporting parents' rights. In addition to Parents for Choice in Education,[54] a new advocacy group—the Alberta Parents' Union,[55] has been formed. This may help to explain why in February 2024, Alberta Premier Danielle Smith announced a series of new policies to strengthen parental rights.[56] Parental notification will be required for any classroom discussions of "gender identity, sexual orientation or human sexuality," and all such materials will first have to be pre-approved by the Ministry of Education as age appropriate. Schools will not be allowed to change the name or the pronoun of a child under sixteen without prior parental consent. For older children, parental notification will still be required. Last but not least, transgender females (i.e., biological boys) will not be allowed to participate in girls' sports. (As the father of a daughter who played three varsity sports all through high school, I especially appreciate this.)

In addition, Smith announced that her government plans to introduce legislation to ban "top and bottom" gender reassignment surgery for children under seventeen, and to ban hormone therapy for those under fifteen. Smith was explicit in her defence of these policies: "Making permanent and irreversible decisions regarding one's biological sex while still a youth can severely limit that child's choices in the future."[57]

As in the case of Saskatchewan, Premier Smith's initiatives were widely denounced—by Prime Minister Trudeau,[58] the opposition NDP party, and the mainstream media.[59] But federal Conservative Party leader Pierre Poilievre defended Smith and challenged Trudeau: "He should let parents raise kids and let provinces run schools and hospitals."[60] The parent power movement has definitely arrived in Canada.

In April 2024, the Alberta and Saskatchewan policies got a boost from the release of the Cass Report, a study on the use of puberty blockers commissioned by England's National Health Service.[61] The Cass Report found that there is no scientifically reliable evidence that puberty blocking hormones can help children with gender dysphoria. Accordingly, Great Britain has now banned the use of puberty blockers except for clinical research. Sweden has now adopted a similar ban.[62] Predictably, the CBC and the Canadian doctors they interviewed are rejecting the findings of the Cass Report.[63]

But it's too late for Canadian Social Justice / Gender crusaders and their media allies to suppress the findings of the Cass Report. A new "non-partisan, non-religious coalition of Canadian parents, healthcare professionals and others" has formed to challenge the use of puberty blockers, sex-change surgeries and "gender-affirming care" practices.[64] They support policies of parental notification and/or consent and are urging governments to adopt "less radical, more science-based approaches to gender incongruence among minors." Their efforts have been supported by a new study from the Macdonald-Laurier Institute.[65] It reports how other Western nations (France, Holland, Finland, Denmark, and Sweden) and twenty-four US states are adopting similar reforms. This study ends with a clear message: "It is time for Canada to follow the advice of the Cass Review, rethink its approach, and redesign its policies around sensible evidence-based standards."[66] Suffice it to say that Canada's debate on these issues is only beginning.

While academics and the mainstream media have sharply criticized Moe, Smith, and Poilievre for their politically incorrect positions, recent studies suggest that mainstream Canadians are actually supportive of parents' rights policies.[67] On issues such as age limits on gender-reassignment surgery, pronoun use, and restricting women's sports competition to biological women only, Canadians support the "anti-woke" positions by about a 2 to 1 margin. One takeaway from this data is that "there is significant space for right-of-centre parties to increase the prominence of culture wars issues, and an associated electoral risk that left-of-centre parties must manage."[68] The Cass Report will strengthen the position of the parents' rights advocates in Canada.

I, for one, hope this is how things unfold in the coming years. The DEI egalitarians preach toleration, but they are the most intolerant voices in our society. They preach diversity, but then invoke government coercion to enforce a one-size-fits-all uniformity. Freedom of speech, freedom of religion, equality of opportunity, the rights of parents to choose their children's education—all can and are being sacrificed to achieve the new progressives' Quota and Androgyny projects.

Protecting these historical rights—all of which are constitutional pillars of Canada's free and democratic society—is what Bill 208 was intended to do.

The Family as the Moral Foundation of Freedom: The Forgotten Dimension of Liberalism

Paper presented at World Congress of Families II, Geneva, Switzerland; November 14-17, 1999

INTRODUCTION

We gather today at a unique moment in human history. We are standing on an ever-shortening bridge from the second to the third millennium. Surely this is a time to take stock of what has gone before and what lies ahead.

In Europe and North America, we can look back at the century that we are leaving and take just satisfaction in having triumphed over the enemies of justice and freedom, first fascism and then communism. When we look beyond the Western world, we see a growing acceptance of Western institutions—not just our technology and market economy, but also our political institutions and principles of human freedom and equality. Turning our gaze to the future, the twenty-first century seems to hold forth a unique opportunity—the chance to harness the productivity of free markets with the freedom of representative democracy and the rule of law. Could it be that the utopias that seemed within man's reach at the end of the last century will in fact be realized in the next?

For those who consider themselves the friends of liberal democracy—and I am one—this moment should be one of unprecedented optimism. And yet it is not. What happened?

Ironically, as the threats of fascism and communism recede into past, they have been replaced by an uneasy sense of an enemy within. A domestic decay seems to be undermining those very things that we cherish most—our relationships with one another: be it husband and wife; parent and child; grandparents and grandchildren; friends, neighbors and what we used to call "our fellow citizens." In the immortal words of Pogo, "We have met the enemy, and it is us."

This has been called the American paradox—not because it is unique to the US, but because it is there that the contrasts of the paradox are most vivid: the wealthiest nation in the history of mankind cannot stem the growth of poverty and crime in its own cities. The most advanced medical care system in history is not available to one-quarter of Americans. The nation that can send a man to the moon must live in gated communities at home. Old people strive to stay younger longer, and young people to get older faster.

The "American paradox" appears most clearly—and most terrifyingly—in the growing list of schoolyard shootings. The horror of these tragedies is that it is children—our own children—who shoot and are shot. Their crumpled little bodies are like mirrors—reflecting back on us the culture from which they came; and we see ourselves, dimly but disturbingly, as somehow complicit in this slaughter of the innocents. How could this have happened? What is going wrong?

In the wake of the most recent of these tragedies—the shootings this past April at Columbine High School in Colorado—Peggy Noonan captured this sense of social unraveling: "The kids who did this are responsible," she said. "They did it. They killed. But," she added, "they came from a place and a time, and were yielded forth by a culture."[1] What kind of culture was that? According to Noonan,

> What walked into Columbine High School Tuesday was the culture of death... The boys who did the killing ... inhaled too deep the ocean in which they swam ... Think of it this way. Your child is an intelligent little fish. He swims in deep water. Waves of sound and sight, of thought and fact, come invisibly through that water, like radar; they go through him again and again, from this direction and that. The sound from the television is a wave, and the sound from the radio; the headlines [and pictures] on the newsstands, on the magazines, on the ad on the bus as it whizzes by—all are waves. The fish—your child—is bombarded and barely knows it. ... This is the ocean in which our children

swim. This is the sound of our culture. It comes from all parts of our culture and reaches all parts of our culture.

Of course, much of the finger-pointing that went on was pointed at Hollywood, and rightfully so. Sex and violence are nothing new. But their commercialization in the mass media is. And here, Noonan noted something new after Columbine. This time, Hollywood didn't defend themselves with its usual excuse: "'If you don't like it, change the channel.' They now realize something they didn't realize ten years ago: there is no channel to change to. You could sooner remove an ocean than find such a channel."[2]

PUBLIC MORALITY: LIBERALISM'S FORGOTTEN DIMENSION

How has our liberal culture of freedom degenerated into a culture of death? There are, of course, multiple causes: secularization, commercialization, urbanization, technology, the rise of rights and the decline of duties, and of course the weakening of the family. But behind these more immediate causes is a proximate cause: we—not just the Americans but all of us—have forgotten the moral foundations of freedom.

Liberalism's emphasis on individual liberty and equality have obscured the role and importance of the family in sustaining free societies. Liberal democracy is usually understood as only a political or an economic project; a collection of equal, rights-bearing individual citizens; or a collection of individuals rationally pursuing their economic self-interest in free markets. As Joseph Schumpeter said "Capitalism saps the private virtues that transcend self-interest, and motivate citizens to defend free institutions."[3]

This view of liberal democracy as simply a political or an economic project is incomplete. Liberal democracy is also a social project. Just as democracy presupposes a certain political and economic infrastructure, so it requires a certain moral infrastructure. Most of the intellectual founders of modern liberalism recognized the need for "citizens with republican character" and the role of the natural family in producing public morality.

According to Rousseau, it is the experience of family that attaches children first to their relatives and then to their fellow citizens. Conventional bonds, he states, can only be built on natural bonds. He describes the family as "la petite patrie," and challenges his readers if it is not "the good son, the good husband and the good father who makes the good citizen."[4]

American Founding Father James Madison, while a realist about the low side of human nature, also recognized that man is capable of living a life based on rationally conceived principles of justice: "Republican government presupposes the existence of these qualities in a higher degree than any other form."[5]

Alexis de Tocqueville, perhaps the pre-eminent analyst of the dangers as well as the opportunities of modern democracy, was adamant in his defence of the democratic family.[6] "No free communities existed without morals," Tocqueville wrote, and families are the wellsprings of moral sentiment.[7]

In sum, two hundred years ago, at the beginning of this radical experiment called liberal democracy, there was a consensus that a free society presupposes free citizens, and that the family played an important role in producing "republican character." The founders' understanding of liberal democracy as a three-dimensional project—combining a moral as well as a political and economic infrastructure—has been neglected for most of the twentieth century. The moral dimension of their thought was eclipsed by their more stirring appeals to individual liberty and equality. This forgetting of the moral foundations of freedom is the deeper source of our present problems.

CIVIL SOCIETY AND SOCIAL CAPITAL

Recently, however, the moral dimension of liberal democracy—and the family's crucial role in it—has been rediscovered by social scientists. This new body of social science recognizes the importance of the natural family to a properly functioning democracy. The key concepts in this new field of research are "civil society" and "social capital."

Civil society is the network of voluntary associations that fill the gap between individual citizens and the state. These associations are voluntary, and have a wide variety of purposes—social, economic, religious, recreational, political, and educational. Civil society produces the social connectedness and trust that allows individuals to co-operate for mutual benefit and happiness.

Civil society is important because it produces "social capital." Social capital is a new expression for an old concept—civic virtue or public morality. At a minimum, it means not doing harm: obeying the laws and respecting the rights of others. More expansively, it denotes doing good by helping others; an altruism born of the knowledge that one's own happiness is connected to the well-being of those around us. Social capital focuses attention on the institutions that generate "the habits of the heart"; that transform the "me" into the "we." The most important source of social capital is the family.

Harvard political scientist Robert Putnam is the leading exponent of this new school. Putnam's research claims that societies in which civil society is strong enjoy better schools, faster economic development, lower crime, and more effective government.[8] Putnam goes on to argue that American democracy is threatened by the weakening of civil society and declining social capital.

Putnam's work is complemented by the work of sociologists such as Sara McLanahan of Princeton University, David Popenoe of Rutgers University, and Patrick Fagan of the Heritage Foundation. Their research measures the effects of family breakdown on children. McLanahan's research shows that children who grow up with only one biological parent are worse off, on average, than children who are raised in a household with both of their biological parents.[9] Popenoe's studies reach similar conclusions.[10]

McLanahan's studies found that children from single-parent families are twice as likely to drop out of school; twice as likely to have a child before the age of twenty; and twice as likely to be unemployed in their late teens and early twenties. This trend holds regardless of family income, educational background, race, or whether the resident parent remarries. There are also higher correlations with drug and alcohol abuse, sexually transmitted diseases, and criminal behaviour.

What children from single-parent families lose, according to McLanahan, are parental guidance and attention, as well as equal access to community resources. She describes this as a deficit of social capital—"an asset that is created and maintained by relationships of commitment and trust." Social capital, McLanahan concludes, can be just as important as financial capital in promoting children's future success. While Putnam and McLanahan are Americans, the importance of preserving social capital—and the natural two-parent family—is beginning to find its way into public policy debates elsewhere.[11]

These new truths—and really, they are old truths—are good news. After years of producing research that contributed to the weakening of civil society, social scientists are finally recognizing the social and economic value of the traditional family and the moral infrastructure that it helps to sustain.

THE NEW EGALITARIANS

If the rediscovery of the social value of the family is good news, there is bad news on another front. There is another stream of modernity—represented primarily by the gender feminists and gay rights movement—that targets the natural family as public enemy number one. According to the feminist-gay gospel, the great evils of this world are sexism and homophobia, and their breeding ground is the traditional family. Hence, the gay-feminist project has become a social engineering project—to use the coercive power of the state to undermine the existing family and to reconstruct in its place their gender-equal utopias.

These New Egalitarians, as I call them, travel under the banner of human rights. But what exactly do they mean by human rights? Those standards of moral right and wrong that transcend dominant opinion in any one nation? Those minimum conditions of civilized conduct that are recognized by all religions and all codes of ethics? Natural rights—those first principles of individual freedom that limit both what governments can do and how?

No. This new version of human rights has been reduced to a single, monotheistic principle: equality. Moreover, this new equality means not so much economic levelling as moral levelling; not the old Left's socialist program of state-coerced redistribution of wealth, but the new Left's embrace of moral relativism. The embrace of moral relativism is evident in most of the new "human rights" issues: abortion, homosexuality, pornography, euthanasia, legalizing recreational use of drugs.

On all of these issues, we are now told that "freedom of choice" is a basic human right. Competing concerns about the effect of that choice on family members and neighbours—not to mention the character and happiness of the chooser—are dismissed as secondary. The important thing, we are told, is not *what* I choose, but that I be completely free to choose it. It is the *act* of choosing, not the contents of that choice, that matters. The freedom of choice principle is tarted-up as an issue of "individual human dignity," regardless of how undignified or socially destructive the actual choice may be.

The new role of moral relativism in the redefinition of human rights is obvious in such issues as abortion and gay rights. But it is also curiously evident in the death penalty debate. Many of the opponents of capital punishment denounce it as a violation of human rights. Yet these same people, with few exceptions, have no problem with other contemporary forms of taking of human life—such as abortion or doctor-assisted suicide.

Their opposition to capital punishment is not based on the sanctity of human life, a traditional human rights position. Rather, as David Frum recently pointed out, "what offends them is not that the death penalty kills, but that it judges. They object not to a specific punishment, but to the very ideal of justice."[12]

Here is the great paradox in this "new improved" version of human rights. Whereas human rights once stood for something objective and eternal, now it stands for the subjective and the temporal. Whereas once human rights pointed toward what is right always and everywhere, regardless of government policy or public opinion, now it means "what I want, here and now."

I can assure you that no other civilization in the history of mankind—East or West, North or South—has ever had such a low and vulgar definition of the good.

The New Egalitarians further debase the value of the human rights standard by stretching it to cover their most recent cause-du-jour. Despite "great progress," we are routinely told, human rights are still under attack around the globe: Kosovo, Tiananmen Square, Rwanda, East Timor—and yes, in Ohio and Alberta! Suddenly genocide and ethnic cleansing are on a par with supporting private religious schools; torture and political prisoners are equated with opposing pay equity; the Holocaust is lumped together with opposition to state-endorsement of homosexual rights. Indeed, there is hardly an issue on the feminist or gay-rights agenda that is NOT presented as a "human rights issue."

Such rhetorical overkill has become the stock in trade of the so-called Human Rights movement. Its bombastic and self-serving moral imperatives are destroying the very meaning of human rights. Moralistic inflation has the same effect as monetary inflation—it devalues the currency.

A final distinguishing characteristic of the New Egalitarians is their love affair with non-representative, non-accountable institutions: courts, rights bureaucracies, and recently the United Nations. Their recourse to the coercive authority of non-accountable institutions is not by accident. The principal obstacles to the achievement of this brave new world are the present middle-class occupants of the old world—people like us. Since we refuse to be reconstructed voluntarily, they must rely on institutions whose authority is not based on consent and whose exercise of power is not accountable. Just as

Lenin had to create the Communist Party as the "Vanguard of the Proletariat" to construct Marx's workers' paradise, so the courts (and other non-accountable institutions) have become the "Vanguard of the Intelligentsia" in the construction of the new egalitarian utopias.[13]

THE FABRIC OF FREEDOM: RESPONSIBILITY

The New Egalitarians like to present themselves as the party of freedom and accuse the defenders of family and traditional moral principles as authoritarian. This of course is absurd. The constant recourse to non-democratic institutions—courts and other non-accountable bureaucracies—discloses their true authoritarian bend.

But there is a subtler and more dangerous dimension to the moral levelling of the Egalitarians. Their mantra—"Freedom is the right to choose"—regardless of the content of that choice—certainly appears to make them the defenders of the private sphere of human freedom. This private-public distinction easily gives rise to confusion, and we can turn to Alexis de Tocqueville to sort out the truth of the matter.

Modern liberalism clearly expanded the scope of "the private"—individual liberty—by reducing the scope of "the public"—those aspects of individual activity subject to state regulation. Tocqueville, a self-confessed political liberal, approved this change as enhancing the exercise of human freedom. On the other hand, he also saw an implicit threat to liberty in the nascent social atomism that accompanies this change. Tocqueville captured the threat posed by the "privatization" of the regime in the novel phenomenon of "individualism."

An unchecked individualism creates social atomism, a condition that actually favours the expansion of the powers of the state by increasing demands on it. The democratic despotism feared by Tocqueville would occur as civil society withered, leaving behind a mass of increasingly disassociated and self-seeking individuals on one side, and an increasingly powerful state on the other. Because such individuals no longer are inclined to take care of one another, the state's "welfare function" expands accordingly. As individuals exercise less and less self-restraint in their actions toward their "neighbors," the state's police function continues to expand in order to protect personal and property rights.

Tocqueville feared that over time this trend threatened to destroy political liberty. To arrest this trend, Tocqueville recommended that matrix of institutions and traditions that fostered the self-dependence of families and local communities, and the ethical *self*-restraint of individuals. The family is one of these institutions. It is private in that it arises out of a voluntary association, is not part of the state, and is not (generally) subject to state regulation. However, its social consequences give it a political and thus a public significance.

If allowed to succeed, the New Egalitarians will lead us down the path to the soft despotism that Tocqueville both predicted and sought to deter. We will become like sheep rather than citizens. As the true friends of human liberty, we must oppose these crude forms of egalitarianism and libertarianism that emphasize rights while ignoring responsibilities. The weaker the bonds of civil society, the stronger those of the state. These trends must be reversed. Free societies require citizens who meet their responsibilities as well as exercise their rights.

PRO-FAMILY POLICIES

To avoid the soft despotism of New Egalitarians, we must make enlightened family policy a cornerstone of the democratic state. We must incorporate the new truths of civil society and social capital into public policy.

We can do this in two ways. The first is to persuade our governments to require a "family impact" statement for every new policy or law that is being considered. Before legislation is voted on, there should be an investigation and written report that assesses its impact—positive, negative, or neutral—on the following aspects of family life:[14]

- Family income
- Family stability
- Family safety
- Parental rights and responsibilities—especially the right to educate their children in the moral and spiritual traditions of their choice.

Our governments already do this for the natural environment by requiring Environmental Impact Statements (EIS). Why not for the human environment?

At the Second World Congress in Geneva, Mr. Kevin Andrews, the Member of Parliament from Australia, went further still, recommending that governments adopt an explicit family policy.[15] I would second this proposal. It would facilitate opening up the family dimension of economic policies, such as the threat posed to income security programs by our aging population. A more comprehensive approach would create opportunities to educate politicians and the public on the research that shows the positive economic impact of intact families[16] and the negative family impact of big government and over-taxation.[17]

Secondly, we can identify a number of specific areas where pro-family, life-affirming, freedom-enhancing policies should be adopted and/or defended. These policies are based on the proven social advantages of two-parent families and need for a social environment that encourages and strengthens such families.

Personal income tax policies must be revised to support the traditional family rather than put it at a competitive disadvantage. Combined family income—not individuals' income—should be the basis for calculating tax rates. This could be easily achieved by allowing income splitting between parents.

Parental child care must be put on an equal tax footing with commercial or public daycare. So-called "public daycare" should be discouraged. Instead, tax-credits for child care should be equally available to all parents—both those who look after their own children and those who choose child care service *of their choice.*

The family-choice principle should be extended to primary and secondary education. This can be achieved easily and efficiently by expanding the school voucher programs. The state maintains responsibility for the universal availability of primary and secondary education, but parents are given the power to choose the kind of school they want. We know that state monopolies provide inferior service in every other field of human endeavour. Why do we continue to support it in education? This is especially true when we know that the New Egalitarians have targeted the public education system as a primary instrument for their social engineering.

On the subject of education, we must bring back education in moral character that includes more than just toleration. Toleration is an important virtue, but hardly the only one. Under the cult of "non-judgmentalism," we have allowed toleration to crowd out all the other virtues that we value in fellow human beings: honesty, courage, generosity, industriousness, fidelity, modesty, compassion, chastity, moderation. We must help our children to recognize what we all know as adults: that there are otherwise noble individuals who are intolerant; and also very tolerant individuals who are otherwise moral scoundrels and a source of sorrow for all who depend on them.

We must support politicians and political parties that will restrict the explosion of hardcore pornography that has flooded into our societies—especially child pornography. The pornography industry is central to the culture of death. It degrades and harms the people who are used to make these films, and corrupts those who consume it. It teaches us to use others as a means to our own end—pleasure. Since much of this material falls into the hands of impressionable minors, it leads them to confuse sex with love and coarsens relations between the sexes. All of these effects undermine marriage and the family.

On the abortion issue, we must try to win back the ground we have lost in recent decades in the battle for public opinion. In North America, at least, it seems to me that this will best be done by accepting "the right to choose" status quo and refocusing on increasing the probability that young women make the right choice—life. This can be done directly by supporting "informed choice" legislation and mounting the kind of paid media advertising that addresses the issue of choice in a direct and personal manner. Here I have in mind the powerful, thirty-second television spots developed by pro-life groups in Michigan that have helped reduce the rate of abortions among teenagers in that state.

There are also indirect policy options. We should take advantage of the new emphasis in public health on fetal alcohol syndrome. Similarly, the growing acceptance of "open adoption"—which emphasizes the mother's ongoing responsibility for her child—should be well publicized among teenage women. These non-coercive steps would help raise public awareness about life-before-birth and help to nudge public opinion in a pro-life direction.

Last but not least, marriage laws should be strengthened: both by making it more difficult to become married and more difficult to dissolve a marriage. The covenant marriage option adopted recently in some American states appears to be a promising option since it naturally appeals to the optimism of young, engaged couples. Many churches have strengthened their marriage preparation courses. This development should be encouraged and extended to non–church based courses.

On the subject of marriage, I would conclude by stressing the importance of resisting the growing pressure to accept so-called homosexual or gay marriage. Homosexuals have—or should have—the same rights to individual freedom and personal privacy that the rest of us enjoy. But they should not have more. Enlisting the coercive power of the state to force people to "approve" homosexual relations is the antithesis of toleration. Toleration loses any meaning if we are not allowed to continue to disapprove of what we tolerate!

As for gay marriage, it will simply further weaken the institution of marriage and fuel the growing number of fatherless children. As David Frum recently observed, most governments will try to minimize the political costs of legislating gay marriage by framing it in euphemistic terms and extending it to cover a variety of co-habitating adults, including heterosexuals.[18] The French are calling it a "Civil Solidarity Pact." In North America, "registered domestic partnership" is perhaps the most well-known of these euphemisms. These alternatives extend most of the benefits of marriage with many fewer of its responsibilities. These new legal arrangements must be equally available to heterosexual couples, and, because they are convenient, will be used by heterosexual couples.

From this perspective, the argument over gay marriage becomes less about gays and more about marriage. The functional equivalents of gay marriage, Frum argues, will not extend marriage but rather abolish it, and put "a new, flimsier institution in its place." Since the average heterosexual co-habitational relationship lasts less than five years, the real losers will be the increasing number of fatherless children. As Frum puts it, "The gay marriage argument … pits the wishes of adults against the needs of children, the urgings of the self against the obligations of the family."

I would take this analysis one step further. It is not just the "obligations of the family" that are at stake, but the future of our societies. We should recall the adage that civilization may be thousands of years old, but it is only a generation deep. Or, as Thomas Sowell more pointedly observed, "each new generation born [is] in effect an invasion of civilization by little barbarians who must be civilized before it is too late."[19]

This process of "civilizing" can only be done efficiently through intact families. As the late Christopher Lasch observed,

> If reproducing culture were simply a matter of formal instruction and discipline, it could be left to the schools. But it also

requires that culture be imbedded in personality. Socialization makes the individual want to do what he has to do; and the family is the agency to which society entrusts this complex and delicate task.[20]

Where but in the family will one first learn to be his brother's keeper?

CONCLUSION

In 1965, more than thirty years ago, American Senator Daniel Patrick Moynihan argued that the lack of any family perspective explained the failure of many of the anti-poverty programs targeted at Black poverty. Calling for a family policy for America, Moynihan wrote:

> From the wild Irish slums of the Nineteenth century Eastern seaboard, to the riot-torn suburbs of Los Angeles, there is one unmistakable lesson in American history: a community that allows a large number of young men to grow up in broken families, dominated by women, never acquiring any set of rational expectations about the future—that community asks for and gets chaos. Crime, violence, unrest and disorder—most particularly the furious unrestrained lashing out at the whole social structure—that is not only to be expected; it is very near to inevitable. And it is richly deserved.[21]

Moynihan was largely ignored. Today, the level of illegitimacy for all of American society is 33 percent—higher than what existed in the Black community Moynihan was describing in the 1960s. But being ignored and being wrong are two different things. Indeed, Moynihan's message has been proven true time and time again, most recently and most tragically at Columbine High School.

At the opening of the second World Congress of Families, Bishop Njue of Kenya declared, "Without families, you cannot have government." I would qualify this only slightly: "Without families, you cannot have free government."

If democracy is the last best hope for mankind, then surely a more informed family policy is the last best hope for democracy.

POSTSCRIPT

I wrote this in 1999, twenty-five years ago. Recent scholarship confirms the many social, political, and economic benefits that I attributed to strong, intact two-parent families. Scholars warn about the "decline in social capital … the rich networks of relationships that exist not just in families but also in neighborhoods, religious institutions and other civic institutions, and the society-wide trust they generate."[22] University of Virginia sociologist Brad Wilcox's statistical analysis finds that married adults are happier, healthier, more satisfied in life, live longer, and are more financially secure.[23] University of Maryland professor Melissa Kearney's new book reports the economic and social advantages enjoyed by children who are raised by two parents.[24] In a recent article, Wilcox and co-writer Chris Bullivant assert that "the success of these books suggests the pendulum is swinging back from extremist ideologies that have discounted the value of marriage and stable families in American life."[25]

Recent Canadian scholarship confirms that these same trends are happening here.[26] Tim Sargent's statistical study confirms that not only do "children in two-parent families have a much higher standard of living than children in one-parent families," but also that "children raised by their original parents have, on average, better life outcomes than children raised in one-parent families or in stepfamilies."[27] Policy-wise, Sargent draws the same conclusions as I do: "Given the clear individual and social benefits of marriage and children, there is a case for making sure that public policy does not impede—and preferably promotes—family formation and fertility.[28]

After 40 years, the Charter is still one of the worst bargains in Canadian history

Rather than the people's party, today's progressives now see the people as the problem
Ted Morton, Special to the *National Post*, April 14, 2022.
https://nationalpost.com/opinion/ted-morton-after-40-years-the-charter-is-still-one-of-the-worst-bargains-in-canadian-history.

The 40th anniversary of the Charter of Rights is an appropriate time to assess how it has changed the way Canada is governed. Have there been winners and losers? And if so, why?

The biggest losers have been provincial governments, and those of us (both in Quebec and in the West) who would prefer to be governed by legislators who live in our neighbourhoods, who share our concerns, and are elected and accountable to us, rather than by distant, unaccountable judges in Ottawa.

This risk was evident at the outset. The highest priority of Pierre Trudeau, the architect of the Charter, was to blunt the Parti Québécois French-only education and language laws, which were creating an exodus of anglophone voters (and Liberal Party supporters) out of Quebec. The more Anglos that left, the stronger the separatists became. Trudeau understood this. So did PQ Premier René Lévesque. Which is why Quebec refused to sign the Constitution Act in 1982. And still refuses to this day.

Western premiers had similar fears of a strongly centralist bias in Charter interpretation. For a decade they had watched Trudeau's hand-picked Chief Justice, Bora Laskin, strike down provincial laws for reasons of federalism. They justifiably feared a similar bias in Charter interpretation. They would never have agreed to the Charter without the now infamous Section 33 notwithstanding clause. The notwithstanding clause allows a province to insulate a law from judicial veto if it deems the judges have made an incorrect interpretation of the Charter and/or are mandating an unacceptable policy.

Why the "infamous" Section 33? The same groups that have benefited from the Court's Charter activism and their allies in the universities and national media have worked tirelessly and successfully to stigmatize the use of the notwithstanding clause. Other than Quebec, provincial governments have been reluctant to use the notwithstanding power for fear of media attacks and political backlash. The net result is that there are now broad areas of provincial jurisdiction where public policy is essentially set by the Supreme Court and its interest group supporters—a coalition that I have dubbed the "Court Party." Like its 18th century predecessor, today's Court Party prefers and benefits from a political system in which certain key decisions are made by government officials unaccountable to the rest of us who have to live with consequences of those decisions.

From a provincial point of view, the Charter of Rights and Freedoms was one of the worst bargains ever struck in the history of Canadian federalism. In practice it is little more than the old, discredited power of disallowance in disguise: a federal veto over provincial policy exercised by the Supreme Court rather than by the cabinet. Pierre Trudeau must be smiling from his grave.

Federalism is itself a form of protecting minority rights. Each province is a minority. Quebec first and foremost, because of its unique linguistic and ethnic heritage, but the other provinces as well. But this version of Canadian federalism is being sacrificed on the altar of a new version of minority rights.

Which takes us to the winners' circle. Any policy touching on bilingual education, Aboriginal issues, abortion, LGBT or feminist issues, or prisoner voting rights—if a provincial government does not accede to the interest group's demands, that government can expect to be hauled into court and usually lose.

This is all quite predictable. The Federal cabinet chooses who sits on the Supreme Court, and the Charter doesn't speak for itself. At the end of the day, the Charter means what the judges say it means. What about the costs of going to court? No need to worry if you're on the right ... er, left ... side. The federal Court Challenges Program funds the litigation costs of interest groups that the Liberals support, and who in turn support the Liberals. It's a tidy and efficient little circle. (The Harper government terminated this program, but it was quickly resurrected by the Justin Trudeau's government.)

But why has Canada gone so far, so fast, down this rabbit hole of jurocracy? What happened to "responsible government," parliamentary supremacy and federalism—all traditions that still defined and shaped Canadian politics as recently as the 1970s?

The Charter revolution has been energized by deeper, socio-economic changes that have transformed the politics not just of Canada but the other English-speaking democracies as well. For several decades the middle class has been shrinking. It is dividing between a white collar, upper middle class and a blue collar, lower middle class. The former are more educated, more affluent, more urban, more public sector and more progressive in their values. The latter typically do not have university degrees, are less affluent, work in the private sector, more rural/small town and have more traditional moral and political values. But demographically, they are still a majority.

These growing socio-economic differences are redefining the left-right cleavages in our politics. For those who now call themselves progressives, the principal political goal is no longer about economic redistribution from the few to the many, but rather protecting the few from the many. Rather than the people's party, today's progressives now see the people as the problem.

This movement is what we now know as "identity politics" and its crusade for "social justice." In the new progressive lexicon, equity has replaced equality. Equality was about equal opportunity, equal starting lines. Equity is about equal results. If minorities—women, LGBT people, Black people, people of colour, Indigenous—are not proportionally represented in classrooms, board rooms, committees, etc., the explanation is racism, sexism and all the other new forms of bigotry attributed to those of us who disagree with them.

And what about freedom of speech, freedom of religion, parents' rights, due process of law and property rights? When these impede the new equity/social justice agenda, they can and are being violated. Rather than protecting us from government overreach, the Charter is being interpreted to justify it. These are all now just "reasonable limits." Just ask those arrested and prosecuted during the truckers' freedom convoy. Like federalism, traditional fundamental rights and freedoms are being sacrificed to the new social justice agenda.

This explains progressives' attraction to the Charter and the courts. If the source of these inequities is the unreconstructed majority, progressives can no longer rely on general elections, or their old populist favourites—referendums and recall elections. Instead, they must turn to institutions that are not accountable to Canadian voters, such as courts, human rights bureaucracies, and now even the United Nations. Since these judges and bureaucrats are more educated, more affluent, more urban—they too tend to be more progressive. A perfect match.

The Charter—a parchment document—has not caused the Charter revolution. Nor have nine judges sitting in a marble temple on the south bank of the Ottawa River. At least not by themselves. Changes of this magnitude required powerful support from influential people and groups—well educated, affluent, connected elites—to design, encourage and then support the transformation of Canadian politics that has taken place since 1982.

Is it a done deal? Is there any coming back to a more accountable, less jurocratic, more federal form of democratic government in Canada? I don't know. But there seems to be the beginnings of a counter-movement. *Globe and Mail* columnist Jeffrey Simpson described the surprise election victory of Doug Ford's Conservatives in the 2018 Ontario election as a "populist ... reaction—or a revolt—against 'identity politics,' for whom the elites' messages of 'inclusiveness' seems to include everybody but them." Ford's supporters were less educated, more rural and small town, more blue collar, more likely to work in the private sector and more likely to describe themselves as "poor."

Was the 2018 Ford election a one-off event, not to be repeated? What about the ground-swell of support for the Truckers' Freedom Convoy this past February? The issues were different but the kinds of people who came out to support the truckers were the same. And what about the recent resurrection of the "infamous" notwithstanding power? It has recently been used not just by the Ford government in Ontario but also by Premier Moe in Saskatchewan.

Is the counter-revolution beginning?

POSTSCRIPT (2024)

The notwithstanding clause has enjoyed a renaissance in recent years.[1] Since 2017, New Brunswick (once), Ontario (three times), Quebec (twice), and Saskatchewan (twice) have introduced legislation invoking the NWC power to protect specific policies/statutes from Charter vetoes by local courts. In each instance, the provincial policies being protected were viewed positively by conservatives and negatively by liberal progressives. While the media commentary on the increased provincial use of the NWC continues to be predominantly negative,[2] the NWC has had more positive coverage than in the past.[3] So, has the counter-revolution begun?

F.L. (Ted) Morton Bibliography

Books

Strong and Free: My Journey in Alberta Politics. University of Calgary Press, 2024.

Law, Politics and the Judicial Process in Canada. Fifth edition. Co-edited with Dave Snow. University of Calgary Press, 2024. First edition, 1984.

Moment of Truth: How to Think About Alberta's Future. Co-edited with Jack Mintz and Tom Flanagan. Sutherland House, 2020.

The Charter Revolution and the Court Party. With Rainer Knopff. Broadview Press, 2000.

Morgentaler v. Borowski: Abortion, The Charter and The Courts. McClelland & Stewart, 1992.

Charter Politics. With Rainer Knopff. Carleton University Press, 1992.

Federalism and the Charter: Leading Constitutional Decisions. With Peter Russell and Rainer Knopff. Carleton University Press, 1989.

Constitutional Reform and a Fair Deal for Alberta

Moment of Truth: How to Think About Alberta's Future. Co-edited with Jack Mintz and Tom Flanagan. Sutherland House, 2020.

"Sovereignty Act shows Ottawa that Alberta will continue to fight for its rights." *Calgary Herald*, December 2, 2022. https://calgaryherald.com/opinion/columnists/morton-sovereignty-act-shows-ottawa-that-alberta-will-continue-to-fight-for-its-rights.

"Alberta premiers have a history of challenging the status quo." *Calgary Herald*, October 15, 2022. https://calgaryherald.com/opinion/columnists/ted-morton-alberta-premiers-have-history-of-challenging-status-quo-to-ensure-control-of-our-resources.

"Ottawa would ignore at its peril Alberta's clear desire for equalization reform." *Calgary Herald*, October 30, 2021. https://calgaryherald.com/opinion/columnists/morton-ottawa-would-ignore-at-its-peril-albertas-clear-desire-for-equalization-reform.

"Vote Yes to abolishing the federal equalization program on October 18." *Calgary Herald*, October 13, 2021. https://calgaryherald.com/opinion/columnists/opinion-vote-yes-to-abolishing-the-federal-equalization-program-on-oct-18.

"Alberta's equalization referendum will start dialogue on Canada's future." *Calgary Herald*, February 27, 2021. https://calgaryherald.com/opinion/columnists/morton-albertas-equalization-referendum-will-start-dialogue-on-canadas-future.

"What the Supreme Court's carbon tax ruling means and what to do about it." *C2C Journal*, April 30, 2021. https://c2cjournal.ca/2021/04/what-the-supreme-courts-carbon-tax-ruling-means-and-what-to-do-about-it/.

"Alberta at the Cross-roads: the Status Quo Must Go." Canadian Club of Calgary, October 18, 2020. https://www.youtube.com/watch?v=TvpUS5d-33w.

"The great divide between Edmonton and Ottawa." *National Post*, September 23, 2020. https://nationalpost.com/opinion/ted-morton-the-great-divide-between-edmonton-and-ottawa.

"Securing Alberta's future." With Jack Mintz and Tom Flanagan. *National Post*, September 20, 2020. https://nationalpost.com/opinion/opinion-securing-albertas-future.

"Canada's Constitution is out of step with economic reality." *National Post*, September 20, 2020. https://nationalpost.com/opinion/ted-morton-canadas-constitution-is-out-of-step-with-economic-reality.

"The Prime Minister's dangerous game." *National Post*, February 21, 2020. https://nationalpost.com/opinion/ted-morton-the-prime-ministers-dangerous-game.

"We shouldn't be fighting with ourselves over Alberta's deficit but with Ottawa." *Calgary Herald*, November 26, 2020. https://calgaryherald.com/opinion/columnists/morton-we-shouldnt-be-fighting-with-ourselves-over-albertas-deficit-but-with-ottawa.

"Alberta has been targeted for its tax dollars by design." *Calgary Herald*, August 8, 2020. https://calgaryherald.com/opinion/columnists/morton-alberta-has-been-targeted-for-its-tax-dollars-by-design.

"More than ever, Canada needs a national infrastructure corridor." *Calgary Herald*, June 27, 2020. https://calgaryherald.com/opinion/columnists/morton-more-than-ever-canada-needs-a-national-infrastructure-corridor.

"It's sales tax time for Alberta without costing a penny more." *Calgary Herald*, April 25, 2020. https://calgaryherald.com/opinion/columnists/morton-its-sales-tax-time-for-alberta-without-costing-a-penny-more.

"The Status Quo Must Go." Economic Education Association of Alberta, July 23, 2019. https://www.youtube.com/watch?v=c1-98qbohCI.

"Screwing the West to Pay the Rest: Referendum Time?" *C2C*, April 3, 2018. https://c2cjournal.ca/2018/04/screwing-the-west-to-pay-the-rest/.

"Liberal Party Wins, Canada Loses." In David Schneiderman, ed., *The Quebec Decision: Perspectives on the Supreme Court Ruling on Secession*. Lorimer, 1999. 120–23.

"Empowering Quebec: The Unity Strategy that Wasn't." *Gravitas* (Summer, 1996). 8–11.

"The Effect of the Charter of Rights on Canadian Federalism." *Publius* 25, no. 3 (Summer 1995). 173–88. https://www.jstor.org/stable/3330693.

"Judicial Politics Canadian-Style: The Supreme Court's Contribution to the Constitutional Crisis of 1992." In Curtis Cooke, ed., *Constitutional Predicament: Canada After the Referendum of 1992*. McGill-Queen's University Press, 1994. 132–48.

"The Charter Revolution and the Court Party." *Osgoode Hall Law Journal* 30, no. 3 (1992). 627–52. https://digitalcommons.osgoode.yorku.ca/cgi/viewcontent.cgi?article=1718&context=ohlj.

"How Not to Amend the Constitution." *Canadian Parliamentary Review* 12, no. 4 (Winter, 1989–90). 9–10. http://www.revparl.ca/english/issue.asp?param=131&art=831.

Energy and Pipeline Politics

"Someone tell Trudeau: energy is now about security." *Financial Post*, January 19, 2023. https://financialpost.com/opinion/trudeau-energy-security.

"Stars are aligning for a better deal for Alberta and all provinces." *Calgary Herald*, July 16, 2022. https://calgaryherald.com/opinion/columnists/morton-stars-are-aligning-for-a-better-deal-for-alberta-and-all-provinces.

"Excess profits tax would kill investment, alienate the West." *National Post*, June 8, 2022. https://nationalpost.com/opinion/ted-morton-excess-profits-tax-would-kill-investment-alienate-the-west.

"Line 5 fiasco shows Trudeau is a failure on energy policy." *National Post*, May 18, 2021. https://nationalpost.com/opinion/ted-morton-line-5-fiasco-shows-trudeau-is-a-failure-on-energy-policy.

"Canada may win the Line 5 battle, but we're still losing the war." *National Post*, May 13, 2021. https://nationalpost.com/opinion/ted-morton-canada-may-win-the-line-5-battle-but-were-still-losing-the-war.

"What the Supreme Court's Carbon Tax Ruling Means and What to do About it." *C2C Journal*, April 30, 2021. https://c2cjournal.ca/2021/04/what-the-supreme-courts-carbon-tax-ruling-means-and-what-to-do-about-it/.

"Alberta's pipeline problem is not from want of sharing." *Financial Post*, February 2, 2021. https://financialpost.com/opinion/ted-morton-albertas-pipeline-problem-is-not-from-want-of-sharing.

"Trudeau's nightmare comes true as he's forced to choose between climate activists and national unity." *Financial Post*, February 20, 2020. https://financialpost.com/opinion/ted-morton-trudeaus-nightmare-comes-true-as-hes-forced-to-choose-between-climate-activists-and-national-unity.

"Another Canadian oil company flees Trudeau and Notley for the US." *Financial Post*, November 6, 2018. https://financialpost.com/opinion/ted-morton-another-canadian-oil-company-flees-trudeau-and-notley-for-the-u-s.

"The Trudeau Liberals are campaigning on strangling our oil industry." *Financial Post*, March 6, 2018. https://financialpost.com/opinion/ted-morton-the-trudeau-liberals-are-campaigning-on-strangling-our-oil-industry.

"Keystone to American Prosperity." 2015. https://www.youtube.com/watch?v=BCiXz1a6jto.

"Export Pipelines and Provincial Rights: How Best to Get to the West Coast and Asian Markets," *School of Public Policy Communique* 5, no. 2 (February 2013). https://papers.ssrn.com/sol3/papers.cfm?abstract_id=2240576.

Alberta Politics and Policies

"Woke is killing free speech on campuses and here are five ways we fight back." *Western Standard*, March 13, 2023. https://www.westernstandard.news/opinion/morton-woke-is-killing-free-speech-on-campuses-and-here-are-five-ways-we-fight-back/article_c733fd42-c1b9-11ed-a484-af3ff6fe70e2.html.

"Racial discrimination at the University of Calgary." *Western Standard*, December 6, 2022. https://www.westernstandard.news/opinion/morton-racial-discrimination-at-the-university-of-calgary/article_ffbe65d0-74b6-11ed-89bd-e34078cc3267.html.

"Now Hiring by Skin Colour! The University of Calgary's "Inclusion" Policy that Discriminates Against Nearly Everyone." *C2C Journal*, November 30, 2022. https://c2cjournal.ca/2022/11/now-hiring-by-skin-colour-the-university-of-calgarys-inclusion-policy-that-discriminates-against-nearly-everyone/.

"Why Alberta Needs a Fiscal Constitution." *University of Calgary School of Public Policy Research Papers* 11, no. 25. 2018. https://papers.ssrn.com/sol3/papers.cfm?abstract_id=3251587.

"The North West Sturgeon Upgrader: Good Money after Bad?" *University of Calgary, School of Public Policy SPP Communique* 7, no. 3, April 2015. https://www.policyschool.ca/wp-content/uploads/2016/03/north-west-sturgeon-upgrader-morton.pdf.

"The Siren Song of Economic Diversification: Alberta's Legacy of Loss," with Meredith McDonald. *University of Calgary School of Public Policy Research Papers* 8, no. 13. March 2015. https://www.policyschool.ca/wp-content/uploads/2016/03/siren-song-economic-diversification-morton-mcdonald.pdf.

"Leadership Selection in Alberta, 1992–2011: A Personal Perspective." *Canadian Parliamentary Review* 36, no. 2 (Summer 2013). 31–38. http://revparl.ca/36/2/36n2_13e_Morton.pdf.

The Supreme Court and the Court Party

Law, Politics, and the Judicial Process in Canada. Fifth edition. Co-edited with Dave Snow. University of Calgary Press, 2024. First edition, 1984.

The Charter Revolution and the Court Party. With Rainer Knopff. Broadview Press, 2000.

Morgentaler v. Borowski: Abortion, The Charter and The Courts. McClelland and Stewart, 1992.

"Judicial Appointments in Post-Charter Canada: A System in Transition." In Kate Malleson and Peter H. Russell, eds., *Appointing Judges in an Age of Judicial Power: Critical Perspectives from Around the World*. University of Toronto Press, 2006. 56–79.

"Taking Section 33 Seriously," in Daniel Cere and Douglas Farrow, eds., *Divorcing Marriage: Unveiling the Dangers in Canada's New Social Experiment*. McGill-Queen's University Press, 2004. 135–54. https://www.degruyter.com/document/doi/10.1515/9780773572874-011/html.

"Can Judicial Supremacy Be Stopped?" *Policy Options* (October 2003). 25–29. https://policyoptions.irpp.org/wp-content/uploads/sites/2/assets/po/who-decides-the-courts-or-parliament/morton.pdf.

"Dialogue or Monologue?" in Paul Howe and Peter H. Russell, eds., *Judicial Power and Canadian Democracy*. McGill-Queen's University Press, 2001. 111–17.

"Feminists and the Courts: Measuring Success in Interest Group Litigation in Canada." With Avril Allen. *Canadian Journal of Political Science* 34, no. 1 (March 2001). 55–84. https://www.cambridge.org/core/journals/canadian-journal-of-political-science-revue-canadienne-de-science-politique/article/abs/feminists-and-the-courts-measuring-success-in-interest-group-litigation-in-canada/9DF529F507A79F0890DF 102894C440EE.

"Judges, The Court Party and the Charter Revolution." With Rainer Knopff. *Policy Options* (April 2000). 55–60.

"The Charter Revolution and the Court Party." *Osgoode Hall Law Journal* 30, no. 3 (1992). 627–52. https://digitalcommons.osgoode.yorku.ca/cgi/viewcontent. cgi?article=1718&context=ohlj.

"Vriend v. Alberta: Judicial Power at the Crossroads?" *Canada Watch* 7, nos. 4–5 (1999). 77–79.

"The Supreme Court as the Vanguard of the Intelligentsia: The Charter Movement as Post-Materialist Politics." With Rainer Knopff. In Janet Ajzenstat, ed., *Canadian Constitutionalism, 1791–1991*. Ottawa: Canadian Study of Parliament Group, 1992. 57–80.

"Judicial Review and Conservatism in the United States and Canada." In Barry Cooper, Allan Kornberg, and William Mishler, eds., *The Resurgence of Conservatism in the Anglo-American Democracies*. Duke University Press, 1988. 163–84.

"The Political Impact of the Canadian Charter of Rights and Freedoms." *Canadian Journal of Political Science* (March 1987). 31–55. https://www.cambridge.org/core/journals/ canadian-journal-of-political-science-revue-canadienne-de-science-politique/ article/abs/political-impact-of-the-canadian-charter-of-rights-and-freedoms/ B30FAF444810C9892CEC472E0BE60861.

Notes

NOTES TO CHAPTER 1

1   Alexander Butcher, winner of the Orwell Youth Prize 2016, quoted by the Orwell Foundation, https://www.orwellfoundation.com/the-orwell-youth-prize/2018-youth-prize/previous-winners-youth/2016-winners/if-liberty-means-anything-at-all-it-means-the-right-to-tell-people-what-they-do-not-want-to-hear-alexander-butcher/. By permission of estate of Sonia Brownell Orwell.

2   Arthur M. Schlesinger, *The Bitter Heritage: Vietnam and American Democracy, 1941–1966* (Boston: Houghton Mifflin, 1967).

3   See David Weinstein and Avihu Zakai, *Jewish Exiles and European Thought in the Shadow of the Third Reich: Baron, Popper, Strauss, Auerbach* (Cambridge: Cambridge University Press, 2017), pp. 131–92.

4   See Matthew Continetti, *The Right: The Hundred Year War for American Conservatism* (New York: Basic Books, 2022), pp. 132–33, 205, 292–93, 301–2.

5   *Dred Scott v. Sandford*, 60 U.S. (19 How.) 393 (1857).

6   *Plessy v. Ferguson*, 163 U.S. 537 (1896).

7   *Reference re meaning of the word "Persons" in s. 24 of British North America Act*, [1928] SCR 276.

8   Allan Bloom, *The Closing of the American Mind* (New York: Simon and Schuster, 1987).

9   Defense Casualty Analysis System, "World War II," https://dcas.dmdc.osd.mil/dcas/app/conflictCasualties/ww2.

10 Zbigniew Brzezinski, *Out of Control: Global Turmoil on the Eve of the Twenty-First Century* (New York: Scribner, 1993).

11 Yana Gorokhovskaia, Adrian Shahbaz, and Amy Slipowitz, "Marking 50 Years in the Struggle for Democracy," *Freedom House*, https://freedomhouse.org/report/freedom-world/2023/marking-50-years.

12 Continetti, *The Right*, pp. 244–47.

13 Michael Novak, *Three in One: Essays on Democratic Capitalism, 1976–2000,* ed. Edward W. Younkins (Lanham, MD.: Rowman & Littlefield, 2001), pp. 3–5.

14 R. Kent Weaver and Bert A. Rockman, *Do Institutions Matter?: Government Capabilities in the United States and Abroad* (Washington, DC: Brookings Institution, 1993).

15 Jake Fuss and Evin Ryan, "Examining Federal Debt in Canada by Prime Ministers Since Confederation, 2022," *Fraser Institute,* July 2022, https://www.fraserinstitute.org/sites/default/files/examining-federal-debt-in-canada-by-prime-ministers-since-confederation-2022.pdf.

16 Michael Babad, "'Honorary' Third World then: How WSJ describes Canada now," *Globe and Mail*, February 8, 2012, https://www.theglobeandmail.com/report-on-business/top-business-stories/honorary-third-world-then-how-wsj-describes-canada-now/article4202469/.

17 F.L. Morton, *Morgentaler v. Borowski: Abortion, the Charter and the Courts* (Toronto: McClelland and Stewart, 1992); Rainer Knopff and F.L. Morton, *Charter Politics* (Scarborough: Nelson Canada, 1992).

18 "Political scientist awarded human rights research prize," *University of Calgary Gazette,* January 30, 1995, p. 1; "SHHRC Awards Laskin Fellowship." *CAUT Bulletin*, March 1995, p. 4.

19 See F.L. Morton, "Judicial Politics Canadian-Style: The Supreme Court's Contribution to the Constitutional Crisis of 1992," in *Constitutional Predicament: Canada after the Referendum of 1992*, ed. Curtis Cook (McGill-Queen's University Press, 1994).

20 Both were attempts by the Mulroney Conservative government to reconcile Quebec to Canada's post-1982 constitution—the new power of the courts to nullify provincial legislation for violating the Charter of Rights and the new amending formula in which Quebec no longer had a unilateral veto. Meech was a set of concessions to Quebec—constitutional recognition of Quebec as a "distinct society" and a restoration of its veto power with respect to Senate reform. Charlottetown included watered-down versions of both, plus some additional confusing and contradictory concessions to other groups that had opposed Meech.

21 Jeffrey Simpson, "That's not a machine gun in the violin case, it's a political manifesto," *Globe and Mail*, January 29, 1992, p. 18.

22 David J. Rovinsky, "The Ascendancy of Western Canada in Canadian Policymaking," *Policy Papers on the Americas* 9, no. 2, February 16, 1998, https://www.csis.org/analysis/policy-papers-americas-ascendancy-western-canada-canadian-policymaking-volume-ix-1998.

23 Adam B. Masters and John Uhr, *Leadership Performance and Rhetoric* (Cham, Switzerland: Palgrave MacMillan, 2017), pp. 2, 3, 8, 135.

NOTES TO CHAPTER 2

1 See Peter McCormick, David Elton, and Casey Vander Ploeg, "Electing Alberta Senators – Senate Reform Step #2: Moving from Precedent to Practice," *Canada West Foundation*, March 1998, https://cwf.ca/wpcontent/uploads/2015/12/CWF_ElectingAlbertaSenators_MovingPrecedentPractice_Report_MAR1998.pdf.

2 David Kenney Stewart and Keith Archer, *Quasi-Democracy? Parties and Leadership Selection in Alberta* (Vancouver: UBC Press, 2000), pp. 30, 48.

3 Mark Lowey, "Political science prof aims at Senate seat," *Calgary Herald*, May 28, 1998, p. B3.

4   Peter Menzies, "Morton looking to run for senator-in-waiting," *Calgary Herald*, May 27, 1998, p. A16.

5   *Reference re Secession of Quebec*, [1998] 2 S.C.R. 217.

6   Ted Morton, "More French Kissing," *Calgary Sun*, August 21, 1998.

7   Sheldon Alberts, "Retiring senator supports elected upper chamber," *Calgary Herald*, August 29, 1998, p. A14.

8   Unsigned Editorial, "The real thing," *Calgary Herald*, August 30, 1998, A12.

9   George Koch, "Suddenly the Senate race is in the news," *Globe and Mail*, September 3, 1998, p. A19.

10   Sheldon Alberts and Jim Cunningham, "PM told to honor Senate election," *Calgary Herald*, August 29, 1998, p. A1.

11   Erin Anderssen and Daniel Leblanc, "Reform tries to block PM's Senate pick," *Globe and Mail*, August 29, 1998, p. A1; Graham Fraser, "Reform takes on Ottawa in bid to elect senators," *Globe and Mail*, Sept. 1, 1998, p. A3.

12   Lorne Gunter, "Will the federal Grits continue to ignore Alberta?' *Calgary Herald*, September 4, 1998, p. A20.

13   Unsigned Editorial, "No short cuts to a new senate," *Globe and Mail*, September 1, 1998, p. A14.

14   Morton: 3,701, 38%; Brown: 2,361, 24%; Gough: 1,218, 12%; Unger: 835, 9%; Blumell, 768, 8%; Hanley, 481, 5%; Bourke, 406, 4%. Total: 9770.

15   Sheldon Alberts, "Reformers pick stalwarts for Senate fight," *Calgary Herald*, September 13, 1998, p. A1.

16   Allan Chambers, "Reform selects Senate nominees," *Edmonton Journal*, September 13, 1998, p. A1.

17   Joan Bryden and Mario Toneguzzi, "Senate election a joke, says PM," *Calgary Herald*, September 17, 1998, p. A1.

18   Jim Cunningham and Sheldon Alberts, "Klein attacks Senate postings," *Calgary Herald*, September 18, 1998, p. A1.

19   Unsigned Editorial, "We are all mocked," *Calgary Herald*, September 18, 1998, p. A16.

20   "Ralph signs up," *Calgary Sun*, September 20, 1998, p. A1; "Slap in the face: Klein furious as Chrétien appoints senator," *Calgary Sun*, September 18, 1998, p. A1.

21   "Chrétien set to flip-flop on vow to reform chamber of slumbering sops," *Calgary Sun*, September 6, 1998, p. C2.

22   Brock Ketcham, "Appoint winner to Senate: poll," *Calgary Herald*, October 18, 1998, p. A12.

23   Paul Mitchinson, "Calgary neo-cons hunt controversy," *National Post*, July 22, 2000, p. B1.

24   F.L Morton, *Law, Politics, and the Judicial Process in Canada*, 3rd ed. (Calgary: University of Calgary Press, 2002).

25   F.L. Morton, "Provincial Constitutions in Canada," presented at conference on "Federalism and Sub-national Constitutions: Design and Reform," Center for the Study of State Constitutions, Rockefeller Center, Bellagio, Italy, March 22–26, 2004.

26   F.L. Morton, "Taking Section 33 Seriously," in *Divorcing Marriage*, eds. Daniel Cere and Doug Farrow (Montreal/Kingston: McGill-Queen's University Press, 2004), pp. 135–54.

27   F.L. Morton, "Our Turn: A New Course for the West," 5th annual Mel Smith Lecture, Trinity Western University.

28   Brian Galligan and F.L. Morton, "Australian Exceptionalism: Rights Protection without a Bill of Rights," in *Protecting Rights Without a Bill of Rights: Institutional Performance and Reform in Australia*, eds. Tom Campbell, Jeffrey Goldsworthy, and Adrienne Stone (Aldershot, UK: Ashgate Publishing, 2006), pp. 17–40.

29   F.L. Morton, "Senate Envy: Why Western Canada Wants What Australia Has," *Papers on Parliament: Number 39*, Parliament House, Canberra (December 2002), pp. 19–37.

30   Masters and Uhr, *Leadership Performance, and Rhetoric*, pp. 8, 136.

31   *Vriend v. Alberta*, [1998] 1 S.C.R. 493.

32   See Nigel Hannaford, "Modest people break the mould," *Calgary Herald*, January 24, 2006, p. A18.

33   Tyler Dawson, "Kenney announces 'firewall'-style panel in pursuit of a 'fair deal' for Alberta," *National Post*, November 9, 2019, https://nationalpost.com/news/politics/kenney-reveals-fair-deal-plan-to-assess-alberta-run-pension-police-and-tax-collection.

34   Fair Deal Panel, "Report to Government," May 2020, https://open.alberta.ca/publications/fair-deal-panel-report-to-government.

35   Carrie Tait and Alanna Smith, "Danielle Smith unveils sovereignty act in attempt to shield Alberta from federal laws," November 29, 2022, https://www.theglobeandmail.com/canada/alberta/article-danielle-smith-sovereignty-act-alberta-announcement/.

36   Sheldon Alberts, "Klein urged to trim ties to Ottawa," *National Post*, January 26, 2001, p. A1.

37   Stephen Harper, Tom Flanagan, Ted Morton, Rainer Knopff, Andrew Crooks, and Ken Boessenkool, "The Alberta Agenda," *Policy Options*, April 1, 2001.

38   See Sheldon Alberts, "Recipe for autonomy," *National Post*, January 27, 2001, p. B1.

39   Tom Flanagan, "Legends of the Calgary School: Their Guns, Their Dogs, and the Women Who Love Them." *Voeglin View*, January 25, 2015, https://voegelinview.com/legends-calgary-school-guns-dogs%E2%80%80%A8and-women-love/.

40   Pat Beauchamp, Director/Chairman; Ryan Cassell, Director/President; Garry Schirrmacher, Director; Jennifer Evaskevich, Secretary and Treasurer; Marv Jones, Chairman of the Advisory Committee.

41   Warren Green, Claresholm; Alan Warnock, Airdrie; Ken Cameron, Drayton Valley; Darryl Laycraft, High River; Richard Wambeke, High River; Neil Wilson, Nanton; Owen Sinclair, Pincher Creek; Faye Engler, St. Albert; Garry Schirrmacher, Stony Plain.

42   "Alberta Agenda launched in Drayton Valley," *The Western Review*, March 18, 2003, p. 5.

43   James Cudmore, "Province mistreated by Ottawa: Klein Responds to Alberta Six," *National Post*, February 8, 2001, p. A6.

44   Tom Olsen, "Klein wary of 'arrogant' Ottawa Grits," *Calgary Herald*, November 16, 2003, p. A5; Brian Laghi, "Klein cites list of grievances for Martin," *Globe and Mail*, November 20, 2003, p. A4.

45   Ken Boessenkool, "Albertans are moving beyond alienation," *National Post*, November 18, 2003, p. A16.

46   Tom Barrett, "Klein assembles 'firewall' panel," *Calgary Herald*, November 15, 2003, p. A14.

47   Dawn Walton, "Seeking to address Alberta's anger," *Globe and Mail*, March 8, 2004, p. A7.

48   Ron Duffy, Lacombe; Jim Chatenay, Penhold; Martin Hall, Vulcan; Rod Hanger, Three Hills; Noel Hyslip, Vulcan: Ike Lanier, Lethbridge; Bill Moore, Red Deer; Jim Ness, New Brigden; Mark Peterson, Cereal; Rick Strankman, Altario; John Turcato, Taber; and Darren Winczura, Viking.

49   CBC News, "Alberta farmers jailed over wheat exports," October 31, 2002, https://www.cbc.ca/news/canada/alberta-farmers-jailed-over-wheat-exports-1.329406.

50   *Reference re Firearms Act (Can.),* [2001] 1 S.C.R. 783.

51   See, e.g., F.L. Morton and Avril Allen,"Feminists and the Courts: Measuring Success in Interest Group Litigation in Canada," with Avril Allen, *Canadian Journal of Political Science* 34, no. 1 (March 2001), pp. 55–84. https://www.cambridge.org/core/journals/canadian-journal-of-political-science-revue-canadienne-de-science-politique/article/abs/feminists-and-the-courts-measuring-success-in-interest-group-litigation-in-canada/9DF529F507A79F0890DF102894C440EE.

52   Ted Morton, "Gun control legal battle lost, but the war is far from over," *Calgary Herald*, June 22, 2000, p. A3.

53   Ted Morton, "A week in the life of a gun registry," *National Post*, January 9, 2003, p. A4.

54   Jane Taber and Jill Mahoney, "Ottawa protest and arrests herald federal gun laws," *Globe and Mail,* January 2, 2003, https://www.theglobeandmail.com/news/national/ottawa-protest-and-arrests-herald-federal-gun-laws/article25276635/.

55   CBC News, "Lacombe found guilty of carrying gun," May 13, 2004, https://www.cbc.ca/news/canada/edmonton/lacombe-found-guilty-of-carrying-gun-1.492430.

56   See Ted Morton, "The Status Quo Must Go," in *Moment of Truth: How to Think about Alberta's Future,"* eds. Jack M. Mintz, Ted Morton, and Tom Flanagan (Toronto: Sutherland House, 2020).

57   Jim Chatenay, Farmers for Justice; Geoffrey Hale, University of Lethbridge; Link Byfield, Alberta Report, Edmonton; Roy Beyer, Canada Family Action Coalition, Edmonton; Dale Blue, Responsible Firearms Association of Alberta, Hardisty; Ron Duffy, Farmers for Justice, Blackfalds; Bruce Hutton, Law-Abiding Unregistered Firearms Association, Rocky Mountain House; Chris Matthews, Canadian Alliance, Calgary; Greg Fletcher, oil and gas, Calgary; Stan Church, lawyer and rancher, Calgary; Rick Sears, cattle feed lots, Nanton; Rod Blair, oil and gas, Calgary; Andy Crooks, Lawyer and Firewall signer, Calgary; Hermina Dykxhoorn, Alberta Federation of

Women United for Families, Calgary; Peggy Anderson, Constituency office manager for MP Jason Kenney, Calgary; Pat Beauchamp, Alberta Residents League, Calgary; David Pope, Alberta Property Rights Initiative, Highwood; Danielle Smith, Alberta Property Rights Initiative, Calgary.

58 Ted Byfield, "Why Ted Morton should become premier," *Edmonton Sun*, April 6, 2003.

59 Tom Olsen, "Firewall group eyes premier's office," *Edmonton Journal*, July 27, 2003, p. A1.

60 Graham Thomson, "Race is on to replace Ralph Klein as Tory leader," *Edmonton Journal*, November 13, 2004, p. A1.

61 "Morton wins Foothills-Rockyview nod," *Cochrane Times*, June 23, 2004, p. 24; "Calgarian wins nomination," *Western Wheel*, June 23, 2004, p. 1.

62 "Nomination will not be appealed," *Western Wheel*, June 30, 2004, p. 1.

63 Tom Olsen, "Klein wants election this fall, so be ready," *Calgary Herald*, June 16, 2004, p. A8.

64 "Premier-in-waiting?" *Western Standard*, August 30, 2004.

65 Jason Markusoff, "Tory candidate hits ditch," *Edmonton Journal*, October 24, 2004, p. A8.

66 Graham Thomson, "Race is on to replace Ralph Klein as Tory leader," *Edmonton Journal*, November 13, 2004, p. A1.

67 "Controversy strikes riding on eve of election," *Cochrane Times*, November 24, 2004, p. 3.

68 The full text of the message was: "This is an important message for voters in Foothills-Rocky View regarding tomorrow's election for MLA. Recent news reports have revealed a voter fraud investigation targeting PC Candidate Ted Morton's campaign. These reports suggest many votes cast for Ted Morton during the Nomination Election may have been cast illegally. This vote fraud investigation does not impact Ted Morton's eligibility for tomorrow's election. Should the investigation find Ted Morton's campaign guilty of voter fraud, a by-election would be held to elect a new MLA. Again, the voter fraud investigation targeting PC Candidate Ted Morton's campaign does not disqualify Ted Morton from running in tomorrow's election."

69 "Allegations dog Foothills-Rocky View Tories," *Cochrane Eagle*, November 24, 2004. p .7.

70 "Controversy strikes riding on eve of election," *Cochrane Times*, November 24, 2004, p. 2.

71 Michelle Lang, "RCMP will check Morton complaint," *Calgary Herald*, December 7, 2004, p. B3.

72 Suzanne Wilton, "MLA angry over autodial attack," *Calgary Herald*, November 24, 2004, p. A1.

73 Graham Thomson, "Race is on to replace Ralph Klein as Tory leader," *Edmonton Journal*, November 13, 2004, p. A1.

74 Elections Alberta, "General Elections," https://www.elections.ab.ca/resources/reports/general-elections/.

NOTES TO CHAPTER 3

1   *Reference re Same-Sex Marriage*, [2004] 3 S.C.R. 698.

2   *Vriend v. Alberta*, [1998] 1 S.C.R. 493.

3   David Rayside, Jerald Sabin, and Paul Thomas, "Faith and Party Politics in Alberta: Or 'Danielle, this is Alberta, not Alabama'," presented at the Canadian Political Science Association, University of Alberta, Edmonton, AB, June 13–15, 2012. https://cpsa-acsp.ca/papers-2012/Rayside-Sabin-Thomas.pdf; Paula Simons, "How the Vriend case established LGBTQ rights 20 years ago in Alberta—and across Canada," *Edmonton Journal*. March 15, 2018, https://edmontonjournal.com/news/insight/paula-simons-how-the-vriend-case-established-lgbtq-rights20years-ago-in-alberta-and-across-canada.

4   *M. v. H.*, [1999] 2 S.C.R. 3.

5   For an explanation and defence of the Section 33 Notwithstanding Clause, see F.L. Morton, "Taking Section 33 Seriously," in *Divorcing Marriage*, eds. Daniel Cere and Doug Farrow (Montreal/Kingston: McGill-Queen's University Press, 2004), pp. 135–54.

6   Rick Bell, "Premier says province will stick to its guns," *Calgary Sun*, December 18, 2005.

7   Niels Veldhuis and Jason Clemens, "Beginning of the end of Alberta Advantage," *Fraser Institute,* 2007, https://www.fraserinstitute.org/article/beginning-of-the-end-of-alberta-advantage.

8   Donald Savoie, "Power at the Apex: Executive Dominance," in *Canadian Politics*, 6th ed., eds. James Bickerton and Alain G. Gagnon (Toronto: University of Toronto Press, 2014), pp. 135–52.

9   G. Bruce Doern and Glen Toner, *The Politics of Energy: The Development and Implementation of the NEP* (Toronto: Methuen, 1985), p. 40.

10 Paul Stanway, "New contenders line up to replace Ralph," *Edmonton Sun*, March 9, 2005, p. 11.

11 Nigel Hannaford, "Morton sets out leadership case," *Calgary Herald*, March 12, 2005, p. A18.

12 Paul Stanway, "Force for change," *Calgary Sun*, March 27, 2005.

13 Ted Byfield, "Premier Klein makes heir-raising play," *Calgary Sun*, April 17, 2005, p. 33.

14 Ted Morton, "Courts have no place in same-sex marriage debate," *Edmonton Journal*, April 4, 2005, p. A15.

15 Graham Thomson, "Tories drop same-sex marriage fight," *Edmonton Journal*, April 5, 2005, p. A14.

16 Thomson, "Tories drop same-sex marriage fight," p. A14.

17 Legislative Assembly of Alberta, Alberta Hansard, May 1, 2006 (Ted Morton), p. 18, https://docs.assembly.ab.ca/LADDAR_files/docs/hansards/han/legislature_26/session_2/20060501_1330_01_han.pdf#page=18.

18 Legislative Assembly of Alberta, Alberta Hansard, May 1, 2006 (Ted Morton), p. 18.

19   Legislative Assembly of Alberta, Alberta Hansard, May 8, 2006, https://docs.assembly. ab.ca/LADDAR_files/docs/hansards/cpl/legislature_26/session_2/20060222_1500_01_ cpl.pdf, pp. 1354–57.

20   Legislative Assembly of Alberta, Alberta Hansard, May 8, 2006, pp. 1357–61.

21   Archie McLean, "Gay bill dies on the table," *Edmonton Journal*, August 29, 2006, p. A6.

22   Darcy Hinton, "MLA's gay-marriage bill dies a quiet death," *Edmonton Sun*, August 29, 2006.

23   Legislative Assembly of Alberta, Alberta Hansard, May 8, 2006, https://docs.assembly. ab.ca/LADDAR_files/docs/hansards/cpl/legislature_26/session_2/20060222_1500_01_ cpl.pdf, p. 1733.

24   Archie McLean, "Gay bill dies on the table," p. A6.

25   Graham Thomson, "Morton may be cheering his bill's death," *Edmonton Journal*, August 28, 2006, p. A16.

26   Colby Cosh, "Ted Morton's cunning bill," *National Post*, September 1, 2006, p. A13.

27   Kelly Cryderman, "Morton's same-sex bill described as a 'wedge' issue," *Calgary Herald*, September 4, 2006, p. A7.

28   Paul Jackson, "Leadership race is tearing party fabric," *Edmonton Sun*, August 31, 2006, p. 11.

29   Naomi Lakritz, "Give up on the anti-gay rant," *Calgary Herald*, August 31, 2006, p. A14.

30   Paul Stanway, "No compromise," *Edmonton Sun*, August 29, 2006.

NOTES TO CHAPTER 4

1   Katherine Harding and Dawn Walton, "Pushed by party, Klein to quit early," *Globe and Mail*, April 5, 2006, https://www.theglobeandmail.com/news/national/pushed-by- party-klein-to-quit-early/article706225/.

2   Dean Bennett, "Morton makes waves in Alberta Tory leadership race," *CNEWS*, November 19, 2006 http://cnews.canoe.ca/CNEWS/Canada/200611/19/pf-2417706.html (URL no longer functional).

3   Tom Olsen, "Departure could be messy affair," *Calgary Herald*, March 15, 2006, p. A5.

4   See Peter L. Berger and Richard John Neuhaus, *To Empower People: The Role of Mediating Structures in Public Policy* (Washington, DC: American Enterprise Institute for Public Policy Research, 1996).

5   See Marvin N. Olasky, *The Tragedy of American Compassion* (Washington, DC: Regnery Gateway, 1995).

6   See Claudia Hepburn and John Merrifield, "School Choice in Sweden: Lessons for Canada," *Fraser Institute* (November 2006), https://www.fraserinstitute.org/sites/ default/files/SchoolChoiceinSweden.pdf.

7   See Chris Wattie, "Funding of private schools improves public system, study finds," *National Post*, November 30, 2006, p. A10.

8   Kelly Cryderman, "Edmonton high on Tory agenda," *Calgary Herald*, November 14, 2006, p. A1; Tom Olsen, "Smoking ban heats up evening," *Calgary Herald*, November 14, 2006, p. A4.

9   Delon Shurtz, "Morton's swing south resonates with average everyday Albertans," *Lethbridge Herald*, December 2, 2006, p. A1.

10 Graham Thomson, "Morton Tory leadership campaign showing surprising strength," *Edmonton Journal*, November 18, 2006, p. A19.

11 Sarah O'Donnell, "Morton gets tune up on foes," *Calgary Herald*, November 22, 2006, p. A5.

12 YouTube, "Ted Morton Is the Man," https://www.youtube.com/watch?v=ZFoJGa439j4.

13 Tony Seskus, "Unwavering Morton a 'true, blue' Tory," *Calgary Herald*, September 21, 2006, p. A19.

14 Thomson, "Morton Tory leadership campaign showing surprising strength," p. A19.

15 Jason Fekete, "Dinning, Morton virtually tied in Tory race," *Calgary Herald*, November 23, 2006, p. A1.

16 *Calgary Sun,* "Dinning has what it takes," November 19, 2006, p. 29.

17 *Globe and Mail*, "Alberta's Tories need a leader with vision," November 18, 2006, p. A22.

18 "Lougheed backs Dinning," *Calgary Sun*, November 19, 2006, pp. 1, 5.

19 Lorne Gunter, "Morton Alberta's best choice for leader," *Edmonton Journal*, November 19, 2006, p. A18.

20 Joe Woodard, "The corner can be turned," *Western Standard*, December 4, 2006, p. 5.

21 Licia Corbella, "Ted Morton wins my vote," *Calgary Sun*, November 23, 2006, p. 15.

22 See Kelly Cryderman, "Geography plays key role in results: Dinning takes Calgary, south goes to Morton," *Calgary Herald*, November 27, 2006, p. A3.

23 Paul Stanway, "A battle for Tory souls," *Edmonton Sun*, November 28, 2006, p. 11.

24 Darcy Hinton, "Three hopefuls continue the race," *Calgary Sun*, November 26, 2006, p. 4.

25 Graham Thomson, "Fear and loathing in the home stretch," *Edmonton Journal*, November 29, 2006, p. A20.

26 Paul Stanway, "A battle for Tory souls," *Edmonton Sun*, November 28, 2006, p. 11.

27 "Mar predicts PC loss," *Edmonton Sun*, November 28, 2006, p. 19; Tony Seskus and Kelly Cryderman, "Leadership campaigns hit final leg of contest hard," *Calgary Herald*, December 1, 2006, p. A8.

28 Dawn Walton and Katherine Harding, "Is this man too 'scary' for Alberta?" *Globe and Mail*, December 1, 2006, p. A4.

29 Andrea Sands, "Temporary Tories cast leadership votes to head off Morton," *Edmonton Journal*, December 3, 2006, p. A2.

30 Kevin Libin, "Alberta Liberals run scared to PCs," *National Post*, December 1, 2006, p. A10.

31   Andrea Sands, "Temporary Tories cast leadership votes to head off Morton," *Edmonton Journal*, December 2, 2006, p. A2.

32   Tony Seskus, "Front-runners come out swinging for final round," *Calgary Herald*, November 28, 2006, p. A4.

33   Jason Fekete, "Federal Tories fight for Morton," *Calgary Herald*, November 28, 2006, p. A1.

34   Tony Seskus, "Dinning-Morton trading body blows," *Calgary Herald*, November 29, 2006, p. A3.

35   Norm Lebus, "Morton building on momentum," *Medicine Hat News*, December 2, 2006.

36   Tom Olsen, "Guess winner at your peril," *Calgary Herald*, December 2, 2006, p. A5.

37   Jason Markusoff, Archie McLean, Sarah O'Donnell, and Trish Audette, "Stelmach win stuns Tories," *Edmonton Journal*, December 2, 2006, p. A1.

38   Thomson, "Morton Tory leadership campaign showing surprising strength," p. A19.

39   See Faron Ellis, *The Limits of Participation: Members and Leaders in Canada's Reform Party* (Calgary: University of Calgary Press, 2005), pp. 160, 169.

40   Archie McLean, "'Maybe we should have kept our foot on the pedal'," *Edmonton Journal*, December 3, 2006, p. A4.

NOTES TO CHAPTER 5

1   "The New Nationalism," Osawatomie, Kansas, August 31, 1910, https://web.archive.org/web/20160527121424/http://www.theodore-roosevelt.com/images/research/speeches/trnationalismspeech.pdf.

2   *Oil Sands Magazine*, "Oil Sands Operations: Bitumen Production," https://www.oilsandsmagazine.com/projects/bitumen-production.

3   Action for Agriculture, "About Us," https://sites.google.com/a/actionforagriculture.com/public/home/about-us.

4   ALCES, "Our Team," https://www.alces.ca/about/.

5   There is another important factor—support, indifference, or opposition from bureaucrats. In today's modern welfare state, the career civil servants are the permanent government. MLAs, ministers, and premiers come and go. Senior civil servants do not. Plus, they have policy knowledge that elected representatives do not. And in this business, knowledge is power. I do not include it here because without exception, all these policy initiatives were supported by the senior civil servants in the SRD ministry. I had a similar experience when I was minister of finance (2010), but a very different experience during my brief stint as minister of energy (2011–12).

6   In 2007, an oil company applied to directional-drill into an oil formation below Marie Lake. The lease had already been sold by the Department of Energy, but residents along the shores of the lake strongly opposed the well. Approval involved sign-off by three different ministries—Energy, Environment, and SRD. The three ministers involved—Mel Knight, Rob Renner, and I—met with Premier Stelmach and unanimously recommended approval of the well. We advised that there was no threat to either water quality or to residences and wildlife along the shores. A similar directional well had

been drilled and completed adjacent to Sylvan Lake with no adverse effects. Several hours later, Premier Stelmach announced that the well would not be allowed. There was no public explanation. Inside, we all knew that several of the lakeshore residents opposed to the well were friends of the premier. See Alberta Outdoorsmen Forum, "Marie Lake – Update," September 6, 2007, http://outdoorsmenforum.ca/showthread. php?t=5922.

7   During my tenure as minister of SRD I introduced and passed three other bills, but none of them fall into this policy area.

8   Government of Alberta, *OH Ranch Heritage Rangeland Management Plan,* February 2010, https://www.albertaparks.ca/media/447228/ohranchmgmtplan.pdf.

9   Government of Alberta, "Heritage designation preserves ecological legacy of 125-year-old ranch," September 13, 2008, https://www.alberta.ca/release. cfm?xID=243375864F680-00AD-F2E5-54F5C4C5F9CED333.

10   Valerie Fortney, "Deal preserves historic ranch," *Calgary Herald,* September 30, 2014, p. A2.

11   For more detail, see Don H. Meredith, "Sunday Hunting," Don H. Meredith Professional Writing Services (first published in the October 2007 *Alberta Outdoorsmen*), 2007, https://www.donmeredith.ca/published-writing-list/sunday-hunting.

12   Legislative Assembly of Alberta, Alberta Hansard, May 5, 2997, p. 442, https:// docs.assembly.ab.ca/LADDAR_files/docs/hansards/han/legislature_27/ session_1/20080505_1330_01_han.pdf.

13   "Major water users in southern Alberta agree to curb consumption during drought," Stephen Tipper, *Calgary Herald,* April 19, 2024, https://calgaryherald.com/news/major-water-users-in-southern-alberta-agree-to-curb-consumption-during-drought.

14   *Alberta Land Stewardship Act,* SA 2009, c A-26.8, Part 3, "Conservation and Stewardship Tools," ss. 23 –49.

15   *Alberta Land Stewardship Act,* Part 2, "Nature and Effect of Regional Plans and Compliance Declarations," ss. 12–22.

16   *Alberta Land Stewardship Act,* "Legal nature of regional plans," s. 13.

17   Ecojustice, "Greater sage-grouse numbers continue to climb in Alberta, Saskatchewan," June 27, 2016, http://www.ecojustice.ca/pressrelease/greater-sage-grouse-numbers-continue-climb-alberta-saskatchewan/#sthash.b3rI18xu.dpuf.

18   *Species at Risk Act,* SC 2002, c. 29, s. 64.

19   This controversy arose because of a different section of ALSA, s. 19, which explicitly states: "No person has a right to compensation by reason of this Act, a regulation under this Act, a regional plan or anything done in or under a regional plan; except either (a) as expressly provided for under Part 3, Division 3, or (b) as provided for under another enactment." ALSA critics, especially the Wildrose Party, achieved a lot of political mileage by publicly citing the first clause of s. 19 and ignoring subsections (a) and (b). To mitigate this confusion, s. 19 was amended in 2011 to explicitly state that a private landowner has a legal right to compensation for any decrease in the value of his property caused by a regional plan. Section 19.1 also affirms the right of a dissatisfied

landowner to appeal the amount of compensation to a Court of King's Bench—the same right enjoyed under *eminent domain*. See *Alberta Land Stewardship Act*, s. 19.1.

20 Government of Alberta, "Alberta Land Trust Grant Program," https://www.alberta.ca/alberta-land-trust-grant-program.

21 Updated 2023 data provided by Justin Thompson, Executive Director, Southern Alberta Land Trust Society (personal correspondence, October 24, 2023).

22 Personal correspondence with Robyn Saude, Director of the Bow Habitat Station, October 16, 2023.

23 Quoted in Aldo J. Leopold, Baird Callicott, and Susan L. Flader, *The River of the Mother of God: And Other Essays by Aldo Leopold* (Madison, WI: University of Wisconsin Press, 1992), p. 202.

24 Leopold, Callicott, and Flader, *The River of the Mother of God,* p. 202.

25 Alberta Beef Producers, Alberta Fish & Game Association, Hunting for Tomorrow Foundation, Western Stock Growers' Association, Alberta Conservation Association, Alberta Association of Municipal Districts and Counties, Municipal District of Pincher Creek.

26 Conservation and Stewardship Working Group, *Final Report,* November 2007, https://landuse.alberta.ca/Documents/LUF_Multi-Stakeholder_Working_Groups_Roll-up_Report-Conservation_and_Stewardship_Report_Pages_123_to_160-2001-11.pdf.

27 Rainer Knopff and Cormack Gates, "Hunting for Habitat: The Rise and Fall of an Alberta Proposal for the Private Production of Ecological Goods and Services," *Frontier Centre for Public Policy*, FCPP Policy Series No. 146 (February 2013), p. 14.

28 For a more detailed explanation of the Hunting for Habitat program, see Knopff and Gates, "Hunting for Habitat."

29 On file with author; URL to original source no longer functional.

30 Hanneke Brooymans, "Elk program cut in half," *Edmonton Journal*, March 20, 2008, p. B8.

31 See Government of Alberta, *2009–10 Recreational Access Management Pilot Study Year 1 Report*, September 2010, https://open.alberta.ca/dataset/42097ece-04e7-4d75-b905-ccc766cd6bc0/resource/736c846f-38af-4a4d-90de-442bfb7854fa/download/2010-2009-10-ramp-programpilotstudyyear1report-sep-2010.pdf.

32 UBA's other founding directors included Don Douglas, Jimmy Miles, Quincy Smith, Tim Swinton, and Bill Turnbull.

33 Todd Zimmerling, Alberta Conservation Association; Bob Haysom, Pheasants Forever; Perry McCormick, Ducks Unlimited Canada; Kelly Semple, Hunting for Tomorrow; Larry Simpson, Nature Conservancy of Canada; Jeff Leighton, Alberta Fish & Game Association; Corey Jarvis, Alberta Professional Outfitters Society; Doug Jones/Ed McWilliams, Canadian Badlands.

34 "Alberta Pheasant Hunting Economic Impact Study," Serecon Management Consulting, Inc. (Edmonton, AB, December 22, 2011).

35 Upland Birds Alberta, *Alberta's Pheasant Release Program: Restoring the Past and Building for the Future*, submitted to the Government of Alberta, February 8, 2012, p. 16.

36   Annalise Klingbeil, "'Hunting is becoming a bit of a lost art': Pheasant festival about more than blasting birds," *Calgary Herald,* October 24, 2016, https://calgaryherald.com/news/local-news/hunting-is-becoming-a-bit-of-a-lost-art-pheasant-festival-about-more-than-blasting-birds.

37   These data were provided to me by the ACA.

38   Livingstone Landowners Group, "Videos," https://www.livingstonelandowners.net/videos-1.

39   CTV Calgary, "Federal, provincial finance ministers agree on private pension plan," *CTV News,* December 21, 2010, http://calgary.ctvnews.ca/federal-provincial-finance-ministers-agree-on-private-pension-plan-1.587934.

40   Kelly Cryderman, "Morton says mining proposal should wait," *Calgary Herald*, January 10, 2011, p. A3.

41   CBC News, "More people left Alberta than moved to the province in the second quarter of 2020," *CBC News,* October 1, 2020, https://www.cbc.ca/news/canada/calgary/provincial-migration-alberta-q2-2020-1.5746066.

42   See Vaclav Smil, *How the World Really Works: The Science Behind How We Got Here and Where We're Going* (New York: Penguin Publishing Group, 2022).

43   Ted Morton, "Someone tell Trudeau: Energy is now about security," *Financial Post,* January 19, 2023, https://financialpost.com/opinion/trudeau-energy-security.

44   See Ted Morton, "Keystone to American Prosperity," YouTube, uploaded October 22, 2014, https://www.youtube.com/watch?v=BCiXz1a6jto.

NOTES TO CHAPTER 6

1   See F.L. Morton and Meredith McDonald, "The Siren Sound of Economic Diversification: Alberta's Legacy of Loss," *School of Public Policy Research Papers* 8, no. 13 (March 2015), https://www.policyschool.ca/wp-content/uploads/2016/03/siren-song-economic-diversification-morton-mcdonald.pdf.

2   Morton and McDonald, "Siren Sound."

3   Alberta Financial Management Commission, *Moving from Good to Great: Enhancing Alberta's Fiscal Framework* (Edmonton: Government of Alberta, 2002).

4   Memo from Ministry of Finance and Enterprise, December 2008.

5   "Stelmach sells out Albertans," Scott Hennig, November 15, 2007, https://www.taxpayer.com/news-room-archive/Stelmach%20sells%20out%20Albertans.

6   See Mark Milke, "Alberta's $22-billion Lost Opportunity: How Spending Beyond Inflation + Population Growth Created Alberta's Red Ink," *Fraser Institute*, February 2015.

7   Under the new rule, a $500 charitable contribution is entitled to a refundable tax credit of $83 for provincial income tax and $117 for federal, resulting in net cost to the taxpayer of $300. For $1,000 worth of charitable contributions, the comparable figures are $188 and $262, for a net cost of $550.

8   In addition to William Hunter, the chair, the committee consisted of Evan Chrapko, Judith Dwarkin, Ken McKenzie, André Plourde, and Sam Spanglet.

9   Alberta Royalty Review Panel, "Our Fair Share: Report of the Alberta Royalty Review Panel," September 18, 2007, https://open.alberta.ca/dataset/923f6129-544f-4ba9-91b0-68cfb58f4920/resource/d0ab5af8-cdca-454a-bf4d-99a6af0b16b7/download/3981408-2007-our-fair-share-report-alberta-royalty-review-panel-final-report.pdf.

10   Government of Alberta, *The New Royalty Framework*, October 25, 2007, https://open.alberta.ca/dataset/adaf8c18-1817-43dc-ac75-9570c4b49e11/resource/6645fe59-bf45-4081-8773-a90ad02c2f20/download/royaltyoct25.pdf.

11   "A message from Premier Ed Stelmach," in Government of Alberta, *The New Royalty Framework*, October 25, 2007, p. iii.

12   CBC News, "Stelmach promises to erase health care premiums," *CBC News,* February 4, 2008, https://www.cbc.ca/news/canada/edmonton/stelmach-promises-to-erase-health-care-premiums-1.697296.

13   CBC News, "Alberta budget to eliminate health-care premiums by 2009," *CBC News,* April 22, 2008, https://www.cbc.ca/news/canada/edmonton/alberta-budget-to-eliminate-health-care-premiums-by-2009-1.695584.

14   Naheed Nenshi, "The election's biggest loser is not who you think," *Calgary Herald,* March 13, 2008, p. A16.

15   CBC News, "Stelmach defends oilsands in Washington," *CBC News,* January 16, 2008, https://www.cbc.ca/news/canada/calgary/stelmach-defends-oilsands-in-washington-1.707445.

16   CBC News, "Alberta premier confident U.S. will remain major energy customer," *CBC News,* January 18, 2008, https://www.cbc.ca/news/canada/edmonton/alberta-premier-confident-u-s-will-remain-major-energy-customer-1.707444.

17   Jack Mintz, *Preserving Prosperity: Challenging Alberta to Save* (Edmonton: Alberta Financial Investment and Planning Advisory Commission, December 2007).

18   When Klein had announced these rebates in January 2001, I had written a guest column in the *Calgary Herald* denouncing them as a "policy disaster" and pointed out that they had already elicited calls from a federal NDP Member of Parliament for a national consumer protection program against high natural gas prices—a policy that would clearly harm Alberta. Ted Morton, "Energy price shield a policy disaster," *Calgary Herald,* February 6, 2001, p. A15.

19   The others included: education and job training; jobs over raises for the public sector; completing the competitiveness review (i.e., fixing the NRF); and communicating to Albertans that dealing with the effects of the recession would have to be a "shared effort."

20   Gillian Steward, "Ed Stelmach's worst nightmare?" *Toronto Star,* January 19, 2010, http://www.thestar.com/opinion/2010/01/19/steward_ed_stelmachs_worst_nightmare.html.

21   By the end of Fiscal Year 2010–11, the final deficit was $3.4 billion, which was not the largest in Alberta's history. That dubious distinction goes to Budget 1992–93.

22   Government of Alberta, "New cabinet team will ensure Alberta is stronger than ever," January 13, 2010, http://www.alberta.ca/release.cfm?xID=27634296588A5-FF21-1A16-60456BB10F8E0513.

NOTES TO CHAPTER 7

1 By the end of Fiscal Year 2010–11, the final deficit was $3.4 billion, which was not the largest in Alberta's history. That dubious distinction goes to Budget 1992–93. That record, unfortunately, was subsequently broken six years in a row, from 2015 to 2020. These six consecutive deficits added $61 billion dollars of new GOA debt.

2 Government of Alberta, *Budget 2010: Striking the Right Balance,* February 9, 2010, https://open.alberta.ca/dataset/9b737a16-9534-4b46-817b-889cd5e25681/resource/abe9e091-5ef8-44ba-8c28-569772bdea06/download/speech.pdf.

3 Jim Dinning, "APP panel committed to engaging with Albertans," *Calgary Herald,* October 24, 2023. https://calgaryherald.com/opinion/columnists/opinion-app-panel-committed-to-engaging-with-albertans-dinning.

4 The group included Tim Hearn (Imperial Oil); Murray Edwards (CNRL); George Gosbee (AltaCorp Capital); Nancy Southern (ATCO); Hal Kvisle (TransCanada Pipelines); Bill Sembo (Royal Bank of Canada); Ross Grieve (PCL Construction); and Ron Mathison (MATCO).

5 Troy Riddell and F.L. Morton, "Government Use of Strategic Litigation: The Alberta Exported Natural Gas Tax Reference," *American Review of Canadian Studies* 34, no. 3 (2004), pp. 485–509.

6 Archie McLean, "Alberta challenges Ottawa over securities regulator," *Edmonton Journal,* February 6, 2010, p. C5.

7 Government of Quebec and Government of Alberta, "Alberta and Quebec Urge Provinces to Resist Federal Push on National Securities Regulator," September 13, 2010, http://www.finances.gouv.qc.ca/documents/Communiques/en/COMEN_20100913.pdf.

8 McLean, "Alberta challenges Ottawa," p. C5.

9 Ted Morton, "Messing with very good thing: Alberta's security regulator has served us well," *Calgary Herald,* June 1, 2010, p. A11.

10 Morton, "Messing with very good thing," p. A11.

11 Jeffrey MacIntosh, "The Feds' weak case," *Financial Post,* June 1, 2010, https://financialpost.com/opinion/the-feds-weak-case.

12 Thomas J. Courchene, "A Single National Securities Regulator? Public Policy and Political Economy Perspectives," Queen's University, School of Policy Studies, June 26, 2010.

13 Janet McFarland, "Alberta court rejects plan for national securities regulator," *Globe and Mail,* March 8, 2011, https://www.theglobeandmail.com/report-on-business/alberta-court-rejects-plan-for-national-securities-regulator/article574822/.

14 *National Post,* "Quebec Court of Appeal opposes federal securities regulator," April 1, 2011, https://nationalpost.com/news/quebec-court-of-appeal-opposes-federal-securities-regulator.

15 Drew Hasselback and Barbara Shecter, "Supreme Court rules against Ottawa's single-regulator move," *Financial Post,* December 22, 2011, https://financialpost.com/legal-post/supreme-court-rejects-national-securities-regulator-plan.

16 *Reference re Securities Act,* [2011] 3 SCR 837, para. 7.

17 MacIntosh, "The Feds' weak case."

18 See Ted Morton, "What the Supreme Court's Carbon Tax Ruling Means—and What to Do about It," *C2C Journal*, April 30, 2021, https://c2cjournal.ca/2021/04/what-the-supreme-courts-carbon-tax-ruling-means-and-what-to-do-about-it/.

19 See Catherine Browlee and Mike Martens, "Business leaders backing Alberta in Supreme Court fight against Bill -C-69," *Calgary Herald*, March 22, 2023, https://calgaryherald.com/opinion/opinion-business-leaders-backing-alberta-in-supreme-court-fight-against-bill-c-69.

20 Teresa Wright, "Quebec intervenes in Saskatchewan's challenge of carbon tax," *Montreal Gazette*, July 8, 2019, https://montrealgazette.com/news/quebec/p-e-i-quebec-intervene-in-saskatchewans-legal-challenge-of-carbon-tax.

21 Robert Mansell, "Alberta's fiscal contribution to confederation," in *Moment of Truth: How to Think About Alberta's Future*, eds. Jack Mintz, Ted Morton, and Tom Flanagan (Toronto: Sutherland House, 2020), pp. 117–20.

22 Government of Alberta, "Alberta Pension Plan," https://www.albertapensionplan.ca/.

23 Canadian HR Reporter, "Ottawa, Ontario propose expanding CPP," June 14, 2010, https://www.hrreporter.com/news/hr-news/ottawa-ontario-propose-expanding-cpp/313036.

24 Lisa Schmidt, "Morton warns Ottawa on pension premiums," *Calgary Herald*, June 12, 2010, p. A4.

25 Don Braid, "Ottawa's last minute pension ploy nothing to snort at," *Calgary Herald*, June 12, 2012, p. A4.

26 CTV Calgary, "Federal, provincial finance ministers agree on private pension plan," *CTV News,* December 21, 2010, http://calgary.ctvnews.ca/federal-provincial-finance-ministers-agree-on-private-pension-plan-1.587934.

27 CBC News, "Flaherty: Pooled pension consensus reached," *CBC News,* December 20, 2010, https://www.cbc.ca/news/politics/flaherty-pooled-pension-consensus-reached-1.901721.

28 CBC News, "Pooled pension consensus reached."

29 CTV Calgary, "Ministers agree on private pension plan."

30 This section is an edited and updated version of a study I published in 2015. Ted Morton, "The North West Sturgeon Upgrader: Good Money after Bad?" *School of Public Policy Research Papers* 7, no. 3 (April 2015), https://www.policyschool.ca/wp-content/uploads/2016/03/north-west-sturgeon-upgrader-morton.pdf.

31 By 2014, of the 113 bitumen extraction projects in Alberta, only six were mines.

32 By 2010, there were only five upgraders operating in Alberta: Suncor (1967), Syncrude (1978), Scotford (2003), CNRL Horizon (2009), and CNOC Nexen Long Lake (2009). See IHS CERA, "Extracting Economic Value from the Canadian Oil Sands: Upgrading and Refining in Alberta (or not)?" March 2013.

33 IHS CERA, "Extracting Economic Value," p. 1.

34 The NWU was owned by the North West Redwater Partnership, a joint venture between Ian MacGregor and Canadian Natural Resources (CNRL) and its CEO, Murray Edwards.

35 This group included Premier Stelmach; his chief of staff, Ron Glen; Doug Horner, the new deputy premier; President of Treasury Board Lloyd Snelgrove; Alison Redford, the new minister of justice; the deputy minister of energy; and myself. Stelmach rarely attended, and the meetings were chaired by Glen.

36 G. Bruce Doern and Glen Toner, *The Politics of Energy: The Development and Implementation of the NEP* (Toronto: Methuen Publications, 1985), p. 40.

37 Standing Committee on Alberta's Economic Future, *Review of the BRIK (Bitumen Royalty-in-Kind) Program*, Legislative Assembly of Alberta, 1st sess., 28th Legislature, May 2013, http://albertaenergyplus.ca/wp-content/uploads/2013/05/AEF-Report-BRIK_web-version.pdf, p. 17.

38 Standing Committee on Alberta's Economic Future, *Review of BRIK*.

39 IHS CERA, "Extracting Economic Value from the Canadian Oil Sands: Upgrading and Refining in Alberta (or not)?" March 2013.

40 Canadian Energy Research Institute, *Refining Bitumen: Costs, Benefits and Analysis*, Study No. 145 (December 2014), p. 13. The study also found that NWU's incremental benefits were primarily limited to enhanced oil recovery (EOR) and reduced emissions through carbon capture and storage (CCS), and restoration of wetlands. On the downside, CERI identified the same risks and liabilities described in this study: no cap on final capital costs; uncertain light/heavy oil differentials—both "at potential expense to the government and by extension society" (pp. 11–13).

41 Kelly Cryderman, "Refinery deal cost Alberta government a bundle, but it will end up making a profit," *Globe and Mail*, April 27, 2023, https://www.theglobeandmail.com/canada/alberta/article-refinery-deal-cost-alberta-government-a-bundle-but-it-will-end-up/.

42 Robert Tuttle, "Alberta project proving costly to taxpayers," *Calgary Herald*, February 16, 2019, p. A16.

43 Mel Knight, 2006–2009; Ron Liepert, 2010–11; Ted Morton, 2011–12; Ken Hughes, 2012–13; Diana McQueen, 2013–14; Frank Oberle, 2014–15.

44 See Ted Morton and Meredith McDonald, "The Siren Song of Diversification: Alberta's Legacy of Loss, 1973–1993," *School of Public Policy Research Papers* 8, no. 15 (March 2015), https://www.policyschool.ca/wp-content/uploads/2016/03/siren-song-economic-diversification-morton-mcdonald.pdf.

45 Morton and McDonald, "Siren Song of Diversification."

NOTES TO CHAPTER 8

1 Don Braid, "Tories in turmoil over budget," *Calgary Herald*, January 19, 2011, p. A4.

2 Tony Seskus and Jason Fekete, "A political meltdown without precedent," *Calgary Herald*, January 30, 2011, p. A4.

3 Josh Wingrove, "Alberta to lead Canada's economic recovery, Premier says," *Globe and Mail*, January 2, 2011, https://www.theglobeandmail.com/news/national/alberta-to-lead-canadas-economic-recovery-premier-says/article563395/.

NOTES TO CHAPTER 9

1 "Albertans down on Stelmach," *Calgary Sun*, December 3, 2010, p. 7.

2 Chris Varcoe, "New poll shows Tories on top but losing ground," *Calgary Herald*, November 5, 2009; Tom Flanagan, *Winning Power: Canadian Campaigning in the Twenty-First Century* (Montreal: McGill-Queen's University Press, 2014), p. 164.

3 Don Braid, "Stakes are high for ambitious Ted Morton in Highwood," *Calgary Herald*, December 24, 2010, p. A4.

4 There is a third version of why Stelmach resigned that morning: that in late December "a delegation of PC Party notables travelled from Calgary to Edmonton to apprise the premier that, in their opinion, the party could not realistically expect to win the next election should he remain at the helm." If this account is accurate, I was not aware of it, and no one has ever told me about such a "delegation" after the fact—which I find surprising. See Bohdan Harasymiw, "Alberta's Premier Ed Stelmach: The Anomalous Case of Leadership Selection and Removal in a Canadian Province," *American Review of Canadian Studies*, 44, no. 2 (2014), pp. 216–33.

5 Josh Wingrove, Renata D'Aliesio, and Nathan Vanderklippe, "Conservative showdown prompts Stelmach resignation," *Globe and Mail*, January 26, 2011, https://www.theglobeandmail.com/news/politics/conservative-showdown-prompts-stelmachs-resignation/article563505/.

6 See Colby Cosh, "The Prairie putsch to replace Ed Stelmach," *Maclean's*, February 4, 2011, https://macleans.ca/news/canada/the-prairie-putsch/.

7 Josh Wingrove, "Ted Morton vows to merge Alberta conservatives with upstart Wildrose," *Globe and Mail*, January 27, 2011, https://www.theglobeandmail.com/news/politics/ted-morton-vows-to-merge-alberta-conservatives-with-upstart-wildrose/article563819/.

NOTES TO CHAPTER 10

1 Graham Thomson, "Ted Morton and the curse of The Front-runner," *Edmonton Journal*, February 8, 2011, p. A11.

2 Don Braid, "Kinder, gentler Morton emerges in Tory leadership turf war," *Calgary Herald*, February 3, 2011, p. A4.

3 Jen Gerson, "Wildrose godfather Ted Morton may end up on losing side of Alberta's conservative civil war," *National Post*, April 20, 2012, https://nationalpost.com/opinion/analysis-wildrose-godfather-ted-morton-may-end-up-on-losing-side-of-albertas-conservative-civil-war.

4 Braid, "Kinder, gentler Morton emerges."

5 Don Braid, "Stelmach still not out of the Wildrose woods," *Calgary Herald*, January 5, 2011.

6 "The Race is On," *PC People*, July 2011, p. 14.

7 Braid, "Kinder, gentler Morton emerges."

8 The bighorn sheep is Alberta's official mammal; "Strong and Free" is the translation of Alberta's official motto, "Fortis et Liber." See Michael Wood, "New plates on the table," *Calgary Sun*, July 20, 2011, p. 18.

9   *Globe and Mail*, "How Alberta PCs can ward off Wildrose," July 30, 2011, https://www.theglobeandmail.com/opinion/editorials/how-alberta-pcs-can-ward-off-wildrose/article588773/.

10   Karen Kleiss, "Watchdog probes Morton's use of secondary email," *Calgary Herald*, September 9, 2011, p. A4.

11   Don Braid, "Charges could hurt Morton's bid for PC crown," *Calgary Herald*, September 9, 2011, p. A4.

12   Gerson, "Wildrose godfather Ted Morton."

13   Tom Flanagan, *Winning Power: Canadian Campaigning in the Twenty-First Century* (Montreal: McGill-Queen's University Press, 2014), p. 171. He once had paid a political consultant, Kelly Charlebois, almost $390,000 for consultations without any tangible evidence—i.e., written reports—of what work Charlebois had done.

14   Kim Guttormson and James Wood, "Mar bears brunt of attacks as rivals take shots in debate," *Calgary Herald*, September 29, 2011, p. A4.

15   Don Braid noted,
     "The second round begins with nearly everyone expecting Mar to win." Don Braid, "Options still open for defeated candidates," *Calgary Herald*, September 19, 2011, p. A5.

16   Tom Flanagan, "The Redford Effect: Stagecraft, State Craft and Rhetorical Pragmatism," *Policy Options*, November 1, 2011, https://policyoptions.irpp.org/magazines/continuity-and-change-in-the-provinces/the-redford-effect-stagecraft-statecraft-and-rhetorical-pragmatism/.

17   Deborah Yedlin, "A power plan for the future," *Calgary Herald*, February 25, 2012, p. D1.

18   Darcy Henton, "High-voltage controversy may shock Tories' Morton," *Calgary Herald*, April 15, 2012, p. A4.

19   Shari Narine, "Chief claims racism behind government's decision," *Alberta Sweetgrass* 19, no. 4 (2012), https://www.ammsa.com/publications/alberta-sweetgrass/chief-claims-racism-behind-government's-decision.

20   Licia Corbella, "Posh promises and bad budgeting lead to a mess," *Calgary Herald*, February 20, 2013, p. A11.

21   Bill Graveland, "Alberta Tories promise to establish 140 family care clinics across province," *Global News*, April 2, 2012, https://globalnews.ca/news/229486/alberta-tories-promise-to-establish-140-family-care-clinics-across-province-2/.

22   Flanagan, *Winning Power*, p. 177.

23   James Wood, "Wildrose revisiting 'firewall' ideas," *Calgary Herald*, April 14, 2012, p. A7.

24   Wood, "Wildrose revisiting 'firewall' ideas."

25   Flanagan, *Winning Power*, p. 177–83.

26   Flanagan, *Winning Power*, pp. 61, 179

27   Flanagan, *Winning Power*, p. 192.

28   Flanagan, *Winning Power*, p. 192.

29   Jen Gerson, "Wildrose godfather Ted Morton."

30 Tom Flanagan makes the same point: "In historical perspective, Wildrose did quite well. Danielle Smith was a new leader, seeking a seat in the legislature for the first time, and Wildrose was essentially a new party." Only twice in Canadian history has a new party with a new leader actually won an election. Flanagan, *Winning Power*, p. 186.

31 Flanagan, *Winning Power*, p. 32.

32 Flanagan, *Winning Power*, p. 56.

33 David K. Stewart and Keith Archer, *Quasi-Democracy? Parties and Leadership Selection in Alberta* (Vancouver: UBC Press, 2000), p. 40.

34 David K. Stewart and Lisa Young, "Leadership Primaries in a Single-Party Dominant System," presented at the European Consortium for Political Research, University of Antwerp, April 2012, pp. 18–19.

35 Stewart and Young, "Leadership Primaries," pp. 8–9, draw the same regional parallel.

36 As Graham Thomson noted, "not only have the PCs stalled, but the 'conservative' flank of the party has deserted it." Graham Thomson, "Second-ballot curse could still scupper Mar's leadership bid," *Edmonton Journal*, September 20, 2011, p. A2.

37 See David Taras, "Politics, Alberta Style: The Rise and Fall of the Progressive Conservatives, 1971–2015," and Duane Bratt, "Death of a Dynasty: The Tories and the 2015 Election," both in *Orange Chinook: Politics in the New Alberta*, eds. Duane Bratt, Keith Brownsey, Richard Sutherland, and David Taras (Calgary: University of Calgary Press, 2019). See also Josh Wingrove, "Seven stumbles and a funeral: Why Alberta's Premier Alison Redford had to quit," *Globe and Mail*, March 20, 2014, https://www.theglobeandmail.com/news/politics/seven-stumbles-and-a-funeral-why-albertas-premier-alison-redford-had-to-quit/article17586488/; Laurie Adkin, "The End of Alison: The multiple meanings of the Redford resignation," *Alberta Views*, May 1, 2014, https://albertaviews.ca/the-end-of-alison/.

38 Stewart Shaw, "Premier showed arrogance and sense of entitlement: poll," *CTV News*, March 19, 2014, https://edmonton.ctvnews.ca/premier-showed-arrogance-and-sense-of-entitlement-poll-1.1736430.

39 Duane Bratt makes the same point. Bratt, "Death of a Dynasty," p. 42.

40 Jen Gerson, "Alberta budget 2013 marked by billions in deficit spending, service cuts," *National Post*, March 7, 2013, https://nationalpost.com/news/politics/alberta-budget-2013.

41 Gerson, "Alberta budget 2013."

42 Stockwell Day, Steve West, Greg Melchin, Lloyd Snelgrove, Lyle Oberg, and Ted Morton, "Letter: It's time to return to Klein's accounting rules," *Calgary Herald*, June 27, 2014, https://calgaryherald.com/opinion/letter-its-time-to-return-to-kleins-accounting-rules.

43 Bratt, "Death of a Dynasty," p. 43.

44 Prentice received 17,963 votes, McIver, 2,742, and Lukaszuk, 2,681.

45 In addition to Danielle Smith, the other Wildrose MLAs who crossed to join the PCs were Rob Anderson, Jason Hale, Blake Pedersen, Bruce McAllister, Jeff Wilson, Gary Bikman, Rod Fox, and Bruce Rowe.

46   Duane Bratt agrees that the floor-crossing strategy backfired on both sides, PC and Wildrose. Bratt, "Death of a Dynasty," p. 48.

47   Karen Kleiss, "Nine Wildrose MLAs cross floor to join governing PC party," *Edmonton Journal*, December 18, 2014, https://edmontonjournal.com/news/local-news/nine-wildrose-mlas-cross-floor-to-join-governing-pc-party.

48   Ted Morton, "Public-sector workers need to help balance budget too," *Calgary Herald*, March 31, 2015, https://calgaryherald.com/opinion/columnists/morton-public-sector-workers-need-to-help-balance-budget-too.

49   CBC News, "#PrenticeBlamesAlbertans goes viral after Jim Prentice's 'look in the mirror' comment," *CBC News*, March 5, 2015, https://www.cbc.ca/news/canada/edmonton/prenticeblamesalbertans-goes-viral-after-jim-prentice-s-look-in-the-mirror-comment-1.2982524.

50   The Canadian Press, "What every Alberta premier needs: Jim Prentice buys 1956 Thunderbird for $71,000 at Arizona auction," *National Post,* January 20, 2015, https://nationalpost.com/news/canada/a-car-fit-for-the-alberta-premier-jim-prentice-buys-1956-thunderbird-for-71000-at-arizona-auction.

51   See Bratt, "Death of a Dynasty," p. 49.

52   CBC News, "Jim Prentice resignation as MLA too fast, strategist says," *CBC News*, May 6, 2015, https://www.cbc.ca/news/canada/calgary/jim-prentice-resignation-as-mla-too-fast-strategist-says-1.3063084.

53   This is the subtitle of the Bratt et al.'s 2019 book, *Orange Chinook: Politics in the New Alberta*.

54   Colby Cosh, "The Death of the Alberta PC Dynasty," *Maclean's*, May 7, 2015, https://macleans.ca/politics/the-death-of-the-alberta-pc-dynasty/.

55   Taras, "The Rise and Fall of the Progressive Conservatives," p. 19.

56   Flanagan, *Winning Power*, pp. 58–59. I also want to credit a former student, Morgan Nagel, for bringing my attention to this strategic error in the Prentice PC 2015 campaign.

57   Cosh, "The Death of the Alberta PC Dynasty."

NOTES TO CHAPTER 11

1   Duane Bratt agrees that the PCs loss in 2015 was not simply Jim Prentice's fault. Bratt attributes the PC's demise to vote splitting with the Wildrose Party and agrees that this schism started with Stelmach and accelerated under Redford. Duane Bratt, "Death of a Dynasty: The Tories and the 2015 Election," in *Orange Chinook: Politics in the New Alberta*, eds. Duane Bratt, Keith Brownsey, Richard Sutherland, and David Taras (Calgary: University of Calgary Press, 2019), p. 52.

2   Everyone who has written about this agrees that Stelmach's New Royalty Framework was a political disaster for the PCs and jump-started the then-tiny Wildrose Party. See Tom Flanagan, *Winning Power: Canadian Campaigning in the Twenty-First Century* (Montreal: McGill-Queen's University Press, 2014), pp. 164–65; David Taras, "Politics, Alberta Style: The Rise and Fall of the Progressive Conservatives, 1971–2015," in *Orange Chinook: Politics in the New Alberta*, eds. Duane Bratt, Keith Brownsey, Richard

Sutherland, and David Taras (Calgary: University of Calgary Press, 2019), p. 28; Bratt, "Death of a Dynasty," p. 38.

3   Sheila Pratt, "Alberta's Redford revolution," *Edmonton Journal*, October 9, 2011, p. A1.

4   David K. Stewart and Anthony M. Sayers, "Responding to Challenge: An Analysis of the 2011 Alberta Progressive Conservative Leadership Election" presented at the Annual Meeting of the Canadian Political Science Association University of Alberta, June 2012, pp. 8–9, https://www.cpsa-acsp.ca/papers-2012/Stewart-Sayers.pdf.

5   Stewart and Sayers, "Responding to Challenge," pp. 8–9.

6   David K. Stewart and Lisa Young, "Leadership Primaries in a Single-Party Dominant System," presented at the European Consortium for Political Research, University of Antwerp, April 2012, p. 19.

7   Tom Flanagan, "The Redford Effect: Stagecraft, Statecraft and Rhetorical Pragmatism," *Policy Options*, November 1, 2011, https://policyoptions.irpp.org/magazines/continuity-and-change-in-the-provinces/the-redford-effect-stagecraft-statecraft-and-rhetorical-pragmatism/.

8   Josh Wingrove, "Seven stumbles and a funeral: Why Alberta's Premier Alison Redford had to quit," *Globe and Mail*, March 20, 2014, https://www.theglobeandmail.com/news/politics/seven-stumbles-and-a-funeral-why-albertas-premier-alison-redford-had-to-quit/article17586488/.

9   Ted Morton, "Leadership Selection in Alberta, 1992–2011: A Personal Perspective," *Canadian Parliamentary Review* 36, no. 2 (2013), pp. 31–38, http://revparl.ca/36/2/36n2_13e_Morton.pdf.

10 Taras ignores the flawed leadership process; mentions the Wildrose Party only once; and only obliquely references vote splitting. Taras, "The Rise and Fall of the Progressive Conservatives," p. 19.

11 Elections Alberta, General Elections, https://www.elections.ab.ca/resources/reports/general-elections/.

12 Flanagan, *Winning Power*, pp. 50–52.

13 Taras makes the same point: "For those wishing to move up the political ladder, the Tories were the only game in town." Taras, "The Rise and Fall of the Progressive Conservatives," p. 28.

14 Bratt and Foster use the principled/pragmatist distinction to explain the historical pattern of Canadian conservative parties splintering and then merging again to form new parties. This analysis is sensible as far as it goes, but it ignores the regional factor—Western Canadian discontent with the status quo—as the force that has driven almost all of the splintering of Canada's conservative parties. See Duane Bratt and Bruce Foster, "The fragility of a 'big tent' conservative party," *CBC News*, July 25, 2019, https://www.cbc.ca/news/canada/calgary/conservative-party-splitting-merging-western-canada-1.5220417.

15 See Taras, "The Rise and Fall of the Progressive Conservatives," pp. 25–26.

16 Daniel Yergin, *The Quest: Energy, Security, and the Remaking of the Modern World* (New York: Penguin Press, 2011), pp. 109–10.

17 Yergin, *The Quest*, p. 108.

18   Yergin, *The Quest*, p. 108.

19   *Calgary Herald*, "Stelmach's Royalty Review and the Rise of Wildrose," April 4, 2012, https://calgaryherald.com/news/politics/stelmachs-royalty-review-and-the-rise-of-wildrose.

20   Alberta New Democratic Party, *Leadership for What Matters*, 2015, https://albertapolitics.ca/wp-content/uploads/2015/10/Alberta-NDP-Election-Platform-2015-.pdf.

21   Lou Arab, "Vote for your boss," *The United Leader (CUPE Alberta)*, Summer 2010, https://alberta.cupe.ca/files/2014/10/United-Leader-2010-07.pdf.

22   CBC News, "NDP oil royalty rate review earns praise from Ed Stelmach," *CBC News*, June 16, 2015, https://www.cbc.ca/news/canada/edmonton/ndp-oil-royalty-rate-review-earns-praise-from-ed-stelmach-1.3115223.

23   Yergin, *The Quest*, 109.

24   Ron Kneebone and Margarita Wilkins, "50 Years of Government of Alberta Budgeting," *School of Public Policy Briefing Paper* 11, no. 26 (October 2018), https://www.policyschool.ca/wp-content/uploads/2018/10/50-Years-AB-Budget-Kneebone-Wilkins.pdf.

25   Sammy Hudes, "How Alberta went from Klein's 'paid in full' years to record debt in 2021 budget," *Calgary Herald*, February 26, 2021, https://calgaryherald.com/news/politics/how-alberta-went-from-kleins-paid-in-full-years-to-record-debt-in-2021-budget.

26   Darcy Henton, "Alberta's debt tops $11.9B with annual servicing cost of $714M," *Calgary Herald*, July 20, 2015, https://calgaryherald.com/news/politics/albertas-debt-tops-11-9b-with-annual-debt-service-cost-of-714m-report.

27   Livio Di Matteo, "A brief fiscal history of Alberta—marked by spending spikes," *Fraser Institute*, February 22, 2021, https://www.fraserinstitute.org/blogs/a-brief-fiscal-history-of-alberta-marked-by-spending-spikes.

28   Government of Alberta, *Budget 2019 Fiscal Plan: A Plan for Jobs and the Economy 2019–23* (Edmonton: Government of Alberta, 2019), p. 168.

29   Robert Mansell, "Fiscal Restructuring in Alberta: An Overview," in *A Government Reinvented: A Study of Alberta's Deficit Elimination Program*, eds. Christopher Bruce, Ronald Kneebone, and Kenneth McKenzie (Toronto: Oxford University Press, 1997), p. 24.

30   Laurie Watson, "The Alberta government has tapped its 'rainy-day fund' to...," *UPI*, September 8, 1982, https://www.upi.com/Archives/1982/09/08/The-Alberta-government-has-tapped-its-rainy-day-fund-to/9999400305600/.

31   Government of Alberta, *Heritage Savings Trust Fund: 2021–22 Annual Report*, 2022, https://open.alberta.ca/dataset/3675e470-646e-4f8a-86a7-c36c6f45471a/resource/a70d648a-4001-4293-a3a0-7fd98aedfd5a/download/2021-22-heritage-fund-annual-report.pdf, at p. 11.

32   NRRR calculated from historical data found at Government of Alberta, "Historical Royalty Revenue," https://open.alberta.ca/opendata/historical-royalty-revenue.

33 Herb Emery and Ron Kneebone, "Alberta's Problems of Plenty," *Policy Options*, May 2011, p. 11, http://irpp.org/wp-content/uploads/assets/po/provincial-deficits-and-debt/emery.pdf.

34 See Government of Alberta, "Alberta Heritage Savings Trust Fund Historical Timeline," February 24, 2022, https://open.alberta.ca/dataset/80ee4142-17f2-4bc7-b30b-18afd3dfe5c8/resource/1c95d123-fa1d-49e3-ad25-98599aba2fb4/download/heritage-fund-historical-timeline.pdf.

35 Quoted in Hudes, "Klein's 'paid in full.'"

36 CBC News, "#PrenticeBlamesAlbertans goes viral after Jim Prentice's 'look in the mirror' comment," *CBC News*, March 5, 2015, https://www.cbc.ca/news/canada/edmonton/prenticeblamesalbertans-goes-viral-after-jim-prentice-s-look-in-the-mirror-comment-1.2982524.

37 Jason Clemens and Robert P. Murphy, "Reforming Alberta's Heritage Fund: Lessons from Alaska and Norway," *Fraser Institute*, March 4, 2013, https://www.fraserinstitute.org/studies/reforming-albertas-heritage-fund-lessons-from-alaska-and-norway.

38 On a personal note, my father, Warren A. Morton, played a role in creating Wyoming's Permanent Mineral Trust Fund (PWMTF) in 1975. At the time he was an elected member of the Wyoming House of Representatives. The fund was based on income from Wyoming's severance taxes on oil, gas, coal, and other natural resource extraction. The fund is managed by the state government and invests in stocks and bonds. The enabling legislation allows the government to use the fund's annual earnings to pay for government programs, but it is not allowed to sell or spend the fund's principal balance. https://www.investopedia.com/terms/p/permanent-wyoming-mineral-trust-fund.asp.

39 Ted Morton and Meredith McDonald, "The Siren Song of Economic Diversification: Alberta's Legacy of Loss," *School of Public Policy Research Papers* 8, no. 13 (2015), https://www.policyschool.ca/publications/siren-song-economic-diversification-albertas-legacy-loss/.

40 Government of Alberta, "Putting Alberta's Growing Savings to Work for Our Future," Press release, March 4. 2014, http://www.alberta.ca/release.cfm?xID=359728D5EF19F-D565-C959-7EFD9867C9BC38F7.

41 F.L. Morton, "Why Alberta Needs a Fiscal Constitution," *School of Public Policy Research Papers* 11, no. 25 (2018), https://www.policyschool.ca/wp-content/uploads/2018/09/Fiscal-Constitution-Morton-final.pdf.

42 Government of Alberta, *2022–23 Final Results: Year End Report*, https://open.alberta.ca/dataset/7714457c-7527-443a-a7db-dd8c1c8ead86/resource/e700b94a-bf65-49d1-bdac-af4915338c2c/download/tbf-goa-2022-2023-final-results-year-end-report.pdf.

43 Taras, "The Rise and Fall of the Progressive Conservatives," p. 22.

44 Taras, "The Rise and Fall of the Progressive Conservatives," p. 22.

45 David K. Stewart and Anthony M. Sayers, "Divisions among Alberta's 'Conservatives'," in *Blue Storm: The Rise and Fall of Jason Kenney*, eds. Duane Bratt, Richard Sutherland, and David Taras (Calgary: University of Calgary Press, 2023), p. 85.

46 Graham Thomson, "Race is on to replace Ralph Klein as Tory leader," *Edmonton Journal*, November 14, 2004, p. A1.

47   Colby Cosh, "The Death of the Alberta PC Dynasty," *Maclean's*, May 7, 2015. https://macleans.ca/politics/the-death-of-the-alberta-pc-dynasty/.

48   Flanagan, *Winning Power*, p. 67.

49   Frontier Centre for Pubic Policy, "Screw the West, We'll Take the Rest," July 9, 2020, https://fcpp.org/2020/07/09/screw-the-west-well-take-the-rest/.

50   Faron Ellis, *The Limits of Participation: Members and Leaders in Canada's Reform Party* (Calgary: University of Calgary Press, 2005), p. 177.

51   Bratt and Foster, "The fragility of a 'big tent' conservative party."

52   James Wood, "Lukaszuk and Kenney exchange glances, not words, at Harper fundraiser," *Calgary Herald*, July 9, 2012, https://calgaryherald.com/news/politics/lukaszuk-and-kenney-exchange-glances-not-words-at-harper-fundraiser.

NOTES TO CHAPTER 12

1   Samuel Issacharoff, *Outsourcing Politics: The Hostile Takeovers of Our Hollowed out Political Parties, Houston Law Review*, 54, no. 4 (2017), pp. 845–80.

2   Tom Flanagan, *Winning Power: Canadian Campaigning in the Twenty-First Century* (Montreal: McGill-Queen's University Press, 2014), pp. 53–56.

3   Flanagan, *Winning Power*, pp. 65, 67.

4   Flanagan, *Winning Power*, p. 56.

5   Ted Morton, "Let's stand up to Ottawa and get a better deal," *Calgary Herald,* March 20, 2017, https://calgaryherald.com/opinion/columnists/morton-lets-stand-up-to-ottawa-and-get-a-better-deal.

6   F. L. (Ted) Morton, "Response to Federal Carbon Pricing: Equalization Reform," *Manning Centre*, March 2017.

7   *Reference re Secession of Quebec*, [1998] 2 S.C.R. 217.

8   Emma Graney, "UCP leadership candidate Brian Jean vows referendums on photo radar, equalization payments," July 26, 2017, https://edmontonsun.com/2017/07/26/brian-jean-to-unveil-policy-on-democratic-reform-personal-freedoms.

9   James Keller, "Albertans reject equalization payments and permanent daylight time in referendum," *Globe and Mail*, October 26, 2021, https://www.theglobeandmail.com/canada/alberta/article-albertans-vote-to-end-equalization-in-ballot-question-designed-to/.

10   Bratt, Sutherland, and Young also note a rise in separatist sentiment in Alberta following the Liberals' re-election in 2019. Duane Bratt, Richard Sutherland, and Lisa Young, "Introduction: Jason Kenney and the Perfect Storm," in *Blue Storm: The Rise and Fall of Jason Kenney*, eds. Duane Bratt, Richard Sutherland, and David Taras (Calgary: University of Calgary Press, 2023), p. 6.

11   Danielle Smith, "How Alberta can stop acting like Canada's doormat," October 18, 2019, *Edmonton Journal*, https://edmontonjournal.com/opinion/columnists/smith-how-alberta-can-stop-acting-like-canadas-doormat.

12   Fair Deal Panel, "Report to Government," May 2020, https://open.alberta.ca/publications/fair-deal-panel-report-to-government.

13 Stewart and Sayers, "Divisions among Alberta's 'Conservatives'," pp. 96–97.

14 Formally called the *Alberta Sovereignty Within a United Canada Act*; see Carrie Tait and Alanna Smith, "Danielle Smith unveils sovereignty act in attempt to shield Alberta from federal laws," *Globe and Mail,* November 29, 2022, https://www.theglobeandmail.com/canada/alberta/article-danielle-smith-sovereignty-act-alberta-announcement/.

15 Jared J. Wesley, "Albertans and the Fair Deal," in *Blue Storm: The Rise and Fall of Jason Kenney,* eds. Duane Bratt, Richard Sutherland, and David Taras (Calgary: University of Calgary Press, 2023), p. 106.

16 https://www.cbc.ca/news/canada/edmonton/sovereingty-act-clean-electricity-regulations-1.7041533.

17 Jesse Hartery and Geoffrey Sigalet, "Equally Sovereign: Alberta and the New Provincial Rights Movement," in *From Multilateral Failures to Unilateral Successes? New Trends in Formal Constitutional Amendments,* ed. David Guénette, Catherine Mathieu, and Félix Mathieu (McGill-Queen's University Press, forthcoming).

18 Chris Varcoe, "'There's a big fight coming'—Smith throws down gauntlet in energy feud with Ottawa," *Calgary Herald,* May 30, 2023, https://calgaryherald.com/opinion/columnists/varcoe-smith-throws-down-gauntlet-in-energy-feud-with-ottawa.

19 See Thomas Flanagan and Mark Milke, "Alberta's Real Constitution: The Natural Resources Transfer Agreement," in *Forging Alberta's Constitutional Framework,* eds. Richard Connors and John M. Law (Edmonton: University of Alberta Press, 2005), pp. 165–90.

20 See Tom Flanagan, "Legends of the Calgary School: Their Guns, Their Dogs, and the Women Who Love Them," *Vogelin View,* January 25, 2015, https://voegelinview.com/legends-calgary-school-guns-dogs%E2%80%A8and-women-love/; Jeffrey Simpson, "That's not a machine gun in the violin case, it's a political manifesto," *Globe and Mail,* January 29, 1992, p. 18; David J. Rovinsky, "The Ascendancy of Western Canada in Canadian Policymaking," *Policy Papers on the Americas* 9, no. 2, February 16, 1998, https://www.csis.org/analysis/policy-papers-americas-ascendancy-western-canada-canadian-policymaking-volume-ix-1998.

21 Jack Mintz, Ted Morton, and Tom Flanagan (eds.), *Moment of Truth: How to Think About Alberta's Future* (Toronto: Sutherland House, 2020).

22 This includes Derek Burney, who served as chief of staff to Prime Minister Brian Mulroney and Canada's ambassador to the United States; Donald Savoie, Canada Research Chair in Public Administration at l'Université de Moncton, fellow of the Royal Society of Canada, and an officer of the Order of Canada; Herb Emery, holder of the Vaughan Chair in Regional Economics at the University of New Brunswick; and Fen Osler Hampson, Chancellor's Professor at Carleton University and fellow of the Royal Society of Canada.

23 See Donald Savoie, "Western Canadians: Victims Searching for a Voice," in *Canada: Beyond Grudges, Grievances and Disunity* (McGill-Queens University Press, 2023), pp. 82–101.

24 Adam B. Masters and John Uhr, *Leadership Performance and Rhetoric* (Cham, Switzerland: Palgrave MacMillan, 2017), p. 136. John Uhr is *professor emeritus* at

Australian National University in Canberra, Australia. We were graduate students together at the University of Toronto in the mid-1970s.

25 Drew Postey and Josh Lynn, "Sask. school pronoun policy becomes law," *CTV News,* October 20, 2023, https://regina.ctvnews.ca/sask-government-s-parents-bill-of-rights-becomes-law-1.6609978.

26 Andrew Waugh and John Chilibeck, "N.B. premier prepared to call election over LGBTQ schools policy," *National Post,* June 8, 2023, https://nationalpost.com/news/n-b-premier-prepared-to-call-election-over-lgbtq-schools-policy.

NOTES TO APPENDIX 1

1 Seymour Martin Lipset, "The Industrial Proletariat and the Intelligentsia in a Comparative Perspective," in *Consensus and Conflict: Essays in Political Sociology* (New Brunswick and Oxford: Transaction Books, 1985), pp. 187, 196.

2 Lipset, "The Industrial Proletariat," pp. 196, 194.

3 Ronald Inglehart, *Culture Shift in Advanced Industrial Society* (Princeton: Princeton University Press, 1990), pp. 321, 325, 331. Also see F.L. Morton and Rainer Knopff, *The Charter Revolution and the Court Party* (Peterborough: Broadview Press, 2000), pp. 77–80.

4 Andrew Sullivan, "We all live on campus now," *Intelligencer,* February 9, 2018, https://nymag.com/intelligencer/2018/02/we-all-live-on-campus-now.html.

5 See Morton and Knopff, *Charter Revolution and the Court Party,* pp. 77–80.

6 "Political scientist awarded human right research prize," *University of Calgary Gazette,* January 30, 1995, p. 1; "SHHRC Awards Laskin Fellowship," *CAUT Bulletin,* March 1995, p. 4.

7 Jordan Peterson, "Why I am no longer a tenured professor at the University of Toronto" *National Post,* January 19, 2021, https://nationalpost.com/opinion/jordan-peterson-why-i-am-no-longer-a-tenured-professor-at-the-university-of-toronto.

8 Peterson, "Why I am no longer a tenured professor."

9 Chrisopher Rufo, "How we squeezed Harvard to push Claudine Gay out," *Wall Street Journal,* January 4, 2024, https://www.wsj.com/articles/how-we-squeezed-harvard-claudine-gay-firing-dei-antisemitism-culture-war-a6843c4c

10 Margaret Wente, "How Tom Flanagan went from respected political scientist to pariah," *Globe and Mail,* April 25, 2014. https://www.theglobeandmail.com/news/politics/how-tom-flanagan-went-from-respected-political-activist-to-pariah/article18232689/.

11 Dylan Short, "Mount Royal professor who questioned Indigenization policies, BLM movement has been removed from school staff," *Calgary Herald,* January 5, 2022, https://calgaryherald.com/news/local-news/mount-royal-professor-who-questioned-indigenization-policies-blm-movement-has-been-removed-from-school-staff.

12 F.L. Ted Morton, "Now Hiring by Skin Colour! The University of Calgary's "Inclusion" Policy that Discriminates Against Nearly Everyone," *C2C Journal,* November 30, 2022, https://c2cjournal.ca/2022/11/now-hiring-by-skin-colour-the-university-of-calgarys-inclusion-policy-that-discriminates-against-nearly-everyone/.

13   Ted Morton, "New World View Poses Danger to Free Speech," *Calgary Herald*, March 4, 2023, p. A13.

14   Ted Morton, "Racial discrimination at the University of Calgary," *Western Standard*, December 6, 2022, https://www.westernstandard.news/opinion/morton-racial-discrimination-at-the-university-of-calgary/article_ffbe65d0-74b6-11ed-89bd-e34078cc3267.html.

15   "The Viewpoint Diversity Crisis at Canadian Universities," Christopher Dummitt and Zachary Patterson, Macdonald Laurier Institute, September 15, 2022, https://macdonaldlaurier.ca/the-viewpoint-diversity-crisis-at-canadian-universities/.

16   John von Heyking, "Why Exclude Oedipus?: On the Incoherent Statism of Same Sex Marriage," *The Interim*, September 2006, https://opus.uleth.ca/bitstream/handle/10133/2521/SSM-Interim-Aug2006.pdf?sequence=1&isAllowed=y.

17   Douglas Farrow, "Let's have a responsible vote on same sex marriage," letter to the *National Post*, June 17, 2006 (quoted in von Heyking, "Why Exclude Oedipus?").

18   David Rayside, Jerald Sabin, and Paul Thomas, "Faith and Party Politics in Alberta: Or 'Danielle, this is Alberta, not Alabama'," presented at the Canadian Political Science Association, University of Alberta, Edmonton, AB, June 13–15, https://cpsa-acsp.ca/papers-2012/Rayside-Sabin-Thomas.pdf, p.11.

19   CBC News, "Alberta passes law allowing parents to pull kids out of class," *CBC News*, June 2, 2009, https://www.cbc.ca/news/canada/alberta-passes-law-allowing-parents-to-pull-kids-out-of-class-1.777604 .

20   Bruce Pardy, "Human rights have become a zero-sum game," *National Post*, June 19, 2017, p. A11.

21   Pardy, "Human rights have become a zero-sum game," p. A11.

22   See Glenn Blackett, "Wokeness captures Alberta's Law Society," *Western Standard*, February 2, 2023. https://www.westernstandard.news/opinion/blackett-wokeness-captures-albertas-law-society/article_80262310-95b0-11ed-866f-a73cc74a2c8d.html.

23   Jonny Wakefield, "Law Society of Alberta votes to uphold mandatory education after Indigenous culture course comes under fire," *Edmonton Journal*, February 6, 2023, https://edmontonjournal.com/news/crime/law-society-of-alberta-votes-to-uphold-mandatory-education-after-indigenous-culture-course-comes-under-fire.

24   Bill 16 was ordered for second reading on August 30, 2022 (after being reintroduced after the election), but as of writing (March 2024), nothing appears to have happened since. Legislative Assembly of Ontario, "Bill 16, Racial Equity in the Education System Act, 2022," https://www.ola.org/en/legislative-business/bills/parliament-43/session-1/bill-16/status.

25   Barbara Kay, "Ontario's Bill 67 is critical race theory in a thin disguise," *Western Standard*, March 14, 2022, https://www.westernstandard.news/opinion/kay-ontarios-bill-67-is-critical-race-theory-in-a-thin-disguise/article_32507878-8117-57cb-9b67-0fb41b4f64cf.html.

26   Kay, "Ontario's Bill 67 is critical race theory in a thin disguise."

27   Kay, "Ontario's Bill 67 is critical race theory in a thin disguise."

28 Eva Ferguson, "Supporting students' right to self-identify," *Calgary Herald*, January 14, 2016, p. A4.

29 Government of Alberta, *Guidelines for Best Practices—Creating Learning Environments that Respect Diverse Sexual Orientations, Gender Identities and Gender Expressions* (Edmonton, Government of Alberta, 2016), https://open.alberta.ca/dataset/f76ede77-626b-4c19-b649-43a3c6a448e8/resource/5431a12d-d051-4116-8062-7596f2689adc/download/91383-attachment-1-guidelines-final-2016.pdf.

30 Tom Vernon, "Calgary bishop slams LGBTQ rules; calls Alberta NDP 'anti-Catholic'," *Global News,* January 14, 2016, https://globalnews.ca/news/2454320/calgary-bishop-slams-lgbtq-rules-calls-alberta-ndp-anti-catholic/.

31 Ted Morton, "Parents' choice in education is a human right," *Calgary Herald*, February 13, 2016, p. A11.

32 Donna Trimble, "An Alberta mother's call to action: When parents lose rights, children are endangered," *Calgary Herald*, January 18, 2016, https://calgaryherald.com/opinion/columnists/an-alberta-mothers-call-to-action-when-parents-lose-rights-children-are-endangered.

33 Arian Campo-Flores, "Florida moves to restrict teaching about sexual orientation," *Wall Street Journal*, February 25, 2022, https://www.wsj.com/articles/florida-moves-to-restrict-teaching-about-sexual-orientation-11645794000.

34 Peggy Noonan, "San Francisco schools the Left," *Wall Street Journal*, February 17, 2022, https://www.wsj.com/articles/san-francisco-school-board-teachers-elections-recall-vote-racist-woke-closures-remote-learning-crt-11645130926.

35 Moms for Liberty, https://www.momsforliberty.org.

36 Anna Betts, "University of Florida eliminates all D.E.I.-related positions," *New York Times*, March 2, 2024, https://www.nytimes.com/2024/03/02/us/university-florida-dei.html.

37 Jessica Bryant and Chloe Appleby, "These States' Anti-DEI Legislation May Impact Higher Education," *Best Colleges,* February 26, 2024, https://www.bestcolleges.com/news/anti-dei-legislation-tracker/.

38 Michael Lind, "The Power-Mad Utopians," *Tablet*, January 30, 2023, https://www.tabletmag.com/sections/news/articles/power-mad-progressive-utopianism-must-be-stopped.

39 This is the title and subtitle of his book-length version of his critique. Michael Lind, *The New Class War: Saving Democracy from the Managerial Elite* (Portfolio/Penguin, 2020).

40 Rufo, "How we squeezed Harvard."

41 CBC News, "Day lashes out against Liberal attacks and the CBC," *CBC News,* November 15, 2000, https://www.cbc.ca/news/canada/day-lashes-out-against-liberal-attacks-and-the-cbc-1.215070.

42 Jeffrey Simpson, "How Ontario became Ford Nation," *Globe and Mail*, June 9, 2018, https://www.theglobeandmail.com/opinion/article-how-ontario-became-ford-nation/.

43 Dave Snow, "How Canadian media covered Claudine Gay's resignation from Harvard," *The Hub,* January 23, 2024, https://thehub.ca/2024-01-23/dave-snow-how-the-canadian-media-covered-claudine-gays-resignation-from-harvard/.

44 Eric Kaufmann, "Canadians aren't actually 'woke'," *The Hub,* February 15, 2024, https://thehub.ca/2024-02-15/eric-kaufmann-canadians-are-not-actually-woke/.

45 Aristotle Foundation for Public Policy, https://aristotlefoundation.org.

46 Mark Milke, ed., *The 1867 Project: Why Canada Should be Cherished not Cancelled* (Aristotle Foundation for Public Policy, 2023).

47 Christopher Dummitt and Zachary Patterson. "Political homogeneity, self-censorship and Threats to Academic Freedom," *Macdonald-Laurier Institute,* September 15, 2022, https://macdonaldlaurier.ca/the-viewpoint-diversity-crisis-at-canadian-universities/.

48 The Hub Staff, "Senior university administrator: Universities are no longer a 'safe space' for debate," *The Hub,* January 13, 2024, https://thehub.ca/2024-01-13/universities-are-no-longer-a-safe-space-for-debate/.

49 Sean Speer, "Reform is coming for entitled universities—one way or another," *The Hub,* December 11, 2023, https://thehub.ca/2023-12-11/sean-speer-reform-is-coming-for-entitled-universities-one-way-or-another/.

50 Adam Hunter, "Sask. Parental Bill of Rights introduced, notwithstanding clause to be invoked," *CBC News,* October 12, 2023, https://www.cbc.ca/news/canada/saskatchewan/sask-bill-137-notwithstanding-clause-1.6993335.

51 This the most recent acronym for "Two-Spirit, Lesbian, Gay, Bisexual, Transgender, Queer and/or Questioning, Intersex, Asexual," and "the plus reflects the countless affirmative ways in which people choose to self-identify." See Middlebury Institute of International Studies, "2SLGBTQIA+", https://www.middlebury.edu/institute/about/diversity-equity-and-inclusion-dei/lgbtq.

52 Heather Mallick, "If Premier Scott Moe can misuse the notwithstanding clause, so can we," *Toronto Star,* October 15, 2023, https://www.thestar.com/opinion/star-columnists/if-premier-scott-moe-can-misuse-the-notwithstanding-clause-so-can-we/article_2c3d8330-ffe1-590e-bd2e-c52e377d8c63.html.

53 Caitlin Salvino and Nathalie Des Rosiers, "Saskatchewan's use of the notwithstanding clause reveals its fundamental flaw," *Policy Options,* September 29, 2023, https://policyoptions.irpp.org/magazines/september-2023/saskatchewan-notwithstanding/.

54 Parents for Choice in Education, https://www.parentchoice.ca.

55 Alberta Parents' Union, https://www.albertaparentsunion.ca.

56 Tyler Dawson, "Alberta's new transgender rules: From restricted treatments to pronouns and parental rights," *Calgary Herald,* January 31, 2024, https://calgaryherald.com/news/canada/danielle-smith-alberta-transgender-pronoun-rules/wcm/16770f15-ac08-4602-9e04-f54c308a7605.

57 Michelle Bellefontaine, "Danielle Smith unveils sweeping changes to Alberta's student gender identity, sports and surgery policies," *CBC News,* January 31, 2024, https://www.cbc.ca/news/canada/edmonton/danielle-smith-unveils-sweeping-changes-to-alberta-s-student-gender-identity-sports-and-surgery-policies-1.7101053.

58 Peter Zimonjic, "Trudeau says Premier Smith's new transgender policies target 'vulnerable' youth," *CBC News,* February 2, 2024, https://www.cbc.ca/news/politics/trudeau-responds-danielle-smith-trans-policies-1.7103250.

59   Phil Heidenreich, "Alberta Opposition leader, federal ministers react to premier's policy affecting transgender youth," *Global News,* February 1, 2024, https://globalnews.ca/news/10266063/alberta-smith-policy-politicians-react-transgender/.

60   John Paul Tasker, "Pierre Poilievre defends Alberta Premier Smith on transgender policies," *CBC News,* February 6, 2024, https://www.cbc.ca/news/politics/pierre-poilievre-danielle-smith-transgender-1.7106283.

61   "The Cass Review: Independent review of gender identity services for children and young people: Final report." April 2024. https://cass.independent-review.uk/home/publications/final-report/.

62   https://www.socialstyrelsen.se/globalassets/sharepoint-dokument/artikelkatalog/kunskapsstod/2023-1-8330.pdf.

63   See https://thehub.ca/2024/05/28/dave-snow-the-groundbreaking-cass-review-on-transgender-care-is-shifting-the-debate-abroad/.

64   Canadian Gender Report, https://genderreport.ca/resources/

65   James Pew, "Canada's dangerous commitment to trans-affirming care for minors," Macdonald-Laurier Institute. May 8, 2024, https://macdonaldlaurier.ca/canadas-dangerous-commitment-to-trans-affirming-care-for-minors-james-pew/.

66   Pew, "Canada's dangerous commitment to trans-affirming care for minors."

67   Eric Kaufmann, "The Politics of the Culture Wars in Contemporary Canada," Macdonald-Laurier Institute, February 15, 2024, https://macdonaldlaurier.ca/canada-less-woke-than-you-think/.

68   Kaufmann, "The Politics of the Culture Wars."

NOTES TO APPENDIX 2

1   Peggy Noonan, "The Culture of Death," *Wall Street Journal,* April 22, 1999.

2   Noonan, "Culture of Death."

3   Joseph Schumpeter, *Capitalism, Socialism and Democracy* (New York: Harper & Brothers, 1942), p. 138.

4   Jean-Jacques Rousseau, *Emile, or On Education,* introduction, translation, and notes by Allan Bloom (New York: Basic Books, 1979), p. 470.

5   *The Federalist Papers,* No. 55.

6   See F.L. Morton, "Sexual Equality and the Family in Tocqueville's *Democracy in America,*" *Canadian Journal of Political Science* 17, no. 2 (1984), 309–24.

7   Alexis de Tocqueville, *Democracy in America,* trans. Henry Reeve, 2 volumes (New York: Schocken Books, 1961), vol. 2, bk. 3, ch. 9, p. 237.

8   Robert D. Putnam, "Bowling Alone: American's Declining Social Capital," *Journal of Democracy* 6, no. 1 (1995), pp. 65–78.

9   Sara McLanahan and Gary Sandefur, *Growing Up with a Single Parent: What Hurts, What Helps* (Harvard University Press, 1994).

10   David Popenoe, *Life Without Father: Compelling New Evidence that Father and Marriage are Indispensable for the Good of the Children and Society* (New York: The Free Press, 1996).

11 For the Canadian experience, see William D. Gairdner, *The War Against the Family: A Parent Speaks Out* (Toronto: Stoddart Publishing, 1992); John Richards, *Retooling the Welfare State* (Toronto: C.D. Howe Institute, 1997), pp. 250–57; also Douglas W. Allen and John Richards, eds., *It Takes Two: The Family in Law and Finance* (Toronto: C.D. Howe Institute, 1999).

12 David Frum, "U.S. Justice is hardly a killing machine," *National Post*, December 15, 1998.

13 This is a major theme in my forthcoming book with Rainer Knopff, *The Charter Revolution and the Court Party* (Peterborough, ON: Broadview Press, [2000]).

14 I have adopted this framework from the Reform Party of Canada's Family Impact Statement.

15 See Kevin Andrews, "Building Family Policy," Plenary Session 5, Word Congress of Families II, Geneva, Switzerland, November 14–17, 1999.

16 See also Bruce Hafen, "A Tribute to Motherhood," Plenary Session 4; David Blankenhorn, "A Preferential Option for the Family;" Plenary Session 8, World Congress of Families II, Geneva, Switzerland, November 14–17, 1999.

17 See David Hartmann, "Economic Change and Family Decline," Plenary Session 7, World Congress of Families II, Geneva, Switzerland, November 14–17, 1999.

18 David Frum, "What gay marriage does to marriage," *National Review*, November 8, 1999.

19 Thomas Sowell, *A Conflict of Visions* (New York: Wilson and Morrow, 1987), p. 150.

20 Christopher Lasch, "The Family in History," *New York Review of Books*, November 13, 1975, p. 33. Also see Christopher Lasch, *Haven in a Heartless World* (New York: Basic Books, 1979), preface and chapters 7 and 8.

21 Daniel P. Moynihan, "A Family Policy for a Nation," *America* (September 18, 1965), pp. 392–93.

22 See James Freeman, "Are family and faith staging a comeback?" *Wall Street Journal*, April 19, 2024, https://www.wsj.com/articles/are-family-and-faith-staging-a-comeback-41436242?mod=hp_opin_pos_6#cxrecs_s.

23 Brad Wilcox, *Get Married: Why Americans Must Defy the Elites, Forge Strong Families, and Save Civilization* (New York, HarperCollins, 2024).

24 Melissa S. Kearney, *The Two-Parent Privilege: How Americans Stopped Getting Married and Started Falling Behind* (Chicago: University of Chicago Press, 2023).

25 Chris Bullivant and Brad Wilcox, "Back from the brink: The intellectual tide is turning on marriage and civil society," *Deseret News*, April 17, 2024, https://www.deseret.com/family/2024/04/17/family-faith-marriage-cultural-elites-deaths-of-despair/.

26 Tim Sargent, "Decline and Fall: Trends in family formation and fertility in Canada since 2001," Macdonald- Laurier Institute, May 2024, p. 4, https://mail.google.com/mail/u/0/#inbox/WhctKKZWnmtpKwpjmZtkmPHPzFRRjGDWnGtzKmKGK XJkDtrDXgZhTjNQnlbxSXSWHzlxXkl.

27 Sargent, "Trends in family formation," p. 4.

28 Sargent, "Trends in family formation," p. 5.

NOTES TO APPENDIX 3

1   Emma Celeste Thornley, "Democracy Notwithstanding: Canada's History of the Notwithstanding Clause and its Role in Human Rights," *Candlelight,* January 31, 2023, https://amnesty.sa.utoronto.ca/2023/01/31/democracy-notwithstanding-canadas-history-of-the-notwithstanding-clause-and-its-role-in-human-rights/.

2   Eleni Nicolaides and Dave Snow, "A Paper Tiger No More? The Media Portrayal of the Notwithstanding Clause in Saskatchewan and Ontario," *Canadian Journal of Political Science* 54, no. 1 (2021), pp. 60–74.

3   Dave Snow, *When Rights Clash: The Notwithstanding Clause and Saskatchewan's Pronoun Policy,* Macdonald-Laurier Institute, October 10, 2023, https://macdonaldlaurier.ca/notwithstanding-clause-and-charter/.

Index

Bill C-38 (*Civil Marriage Act*, 2005), 50, 51, 53, 54, 55
Bitumen-royalty-in-kind (BRIK) program, 165–168, 173–174, 219
Bloom, Allan, 6, 7
Boessenkool, Ken, 26
Bow Habitat Station (2009), 108–11, 150, 312n22. *See also* Kids Can Catch Trout Pond
Braid, Don, 149, 150, 192, 199, 209, 210, 213
British North America Act, 7, 25, 56, 301n7
Brown, Bert, 14, 17, 18, 19
Buckley, Harvey, 33, 34, 38, 88
Byfield, Link, 27, 36, 73, 305n57
Byfield, Ted, 11, 16, 27, 32, 36, 49, 50

C. D. Howe Institute, 142–143, 155, 162, 180, 258
Calgary Flames, 94, 96
"Calgary mafia". *See* Calgary School
"Calgary School", 12, 20, 26, 76, 258, 304n39, 326n20
Canada Pension Plan (CPP), 24, 25, 68, 127, 154, 160, 161–165, 175, 211, 256
Canada West Foundation, 13, 143
Canadian Alliance, 20–24, 26, 29, 31, 33, 40, 64, 67, 78, 82, 84, 142, 188, 248, 272
Canadian Alliance Leadership (2000), 21–24
Canadian Charter of Rights and Freedoms, 11–12, 16, 20, 28, 30, 41–42, 51–52, 56, 263, 266
Canadian Federation of Independent Businesses (CFIB), 162, 165
Canadian Taxpayers Federation, 26, 73, 165, 226
Canadian Wheat Board, 28–32, 37, 67
carbon capture and storage (CCS), 140–141
Carter, Stephen, 219–221
Cass Report, 275, 276
Caucus Policy Committee (CPC), 176, 183, 184, 185
Charlottetown Accord, 11, 13, 37, 302n20
Charter. *See* Canadian Charter of Rights and Freedoms
Cheney, Dick, 139–140
Chestermere-Rocky View (electoral district), 222, 223

Chrétien, Jean, 10, 16, 18, 19, 21, 22, 25, 31, 85
Churchill, Winston, 2, 8, 133, 175, 207
civil society, 28, 69, 259, 280–281, 284, 285
Clark, Joe, 23, 208, 226, 228, 229
climate change, 40, 92, 129, 130, 131, 141, 257, 271
Clinton, Hillary, 270, 272
Colorado College, 1, 3
conservation easement, 94, 95, 102, 106–107, 112
Conservative Party of Canada (CPC), 15, 72, 84, 208, 228, 248–251, 254, 258, 275
Constitution Act, 1867. See British North America Act
Cooper, Barry, 12, 27, 94, 218
Corbella, Licia, 17, 27, 73, 74
COVID-19 pandemic, 129, 256
Critical Race Theory (CRT), 7, 268
Crooks, Andy, 26, 32, 64, 304n37
culture wars, 268, 270, 272–276

Day, Stockwell, 16, 21, 22, 23, 26, 67, 78, 188, 320n42
DEI. *See* diversity, equity, and inclusion
Dinning, Jim, 33, 34, 36, 48, 49, 61, 64–77, 81–85, 138, 150, 155, 170, 194, 208, 212, 214, 216, 236, 238, 250
diversity, equity, and inclusion (DEI), 263–265, 270–276
Duckett, Stephen, 183, 191–192
Ducks Unlimited, 91, 102, 105, 110, 123, 312n33
Duncan, Dwight, 159, 162
dynasty syndrome, 239–241

elections. *See* Alberta Provincial Elections
Energy Resources Conservation Board (ERCB), 173
equalization, 25, 152, 159, 221, 254–256, 295
equalization referendum, 254–256
Evans, Iris, 83, 142–146, 148, 150, 151, 156, 186, 198

"Fair Deal", 24, 37, 84, 221, 254–259
Fair Deal Report, 24, 254–256
federalism, 6, 12, 158–160, 291–293

Plato, 4, 5, 6

Poilievre, Pierre, 15, 259, 275, 276

populism, 72, 73, 135, 137, 256, 258, 273, 294

preferential ballot (voting system), 34, 75, 81, 143, 217, 235–237

Prentice, Jim, 187, 199, 205, 207, 227–233, 235, 237, 239, 240, 246, 249, 320n44, 321n56

private member's bill, 53, 54, 59, 60, 98

Progressive Conservative Association of Alberta. *See* PC leadership campaigns

property rights, 4, 6, 15, 31, 92, 102, 104, 191, 210, 214, 284, 293

provincial elections. *See* Alberta provincial elections

Provincial Hunting Day (2008), 89, 96, 99

Putnam, Robert, 281

Quebec as an adversary, 9, 15–18, 31, 221, 248, 251

Quebec as an ally, 25, 68, 156–160, 163, 165, 256, 259, 291, 292

Quebec Secession Reference (1998), 16, 25, 254

"Ralph Bucks", 46, 47, 242

RCMP, 22, 25, 38, 39, 221, 256

Recreational Access Management Plan (RAMP, 2009), 89, 91, 92, 93, 114–118, 120–121, 150

Redford, Alison, 129, 172, 173, 186–187, 198–200, 206, 207–233, 235–240, 242, 247–252, 317n35, 321n1

Reform Party, 2, 9–21, 27, 30, 33–35, 67, 72, 82, 84, 94, 104, 119, 149, 208, 209, 215, 218, 228, 229, 248–251, 253, 255–256, 259, 310n39, 325n50, 332n14

religious freedom. *See* freedom of religion

"resource curse", 241–248

Rousseau, Jean-Jacques, 6, 279

royalties, 118, 125, 134, 136, 137, 140, 166, 168, 170–172, 178–179, 236, 243, 246

Rufo, Christopher, 272

Russell, Peter, 6, 295, 298, 299

same-sex marriage, 20, 21, 28, 41, 42, 44, 50–61, 67, 68, 85, 261, 262, 266

Saskatchewan Party, 79, 251

Seaman, Doc, 94, 96, 112

section 33 of the Canadian Charter of Rights and Freedoms. *See* notwithstanding clause

securities regulator, 154, 156–160, 175

Senate election. *See* Alberta Senate election (2008)

Senate Reform, 10–14, 19–20, 25, 28, 37, 84, 302n20, 302n1

Senator-in-Waiting, 13–21

shale gas, 178

Sherman, Raj, 148, 183, 191, 222, 239

Sierra Club, 92, 105, 180

Simpson, Jeffrey, 12, 273, 294, 302n21

Smith, Danielle, 24, 27, 79, 155, 161, 191, 204–205, 221, 222, 229, 230, 233, 249, 255–259, 274–276

Snelgrove, Lloyd, 78, 141–146, 151, 176, 183–185, 198, 204, 317n35, 320n42

social capital, 280–281, 285, 290

Social Credit, 72, 85, 149

social engineering, 282, 286

social justice, 58, 61, 262, 263, 268, 275, 293

Solberg, Monte, 14, 16, 78

Sovereign Wealth Funds (SWFs), 244–247

Sovereignty Act. *See* Alberta Sovereignty Act (2022)

Species at Risk Act (SARA, 2003), 103, 104

Stelmach, Ed, 24, 66, 67, 73–86, 87, 89, 90, 96, 99, 116, 118, 128, 130, 133–142, 147–153, 163, 166, 167, 170, 173, 188, 189, 191–220, 226, 232, 233, 235, 236, 239–244, 248, 249, 250, 252, 266, 310n6, 317n35, 318n4, 321n1, 321n2

Strauss, Leo, 6, 72

Sunday Hunting (2008), 96–99

Supreme Court of Canada, 6, 11, 15–16, 21, 25, 28, 30, 41, 42, 51, 55, 57, 85, 158, 159, 254, 266, 292, 296–299, 302n19, 315n15, 316n18

Sustainability Fund, 133–135, 145, 176–178, 181–182, 186, 196

Taras, David, 232, 239–240, 248–249, 322n10, 322n13

"Ted Morton is The Man" (song), 71, 309n12